The Soviet Calculus
of Nuclear War

The Soviet Calculus
of Nuclear War

Edited by
Roman Kolkowicz
University of California, Los Angeles

Ellen Propper Mickiewicz
Emory University

Lexington Books
D.C. Heath and Company/Lexington, Massachusetts/Toronto

Library of Congress Cataloging-in-Publication Data

The Soviet calculus of nuclear war.

Proceedings of a symposium held at the Carter Center, Emory University in May 1984.
Includes index.
Contents: The Soviet Union, the elusive adversary / Roman Kolkowicz—Contemporary
Soviet military policy / Benjamin S. Lambeth—Soviet strategic planning and the control of
nuclear war / Desmond Ball—[etc.]
1. Nuclear warfare—Congresses. 2. Soviet Union—Military policy—Congresses.
I. Kolkowicz, Roman. II. Mickiewicz, Ellen Propper.
UA770.S6577 1986   355'.0335'47   85-45344
ISBN 0-669-11566-5 (alk. paper)
ISBN 0-669-12580-6 (pbk. : alk. paper)

Published simultaneously in Canada
Printed in the United States of America
Casebound International Standard Book Number: 0-669-11566-5
Paperbound International Standard Book Number: 0-669-12580-6
Library of Congress Catalog Card Number: 85-45344

The paper used in this publication meets the minimum requirements of American National
Standard for Information Sciences—Permanence of Paper for Printed Library Materials,
ANSI Z39.48-1984.
∞ ™

The last numbers on the right below indicate the number and date of printing.

10   9   8   7   6   5   4   3   2   1

95   94   93   92   91   90   89   88   87   86

Contents

Preface

This volume is the result of two related efforts to focus attention on the problems of arms races and arms control and to mobilize an informed public opinion on these issues. The first effort resulted in a special double issue of the multidisciplinary journal *Soviet Union*, published in 1983 and also titled "The Soviet Calculus of Nuclear War." This issue brought together a number of articles and short essays addressing posture, doctrine, missions, and capabilities of the Soviet Union with respect to strategic nuclear questions. Some of the contributions to this book were originally published in somewhat different form in that special issue.

At the same time, at the Carter Center of Emory University, the second effort was initiated with the planning of a Consultation on International Security and Arms Control. This consultation was to consist of a research program and a series of three public policy forums, the first of which was a symposium held at the Carter Center in May 1984. The proceedings of that day-long conference are included in this volume. The second forum, also a day-long public program, was held in November 1984 at the Ford Library at the University of Michigan. The final public program was a two-day, nationally-televised conference, chaired by former Presidents Carter and Ford, with the participation of leading officials of the Reagan administration; former secretaries of state and defense and national security advisors; congressmen and senators; scholars and experts in government and academia; and key representatives of the governments of the Soviet Union, Great Britain, the Peoples Republic of China, the Federal Republic of Germany, and Japan. For several days preceding this April 1985 conference, study panels met in private to generate reports on military and strategic issues, diplomatic and political aspects of strategic and arms control questions, and matters of alliances and regional policies. The full proceedings of this conference will be published in 1986.

While the public programs of the consultation were designed primarily for the analysis and exploration of policy issues, a complementary research program conducted by the Project on Politics and War at the University of

California, Los Angeles was designed to address the core issues in the complex network of East/West political and strategic problems. *The Soviet Calculus of Nuclear War* is the first in a series of planned publications. Subsequent volumes will reflect the results of the research program undertaken by the UCLA Project on Politics and War. One of these will examine *The Domestic Sources of Soviet Foreign and Defense Policies*, a long-neglected aspect of Soviet policymaking. Two additional research volumes which are thematically but not institutionally linked with the Carter Center are also planned. One, *The Calculus of Terror: Nuclear Strategy and Its Discontents*, will examine the historical, theoretical and policy relevance of the nuclear deterrence paradigm. The second volume will take a hard look at the nexus between *Arms Races and Arms Control: Lethal Logic, Dangerous Illusions.*

The present book attempts to examine assumptions commonly made not only about our own strategy and the mission capability to support it, but primarily about that of our adversary. The authors were asked to examine some of the key issues in Soviet/U.S. strategic and arms control policies. We in the West have a considerable amount of information on Soviet weapons and technological capabilities, as well as about the economic dimensions of their defense establishment. Yet we remain relatively ignorant about the rest of their complex society: the who, how, where and why of their political and strategic decision-making process. This book goes beyond the conventional threat-assessment and "bean-counting" to take a hard look at the forces, institutions, and people that shape the Soviet calculations about war and peace. The contributors examine Soviet military policy and strategic planning; the weapons procurement process; arms control policymaking; and the economic dimensions of the military juggernaut. Soviet/U.S. negotiating techniques are discussed by distinguished practitioners from several administrations.

The editors of this book served as co-directors of the Consultation on International Security and Arms Control. During the many months of planning and preparation for the public policy and research programs, we benefitted from the vigorous guidance and counsel provided by former Presidents Jimmy Carter and Gerald Ford. To be sure, conferences and books are no substitute for serious diplomacy, strategic decisions, and state policy. However, as President John Kennedy asserted, "In the nuclear age, any misjudgment on either side about the intentions of the other could rain more devastation in several hours than has been wrought in all the wars in human history." Nuclear war and nuclear peace are ultimately decided in the minds of men. The fragile, yet durable system of nuclear deterrence is premised not on trust or good will, but on the calculus of enlightened self-interest; the survival of one depends upon the survival of the other, and upon perceptions of adversary rationality and credibility. Knowledge of the adversary becomes of central and critical importance. As President Kennedy observed, "Channels of communication should be kept very widely open in order to prevent the kind of miscalculation which has led to three wars."

It was with this intent of keeping the channels of communication open that the Consultation and related programs were undertaken by Presidents Carter and Ford: to initiate serious and candid discussions of these vital issues with friends, allies, and adversaries; to involve a wide and diverse public participation in these endeavors; and to make the deliberations and findings of these meetings available to scholars, experts and decision makers. This book is a part of that process.

Roman Kolkowicz
Ellen Mickiewicz

1

The Soviet Union:
The Elusive Adversary

Roman Kolkowicz

> In the thermonuclear age, any misjudgement on either side about the
> intentions of the other could rain more devastation in several hours
> than has been wrought in all the wars of human history.
> —John Kennedy

The Problem of Strategic Narcissism

John Kennedy, the first U.S. president to face the other superpower in a
direct nuclear confrontation in the Cuban missile crisis, fully appreciated
the lethal danger of miscalculation. Kennedy was much taken with Barbara
Tuchman's book *The Guns of August,* which made him acutely aware of
how easily miscalculation can involve countries in war. After the Cuban
missile crisis, he cited the 1914 conversation between two German leaders on
the origins of that war—a former chancellor asking, "How did it all
happen?" and his successor saying, "Ah, if only one knew." Kennedy then
continued, "If this planet is ever ravaged by a nuclear war—if the survivors of
that devastation can then endure the fire, poison, chaos, and catastrophe—I
do not want one of those survivors to ask another, 'How did it all happen?'
and to receive the incredible reply, 'Ah, if only one knew.' "[1] Kennedy's near
obsession with the need to know as much as possible about one's main
adversary, with the overriding need that "channels of communication
should be kept very widely open in order to prevent the kind of miscalculation which has led us to three wars" in his lifetime, is a poignant and
melancholy reminder to us, two decades deeper into the nuclear era.[2] It is the
premise of this chapter that our perceptions of our main adversary—the
Soviet Union—remain ambiguous, that our understanding of Soviet decision making concerning foreign and defense policies is inadequate, and that
we remain largely satisfied with a few entrenched stereotypes that focus
primarily on Soviet military capabilities and ideological clichés.

In a recent thoughtful study, Fritz Ermarth asserted that a major impedi-
ment to the serious study of Soviet strategic thinking "had been the long and

uncritically-held assumption that [Soviet and U.S. strategic thought] had to be very similar."[3] This problem was also examined by Ken Booth in *Strategy and Ethnocentrism*, in which he states that "many strategists, in fact, appear to have what T.E. Lawrence called 'a fundamental crippling incuriousness' about their adversaries."[4] He maintains that this incuriosity is widespread because "few strategists spend time enquiring into the causes and consequences of the conflicts they involve themselves with: these are taken as givens." Strategists, he asserts, are mainly interested in "playing the game." Booth is particularly critical of nuclear strategists who share "a general unwillingness ... to invest much time and effort in studying other countries, including the Soviet Union. Stereotypes satisfy, bureaucratically and psychologically. They also save having to think too much." And yet, he maintains, "strategy, like nature abhors a vacuum; the field of strategy ... must be filled with enemies. Without enemies, strategy is shapeless." Thus, he continues, intolerance of ambiguity is particularly strong for strategists, and enemy images help clear up ambiguities: "If strategists don't have enemies they must invent them" because "a satisfying illusion is often preferable to an uncertain and complicated reality."[5] And since most Western strategists do not take the trouble to study their main adversary, he concludes that "strategic studies divorced from area studies is largely thinking in a void."[6]

Western approaches to East–West strategic relations and to international security have been characterized by a pervasive ethnocentrism, focusing largely on the Western side of the superpower equation. Western theorists have defined and prescribed the theories (massive retaliation, flexible response, deterrence, assured destruction, escalation dominance, limited war, and so forth), the methodologies (game theory, system analysis, quantitative analysis, rational actor models), the language, and the rules of the game for superpower interaction in the postwar period. And in the process, they have largely dismissed the relevance and credibility of Soviet theoretical, analytical, and policy-prescriptive approaches to the same issues, generally finding them to be excessively ideological, theoretically arid and uninteresting, methodologically unsophisticated, and lacking quantitative and numerical precision.

This dismissive and arrogant attitude of the Western strategists toward their Soviet counterparts was characterized by Fritz Ermarth as "three familiar schools of thought on Soviet doctrine arguing past each other: one saying 'whatever they say, they think as we do'; the second insisting 'whatever they say, it does not matter'; and the third contending, 'they think what they say, and are therefore out for superiority over us.'"[7]

The results of this strategic underdevelopment are disturbing, and create an undesirable situation, one harboring potential unintended dangers to international stability and national security. The basis of a stable international system in the nuclear context, one that is to serve both the individual security needs of the countries as well as the system as a whole, is mutual interdependence. Nuclear deterrence, arms control, détente, limited war, crisis management, and others are all premised in concepts of balance, equilibria, and symmetry, and all presuppose a clear, rational, and sustained form of communication, interaction, and signaling between the two political systems. To be sure, knowledge of Soviet and Western technologies and weapons of war is very good. The literature on the quantitative and qualitative characteristics of the weapons, their costs, destructive power, and so on is fast becoming something of a growth industry. Similarly, knowledge and literature on strategic arms control, its procedures, negotiations, agreements, and treaties is burgeoning. Indeed, as a recent study by two highly respected experts on national security problems indicated, "The public has been deluged with missile and warhead counts on both sides. These have been prepared for relative comparison of Soviet and American nuclear power by academics, strategists, the Department of Defense."[8] However, knowledge and understanding of the vital political, social, and prepolicy values and processes in the Soviet Union remain marginal. Who, how, why, where, and when in this important process remain largely enigmatic, so analysts tend to focus attention and responses on Soviet military capabilities, on the threat potential, and on other stereotypes. The public becomes inundated by a kind of "strato-babble," a popularization and vulgarization of nuclear-strategic complexities, whereby experts "first warn us against viewing the strategic nuclear balance purely in quantitative terms of who has the most warheads, missiles, etc." After this rather pro forma warning, however, "most reports then go on to analyze the strategic balance purely in quantitative terms of who has the most missiles, warheads, etc."[9]

I shall examine this situation in Soviet–U.S. strategic relations and try to discern some of its causes and implications for international stability and national security. I shall look at the different historical and political sources of Soviet and U.S. ideas and traditions concerning war and strategy; I shall also examine the reasons for the Western, and specifically U.S., ethnocentrism in the evolution of nuclear strategic doctrines and policies by identifying several groups of strategic experts and their influence on the development of strategic thinking and policy; and finally, I shall look at the implications of this crippling incuriosity about our main adversary among the strategists and consider some alternatives.

Dissimilar Origins of Soviet–U.S. Strategic Thinking

Soviet and U.S. approaches to strategic problems in the nuclear era appear to be similar: the military technologies are similar; both sides generally understand the qualitative and quantitative aspects of the other's weapon systems;

and both sides have been engaged in protracted diplomatic and technical negotiations on strategic arms limitations, with certain mutually acceptable results. Yet the two countries diverge sharply on many fundamental issues regarding the uses, limitations, and purposes of military power, as well as the rules of the game that are to govern it. This divergence, often disregarded by Western technical experts, is of vital importance to our understanding of profound misperceptions along the whole range of strategic and political issues inherent in the superpower relationship.

Traditional Soviet and U.S. approaches to the use of military force in pursuit of national objectives are fundamentally at odds. The roots of modern U.S. strategic theory and doctrine lie in the scientific spirit of the Enlightenment and in the optimistic tradition of democratic liberalism, which envisaged human ability to control, manage, and order conflict by rational scientific and technological means. This tradition was reflected in the words of the English theorist W. Lloyd: "The general who knows these things can direct war enterprises with geometrical precision and lead to a continual war without ever getting into the necessity of giving battle."[10] More recent aspects of this tradition are embodied in the positive and optimistic premises of systems analysis and crisis management and in the vast literature on deterrence.

The traditional U.S. approach to the use of military force has been pugnacious but not "cunning and premeditated; rather it is a romantic impulse that erects boldness and initiative into patriotic tenets, but only in response to provocation."[11] George Kennan saw this trait as wrathful righteousness: "Democracy fights in anger—it fights for the very reason that it was forced to go to war. It fights to punish the power that was rash enough to provoke it—to teach that power a lesson it will not forget."[12] Until recently, U.S. policymakers have "looked on war and peace as two distinctly separate states. War has been viewed not as a continuation of policy but as a failure of diplomacy. ... The American response to war has been to view it as the use of force in a great moral crusade in which there is no room for the deliberate hobbling of American power."[13]

This U.S. tradition was challenged by events in the post–World War II period, particularly by the dismal war in Korea. It was further challenged by the rise of modern deterrence strategists, who rarely if ever asked questions about ethical or normative values, being preoccupied instead with problems of efficiency and economy in the application of force toward a given end. Modern U.S. strategists began to aspire to realpolitik, asserting the "principle that military power should be subordinated to national policy, and that the only legitimate purpose of military force is to serve the nation's political objectives."[14]

These challenges eventually resulted in a new U.S. tradition, a radically different approach to the uses of military power. The evolution of various theories, doctrines, methods, and models of conflict and warfare, under the general heading of deterrence, emptied U.S. strategic thought of much of its political content, yielding abstract metaphors, deductive theories, and conflict management techniques—a veritable science of warfare. Much of this activity, however, was focused on one type of war and on methods for its avoidance: an all-out nuclear war between the two superpowers and their alliance systems.

The Soviet tradition has different origins. One of its key progenitors is Clausewitz, who "rejected both the optimism and dogmatism of the eighteenth century theory"[15] and held that war was neither a scientific game nor an international sport, but an act of violence: "We do not like to hear of generals who are victorious without the shedding of blood" because this leads to an underappreciation of the terrible nature of war and might lead to a condition whereby "we allow our swords to grow blunt . . . until someone steps in with a sharp sword and cuts our arms off our body."[16] Clausewitz was known, with good reason, as one of the "mahdis of mass" who gave theoretical justification to the "rage of numbers" and identified the "idea of war with that of utmost violence."[17]

In the Soviet Union, the spirit of Clausewitz lives on. His ideas permeate contemporary Soviet military theories and defense policies. Party leaders find the Clausewitz dictum that "war has its grammar but not its own logic" most useful in legitimating political primacy over military affairs, since the logic of politics also governs war. The other Clausewitz dictum—that war is merely a continuation of politics by other means—has regained acceptance; after two decades of debate and vacillation, Clausewitz's ideas have again made war rational, thinkable, and possibly winnable. Even some of Clausewitz's earlier works on the military art have been recently rediscovered by the Soviet military and used to rationalize and justify proposals for the offensive, mobile type of theater warfare, with or without the use of nuclear weapons. In short, current Soviet military doctrine has fully regained its object:

> Since war has its origins in a political object, we see that this first motive, which called it into existence, naturally remains the first and highest consideration to be regarded in its conduct. . . . Policy will therefore permeate the whole action of war and exercise a continuous influence upon it . . . for the political design is the object, while war is the means, and the means can never be apart from the object.[18]

Accordingly Clausewitz maintained that war can never be separated from politics and that, should such a separation "occur anywhere, all the threads of the different relations become in a certain sense broken and we have before us a senseless thing without an object."[19]

Clausewitz found avid readers and attentive students among the Marxists and the Bolsheviks. Engels, probably the most sophisticated student of military affairs among them, defined the essential Marxist (and Soviet) approach to military power and war, as distilled from Clausewitz: "Fighting is to war what cash payment is to trade, for however rarely it may be necessary for it actually to occur, everything is directed towards it, and eventually it must take place all the same, and must be decisive."[20] A recent Soviet book on military strategy brought this tradition into the contemporary realm: "In his remarks on Clausewitz' book *Vom Kriege*, V.I. Lenin stressed that 'politics is the guiding force, and war is only the tool and not vice versa.' "[21]

Leon Trotsky, the founder of the Red Army, aptly expressed another Soviet view on war: war "bases itself on many sciences, but war itself is no science, it is a practical art, a skill, a savage and bloody art."[22] He would approvingly quote the Clausewitz maxim that "in practical arts one should not drive the flowers and foliage of theory too high, one should rather keep them close to the soil of experience."[23] This sobering admonition by the great philosopher of war is particularly relevant to our study.

To Western strategic analysts, Soviet writers on strategic and military problems behave like scholastics, adhering to obscure formulations of questionable relevance to the serious study of war and strategy. To Western deterrence theorists, the public formulations of Soviet strategic and limited-warfare concepts and doctrines appear peculiarly simplistic, anecdotal, tautological, and soft in relation to the logically impeccable, tightly-reasoned Western theories of deterrence and limited war. They find Soviet military writings to be excessively politicized and historical, as well as subordinated to the values and whims of political elites; their primitive and unsophisticated approaches exasperate Western analysts. That exasperation is reflected in the remarks of the U.S. editors of *Soviet Military Strategy* by Marshal V.D. Sokolovskii: "Nowhere in this book, as in most Soviet literature as well, are there to be found signs of serious professional interests in concepts like controlled response and restrained nuclear targeting, which have been widely discussed in the West." The editors seem discouraged by a persistent "theme of automacity [*sic*] of global nuclear war," which they interpret not only as serving to reinforce the credibility of Soviet nuclear retaliation "but also to discourage the United States and its allies from entertaining ideas that ground rules of some sort might be adopted for limiting the destructiveness of a war, should one occur."[24]

This Western exasperation with Soviet strategic analysis is reciprocated with equal force: Soviet military and political analysts dismiss much of Western strategic and limited war theory as pretentious, pseudoscientific, and even metaphysical: "The idea of introducing rules and games and artificial restrictions by agreement seems illusory and untenable. It is difficult to visualize that a nuclear war, if unleashed, could be kept within the framework of rules and would not develop into an all-out war. In fact, such proposals are a demogogic trick designed to reassure public opinion."[25] The authoritative volume *Marxism-Leninism on War and Army* vigorously rejected as a "cynical and deliberate falsehood" the idea that the "prudence of the opponents will make it possible to coordinate their nuclear targets against which these weapons would be aimed."[26] The distinguished Soviet strategist, General N. Talenskii, expressed the Soviet position clearly: "When the security of a state is based on mutual deterrence with the aid of powerful nuclear weapons rockets, it is directly dependent on the goodwill and designs of the other side, which is a highly subjective and indefinite factor."[27]

Soviet analysts find Western strategic sophistries objectionable and unacceptable on several grounds.

The first is the apolitical nature of Western military doctrines. In effect, politics is subordinated to the narrower technological and bureaucratic imperatives and to the abstract notions of game theory and formal logic. A recent Rand study assessed this problem quite realistically:

> American strategic thinking—born predominantly of civilian defense specialists bearing legal, technical and distinctly non-military intellectual outlooks—is deeply rooted in the proposition that nuclear war is unwinnable in any practical sense. . . . it has also produced an increasingly predominant belief that deterrence stability (hence U.S. security) is best served by a strategic environment of mutual vulnerability. The Soviets reject "mutual vulnerability" out of hand as an abdication of political responsibility.[28]

The study goes on to describe insistent Soviet disavowals of such Western strategic ideas as demonstration attacks, limited nuclear operations, and slow-motion counterforce duels, treating such U.S. conceptualizations of strategic issues "with alternating bemusement, perplexity and sarcasm."[29] Marshal Grechko shares this Soviet view of "bourgeois military theorists who propagate quite a different viewpoint" from that of communist military analysts, and he is troubled by the fact that Western military theorists "regard war as a mere armed clash between the two sides . . . in other words, they emasculate the political content of the concept of war."[30]

The second objection is the status quo–supportive nature of deterrence and limited war theory and its corollaries. A recent Western critical study of deterrence observed that "deterrence is a policy which, if it succeeds, can only frustrate an opponent who aspires to changing the international status quo." Although the consequences of continuous frustration of expansionist and anti–status quo aspirations are not easily predictable, the study concluded, they are nevertheless "not necessarily benign."[31] Soviet analysts frequently attack what they perceive as this pernicious Western attempt to impose their own rules of the political and strategic game upon socialist countries and on countries in the Third World that are trying to free themselves from colonial or imperialistic shackles: "The development of a new international situation more favorable to the cause of peace in no way signifies an interruption of the strenuous and sharp struggle which Soviet policy is waging. There are no pauses in international relations just as there is no rest in the struggle which accompanies their development."[32]

Marshal of the Soviet Union N.I. Krylov claimed that the "imperialists are trying to lull the vigilance of the world's peoples by having recourse to propaganda devices to the effect that there will be no victors in a future nuclear war. These false affirmations contradict the objective laws of history."[33] General Bochkarev asserted that "Marxist-Leninists are not panicked in the face of the terrifying danger created by imperialism nor do they depict it as a prelude to the end of the world."[34] And General P. Zhilin has stated that détente and deterrence, implicit in peaceful coexistence, neither rule out war nor imply stable peace: "That is why all the talk about an end of the era of wars and the arrival of an era of universal peace is premature and dangerous."[35]

A recent Rand study has asserted that "the center of gravity of Soviet doctrinal discussions is decidedly hostile to this way of thinking" and that the Soviets pay "no homage whatsoever to the abstract concept of stability" assumed in the West under the concept of a "*mutual* assured destruction relationship."[36] Generally, moreover, the concepts of equivalence and balance are seen as "unnatural" by the Soviets because they imply "the enshrinement of the status quo, something alien to every known tenet of Soviet political, ideological and historical doctrine."[37]

Finally, Soviet analysts object to the interdependent, controllable, mutually balanced, and self-constrained nature of Western doctrines of war. They are particularly skeptical of Western claims with respect to the ability to control, limit, and fine tune the applications of force in war. They question claims to omniscience, omnipotence, and ubiquity of cool reason and rationality that are implicit or explicit in many Western studies on limited war. As the Rand study indicated, "If there is little convergence in Soviet and American writing on deterrence, there is even less complementarity in their statements on limited strategic war."[38]

Soviet analysts are particularly vehement in questioning and rejecting sweeping claims on limited war: "To lull the vigilance of the peoples, the U.S. militarists are discussing the possibility of limiting nuclear war." The Soviets deny the idea that prudent opponents will coordinate their nuclear strikes and thus limit the targets, thereby keeping material losses and human suffering at a minimum. Soviet analysts find this idea unappealing, for they would have to "rely on the chance that the aggressors will be prudent and will impose certain limits on the use of nuclear weapons."[39]

There are several fundamental disparities between Soviet and U.S. approaches to strategy, arms control, foreign policy, and the uses of force in pursuit of the national interest. The main reason for the persistence of these conceptual, perceptual, and doctrinal disparities lies in the asymmetrical nature of the two belief systems and in the cultural, historical, and political factors. We are dealing with two orthodoxies, mutually exclusive by their nature, each claiming a monopoly on scientific truth.

At the root of the problem lie different perceptions with respect to deterrence and the uses of force in a nuclear context. Deterrence theory is a uniquely U.S. construct, shaped by certain historical, political, institutional, and idiosyncratic influences and circumstances of the post–World War II period. Deterrence was conceived in its modern sense when it became possible to threaten vast damage and pain while leaving opposing military forces intact. The atomic bomb that ended World War II and the bipolar international system that emerged after the war provided the conditions for modern deterrence theory: "the former made deterrence necessary and the latter made it possible."[40]

The problem with U.S. deterrence theory has been an excessive reliance on deterrence threats and alliance commitments as the primary tool of foreign policy regarding the Soviet Union, a tool that by the mid-1950s had become an inflexible response to almost any perceived communist encroachment. In effect, the specifically U.S. nature of deterrence tended to "reinforce policy makers' tendency to rely too heavily on deterrence strategy and deterrence threats in lieu of the more flexible instruments of inter-nation influence associated with classical diplomacy."[41]

A fundamental flaw of deterrence was that it became theoretically most developed and practically best applied to acute bipolar conflicts where great values were at stake and where the potential for great violence was high. At the same time, this led to a poverty of theoretical and doctrinal development with respect to conflict below the strategic and bipolar level, resulting in the forced application of strategic deterrence doctrine to conflict at lower levels on the threat scale: "This attempt to extend the applications of flexible response into the lower portion of the spectrum is exactly analogous to the earlier attempt to extend, through massive retaliation, the applications of strategic deterrent forces into the next lower portion of the spectrum, to try to deter limited war."[42]

Military theory and doctrine remained rooted in the U.S. tradition, as if trying to bend the laws of warfare in the nuclear era to conform to U.S. preferences: the massive use of strategic rather than conventional or tactical forces, the substitution of technology for manpower because of the high value of human life, the unhobbled use of military force in war, punitive warfare against a despised enemy coupled with an insistence on "unconditional surrender," primacy of military considerations once warfare begins, a clear resolution and conclusion of all wars, and avoidance of entangling ground warfare in remote areas of the world.[43] Because World War II and, to a lesser extent, World War I reinforced these U.S. preferences (not necessarily realities), it seemed sensible to extend them into the postwar period, specifically to relations with the communist world. Thus, the classic U.S. model of war and the strategies for dealing with it may be characterized as a direct confrontation between the two superpowers and their respective alliances, along a central confrontational axis in Europe, across North Atlantic Treaty Organization (NATO) and Warsaw Pact territories, according to clearly demarcated rules, and with the communications and signaling characteristics so highly regarded by deterrence purists. This situation was perceived as a bipolar, either–or confrontation, which by the nature of its terrifying threat and terrible consequences would militate against a suicidal initiation of hostilities by the communists and thus validate the logical-theoretical content and political utility of deterrence strategy. We might call this a cowboy strategy, reflecting distinctly U.S. preferences, styles, and values. It also reflected a set of practical concerns and preferences since this scenario was premised on U.S. advantage and Soviet disadvantage: the United States had the strategic and nuclear trump cards, and the Soviets did not.

The Soviet Union, however, did not comply with U.S. deterrence theories, preferences, or fantasies. Instead of confronting the United States and NATO directly and frontally in the European theater, the Soviets chose to probe, feign, and challenge the United States and its allies in areas remote from Europe. Moreover, the Soviet challenge was undertaken indirectly by proxies and allies. One might say that Soviet military and political behavior reflects a commissar strategy, which is essentially nonconfrontational or, more properly, confrontation avoiding under poor conditions of Soviet advantage and control. This strategy is largely manipulative, deceptive, theoretically inelegant, methodologically unsophisticated, and shrouded in ambiguity. It is a strategy of confrontation and negotiation, one that rejects the stark U.S. either–or deterrence (either stable peace or nuclear incineration) for Moscow's own neither–nor deliberativeness (accepting neither the imperatives of a perfectly stable peace and an atrophied international political process nor the alternative of nuclear suicide). The Soviets view strategic doctrine as a highly politicized means-end process; this contrasts sharply with the U.S. ends-means teleology of Armageddon avoidance.

In the end, deterrence strategy is logically and politically suitable to a conservative, status quo, balance of power state having no territorial designs but with widespread and vital international economic interests; a power enjoying strategic superiority and whose traditional values favor minimal involvement in remote areas; a power that has historically relied on technological and economic means for implementing its foreign policy. It is a policy for dealing with a troublesome and dangerous, but weaker, adversary by launching terrible threats of punishment in order to appeal to the bully's sense of survival.

Soviet strategy is suited to a quasi-revolutionary, expansionist power whose interests lie in changing the international status quo. It is an appropriate strategy for a power that emerged internationally after World War II as a strategic inferior and whose traditions favor the brute force of mass armies, guided primarily by defensive continental strategies and coastal navies, a country having little experience in massive projection of its forces beyond the Eurasian land mass. It is a strategy of a country with universal ideological and global political interests and claims but a country also that is not in a hurry, believing that history and time are on its side.

Deterrence may have been a suitable strategic theory and doctrine for the United States during its period of ascendancy in international affairs. The United States enjoyed clear strategic superiority and a supportive society whose internal goals were in harmony with the external policy goals of the state. It confronted a Soviet Union whose leadership was divided, whose allies were restless and unreliable, and whose military capabilities were inadequate and inferior to those of the West.

Times have changed. The Soviet Union is now a military power at least the equal of the United States and has moved from its continental, defensive military position to that of a global superpower. Soviet strategic doctrines have shown themselves to be more flexible and adaptable than those of the West. While the United States has remained largely committed to deterrence strategy and its variations—despite profound changes in international and regional politics—the Soviet Union has shown an interest in experimenting with various strategic formulations in order to fit strategy to policy and to changing political and technological circumstances. At present Moscow's strategy is double-edged: (1) a strategic nuclear force for the primary purpose of deterring and thus neutralizing the West and (2) flexible and powerful engagement in the vulnerable and vital areas of the Third World, using conventional general-purpose forces.

The United States remains fixated on deterrence and various assured destruction scenarios. Recent efforts to provide flexible, rapid deployment forces capable of hitting pressure points along the Soviets' southward expansionist trajectory are still too incomplete to evaluate properly. U.S. positions on theater nuclear forces and doctrines in Europe are causing the NATO allies much discomfort.[44] The vaunted flexible options policy (resting on such notions as control of escalation through threshold recognition and target distinctions, willingness to compete in pain endurance and risk taking, and war termination through intrawar bargaining) is not much of an improvement and falls short in political credibility.[45] (Presidential directive 59 represents a shift away from the mutual assured destruction doctrine of city busting, but it still limits itself to a central war context. Thus, in the event of a central war, the United States would concentrate on hard targets rather than cities. PD 59, then, does not bear on limited wars as seen in the Soviet context and as discussed in this chapter. It deals essentially with collateral damage limitation in a central war, a concept that is still roundly rejected in Soviet military literature.)

The Image Makers: Why Do We Perceive the Soviets As We Do?

The early postwar period of Soviet–U.S. relations is usually described in terms of rigid bipolarity, two camp doctrines, and intense ideological hostility. This was the cold war at its chilliest, marked by hostile and punitive anti-Soviet doctrines of containment, massive retaliation, and the flexing of U.S. nuclear strategic superiority. U.S. defense policy was formulated by military professionals, and their ideas about war and strategy were largely unchanged from World War II, reflecting U.S. superior strength and a sense of moral righteousness in relation to the communists.

This complacent perception was rudely shaken by the realization that the relationship between the United States and the Soviet Union had become one of a delicate balance of terror and that the Sputnik shock had forever shattered the U.S. sanctuary and safety from wars and aggression elsewhere. Far from retaining full initiative to threaten punitive measures against an adversary, with immunity from retaliation, leaders of the West and emerging strategic elites understood that the nature of the new weapons technology was creating an interdependence between the two sides. A kind of logic derived from these new technologies, they realized, and the previously assumed freedom of policy choices was now constricted by this interdependence.

The realization of the unprecedented U.S. vulnerability to Soviet intercontinental ballistic missiles (ICBMs) shocked Western leaders. These perceptions of vulnerability and interdependence also served to corrode camp discipline and loosen the existing alliance systems. The credibility of the massive U.S. retaliatory umbrella was now questioned. Moreover, the threat of nuclear proliferation and the renewed political activism of the Third World added to the loosening of rigid boundaries between the blocs and introduced a worldwide political activism. Faced with new developments in technology, strategy, and politics, U.S. leaders searched for ideas and policies that would accommodate these changes while preserving and stabilizing the balance of terror. And in this pursuit, they eagerly sought the advice of newly emerging groups of experts in strategic and technical disciplines.

Four major groups of strategic experts have had an overwhelming impact on U.S. perceptions of war, on its understanding of the uses of force for political purposes, and on the techniques of efficiently joining means to given ends. Typically these groups shared a professional and intellectual involvement in the problems of war and politics in the nuclear context. They generally believed that these problems lend themselves to systematic study, that international politics contains a certain causal logic, and that predictable results can be obtained in the international arena by the application of different kinds and levels of threat and coercion. These new elites came largely from academic, intellectual backgrounds and were often associated with large universities, research institutes, or government bureaucracies. They generally rejected absolute solutions for complex political–military problems and instead preferred maximizing objectives within a relatively value-free context. The best known and most active people were associated with the Rand Corporation, the Institute for Defense Analyses, the Hudson Institute, Columbia University, Harvard University, MIT, the bureaucracies of the Pentagon (particularly in the offices of International Security Affairs and Systems Analysis), and the Central Intelligence Agency.

The *logicians* advanced several ideas about politics and warfare in the context of deterrence and the balance of terror. These ideas derived from several assumptions: imperatives of terror (the fear of nuclear weapons and their immense destructive capabilities can serve as a stabilizing and regulating mechanism for most aspects of international politics); nuclear rationalism (the behavior of adversaries, allies, and neutrals, all rational political actors, can be influenced by the threat of proper application of coercion or force; moreover, crises in international affairs can be managed by certain scientific or technocratic methods); transference of logic (the behavior of political actors in a conflict situation can be described and influenced by means of concepts derived from game theory); and economic calculus (military and strategic policy can be best determined by modern techniques that maximize objectives at given costs).

The logicians introduced several important policy ideas. They distinguished between a first and second strike and their respective consequences, and they pointed to certain vulnerabilities in positions of presumed strategic strength. They examined deterrence and forced a rethinking of certain accepted verities about adversary relations. They systematized and clarified the complexities of nuclear warfare. This group included Thomas Schelling, Albert Wohlstetter, Herman Kahn, Morton Halperin, and Henry Rowen.

The logicians alerted policymakers to certain dangers of nuclear confrontation and educated them in the importance of signaling, in the escalation and deescalation of threats, and in understanding the reality of superpower interdependence. They sobered up nuclear hotheads and emboldened those who were intimidated by the unthinkable. The logicians, in domesticating the nuclear monster and warning policymakers to think in terms of what is tolerable and not what is necessarily preferable, introduced a measure of routine and predictability into the policymaking of nuclear deterrence.

The *defense managers* are usually associated with concepts of cost-effectiveness, operations research, and systems analysis. Operating in a narrower intellectual and theoretical context, the defense managers were less preoccupied with values, broad policy objectives, or international politics than with policy implementation within given guidelines. Their primary function was in searching for ways to utilize most effectively available resources for given policy objectives. They can be seen as a logical extension of the logicians. The most innovative and representative individuals of this group, largely associated with the Rand Corporation and the Pentagon Office of Systems Analysis, include Charles Hitch, Alain Enthoven, and E.S. Quade.

The *traditionalists,* individuals such as Bernard Brodie, Henry Kissinger, and Robert Osgood, were largely academicians in the disciplines of political science, history, and sociology. Traditionalists tended to view international relations and the problems of nuclear warfare in terms of the long-standing units and dynamics of politics. While not ignoring the technology and dynamics of nuclear warfare, they stressed the nation-state as the dominant factor in international relations. Some traditionalists based their analyses on the historical continuities of international politics. Others emphasized international alignments such as the balance of power. They tended to stress the role of personality in politics, social values, and psychological problems. Their treatment of political and military problems was less given to the abstractions and logical constructs of the logicians. Traditionalists have made important contributions to the understanding of politics and warfare in the nuclear context; they politicized the abstract universe of the logicians and the defense managers; they pointed to certain important historical continuities in state policy; they humanized the international strategic arena and stressed the importance of common sense, tradition, and ideology in the behavior of states and political actors. The traditionalists also introduced a skepticism about the vast claims to rationality advanced by others in matters of politics and war.

The *kremlinologists,* the so-called area experts, assessed Soviet ideological norms and sociopolitical and economic processes in order to offer predictive propositions regarding Soviet behavior and intentions. Working largely with deductive approaches (totalitarian models and ideological determinants, for example) and using inadequate and frequently distorted Soviet sources for empirical support of given assumptions, the kremlinologists focused their attention on the political processes at the top of the Communist party pyramid. Their research techniques included pairing-off methods (pairing off announced Soviet policy with known or assumed levels of capabilities in one context and projecting the policy in a predictive mode into another capability level); elite conflicts in the party (as an index of systemic stability or instability or as evidence of policy change or maintenance); rosetta stone methods (searching for minute departures in ceremonial ideological declarations as evidence of impending policy change); and capability studies (in which intensive studies of economic documents are aimed at recreating a larger and more credible picture of economic and budgetary policies). The kremlinologists contributed to the U.S. policy process by illuminating the secretive aspects of party and government politics and by offering predictive statements on Soviet psychological and political predispositions and actions. The kremlinologists include Arnold Horelick, Herbert Dinerstein, Thomas Wolfe, Robert Conquest, Raymond Garthoff, Zbigniew Brzezinski, Nathan Leites, and Leon Goure.

There is little doubt that these Western strategic elites have improved and rationalized policymaking during a crucial period of recent history. They have expanded the universe of strategy and policy and described its complexity while introducing an element of order and predictability into policymaking. They have also introduced a number of less desirable influences into the policy process:

> Having believed that the adversary was implacably hostile and subscribed to the view of politics as a zero-sum game, all the elites argued for the primacy of national defense over other societal goals;

> Having accepted the view that policymaking in the nuclear context is so esoteric that only specialists can cope with it, they tended to reject public participation;

> Having accepted the idea that war in the nuclear context is continuation of management by other means, they fell victim to their own illusions by seeing the complexities of international politics as a management problem in which rational means-ends techniques would yield predictable results;

> Having embraced, deliberately or otherwise, a paradigmatic view of politics and war, they mistakenly tended to apply this paradigm to the murky regions of international politics. Overabstraction, scientism, numerology, and technical jargon are all part of the legacy of this professionalism.

Logicians claimed the ability to assess, predict, and even influence adversary behavior, and information based on these claims composed an important aspect of their work and served as major inputs into policymaking. Since most logicians knew little about the Soviet Union, they posited a rational adversary who was seen to have created rational technologies and rational management techniques and was therefore assumed to be rational by U.S. definition. This adversary was supposed to be attuned to U.S. signals and to U.S. perceptions of the rules of the game of deterrence. The logicians were either unaware of, or dismissed as irrelevant, the *kto-kovo* ("who-whom") pervasive institutionalized distrust of Soviet elites, the rather irrational economic and political processes there, the unpredictable nature of Soviet domestic politics, the radically different values and traditions, and ultimately the different political goals of Soviet leaders.

The defense managers operated from a simpler premise: they assumed that the adversary was militarily dangerous and unpredictable. Their task proceeded from the supposition of the worst possible case; they assumed that the adversary would try to destroy the opponent and prepared therefore to deter him from doing so. Nuances in Kremlin politics, bloc politics, or ideological schisms played a minor role in these calculations.

The traditionalists tended to see the Soviets as totalitarian ideologues who were continuing the imperial geopolitical practices of the ancien regimes. Having little knowledge of Soviet internal affairs or their ideological preoccupations, the traditionalists tended to rely on analogies to other totalitarian regimes and so arrived at conclusions that stressed the high threat levels implicit in Soviet leadership. Thus they warned of the need to create the necessary military–economic capabilities to counter such threats.

While seeing in the Soviet adversary a threatening juggernaut, the three groups nevertheless believed that the communist system of government was rational and orderly. The kremlinologists, on the other hand, who were most familiar with the Soviet Union, saw a state that was far from rational or predictable. They described the communist system as one convulsed at times by kinds of civil holy wars, reigns of terror undertaken in the name of obscure ideologies, irrational passions, and social pathologies, and they asserted that the Soviet leaders looked at politics and international relations through distorted prisms of dogma, ignorance, and blind faith. What emerged from kremlinologists' studies was the image of an enormous, modernizing, industrializing society, wracked by permanent insecurity and occasional terror and harboring at its apex a small isolated group of communist mafiosi.

While each strategic group contained well-trained or even brilliant writers and analysts and while they all had a powerful, though uneven, impact on formal U.S. strategy and policy, they rarely talked to each other; in other words, each group labored essentially in isolation, with little interaction or cross-fertilization among them. There has been little effort at a synthesis of these diverse or complementary elements of strategic theories, thus introducing a serious weakness in Western strategic doctrines and theories that developed in a sort of modern tower of Babel with various analysts and theorists articulating their own ideas, listening little to the others, and frequently misunderstanding what the other groups had to say. To be sure, the elegant, striking, and logically consistent theories and methods of the logicians and the defense managers dominated the strategic and policy community, mainly because they provided decision makers with discrete, hard, quantified, and defined policy guidelines, necessary for the management of complex, enormous defense enterprises, involving vast quantities of money, material, and manpower in a radically new military and political environment.

These strategic elites created the illusion that they exercised a constant control and management over events. Their techniques reduced the complex factors in international affairs to simple models, designed to assist policymakers in the selection of options. These techniques led to a depoliticization of strategy and the militarization of politics. The mounting reliance on methods of systems analysis, cost-effectiveness, and game theory influenced the parameters of the policy process, creating a strong interdependence between politics and technology, making policy often a function of technology. A minimization of the soft variables of adversary morale, patriotism, and willingness to sacrifice, the imposition of nation-building techniques on societies alien to such Western sociopolitical values, and the solution of complex political problems by military or managerial techniques: these were some of the consequences of the methods used by the strategic elites. Thus, during the period of what many assumed to be a stabilizing balance of terror, a period when R. McNamara pointed out that "in the end, the root of man's security lies in his mind," U.S. policymakers were receiving disparate advice on the mind and muscle of the Soviet adversary. Policymakers then reduced it to its lowest common denominator: "The Soviet adversary is very threatening and we must therefore prepare for the worst."

The Persistence of Illusion: U.S.–Soviet Arms Control Negotiations

U.S. ethnocentrism and strategic narcissism has strongly affected Soviet–U.S. relations, essentially imposing U.S. strategic ideas and perceptions of the rules of the game on its adversaries without too much thought.[46] A similar, though not identical, problem applies in the case of Soviet–U.S. arms control negotiations, a vital corollary to the strategic deterrence relationship. Once again, the dominant mode of East–West interaction is primarily technical, technological, bureaucratic, quantitative, and procedural. U.S. negotiators, bureaucrats, and analysts operate on the unquestioned assumptions of rough similarily of Soviet and U.S. interests and objectives in these negotiations, and the larger systemic, political, and historical dissimilarities between the two protagonists are rarely considered.

Arms control negotiations are assumed to be one of the most fundamental elements of continuity in the East–West relationship, one that is assumed to be insulated from the various political and military crises affecting these relations. Neither the Soviet invasion of Czechoslovakia in 1968, nor U.S. involvement in Vietnam, nor various Soviet aggressive moves in Africa and the Middle East, nor their invasion of Afghanistan, nor their various offenses in Poland or in the air over the Kamchatka Peninsula have stopped the arms control negotiations. There seems to be an implicit and widespread perception in the West that Soviet and U.S. interests in arms control negotiations are roughly similar; that arms control represents a central and fundamental policy objective of both parties; that arms control is significantly affecting and stabilizing international military and political relations. In short, the public belief in East–West arms control, as one of the signs of sanity and rationality in an otherwise dangerous world, is a powerful sentiment; it is an illusion that is not contingent on empirical verification.

Soviet and U.S. leaders in the last two decades have been conducting extensive negotiations on arms control. These negotiations have resulted in several treaties and agreements whose objectives were to prevent nuclear testing in outer space, in the atmosphere, on land, and underwater; to prevent the proliferation of nuclear weapons beyond the few existing nuclear powers; to prevent the deployment of nuclear weapons in space, on the seabed, and in several designated nuclear-free zones around the globe; to prevent uncontrolled arms races by agreeing to limit arms production and deployment to certain numerical ceilings and ratios; and to prevent accidental, escalatory war spirals through the establishment of hot lines and other means.

These arms agreements were paralleled by two other major Soviet–U.S. policy initiatives that aimed at the normalization and stabilization of a whole range of outstanding issues and in effect constituted the three legs of the post–cold war policy triad between the superpowers. Thus, arms control negotiations and policies coincided with the era of U.S.–Soviet détente and with the achievement of stable nuclear deterrence based on a balanced parity relationship in nuclear and strategic weapons. Arms control was to slow down and reverse the vertical growth and spread of nuclear weapons; détente was to create a favorable diplomatic and political climate for negotiations instead of confrontations between the superpowers; stable nuclear deterrence was to reduce the incentives and increase the risks for the initiation of nuclear warfare. The prevailing and commonsense assumptions and expectations in the West regarding arms control and détente were overwhelmingly benign and positive. It was generally assumed in the West that these policies would serve to stabilize and normalize international relations, would save money, and would reduce the probability of conflict and war.

Arms control was also assumed to be benign and positive. Arms control negotiations and agreements were assumed to bring about the reduction of defense budgets due to reduced arms development and procurement policies resulting from established numerical ceilings and ratios; the reduction and halting of nuclear proliferation; the slowing down of arms races and conventional arms transfers to the industrialized and Third Worlds; and the achievement of an arms control dividend in the form of substantial savings that could be transferred to the nondefense sectors of the society. And yet arms control negotiations have produced little of real substance although they have resulted in several useful secondary achievements, including the ABM Treaty, the Interim Agreement on Offensive Weapons, and the Vladivostok Agreement, among others.

During the past decade of stable deterrence, détente, and arms control negotiations, we have observed an apparent paradox: the decade that witnessed the most stable and reasonable relations between the East and West, when intensive diplomatic efforts were undertaken to harness the arms races and to create peaceful relations in various parts of the globe, was also a decade of the most intensive arms development, arms production, and arms deployment programs and a decade of escalating arms sales in various incendiary parts of the world. The weapons developed and deployed in the past decade are more deadly, more precise, and more costly than ever before.

Although the Strategic Arms Limitations Talks (SALT) achieved some secondary goals, a wide range of weapons is not properly covered under the SALT agreements: mobile launchers with nuclear warheads with tactical and strategic ranges; reloading and cold launch systems that critically reduce the meaning and utility of the SALT agreements on the numbers of silos and launch systems; the cruise missile development, which is likely to complicate greatly the arms control calculus of the past decade; and weapons systems that fall into the so-called grey areas since they can be counted among strategic systems although they are ostensibly of tactical nature. Massive amounts of money are spent annually by both superpowers—in the $30 billion range—on research and development programs of new weapons and more effective military hardware. These create potential pressures to produce and deploy ever newer, better, more deadly, and more effective war technologies. There is little evidence of the arms control dividend, of a reduction of defense budgets, of a slowing down of defense expenditures, of a reduction in the size of standing armies or of conventional arms production, or of a reduction of proliferation pressures.

What emerges from even this sketchy overview of the achievements and failings of a decade-long arms control policy is that while political leaders keep reassuring the public that their policies are workable and successful, the world is becoming a more dangerous place: a place of proliferating arms and military technologies, of qualitative arms races and escalating defense expenditures, and of continued conflicts of interest in various regions of the globe that do not seem to submit to reason or to political control. At the root of this paradox of arms control lies a fundamental disparity of interests and policy objectives between the superpowers, as well as excessive and unrealistic expectations in the West as a result of its failure to perceive this fundamental disparity.

Any study of Soviet–U.S. arms control negotiations needs first to understand how Soviet leaders look at the connection between national security and arms limitation talks because an arms control agreement is presumably a non-zero-sum game situation: both participants must be assured that both stand to gain and that their essential security and policy interests would not be jeopardized in the process. We would therefore want to know how the Soviets see the rules of the game; the opportunities, risks, costs, and limitations inherent in their arms programs and in potential arms control arrangements.

Certain political, cultural, and psychological characteristics of the Soviet system contribute to high levels of threat expectation. A combination of militant ideology and a perception of a hostile international environment has instilled in most Soviet leaders a form of political paranoia in general and a profound mistrust in the West in particular. It has also engendered in them a strong expectation of threat and a corresponding reliance on their own defense capabilities. It has led to a militarization of national priorities in which the defense sector is almost invariably given primacy; a sense of internal vigilance and mobilization of resources and manpower in anticipation of threat; and a basic mistrust in agreements that might impinge on their freedom to pursue optimal defense policies. Soviet leaders were raised on the Leninist philosophy of a basic "Bolshevik belief that enemies strive not merely to contain the Party ... but rather to annihilate it."[47] Stalin spoke of basic contradictions between the two camps, capitalist and socialist, and concluded, "Who will defeat whom? that is the essential question."[48] Khrushchev maintained that the "imperialists walk around the fence of the socialist countries like hungry wolves around a sheep pen."[49] He also warned that "some people watch us with greedy eyes and think how they can disarm us. But what would happen if we disarmed? We would certainly be torn to pieces."[50] Brezhnev alluded to the "dangerous intrigues by the enemies of peace,"[51] while Gorbachev warned that "the Soviet Union has no right to ignore the constantly threatening danger of a new military attack by the predatory imperialists."[52]

Among the reasons for these attitudes of Soviet leaders are their perceptions of a hostile international environment and punitive Western policies. Soviet leaders grew up in a society marked by such anti-Soviet policies as the cordon sanitaire, capitalist encirclement, rollback, massive retaliation, containment, and asserted Western strategic superiority. The Soviet Union was for many years surrounded by a ring of U.S. military bases, making the Soviet Union vulnerable to U.S. retaliatory attacks, while during much of that time the United States remained virtually invulnerable. Moreover, the Soviets were educated by the West to the fact that credible strategic superiority can be translated into various kinds of political, strategic, and diplomatic advantages. This particular lesson did not fail, and the primary Soviet objective after the Cuban missile crisis was to climb out of the pariah position of strategic inferiority and to obtain at least strategic parity with the United States.

And yet the Soviets claim to be seriously interested in arms control. The question now is how arms control fits within broader Soviet policy interests and objectives. First, however, we must examine certain entrenched Western beliefs and misapprehensions about the Soviet Union and U.S.–Soviet relations. Among these beliefs are that the United States can "bleed" them to death economically by forcing them to keep up with it in an intensive arms race; that it can still attain meaningful strategic superiority; and that it can expect an internal political and social upheaval in the Soviet Union or in the communist bloc. Such beliefs are unrealistic and are to some extent wishful thinking. It may be more realistic to assume that the Soviet Union is going to continue its arms program, if necessary, to ensure strategic equality; the Soviet Union is not seriously interested in first strike or surprise attacks on the United States; and the Soviet Union is interested in stabilizing the expensive arms race and would seek to avoid confrontations with the United States in areas of vital interests; however, the Soviet Union is also going to probe in the soft areas of the world for opportunities and expansion, regardless of the SALT outcomes. Thus, while SALT is a desirable Soviet goal, it is not the central and fundamental objective of Soviet policy.

Soviet interests in SALT are limited, instrumental, and essentially political. They are limited to the extent that SALT does not imply any reduction in Soviet military capabilities or in their arms programs. SALT merely formalizes certain current and future strategic ratios between the Soviet Union and the United States. They are instrumental to the extent that SALT served other important Soviet objectives as a *perediska* (a necessary breathing pause) in stabilizing one traditional area of confrontation as the Soviet Union assumes new responsibilities and commitments in the Far East, Asia, and south of the Soviet Union. They are essentially political to the extent that SALT formalizes superpower political equality and symbolically binds the United States to the Soviet Union while excluding China and others from this compact.

SALT does not significantly change the adversary relationship of the United States and the Soviet Union. Any expectations of dramatic departures in Soviet foreign policy are bound to be disappointed. If anything, one would expect a heightened Soviet foreign policy activism in areas of presumed vulnerability, opportunity, and low U.S. interest. Such policy activism is likely to proceed at a slow, uneventful pace, in an unobstructive, nonagressive manner in areas of strong Soviet interest. The Middle East region would appear to be such a target of opportunity and is likely to remain an area of continuing Soviet penetration. Soviet elites find themselves in possession of enormous military power, a power looking for a purpose. That purpose will be shaped by the resolve of their traditional adversary, by probes into vulnerable targets of opportunity, and by the internal politics in the Soviet Union.

Conclusion

U.S. strategic approaches to the Soviet Union may be characterized as a combination of ignorance and arrogance. The essential logical foundations of U.S. theories and doctrines of nuclear deterrence—indeed, their indispensable prerequisite—consists of symmetries, dualisms, balances, and equilibria, all referring to pairings of adversaries and to clear communications and well-understood rules of the game. And yet the creators of this strategic science pay little attention to their own rules and exhibit a crippling incuriosity about the other side. They have only a vague understanding of their main adversary and rarely inquire if and how well it understands these rules of the game.

In the West, nuclear strategy is essentially apolitical and ahistorical; it does not account for the idiosyncratic elements and soft variables in decision making on war and peace. It is a science of war, one created largely by mathematicians, logicians, and economists. It is also a strategy whose founding fathers were not military professionals but civilian intellectuals, academics, and researchers.

In the Soviet Union, the guiding principles that shape and influence their strategic theories and doctrines are those of a professional officer, General von Clausewitz, and his contemporary successors in the Soviet Union are largely military officers. And yet Soviet strategy remains rooted in political formulations and invariably refers to the soft variables and inquires about the larger purposes of military power.

Our understanding of the Soviet Union remains ambiguous. We understand the technology of their weapons, their techniques of negotiation, and their methods of management, but we do not understand very well their concerns and intentions, or the objectives of their politics and military power. And although U.S. strategists and technocrats say that this does not matter, because in the final analysis the Russians think as rationally as do

Western powers, somehow one fails to be reassured. Indeed, one becomes alarmed about the future prospects for world peace and stability.

Notes

1. Theodore C. Sorensen, *Kennedy* (New York: Bantam Books, 1965), p. 578.

2. Ibid.

3. Fritz Ermarth, "Contrasts in American and Soviet Strategic Thought," in *Soviet Military Thinking*, ed. Derek Leebaert (London: George Allen & Unwin, 1981), p. 52.

4. Ken Booth, *Strategy and Ethnocentrism* (New York: Holmes & Meier, 1979), p. 26.

5. Ibid., p. 27.

6. Ibid., p. 147.

7. Ermarth, "Contrasts," p. 53.

8. Paul Bracken and Martin Shubik, "Strategic War: What Are the Questions and Who Should Ask them?" *Technology and Society* 4(1982):166.

9. Ibid.

10. Quoted in H. Rothfels, "Clausewitz," in Edward Meade Earle, ed., *Makers of Modern Strategy* (New York: Atheneum, 1966), pp. 99–100.

11. Robert E. Osgood, *Limited War: The Challenge to American Strategy* (Chicago: University of Chicago press, 1957), p. 34.

12. George Kennan, *American Diplomacy, 1900–1950* (New York: Mentor, 1951), p. 59.

13. Morton Halpern, *Limited War in the Nuclear Age* (New York: John Wiley, 1963), p. 19.

14. Osgood, *Limited War*, p. 46.

15. Rothfels, "Clausewitz," p. 100.

16. Ibid.

17. Ibid.

18. Carl von Clausewitz, *On War* (Moscow: Combat Forces Press, 1953), p. 16.

19. Ibid., p. 596.

20. Quoted in Earle, *Makers of Modern Strategy*, p. 158.

21. Marshal of the Soviet Union V.D. Sokolovskii, *Soviet Military Strategy* (Santa Monica: Rand, 1963), p. 98.

22. Quoted in Isaac Deutscher, *The Prophet Armed* (Oxford: Oxford University Press, 1976), p. 482.

23. Ibid.

24. See the Introduction to Sokolovskii, *Soviet Military Strategy*, by H.S. Dinerstein, Leon Goure, and Thomas W. Wolfe, pp. 44–45.

25. G.D. Arbatov, *Problemy mira i sotsializma* 2(February 1974):46.

26. *Marxism-Leninism on War and Army* (Moscow: Progress Publishers, 1972), p. 100.

27. N. Talenskii, "Anti-Missile Systems and Disarmament," in John Erickson, *The Military-Technical Revolution* (New York: Institute for the Study of the USSR, 1966), pp. 225–257.

28. See Benjamin S. Lambeth, "The Political Potential of Soviet Equivalence," *International Security* (Fall 1979):27.

29. Ibid., p. 31.

30. Marshal of the Soviet Union A.A. Grechko, *The Armed Forces of the Soviet Union* (Moscow: Progress Publishers, 1977).

31. Alexander L. George and Richard Smoke, *Deterrence in American Foreign Policy* (New York: Columbia University Press, 1974), p. 5.

32. Editorial, *Kommunist* (June 1972).

33. Marshal of the Soviet Union N.I. Krylov, "The Instructive Lessons of History," *Sovietskaia Rossiia*, August 30, 1969.

34. Quoted in Leon Goure et al., eds., *The Role of Nuclear Forces in Current Soviet Strategy* (Miami: Center for Advanced International Studies, 1974), p. 61.

35. General P. Zhilin, "The Military Aspects of Detente," *International Affairs* (Moscow) 12(1972):25.

36. Jack L. Snyder, *The Soviet Strategic Culture: Implications for Limited Nuclear Operations* (Santa Monica: Rand, 1977), p. 18.

37. Lambeth, "Political Potential," p. 28.

38. Snyder, *Soviet Strategic Culture*, p. 19.

39. *Marxism-Leninism on War and Army*, p. 99.

40. George and Smoke, *Deterrence*, p. 20.

41. Ibid., p. 7.

42. Ibid., p. 45.

43. It is ironic that U.S. preferences were largely unfulfilled and that U.S. troops in effect became bogged down in Asian lands (Korea and Vietnam) where strategic preponderance meant little in the conduct and outcome of either war.

44. See Uwe Nehrlich, "Theatre Nuclear Forces in Europe: Is NATO Running Out of Options?" *Washington Quarterly* (Winter 1980).

45. Snyder, *Soviet Strategic Culture*, p. 19.

46. This section is based on my congressional testimony concerning arms control issues: "Soviet Objectives in Arms Control," prepared for the U.S. Senate, Committee on Foreign Relations, Subcommittee on Arms Control, April 1970, pp. 591–602; "The Political and Military Implications of the Moscow Agreements," prepared for the U.S. Senate, Committee on Foreign Relations, June 1972, pp. 142–174; "The Future of Arms Control," prepared for the U.S. Senate, Committee on Foreign Relations, Subcommittee on Arms Control, Oceans, International Operations and Environment, January 1982, pp. 116–124.

47. Nathan Leites, *A Study of Bolshevism*, (Glencoe, IL: The Free Press, 1953), p. 8.

48. "Report to the Fourteenth Conference of the Russian Communist Party," May 9, 1925.

49. Radio Moscow, August 24, 1959.

50. Radio Moscow, October 10, 1955.

51. Radio Moscow, July 3, 1965.

52. *Pravda,* July 25, 1984, p. 1.

2
Contemporary Soviet Military Policy

Benjamin S. Lambeth

T he U.S. defense community and the attentive public are once again in the throes of a wide-ranging debate over the nature of the Soviet military challenge. This debate has been partly abetted by a skillful Soviet effort to project a contrast between Soviet "reasonableness" and U.S. obduracy in the superpower relationship. Mainly, however, it has stemmed from a steady erosion of the fragile national consensus regarding Soviet motivations and their implications for Western security that was first formed in the aftermath of the Soviet invasion of Afghanistan.

The sources of this resurgent disagreement over the Soviet threat (and, relatedly, over the appropriate agenda for U.S. defense planning) are internal and external. On the first count, the massive increases in defense spending sought by the Reagan administration have not resonated well among many constituencies in the light of pervasive economic difficulties, mounting pressures for budgetary stringency, and the administration's lack of success in articulating a coherent strategy that might justify its program proposals.[1] On top of this, the substantial toughening of the administration's declaratory rhetoric toward the Soviet Union has conjured up widespread popular fears of an increased danger of nuclear war.[2] Not only has this exacerbated the administration's effort to place the U.S. defense posture back on a strong footing, but it has also given rise to increasingly vocal congressional and popular demands for a negotiated nuclear freeze, which most defense analysts believe would be highly premature given the numerous military imbalances that currently favor the Soviet Union.[3]

In the external realm, these domestic difficulties have been compounded by a powerful blend of nervous indecision within NATO and a carefully orchestrated Soviet propaganda campaign aimed at discrediting official U.S. depictions of the Soviet strategic threat.[4] This latter effort, coupled with Moscow's ongoing "peace offensive" and vigorous advocacy of all varieties of arms control, has fostered a rising groundswell of neopacifism and resistance to nuclear force modernization in Western Europe and thereby deepened further the traditional division of outlook between the United States and NATO. It has also lent encouragement to those within and around the U.S. defense community who have always been disposed to interpret Soviet military programs and behavior in the most benign possible light. The fact that Soviet power and assertiveness have continued to grow uninterrupted in the years since the collapse of détente, with motivations clearly inimical to Western security interests, has failed to produce a commonly agreed Western understanding of the problem, let alone a military response appropriate to its demands.

Much of the reason for this continued confusion over the nature of Soviet military activity lies in the tendency of U.S. defense debates to fixate on technological marginalia rather than on the more basic premises that have driven Soviet military programs over the past decade and a half. This discussion aims to help correct that misdirected focus. It is not principally concerned with hardware specifics, such as the numbers and performance characteristics of Soviet weapons. Although these specifics cannot be ignored by defense planners, they are less important for informing a purposeful defense policy than awareness of the broader underpinnings of Soviet military conduct: how the Soviets perceive their security predicament, why their programs have assumed the shape they have, and what these programs reveal about underlying Soviet strategic goals.

Concentration on the material elements of Soviet power to the exclusion of these larger matters obstructs consideration of the important operational axioms that shape the context in which Soviet defense decisions are made. Yet these broader axioms that make up Soviet strategy and constitute the key link between Soviet budget planning and force capabilities are critical to a correct understanding of the Soviet strategic challenge. It is not any specific weapon (or combination of weapons) in the Soviet inventory that fundamentally gives rise to the Western security problem. More important is the overarching strategic vision that lends direction and purpose to Soviet military programs. Without proper appreciation of this, U.S. and NATO responses to Soviet force improvements are bound to remain episodic and shortsighted, reactive solely to the hardware manifestations of Soviet strategy rather than to the strategy itself.

Another cost of concentrating narrowly on hardware rather than on Soviet strategic concepts is the tendency to perpetuate the myth that the two superpowers are engaged in a purely technological arms race divorced from any broader political context. Of course, the Soviet Union and the United States employ comparable systems in their respective arsenals, but a perspective on these tangibles that ignores their underlying rationales can easily mislead us into believing that both sides are driven by common views of the security problem and are pursuing similar strategies toward similar ends. The truth is that the superpowers are worlds apart in their view of the deterrence dilemma and speak anything but a common strategic language.

To be sure, certitudes about the sources of Soviet military conduct are not easy to come by. Although the Churchillian image of the Soviet Union as a "riddle wrapped in mystery inside an enigma" is inappropriate to the transparent facts of Soviet military capability, we still have few reliable insights into the inner workings of Soviet defense decision making. The Soviet Union does not publish annual military budget figures, posture statements, its equivalent of U.S. congressional deliberations, and other sorts of raw data freely available in the West. As a consequence, many of the factors that influence the Soviet force posture remain obscure. Moreover, even overt indicators like doctrine are not always self-explanatory. Fritz Ermarth and others who have pondered the dilemmas of threat assessment over the years have drawn a useful distinction between what they have termed intelligence secrets and intelligence mysteries. The former involve data that we are prevented from uncovering (the nature of Soviet war plans, weapons capabilities, targeting objectives, and so on). The latter involve intangibles that may not be entirely clear even to the Soviets. These are supremely matters of interpretation rather than fact and must be derived largely through analysis and informed inference. The relationship between doctrine and policy, the interactive influences between technology and strategy, and what the Soviet leadership might do in a given contingency are examples of this class of questions.[5]

It is to this latter category of concerns that this chapter is directed. It will review the major conceptual inputs into Soviet military planning, indicate important distinctions between Soviet and U.S. approaches where appropriate, and survey the changing nature of Soviet military capabilities so as to underscore their growing congruence with long-standing Soviet strategy.

Doctrinal Basis of Soviet Defense Policy

The central elements of Soviet thought on the requirements of deterrence are embodied in Soviet military doctrine, a formal body of authoritative precepts on the nature of the threat and its imperatives for Soviet weapons acquisition and use. This doctrine is a product of the services, the military academies, and the General Staff. It is continually reviewed at the top echelons of the Defense Ministry and carries the endorsement of the party leadership. Unlike the strategic doctrines of the United States, which have been repeatedly buffeted over the years by budgetary pressures and shifting fashions in strategy as each successive administration has sought to reshape U.S. defense policy into its own preferred image, Soviet doctrine has remained remarkably constant since it began to crystallize in the early 1960s. It is described by Soviet writings as a comprehensive body of views on the nature and demands of modern war that enjoys the status of accepted national policy.

In its fundamentals, Soviet doctrine combines a Hobbesian world outlook with Clausewitzian teachings on war. Soviet military theory regards the superpower relationship as one dominated by irreconcilable conflict and laden with dangers of war sufficient to oblige Soviet planners to undertake every measure necessary for its eventuality. Although the Soviets concede that the destructiveness of nuclear weapons has dramatically reduced the likelihood of such a war, they maintain that it could nonetheless occur through accident, inadvertence, or willful enemy aggression. Given the awesome consequences of nuclear war, deterrence is the top Soviet priority. Yet unlike many in the West, the Soviets reject the complacent notion that deterrence is automatically guaranteed merely by the existence of large inventories of nuclear weapons on both sides. Instead they recognize that deterrence can fail despite the best efforts of each side to preserve it.

In these circumstances, the Soviets feel compelled to maintain a capacity to take prompt measures aimed at seizing and holding the operational initiative in any crisis in which war sooner or later has become inescapable. One of the problems for Soviet–U.S. stability posed by this Hobbesian view of the threat is the inability of Soviet leaders to settle on any natural end point to their efforts at arms accumulation. Instead they appear determined to seek absolute security regardless of the cost in terms of resultant East–West tension. Although this orientation does not bespeak any inherent Soviet tendencies toward aggressiveness, it implies a situation of absolute insecurity for everybody else. This, for good reason, is unacceptable to the United States and goes far toward explaining the persistence of superpower arms competition notwithstanding efforts to ameliorate it through arms control negotiations.[6]

This belief that war is a continuing possibility requiring relentless force improvement leads to a corollary in Soviet strategic thinking: that victory for the Soviet Union, even in unrestricted nuclear warfare, is theoretically attainable if the proper measures are undertaken. Here Soviet theory follows a path markedly divergent from that pursued by the United States since the beginning of the nuclear age. U.S. views on the nuclear issue have their origins in a body of academic writings running back to the late 1940s, when the revolutionary implications of Hiroshima were first being pondered in U.S. intellectual and scientific circles. The consensus that emerged from this ferment and gradually came to shape authoritative U.S. civilian leadership thinking held that the advent of nuclear weapons marked a fundamental disjuncture in the trend line of arms development that had characterized all prenuclear history. Because of their unprecedented damage potential, nuclear weapons had, in this view, invalidated all preexisting rules of strategy and made war involving their use unacceptable as a tool of policy. Since no one could rationally contemplate meaningful victory in such a war, this argument went, deterrence had become the sole legitimate function of military power and thus the only appropriate goal of strategic planning.[7]

Over the nearly four decades since this initial groundswell of theorizing, these ideas have remained persistent undercurrents in the various permutations of U.S. nuclear policy. Robert McNamara's flirtations with a counterforce doctrine, Secretary James Schlesinger's reforms aimed at imposing a measure of controllability on nuclear crises through development of selective targeting, and the more recent attempts to refine U.S. options even further by means of PD59 and subsequent amendments to U.S. nuclear planning guidance have all sought to provide U.S. leadership with alternatives other than suicide or surrender. Yet despite these efforts to acquire more flexible options, neither the public rhetoric of any U.S. president (including Reagan) nor the hardware ingredients of the U.S. nuclear posture have shown a substantial departure from the abiding disbelief in the winnability of nuclear war that has influenced U.S. nuclear policy since its earliest years.[8] Despite notable advances in the operational capabilities of U.S. forces and comparable increases in the sophistication and coverage of U.S. targeting plans, the U.S. arsenal still lacks any significant means of defense against nuclear attack and relies heavily on mutual vulnerability for preserving deterrence.

For their part, the Soviets have shown no attraction to this intellectual baggage that has been associated with U.S. defense planning throughout the postwar years. They reject mutual assured destruction as a consummate abandonment of leadership responsibility. Instead they have sought to prevent war by relying on the classic injunction, *si vis pacem, para bellum* (To achieve peace, prepare for war). In modern terms, they have long articulated a deterrent strategy based on denial rather than punishment. Moreover, not only have they sought to deny the West a credible war option, they have gone the significant further step of striving to develop a plausible war-waging option of their own. They have done this not merely out of doctrinal preference but out of their conviction that the responsibilities of national stewardship allow no other choice.[9]

This distinctive approach has led the Soviets to adopt and refine what has come to be called in the West a war-fighting survival doctrine.[10] That they have done so does not mean the Soviets are spoiling for war or have confidence that any victory worth having would actually be attainable by the Soviet Union, even in the most optimistic scenario Soviet planners might entertain. It does mean, however, that Soviet leaders regard mutual assured destruction as a suicide pact and would prefer even pyrrhic victory to a pyrrhic defeat. In their view, a force capable of dominating events in war is more likely to ensure deterrence in peacetime and crises than is one—whether for reasons of choice or neglect—that lacks those operational attributes. There is a vast difference between a theory of war that includes a well-defined image of victory and high confidence in its attainability (neither of which the Soviets show any evidence of possessing) and the idea that a credible war-waging posture for worst-case contingencies is something worth having in principle. It would be a considerable exaggeration to assert that the Soviet leadership is anywhere close to harboring self-satisfied convictions that it "could fight and win a nuclear war," as one periodically hears from some quarters in the ongoing defense debate.[11] Nevertheless, Soviet strategic planning takes place in a conceptual universe fundamentally unlike that of the Western powers and has force posture implications that are anything but good news for U.S. and NATO security.

Impact of Doctrine on Force Posture

A closer approximation of Soviet strategic goals than either the war-fighting or victory formulas may lie in the notion that military planning should aim to provide the Soviet armed forces a capability to control events at all levels of conflict, ranging from local and theater conventional war to unrestricted intercontinental nuclear warfare. The more one becomes captured by the technical details of Soviet hardware and combat repertoires, the easier it is to forget that the main motivation for Soviet force improvement remains deterrence, not war. In this image of preparedness, elusive absolutes like superiority and victory are less important than the maintenance of a force whose attributes, in an inherently uncertain world, might impose an asymmetrical burden of anxiety on the Soviet Union's adversaries and thereby augment deterrence on terms congenial to Soviet interests.

Put differently, it is plausible that the Soviet buildup over the past fifteen years has not sought so much a high-confidence capability to achieve victory in war as a capacity to secure and enforce the fruits of victory without the need to resort to war. Richard Pipes argues that Lenin and his successors effectively turned Clausewitz on his head by "transforming politics into the waging of war by other means."[12] This idea is compatible with the apparent contradiction between the Soviet Union's propensity to engage in global interventionism and its well-developed aversion to risk.[13] It makes particular sense in the light of the Soviet belief that nuclear weapons have not invalidated the legitimacy of intimidation strategies even as they have rendered them far more dangerous.

One way out of this dilemma for the Soviets is a force development approach that tries to make the best of all worlds by providing Moscow advantages in military muscle whose actual combat effectiveness might be problematic yet whose capabilities (as perceived by adversaries) might be sufficient to allow Soviet leaders to pursue their ambitions in an environment in which the danger of war would be minimized. Whether this logic entirely reflects private Soviet leadership thinking, one can observe enough disturbing trends working to the Soviet advantage that have emanated from the changed correlation of forces over the past decade to appreciate its attractions.

To cite some examples, Moscow's attainment of parity in central systems has all but neutralized the capacity of the U.S. strategic posture to ensure escalation dominance in Europe and has thereby substantially decoupled the latter from its erstwhile role as a linchpin of NATO's defense. At the same time, by successfully exploiting a decade of SALT negotiations to help postpone the development of increased U.S. hard target kill capabilities, the Soviets have thus far avoided what almost surely would otherwise have been massive pressures to ensure the continued survivability of their own ICBM forces. This, in turn, has freed them to concentrate on improving their theater nuclear capabilities through extensive deployment of the SS-20 and follow-on systems. Finally, under this expanded umbrella of intercontinental and theater nuclear capabilities, the Soviets have continued to broaden their conventional options through improvements in ground force versatility and acquisition of new, deep penetration tactical fighter assets.

The result has been to alter considerably the former NATO–Warsaw Pact imbalances that favored the Western powers during the days of U.S. strategic superiority. It would be wrong to attribute solely to the changed strategic balance all the current ills of NATO (renascent pacifism and popular antinuclear sentiment, deepening separatism, unresolved disagreements over theater nuclear force modernization, and flagging appreciation and support for U.S. global concerns that bear heavily on NATO's security, among others). There is little doubt, however, that the growing convergence of Soviet doctrine and capabilities has created problems for the alliance that have yet to be met by an equally coherent Western response.

Formal doctrine is far more influential in governing the direction and character of Soviet force development than it tends to be in pluralistic societies, where doctrine is frequently a less than authoritative statement of highest-level national goals. In the United States, military doctrine is more often than not a reflection of narrow service or other parochial interests. As such, it has to contend with a variety of cross-cutting secular interests, institutional pressures, and budgetary demands in the continuing process of force improvement. This is why U.S. declaratory policy, research and development (R&D) planning, action policies, contingency plans, and force deployments have so often been out of phase with each other. The inevitable results have been strategy–force mismatches, dramatic shifts in the slogans of U.S. national security policy, and periodic domestic crises (like the one currently facing the Reagan defense program) over funding practices that show no obvious connection to any unifying theme. The Soviet Union is hardly immune in day-to-day governmental activity to its own version of bureaucratic politics, organization processes, and related strains that are part and parcel of politics in any modern industrial society. Nevertheless, it remains a distinctive feature of totalitarian systems—not only in the military sphere but in other realms—that while their leaders may be wrong, they are rarely confused about their goals.

This has not always been true in the case of the Soviet Union, however. It would thus be wrong to infer from the foregoing remarks that there is anything automatic about the connectivity between Soviet doctrine and force structure. Although in recent years there has emerged a very close correlation between the two, the essential catalyst bringing them into harmony has been the Soviet political process. The changed character of party support of military interests, and not doctrine in isolation, has been the real force behind the major gains in size and versatility enjoyed by the Soviet armed forces since the advent of the Brezhnev regime. After all, the basic content of Soviet doctrine has remained relatively stable since the early 1960s, when the initial post-Stalin military debates finally produced the broad policy consensus reflected in Marshal Sokolovskii's *Voennaia Strategiia*.[14] Such basic themes as surprise, shock, simultaneity, mass, momentum, superiority, and the feasibility of victory have long been familiar refrains of the Soviet military literature. What has changed has not been doctrine but the Soviet force posture itself. That development can be explained only by the disposition of the current leadership to underwrite the edicts of doctrine with appropriate resource allocations.

Throughout the Khrushchev era, the party and armed forces were locked in an adversary relationship. Khrushchev delighted in heaping scorn on what he termed those "thick-headed types you find wearing uniforms."[15] He once remarked during an interview, "I do not trust the advice of generals on questions of strategic importance."[16] His own military policies—including plans for massive manpower reductions, his dismissal of air and naval forces as being obsolete in the nuclear age, his propensity to rely on a minimum deterrent based solely on strategic missiles, and ultimately his abortive venture in Cuba in 1962—were informed by notions that lay well outside the mainstream of professional Soviet military thought. Although Khrushchev's failings in the military realm were by no means the only ones that led to his undoing in 1964, he clearly had no use for martial values and was anything but a willing supporter of the military's institutional interests. In the aftermath of his ouster, Chief of the General Staff Zakharov transparently indicated the military's relief when he openly scored the "harebrained schemes" and so-called strategic farsightedness of "persons who lack even a remote knowledge of military strategy."[17]

Obviously things have changed a great deal in the intervening years. Essentially subsequent Soviet leaders appear to have accepted Soviet military doctrine as their own belief system and agreed, at least in principle, to observe its teachings as appropriate guides for Soviet force development. Perhaps the most revealing measure of this transformation, aside from the Soviet buildup itself, has been the virtual disappearance of those party–military animosities that dominated the Khrushchev era, especially the sharp cleavages over resource allocations and institutional roles that formerly divided the civilian and military leadership. This convergence of party and military views on the needs of Soviet security grew steadily during Brezhnev's incumbency and remains solidly entrenched. Today military interests are well represented in a variety of high-level governmental organs, ranging from the Defense Council and the Military-Industrial Commission to the CPSU Central Committee and the Politburo itself. This reaffirms that whatever doctrine may insist upon, it is conscious leadership choice—in the Soviet Union no less than elsewhere—that most heavily affects the character and direction of military investment programs. What is distinctive about the Soviet case is that harmony between doctrine and programs (given the necessary leadership cooperation) is made all the easier when adjudication of internal conflicts can be carried out with the iron discipline that has long been a hallmark of the Soviet political process.

Character and Goals of the Soviet Military Buildup

Throughout the post-Khrushchev era, a major motivation of the leadership has been to add substance to the image of Soviet power and thereby invest Soviet doctrine with a degree of credibility it plainly lacked during Khrushchev's tenure in office. The impetus for this redirection of effort can be traced to a number of embarrassments the Soviet Union sustained because of Khrushchev's failure to provide adequate material support to the Soviet military. These included the explosion of the missile gap myth through U-2 and satellite photography, the failure of Soviet threats to command U.S. respect during the Berlin crisis and other confrontations of the late 1950s, and particularly the humiliating debacle the Soviet Union experienced as a result of superior U.S. power and resolve during the Cuban missile crisis. The effect of these accumulated insults to Soviet pride was to instill in the new leadership a firm determination never again to tolerate such effrontery on the part of its major enemy.[18]

Although details are hard to come by, the military programs of the Brezhnev era that have yielded such an impressive force posture today most likely did not emanate from a single Soviet decision. At the outset, the new leadership was probably concerned mainly with eliminating the pronounced numerical inferiority that had hitherto characterized the Soviet position in the strategic balance. Most notably by means of the SS-11 (a small, relatively cheap, and technically retrograde ICBM by prevailing Soviet standards), Khrushchev's successors initially sought primarily to close the quantitative gap with the United States as quickly as possible and may well not have nurtured more ambitious strategic goals.

With the deepening U.S. involvement in Vietnam and consequent slackening of U.S. effort in the strategic sphere, however, the Soviets may have sensed an opportunity to press ahead toward more expansive force improvements, possibly including even a reversal of the former strategic imbalance to the Soviet Union's decisive advantage. Such a perception may have been encouraged by the beginnings of SALT and détente, which reflected a growing U.S. willingness to settle for some vaguely defined nuclear parity and to forgo further arms competition in the interests of stability, a concept long anathema to Soviet military logic.

By the end of the 1960s, the Soviet Union had entered into a military construction effort aimed at providing the means to fight credibly across the entire range of conflict, nuclear and conventional. Whatever deliberations and decisions that may have gone before it, this buildup represented an impressive confirmation of the leadership's commitment to the all-arms rhetoric that for years had dominated Soviet military declaratory policy.

One of the more disturbing features of the Soviet defense effort for U.S. and NATO planners is the absence of any apparent sizing criteria for determining its ultimate magnitude. Instead the Soviet leadership appears determined to acquire as much weaponry as its armed forces can readily assimilate, within the limits of technical and budgetary constraints and the willingness of the United States to tolerate it without being provoked into determined countermeasures. This prospect is not encouraging for the future of arms control or Soviet–U.S. relations, but it is a natural outgrowth of the pronounced combat orientation of Soviet military doctrine. Given its pervasive war-fighting focus and consequent open-ended demand for military hardware, Soviet doctrine recognizes no measures of sufficiency or arbitrary stopping points in the acquisition of weapons and materiel. To be sure, the Soviets can probably be counted on to observe the letter of verifiable arms control agreements to which they are signatories. Beyond that they are likely to continue pressing for every quantitative and qualitative advantage in relative military power that their military structure can accommodate.

One of the certitudes of Soviet doctrine is that there are no certitudes in war. As a consequence commanders require as much strength as they can get to hedge against the tendency of things to devolve in unexpected ways in the confusion of battle. Particularly if resource constraints are not a major influence on military programs (as appears to be the case in the Soviet Union), one of the surest ways to minimize risk and uncertainty in strategic planning is to overinsure against anticipated needs with large numbers of first-echelon and reserve forces, whether intercontinental nuclear weapons or general-purpose assets. Aside from the leadership's principled support for a robust military posture, there is probably no other single factor behind the continuing Soviet force expansion effort more influential than the notion that one can never have enough strength to operate comfortably in the fog of war.

Interestingly there is little uniquely Soviet about this approach to military requirements. Not only their stress on the importance of numbers but virtually all their doctrinal edicts (on the commanding importance of the offensive, on the indispensability of maintaining the initiative, on the necessity of tailoring ends to means and not attempting the impossible, and so on) can be traced back to the nineteenth-century European military classics.[19] The profound differences that separate Soviet strategy from that of the United States mainly reflect dissimilarities between the Soviet and U.S. strategic cultures, not any inherent incapacity of one side or the other to appreciate military logic. U.S. strategic concepts are largely artifacts of civilian decision makers who have set the drumbeat of U.S. national security policy over the years. Although the services continue to predominate in formulating action policy (the single integrated operating plan (SIOP), rapid deployment force (RDF) plan, and similar contingency options), they have only tangential influence on resource allocation, which ultimately determines the size and composition of U.S. forces.

In the Soviet case, by contrast, those responsible for formulating doctrine and strategy, setting R&D requirements, selecting weapons for deployment, and sizing the forces all wear uniforms and are virtually indistinguishable from one another. Put differently, contemporary U.S. defense policy is less characteristically American than merely civilian. Soviet strategic views, for their part, are less uniquely Soviet than simply military. The differences between the two stem principally from asymmetries in the composition of the strategic elites of the two countries rather than from any more deeply rooted societal or intellectual dissimilarities between the superpowers.[20] Most U.S. military professionals would find themselves readily conversant with their Soviet counterparts, and a visitor from the Prussian Kriegsakademie steeped in traditional Clausewitzian philosophy would most likely adjudge the United States, not the Soviet Union, as the country more egregiously out of step with his understanding of military common sense, at least on the issue of strategic nuclear deterrence.

A question of continuing concern to U.S. planners involves the ultimate ends toward which this Soviet effort is directed. Nothing in the available evidence permits much more than informed speculation on this score. Insofar as the outlook for Soviet defense programs is caught up in the uncertain vagaries of domestic politics, even the Soviets themselves probably cannot say for sure what the long-term future holds. Probably the best answer we can give, based on historical precedent and the facts of Soviet organizational life, is that the Soviet leaders are pursuing no master plan beyond simply striving to underwrite Soviet military doctrine to the best of their ability. Those inclined to impute more sinister motivations or unitary purpose to Soviet force improvements fail to appreciate either the Soviet Union's healthy respect for the consequences of war or the extraordinary capacity of the Soviet bureaucratic byzantium to keep the left hand from knowing what the right one is doing.

It would be foolhardy to deprecate the willingness of Soviet leaders to use force in any circumstances in which they felt that necessity left them no alternative. Nevertheless, they are anything but prone to cavalier adventurism —whatever their military capabilities might be. Perhaps the most balanced explanation of the Soviet buildup was that offered over a decade ago by Herbert Goldhamer, who described it as an exercise in banking power against the uncertain requirements of a future crisis whose contours and consequences the Soviets, by definition, could have no way of anticipating.[21]

Developments in Combat Missions and Forces

The emphasis of the Soviet defense effort since Khrushchev has been directed toward striving to close gaps between mission requirements and operational capabilities in all categories of force employment addressed by Soviet doctrine and strategy. Throughout the postwar years, Soviet ground forces have remained more than adequate numerically and qualitatively to support Soviet deterrence requirements and theater war objectives against NATO. Until the present buildup moved into high gear beginning in the late 1960s, however, most other declared Soviet mission needs were left substantially unmet by actual capabilities in the field. In the strategic realm, the peacetime deterrence function could claim a measure of backing by the embryonic missile inventories of the strategic rocket forces and the navy, but it was never clear to Soviet leaders (as Moscow's backdown in the Cuban crisis attested) whether those capabilities would enforce Western restraint when core interests on both sides were at stake. Moreover, the counterforce preemption option that lay at the heart of Moscow's emerging strategy for nuclear war stood devoid of any tangible backstopping due to the gross numerical and performance deficiencies of early generation Soviet ballistic missiles.[22]

Added to this inadequacy were a variety of shortcomings in the composition and strength of other Soviet combat arms. With the Soviet navy essentially a coastal defense force and military transport aviation configured solely for intratheater and rear area resupply, Soviet global power projection assets were all but nonexistent. Soviet tactical airpower remained in the shadow of the ground forces, was restricted to providing only local battlefield interdiction and close air support, and had no independent offensive capabilities. Long-range aviation possessed only a token intercontinental attack capability and was grossly outmatched by the U.S. Strategic Air Command (SAC). Its numerous medium bombers oriented toward peripheral strike missions were outmoded and vulnerable to enemy air defenses. Even the widely proliferated home defense fighters and surface-to-air missiles of air defense forces (PVO) Strany, despite their vast numerical abundance, afforded scant intercept capabilities against U.S. bombers flying in the low-level ingress mode that had become the standard SAC penetration and survival tactic. Despite the numerically imposing size of the Soviet armed forces, the Soviet concept of war remained virtually a paper doctrine for all practical purposes.

Even today the Soviet Union has yet to meet adequately some of the more important of these mission needs, particularly in the realm of homeland defense. Nevertheless, the progressive shakedown of the Soviet mission set and the determined efforts of the Brezhnev regime to match its military requirements with appropriate hardware equities have resulted in a Soviet posture with diverse potential and increased capacity for supporting Soviet global ambitions.

The growing consistency between doctrine and forces, the progressively tighter matching of mission needs with deployed assets, and the fact that most capital Soviet weapons likely to be procured by the end of the 1980s are already observable in R&D or prototype testing suggest that trends in Soviet force improvement during the foreseeable future will be more incremental and less dramatic than those that marked the greater portion of the Brezhnev era. We can expect the Soviets to continue to press hard on the frontiers of technology in search of breakthrough areas (especially in air and missile defense and antisubmarine warfare) that might permit them to alter the strategic balance to their advantage. By and large, however, they will probably continue pursuing their mission support efforts primarily by relying on their tried and proved approach of gradual product improvement rather than radical innovation.[23]

With the mounting buy-in costs of complex and sophisticated weaponry (to which the Soviets are no more immune than anyone else) and the steadily expanding lead times between concept definition and operational deployment of such weapons, Soviet planners will most likely be driven increasingly to reassess their traditional practice of routinely substituting quantity for quality. The result, if this occurs, will necessarily be a steady decline in the numerical growth of Soviet forces, although this may be offset by commensurate improvements in their performance and combat leverage. Interestingly, a by-product of this development could well be a Soviet military management system increasingly plagued by the same sorts of maintainability problems and cost versus quality trade-off dilemmas that have recently risen to such public notoriety in the United States.[24]

In the realm of intercontinental attack, the main Soviet emphasis will continue to be placed on acquiring a comprehensive hard target capability against U.S. land-based ICBMs that will give the Soviet Union a credible preemption option and also permit retention of substantial reserve forces for follow-on operations. Barring a complete collapse of the arms control process, the overall numbers of ICBMs and submarine-launched ballistic missiles (SLBMs), both launchers and warheads, will probably remain capped by tacit Soviet obeisance to prevailing SALT II restrictions. Within these numerical constraints, however, we can expect to see steady Soviet improvements in accuracy and targeting flexibility.

In the event that MX, with its own appreciable counterforce capability, should ever see the light of day in a survivable basing mode, Soviet planners will also want to hedge against this threat with appropriate countermeasures. A high-confidence U.S. silo killing capability could be very disruptive to Soviet strategic planning since the Soviet Union relies on fixed ICBMs to a far greater extent than the United States does. Such countermeasures could come in the form of both increased Soviet silo hardening efforts and a gradual trend toward land mobility along the lines of the SS-20, perhaps in their fifth-generation ICBMs now in advanced development. Finally, we might see over the coming decade a gradual blurring of the former distinctions between land- and sea-based missile forces as the Soviet Union continues to perfect SLBMs with increased accuracy and intercontinental ranges that would allow them to be launched from protected sanctuaries beyond the reach of Western antisubmarine warfare (ASW).

Soviet prospects for aerospace defense look substantially less appealing because of the numerous difficulties that will continue to frustrate Soviet efforts to deal with enemy penetration capabilities that either exist now or lie on the immediate horizon. Much has been made of Soviet R&D efforts in lasers and directed-energy weapons. Most knowledgeable observers agree, however, that any deployable Soviet capability of this sort will not be available until the latter years of this century at the earliest. As for more near-term possibilities, the Soviets are known to be developing airborne warning and communications system (AWACS)-type battle management platforms; improved interceptors with look-down–shoot-down capabilities against bombers and cruise missiles; advanced surface-to-air missiles for engaging low- and medium-altitude air-breathing threats; and better exoatmospheric antiballistic missiles (ABMs) for engaging enemy ballistic missiles. Constraints imposed by the ABM Treaty (assuming it survives the years ahead relatively intact), however, are likely to inhibit any major Soviet deployment efforts in the last category. The numerous tactical circumstances that appear likely to continue favoring the penetrativity of aerodynamic vehicles (particularly once low-observability stealth systems become operationally available toward the end of the 1980s) also promise to render Soviet efforts to deal with these threats a continued uphill battle. Probably the only realistic counsel of optimism for Soviet planners in the realm of home defense is the hope that a truly effective Soviet counterforce capability might be able to draw down U.S., British, and French nuclear offensive forces in a preemptive attack, thereby offering Soviet air defenses the comparative advantage of dealing with a heavily upgraded offensive threat from a fully generated alert posture. The likelihood that even such a degraded enemy capability would still be able to inflict grave retaliatory damage on the Soviet Union promises to remain a major factor inhibiting the Soviets from indulging in excessive risk taking.

For lesser levels of conflict, the Soviet armed forces are on a much more positive footing. The Soviet ground forces have undergone fewer dramatic changes than other force elements in recent years as a consequence of their enduring mission charter and their persistent numerical strength. Indeed, notwithstanding some overall manpower growth during the past decade, the ground forces have sustained a perceptible adverse shift in their tooth-to-tail ratio as a result of heightened allocations of troop strength to battlefield support and command and control functions. Nevertheless, the gradual tapering off of Soviet ground force manning promises to be more than offset by ongoing Soviet efforts to achieve greater flexibility, versatility, and operational leverage through emphasis on increased interchangeability between armored and motorized rifle divisions. These efforts stand to be supplemented by collateral activities aimed at developing specialized divisions with capabilities tailored for discrete missions (such as airborne operations and remote power projection) and discrete theaters of operations (China or the Persian Gulf) that lie outside the boundaries of traditional Soviet planning for the European scenario.[25]

As for in-theater strategic forces, the expanding SS-20 inventory, along with other Soviet nuclear systems deployed opposite NATO, has amplified the leverage of the Soviet ICBM posture in defusing NATO's former advantage in escalation dominance. With Soviet parity in central forces now holding U.S. intercontinental attack assets at bay and Moscow's strengthened theater nuclear capabilities pressing hard on the credibility of NATO's threat to escalate with its own nuclear forces, the Soviet Union has increasingly moved toward a position where it could dominate a NATO–Warsaw Pact war as a result of its superior conventional capabilities.

In the tactical air realm, frontal aviation has decisively shed its former status as a subordinate adjunct of the ground forces and has acquired both the mission and the necessary hardware to conduct deep offensive strikes against virtually the entire NATO rear area. Because of its continued lack of adequate hard structure conventional munitions, frontal aviation remains incapable of destroying aircraft shelters and runways with high confidence and would be hard put to disarm NATO's theater nuclear forces in a surprise air offensive. Nevertheless, it has an impressive capability for severely hampering NATO's fighter sortie generation capability. This, in turn, could contribute substantially to the pact's ability to achieve theater air superiority under the protective umbrella of a Soviet nuclear preemptive threat.[26] In such circumstances, combined Soviet and Warsaw Pact ground elements might have enough time to carry out a conventional blitzkrieg aimed at seizing and consolidating a large portion of NATO territory. This capacity to hamper effective NATO conventional opposition is even more disconcerting if one also considers the possible use of chemical weapons, which currently remain a virtual Soviet monopoly.[27]

None of this is to say that NATO planners are without effective counterthreats and options that might disincline Soviet decision makers from attempting such a campaign in most conditions of East–West crisis. Were a conventional war between NATO and the Warsaw Pact to occur for whatever reason, however, the Soviet side would be able to call on disturbingly effective capabilities for prosecuting it toward a favorable conclusion, so long as its opponents remained unable or unwilling to raise the stakes through nuclear escalation.[28]

Finally, the Soviets have made major strides over the past decade in their capabilities for war at sea and power projection. On the first count, the Soviet navy has moved well beyond its traditional role as a spoiler of enemy naval activities and has become a truly multimission service with global reach. Its expanded mission set now includes strategic nuclear attack, antisubmarine warfare, and selective sea control in open ocean areas increasingly removed from Soviet shores. Within these broadened mission areas, Soviet naval weapons and forces continue to improve and offer new combat options to Soviet planners. Examples include the nuclear cruiser *Kirov*, the *Alfa* fast-attack submarine (probably intended for use against U.S. carrier battle groups), and the prospective development of a large deck carrier intended for launching and recovering high-performance fighter aircraft.[29]

For peacetime and intracrisis power projection, the Soviet navy has increased its heavy-lift transport capability and is acquiring the rudiments of a credible assault force through such platforms as the *Ivan Rogov* roll-on-roll-off amphibious landing craft. The lift and remote deployment potential of the navy is complemented by the expanded assets of military transport aviation. The latter's new-found operational leverage was first vividly displayed during the Soviet invasion of Czechoslovakia in 1968. It has periodically supported Soviet foreign policy in subsequent years with equally effective and professional service in such areas as Angola, Ethiopia, and—most recently—Afghanistan.

Soviet air and sealift capabilities will undoubtedly continue to grow in the coming decade in consonance with Moscow's determination to seek increased global influence and presence. To support this ambition to the fullest, the Soviet navy will have to improve considerably its present means of resupply, either through development of an overseas basing infrastructure (which has remained elusive) or a substantially reinforced underway replenishment capability. Nevertheless, the Soviet navy has become a mature and sophisticated blue water fleet with unquestioned worldwide mobility. Its evolving missions and capabilities leave little doubt that the Soviet Union has entered the power projection game in a major way.

Overview and Outlook

A dominant hallmark of the Soviet defense buildup since the mid-1960s has been the remarkable continuity of effort that has sustained it. The Soviet leaders see themselves in a long-term competition with the West for global influence and ascendancy. In this contest, persistence and patience are among their most enduring attributes. Their advantages include an ideologically rooted sense of purpose, an established institutional memory, and a decision-making environment largely unfettered by the sort of internal pressures that so heavily complicate the policy processes of democratic societies. Barring a fundamental change in the structure of Soviet politics, these comparative advantages (if one can call them that) promise to guarantee the Soviets a continued edge in strategic competitiveness for the indefinite future. By contrast, the United States and its NATO allies will necessarily continue to do their own defense planning largely from budget cycle to budget cycle. Given the fractious nature of their internal debates and the inherent tendencies of recurrent leadership turnover to keep their defense programs in continual turmoil, there is little chance that the Western powers can ever match the Soviet Union in the constancy of its strategic vision.[30]

This chapter has emphasized the stability of Soviet military thought over the past two decades, but this does not mean that Soviet operational concepts are unamenable to change. The comprehensive expansion and modernization of Soviet forces since the advent of the Brezhnev regime have brought Soviet combat capabilities into close congruence with long-standing Soviet doctrinal edicts. At the same time, these Soviet postural innovations have increasingly made possible new Soviet force employment options either expressly ruled out or hitherto unaddressed by the Soviet literature.[31] In the years ahead, we can anticipate a steady maturation of Soviet doctrine, contingency plans, and operating repertoires in a way that accommodates the broadened range of options afforded by these new Soviet capabilities. Whatever changes that may occur, however, are unlikely to make life for Western defense planners any easier. While implementation strategies will continue to evolve in parallel with improvements in Soviet technology and capability, the underlying principles of Soviet doctrine that stress the importance of ensuring deterrence through the pursuit of plausible war options show every likelihood of remaining established articles of faith.

Given this prospect for continued doctrinal stability and continued force refinement aimed at lending increased support to Soviet doctrinal principles, any resurgent U.S. effort to draw the Soviets into an arms dialogue based on a common strategic language would most probably be in vain. Far more likely to impress the Soviets will be a measured effort to match U.S. and NATO capabilities with mission needs—without flourish or fanfare—in a way calculated to deprive Soviet operational plans of any realistic possibility of success. Both U.S. and most European defense officials now recognize and accept the necessity of this approach. Those who continue to lament the Reagan defense buildup and the new arms race it threatens to occasion fail to appreciate that current U.S. policy is largely an attempt to make up for numerous years of past failure on the part of the United States to hold up its end of the competition due to preoccupation with the Vietnam war, fixation on misguided mutual assured destruction thinking, and consequent underfunding of a broad variety of strategic and general-purpose force needs.[32] Today the United States and NATO face multiple deficiencies in military capability that constitute equally top priority problems. Restoring U.S. ICBM survivability, replacing the aging B-52, acquiring a credible remote area power projection capability with associated naval and airlift components, and attending to the legitimate demands of tactical air and theater nuclear force modernization are only four among many. The real question is not whether U.S. programs threaten a new arms race or constitute an unprecedented military buildup but whether the fiscal resources and popular support available in the immediate future will be sufficient to sustain these planned force improvements long enough to permit the United States to undo the legacy of their neglect during years past.

Despite the magnitude of this challenge, engaging the Soviet Union in the long-term competition need not be an insurmountable task. What the United States and NATO countries may lack by way of institutional mechanisms for imposing extended discipline on their defense programs is offset by their superior technological prowess and adaptability in the face of changing political–military circumstances. The preceding discussion has emphasized the more disturbing elements of Soviet doctrine and planning. It has not, however, suggested that the Soviet Union is without significant problems in the military realm. This is not the place for a detailed review of those liabilities, but it bears stressing that the Soviet leadership has ample reasons of its own to look to the future with less than exuberant self-confidence. For example, despite the ongoing Afghanistan episode, the Soviet Union has had no direct combat experience of a significant nature since World War II and doubtless harbors genuine uncertainties about how its forces (both material and human) would fare under the stresses of a full-blown confrontation with the West. Relatedly, the rigidities of the Soviet military management system that permit uninterrupted planning and orderly implementation of Soviet defense programs in peacetime may well deny the leadership the flexibility and responsiveness that would be required to cope effectively in a crisis.

Even in peacetime, Soviet leaders face internal and external pressures that almost surely raise valid questions about the limits of achievable military growth. The continued intractability of the Poland situation, for example, offers them a daily reminder of the burdens of empire. The continued presence of a hostile China on the Soviet Union's eastern flank constitutes another planning uncertainty unique to the Soviet leadership and doubtless occasions much circumspection in Soviet contingency planning against the West. The increasingly prominent racial tensions generated by the steady growth in percentage of ethnic minorities in the manpower composition of the Soviet armed forces make up a third ground for legitimate Soviet anxiety by raising questions about how reliable Soviet ground forces would be in any circumstance short of a fundamental threat to Soviet survival.[33] Finally, the Soviet Union—like all other modern powers—is saddled with seemingly irreversible growth trends in the development and procurement costs of capital weapons systems. Every year since 1960, Soviet defense expenditures have increased in percentage of total outlays without interruption, encroaching deeper and deeper on needed investment in other sectors of the economy.[34] The Soviet leaders have thus far appeared willing to accept this burden as a necessary price for meeting their baseline force requirements and show no indication of feeling threatened by the specter of a bilateral military spending contest with the United States. Nevertheless, the increasing strains on the Soviet economy that have been generated by this continuing buildup raise the possibility that they may eventually have to impose more stringent budgetary toplines on their defense effort, with a commensurate tapering off in the rate of Soviet military expansion.

For these and other reasons, the Soviet military challenge should be regarded not merely as a threat but also as an opportunity for purposeful Western counterplanning. To be sure, because stakes are high and the penalties for misjudgment are severe, the pressures to hedge against worst cases are compelling and understandable. Clearly it would be dangerous to underestimate the effectiveness of Soviet forces in an unrestricted war, however valid our assumptions about Soviet caution and risk aversion might be. This does not mean, however, that Western planners are reduced to accepting worst case possibilities as certainties or to engaging Soviet programs head-on in a mindless confrontation of countervailing weapons development. As Major General Jasper Welch has observed, "There is a certain unbecoming fatalism about routinely allowing the Soviet military a free ride on their existing vulnerabilities just because we 'might' be wrong or they 'might' fix them."[35]

Conversely, we must resist the temptation that has recently become fashionable in some political and journalistic circles to discount Soviet strengths on the misguided premise that known Soviet weaknesses constitute an adequate basis for Western complacency. Some of the more excessive efforts of this genre that emphasize Soviet military problem areas such as alcoholism and poor morale—as though these were sufficient to render the

Soviet armed forces incapable of serious combat—border on intellectual irresponsibility.[36] The real analytical challenge before U.S. defense planners lies in the middle ground of soberly recognizing Soviet strengths for what they are and then systematically considering how identifiable Soviet vulnerabilities might be exploited through clever tactics and planning in compensation for U.S. inability to match the Soviet defense effort weapon for weapon and dollar for ruble.

Notes

1. For elaboration, see Kevin N. Lewis, *The Reagan Defense Budget: Prospects and Pressures* (Santa Monica: Rand Corporation, P-6721, December 1981).

2. Among the more notable journalistic tracts that have successfully exploited this mounting undercurrent of popular concern are Jonathan Schell, *The Fate of the Earth* (New York: Alfred Knopf, 1982) and Ground Zero, *Nuclear War: What's in It for You?* (New York: Pocket Books, 1982).

3. See Barry Sussman and Robert G. Kaiser, "Survey Finds 3-to-1 Backing for A-Freeze," *Washington Post,* April 29, 1982—this despite the fact that the same respondents also indicated by two to one their belief that the Soviet Union is ahead of the United States in nuclear weapons and by six to one that the Soviet Union would secretly violate any nuclear freeze agreement the two nations might sign.

4. Spearheading this campaign have been two widely cited Soviet pamphlets written expressly for foreign audiences in response to the Reagan administration's various statements on the Soviet military challenge: *The Threat to Europe* (Moscow: Progress Publishers, 1981) and *Whence the Threat to Peace* (Moscow: Military Publishing House, USSR Ministry of Defense, 1982). Soviet public repudiation of any doctrinal orientation toward offensive war fighting, however, predates President Reagan's election and goes back to the Carter years. See, for example, Don Oberdorfer, "Soviet Marshal Denies Kremlin Seeks Nuclear Superiority," *Washington Post,* August 3, 1979.

5. Even putative matters of fact can entail important elements of ambiguity. An example is the issue of the CEP of the Soviet SS-18 ICBM. The "secret" component of this question—denied to Western observers—is what the Soviets believe to be the accuracy of that weapon, based on evidence provided by their limited flight test experience. The residual mystery concerns what the circular error probability (CEP) of the SS-18 force as a whole actually is. This cannot be confidently known even by the Soviets in the absence of a full-fledged ICBM exchange.

6. For a fuller development of this argument, see Benjamin S. Lambeth, "Soviet Strategic Conduct and the Prospects for Stability," in Christoph Bertram, ed., *The Future of Strategic Deterrence,* Adelphi Papers No. 161 (London: International Institute for Strategic Studies, 1980), pp. 27–38.

7. This perspective was first articulated by Bernard Brodie in his "The Atomic Bomb and American Security," Memorandum No. 18 (New Haven: Yale Institute of International Studies, 1945) and was amplified in his landmark volume, *The Absolute*

Weapon (New York: Harcourt, Brace, 1946). It was reaffirmed in its essentials over three decades later in Brodie's last article before his death in 1978, "The Development of Nuclear Strategy," *International Security* (Spring 1978):65-83.

8. The most recent official expression of this view was Secretary of Defense Casper Weinberger's assertion that despite the Reagan administration's determination to deny the Soviet Union a credible war option, "we do not believe there could be any 'winner' in a nuclear war" (letter to the editor, *Los Angeles Times*, August 25, 1982). Despite the greater than usual heat the Reagan administration has invited upon itself as a consequence of some of its less circumspect pronouncements on nuclear matters, its strategic planning guidance does not differ in its conceptual fundamentals from either that of the Carter administration or the Nixon-Ford administrations.

9. This point was expressed with elegant simplicity by Khrushchev in his memoirs: "If the enemy starts a war against you, then it is your duty to do everything possible to survive the war and to achieve victory in the end." *Khrushchev Remembers*, trans. Strobe Talbott (New York: Bantam Books, 1970), p. 570.

10. By the "Soviets," I am talking about those civilian and military officials at the highest levels of the Soviet defense establishment whose views on the threat and the requirements that stem from it largely govern the complexion of Soviet military programs. Undoubtedly widespread—if often unobservable—differences obtain within this community concerning questions of resource priorities and other implementation matters. It is a premise of this chapter, however, that a broad consensus exists throughout the Soviet elite regarding fundamental Soviet military needs.

11. See, in particular, Richard Pipes, "Why the Soviet Union Thinks It Could Fight and Win a Nuclear War," *Commentary* (July 1977):21-34. A more balanced and qualified treatment of this controversial issue, which resonates well with the argument advanced here, may be found in Stephen Meyer, "Would the Soviets Start a Nuclear War?" *Washington Post*, December 4, 1981.

12. Richard Pipes, "Why the USSR Wants SALT II," Occasional Paper (Washington D.C.: Committee on the Present Danger, September 1979).

13. For further discussion, see Benjamin S. Lambeth, "Uncertainties for the Soviet War Planner," *International Security* (Winter 1983):139-166.

14. See Marshal V.D. Sokolovskii, *Soviet Military Strategy*, with an introduction and commentary by Herbert S. Dinerstein, Leon Goure, and Thomas W. Wolfe (Englewood Cliffs, N.J.: Prentice-Hall, 1963).

15. *Khrushchev Remembers: The Last Testament*, trans. Strobe Talbott (Boston: Little, Brown, 1974), p. 13.

16. Quoted at a Kremlin press conference, *New York Times*, November 9, 1959. Khrushchev's disparaging attitude toward military men was almost legendary. A firm disbeliever in the value of surface combatants in the nuclear age, he would often point to children's toy boats in ponds during strolls through Moscow parks with foreign visitors and refer to them jokingly as "our navy," no doubt to the profound irritation of his admirals. Another symbolic illustration was provided in a remark he reportedly made to Pierre Salinger during a visit at one of the Kremlin's country dachas. The two men were practicing at shooting clay pigeons with shotguns. When

Salinger proved himself clearly the inferior marksman, Khrushchev commented, "Don't feel badly. I've got generals who can't hit anything either." Pierre Salinger, *With Kennedy* (New York: Avon books, 1966), p. 285.

17. Marshal M.V. Zakharov, "The Imperative Demand of Our Time," *Krasnaia Zvezda*, February 4, 1965.

18. The Cuban missile crisis has frequently been touted as a casebook example of successful U.S. coercive diplomacy. Viewed with two decades' hindsight, however, it should more properly be regarded a brilliant tactical victory that produced some very discomfiting long-term consequences for the United States. A former U.S. Ambassador to Moscow reminded us several years ago that the Soviet negotiator during the deliberations leading to the missile withdrawal, Vasiliy Kuznetzov, repeatedly told his U.S. counterpart, John J. McCloy, that "the Soviet Union would never again face a 4-to-1 missile inferiority." Jacob D. Beam, "Dangers of Relying on Weapons Superiority," *Washington Post*, July 15, 1979.

19. Lenin himself insisted that Clausewitz's axiom regarding war as a violent extension of politics constituted the "theoretical foundation for the meaning of every war." Quoted in Edward Meade Earle, "Lenin, Trotsky, Stalin: Soviet Concepts of War," in Earle, ed., *Makers of Modern Strategy* (Princeton: Princeton University Press, 1944), p. 323. For a summary review of how the military classicists (particularly Clausewitz and Jomini) influenced the formation of Soviet military thought during the years prior to World War II, see Raymond L. Garthoff, *Soviet Military Doctrine* (Glencoe, Ill.: Free Press, 1953), pp. 51–58. See also R.H. Baker, "The Origins of Soviet Military Doctrine," *Journal of the Royal United Services Institute* (March 1976):38–43.

20. As Stanley Sienkiewicz has aptly put this point, "The explanation for the Soviet solution to the problem of security in the nuclear age derives more from the fact that it is a solution devised by the *military* profession. ... The notion of sufficiency or parity, on the other hand, is not merely an *American* invention. It is more importantly a *civilian* invention." "SALT and Soviet Nuclear Doctrine," *International Security* (Spring 1978):92.

21. Herbert Goldhamer, *The Soviet Union in a Period of Strategic Parity* (Santa Monica: Rand Corporation, R-889-PR, November 1971).

22. At the time of Khrushchev's ouster in 1964, the Soviet Yankee-class SLBM submarine had not yet been deployed, and the SRF possessed only some 200 SS-7 and SS-8 ICBMs, mostly in soft site launch configurations. By contrast, the United States was well on its way to completing a missile deployment program featuring 1,000 Minuteman ICBMs and 656 Polaris SLBMs.

23. Among the most perceptive analytical treatments of this Soviet weapons acquisition style may be found in Arthur J. Alexander, *R&D in Soviet Aviation* (Santa Monica: Rand Corporation, R-589-PR, November 1970) and his *Armor Development in the Soviet Union and the United States* (Santa Monica: Rand Corporation, R-1860-NA, September 1976). See also Richard D. Ward, "Soviet Practice in Designing and Procuring Military Aircraft," *Aeronautics and Astronautics* (September 1981):24–38, and David Holloway, "Doctrine and Technology in Soviet Armaments Policy," in Derek Leebaert, ed., *Soviet Military Thinking* (London: Allen and Unwin, 1981), pp. 259–291.

24. Much of this notoriety has been occasioned by a recent journalistic critique of U.S. weapons acquisition practices by James Fallows, *National Defense* (New York: Random House, 1981). Fallows makes a major point of contrasting allegedly oversophisticated and unreliable U.S. weapons like the F-15 fighter and the M-1 tank with their cheaper and more serviceable Soviet counterparts. In doing so, he fails to recognize the significant differences in manpower availability and cost that confront the U.S. and Soviet defense establishments, respectively, and largely allow the Soviets to pursue quantity solutions to their military requirements. He also fails to note that the new fighters about to enter the Soviet Air Force inventory are quite comparable (in terms of sophistication and complexity) to those U.S. fighter aircrafts he so roundly deprecates.

25. For further discussion, see John Erickson, *Soviet-Warsaw Pact Force Levels,* USSI Report 76-2 (Washington, D.C.: United States Strategic Institute, 1978); Chris N. Donnelly, "Options in the Enemy Rear: Soviet Doctrine and Tactics," *International Defense Review* 1(January 1980):35–41; and Donald L. Madill, "The Continuing Evolution of the Soviet Ground Forces," *Military Review* (August 1982):52–68.

26. See John Erickson, "Some Developments in Soviet Tactical Aviation (Frontovaia Aviatsiia)," *Journal of the Royal United Services Institute* (September 1975): 70–74; Colin Gray, "Soviet Tactical Airpower," *Air Force Magazine* (March 1977): 62–71; and Colonel Lynn M. Hansen, "The Resurgence of Soviet Frontal Aviation," *Strategic Review* (Fall 1978):71–81. For a brief treatment of some operational impediments that might hinder a successful Soviet air campaign against NATO, see also Joshua M. Epstein, "On Conventional Deterrence in Europe: Questions of Soviet Confidence," *Orbis* (Spring 1982):71–86.

27. See Amoretta Hoeber and Joseph D. Douglass, Jr., "The Neglected Threat of Chemical Warfare," *International Security* (Summer 1978):55–82. U.S. development of chemical weapons was halted during the Nixon administration and has remained moribund ever since. During the Carter years, U.S. officials commonly suggested that a NATO threat to use tactical nuclear weapons would suffice to deter Soviet chemical weapons use. Yet there was and remains good ground for questioning the credibility of such a threat in the absence of a countervailing NATO chemical warfare capability. In 1981, President Reagan sought to reinstitute U.S. development and production of chemical weapons but was turned down by Congress.

28. This would be especially true were the Soviets to withhold attacks against selected countries (for example, France) or indicate a willingness to limit their operations solely to all or part of West Germany. Although there is no evidence that such options are part of Soviet contingency planning, they could be very plausible given the right circumstances of crisis and Soviet war objectives.

29. The Reagan administration has indicated that the Soviets could deploy a nuclear-powered carrier of some 60,000 tons with catapults and an air wing of sixty fighter aircraft toward the end of the 1980s. See *Soviet Military Power* (Washington, D.C.: Department of Defense, 1982), p. 41.

30. Merely to note these Soviet advantages is scarcely to express "discomfort with the messiness of American domestic politics," as imputed by Donald W. Hansen, "Is Soviet Strategic Doctrine Superior?" *International Security* (Winter 1983):66–67. Accepting the complications and occasional irrationalities of a

pluralistic defense process is one of the easier prices to pay for the benefits of life in a democracy. It is pointless, however, to ignore on sentimental grounds the practical effects of the more regimented Soviet approach simply because it happens to be incompatible with Western democratic values.

31. Examples include limited strategic warfare; counterforce-only attacks; selective attacks against enemy command and control facilities; war in space; crisis managment and escalation control; and the use of land-based missiles against targets at sea.

32. The Soviet Union over the past decade has massively outspent the United States in military procurement. Between 1973 and 1979 alone, the Soviets are authoritatively estimated to have exceeded the U.S. effort in this category by some $100 billion. According to a Rand study conducted several years ago, an equivalent sum available to the United States would have completely covered procurement costs (in 1979 dollars) for the following U.S. programs that were planned at that time: the complete B-1 buy; the full MX ICBM force in its racetrack shelter configuration; all programmed Trident missiles and submarines; all 7,000 M-1 tanks planned for deployment, along with a matching number of infantry fighting vehicles and a full complement of new transport aircraft to give them intratheater mobility; and the total package of F-14, F-15, F-16, F-18, and A-10 aircraft intended for U.S. Air Force and Navy tactical airpower modernization. See Arthur J. Alexander, Abraham S. Becker, and William E. Hoehn, Jr., *The Significance of Divergent U.S.–USSR Military Expenditure* (Santa Monica: Rand Corporation, N-1000–AF, February 1979).

33. For further discussion, see S. Enders Wimbush and Alex Alexiev, *The Ethnic Factor in the Soviet Armed Forces* (Santa Monica: Rand Corporation, R-2787, March 1982).

34. See Abraham S. Becker, *The Burden of Soviet Defense: A Political-Economic Essay* (Santa Monica: Rand Corporation, R-2752–AF, October 1981).

35. "A Conceptual Approach to Countering Invasion Threats to NATO" (unpublished manuscript, June 1976), p. 6.

36. A particularly egregious example is Andrew Cockburn, *The Threat: Inside the Soviet Military Machine* (New York: Random House, 1983). See also Les Aspin, "The Soviet Soldier," *New York Times,* June 8, 1982.

3
Soviet Strategic Planning and the Control of Nuclear War

Desmond Ball

Although the objectives of Soviet and U.S. strategic nuclear policy are superficially similar at the most general level—the deterrence of nuclear war and the limitation of damage to their military forces, economic structures, and polities in the event that deterrence fails— each has developed some important differences in the employment policies and force postures in pursuit of these objectives. Central to these differences are the assumptions held by the respective Soviet and U.S. strategic planners regarding the controllability of nuclear war and the approaches each has taken to the design of their national strategic command, control, communications, and intelligence (C³I) systems.[1]

Since the early 1960s, the overriding objective of U.S. strategic nuclear policy has been the development of a strategic posture designed to enable the United States to control any nuclear exchange in order to limit damage at the lowest possible levels while ensuring that the outcomes are favorable to the United States. The notion of controlled response, which was developed by the Kennedy administration in 1961–1962 and which governed the design of SIOP 63 (the single integrated operational plan, or the plan for general nuclear war, which came into effect on July 1, 1962), has been refined but in all essential respects maintained in the concept of escalation control embodied in successive national guidance such as the national security decision memorandum (NSDM) 242, signed by President Nixon on January 17, 1974, PD 59 signed by President Carter on July 25, 1980, and national security decision directive (NSDD) 13 signed by President Reagan in October 1981, and given effect in SIOP 5 of January 1, 1976 and SIOP 6 of October 1, 1983. An extremely wide range of options for the employment of the U.S. strategic nuclear forces has been developed, beginning with the various major attack options (MAOs) and suboptions of SIOP 63 and greatly supplemented by the numerous selective attack options (SAOs), limited nuclear options (LNOs), and regional nuclear options (RNOs), which have been generated by SIOP planners since 1974.[2]

The central theme of these developments has been that the limitation of damage in a nuclear war can best be achieved by controlling escalation so as to terminate any nuclear exchange at the lowest possible level. This has required the United States to develop an extremely sophisticated C³I system to support its own nuclear forces; to design attack options so that Soviet attack characterization and assessment systems could clearly determine the specific intentions behind particular, limited strikes; to have the potential to "hold some vital enemy targets hostage to subsequent destruction" and to control "the timing and pace of attack execution, in order to provide the enemy opportunities to consider his actions"[3]; and insofar as is possible, to give the Soviet Union every incentive to avoid escalation to major urban-industrial attacks. The preservation from destruction or disruption of Soviet C³I systems, including particularly the Soviet national command authorities (NCA), the Soviet attack characterization and assessment systems, and the ability of the Soviet NCA to control its strategic forces, is critical to the success of this approach to damage limitation.

There is no parallel to any of this in Soviet strategic nuclear war planning. On the contrary, Soviet strategic planners believe that the best approach to limiting damage to the Soviet Union is the rapid and wholesale destruction of the ability of the United States and its allies to wage nuclear war. Soviet planners evince no willingness to consider seriously the possibility of limited or controlled strategic nuclear operations. Rather, Soviet strategic policy and targeting doctrine, together with some quite explicit pronouncements, is to the effect that any nuclear exchange would involve simultaneous and unconstrained attacks on a wide range of targets, which would certainly not exclude C³I systems.

There is no evidence that the Soviet strategic planners believe that the damage the Soviet Union would suffer from the resultant U.S. response would be anything less than horrible. On the other hand, they believe that it would be significantly less than that which would pertain in the event that the United States was allowed to control the escalation process and to engage the Soviet Union with its strategic forces fully coordinated and its planners fully informed by timely and accurate intelligence with respect to the deployments and movements of the Soviets' own strategic forces. By attacking the U.S. forces and associated C³I system and thus causing any U.S. response to be less coordinated, more ragged, and much more degraded than it otherwise would be, the casualties that the Soviet Union would be likely to suffer could well be fewer than half what they otherwise might be—perhaps 30 million to 50 million fatalities rather than 50 million to 100 million. Indeed, if the U.S. NCA and other critical elements of the U.S. C³I system were destroyed at the outset of any exchange, Soviet planners could well believe that it might be possible to limit fatalities and damage to much lower levels. This approach to damage limitation is fundamentally different from that embodied in U.S. plans.

Soviet Strategic Doctrine: Implications for the Control of Nuclear War

The most fundamental objective of Soviet strategic policy, as of U.S. strategic policy, is the deterrence of nuclear war: "War with the employment of nuclear weapons can undermine the very foundation for the existence of human society and inflict tremendous damage to its progressive development. Therefore, the most important requirement for progress in our time is the prevention of a new world war."[4] However, unlike U.S. strategic policy, the Soviet view of deterrence involves neither the notion of assured destruction or unacceptable damage nor that of limited or controlled nuclear options. Rather, deterrence of nuclear attack is best achieved by the ability to wage a nuclear war successfully. The better the Soviet forces are equipped and trained to fight a nuclear war, the more effective they will be as a deterrent to a nuclear attack on the Soviet Union. If deterrence fails, these forces will then be used purposefully and massively for military victory.[5]

Soviet discussions of nuclear war invariably stress the importance of the initial nuclear strikes and of seizing the initiative in those strikes. As Marshal Moskalenko wrote in 1969, "In view of the immense destructive force of nuclear weapons and the extremely limited time available to take effective countermeasures after an enemy launches its missiles, the launching of the first massed nuclear attack acquires decisive importance for achieving the objectives of war."[6] Indeed, the notion of anticipating and preempting the attack is pervasive throughout the Soviet literature. For example, a Soviet military text, *Marxism-Leninism on War and Army*, states, "Mass nuclear missile strikes at the armed forces of the opponent and at his key economic and political objectives can determine the victory of one side and the defeat of the other at the very beginning of the war. Therefore, a correct estimate of the elements of the supremacy over the opponent and the ability to *use them before the opponent does* are the key to victory in such a war."[7] Another Soviet text, *Scientific Technical Progress and the Revolution in Military Affairs*, states, "One of the decisive conditions for success in an operation is the anticipating of the enemy in making nuclear strikes, particularly against the enemy's nuclear missile weapons."[8]

Two Soviet military analysts wrote in 1963 that in the event of a nuclear war, the Soviet Union's missiles and bombers "would take off even before the aggressor's first rockets, to say nothing of his bombers, reached their targets."[9] After seizing the initiative, the Soviet forces would move to control events during the conflict. Massive blows against U.S. military, economic-industrial, and political-administrative resources and facilities would frustrate or at least degrade U.S. military operations, thus minimizing damage to the Soviet Union, and would stun the United States into incapacity and eventual surrender.

Soviet nuclear targeting policy follows directly from this doctrinal refrain. In the event of a nuclear war, Soviet strategic forces would be used massively rather than sequentially and against a wide range of nuclear and conventional military targets, command-and-control facilities, centers of political and administrative leadership, economic and industrial facilities, power supplies, and other targets rather than more selectively. Urban areas would not be attacked in pursuit of some arbitrary minimum level of fatalities, but neither would they be avoided if they were near military, political, or industrial targets.

The breadth of Soviet strategic nuclear targeting is shown in the following quotations:

> The Strategic Missile Forces, which form the basis of the combat might of our Armed Forces, are intended for the destruction of the enemy's means of nuclear attack, his large troop formations and military bases, the destruction of the aggressor's defense industry, the disorganization of [his] state and military command and control, and of the operations of his rear and transportation.[10]

> Very important strategic missions of the armed forces can be the destruction of the largest industrial and administrative-political centers, power systems, and stocks of strategic raw materials; disorganization of the system of state and military control; destruction of the main transport centers; and destruction of the main groupings of troops, especially of the means of nuclear attack.[11]

> For the achievement of victory in a present-day nuclear war, if it is unleashed by the imperialists, not only the enemy's armed forces, but also the sources of his military power, the important economic centers, points of military and state control, as well as the areas where different branches of armed forces are based, will be subjected to simultaneous destruction.[12]

Although this wide range of targets would be subject to massive and simultaneous attacks, there are some definite priorities regarding the destruction of particular elements of the U.S. and allied target sets. The primary strategic mission is to destroy enemy military forces, particularly the opposing strategic nuclear forces. As Major General Dzhelaukhov wrote in 1966, "Strategic rockets are regarded as the most important strategic objectives."[13] Also in the primary category are strategic bomber bases, forward-based missiles (FBM) submarine bases and support facilities, nuclear stockpiles, and strategic command-and-control centers.[14] The second target category consists of theater nuclear weapons and associated systems, including tactical and carrier aviation, cruise missiles, tactical missiles, airfields, and tactical command-and-control systems. The third category consists of other military targets, such as large ground troop formations, tank concentrations, reserve forces, storehouses of arms and munitions, equipment and fuel, naval bases, interceptor airfields, antiaircraft artillery and missiles, and associated command-and-control systems and facilities. The fourth category consists of political-administrative targets, such as governmental centers and areas where the political leadership is concentrated. Finally, the fifth category consists of a wide range of economic-industrial facilities, including power stations (perhaps the most important nonmilitary targets in Soviet war planning), stocks of strategic raw materials, oil refineries and storage sites, metallurgical plants, chemical industries, and transport operations (such as "rail centers and marshalling yards, bridges, tunnels, train ferries and trains on land, and ports and vessels on the water").[15]

On the basis of these target sets and the priorities attached to their destruction, it is possible to construct a notional Soviet equivalent of the SIOP: the Russian integrated strategic operational plan (RISOP). The most recent version of RISOP 5, which involves the allocation of about 7,420 strategic warheads and bombs to these target categories in generated and nongenerated situations (where the Soviet forces are intact and on a relatively high level of alert as compared to where they have suffered a U.S. counterforce strike) looks something like that shown in table 3–1.

Table 3–1
Allocation of Soviet RISOP Warheads to Target Categories in Generated and Nongenerated Situations, July 1982

	Generated	*Nongenerated*
Baseline force	7,420	7,420
Weapons deliverable to target	4,840	3,352
Target category		
Strategic C³I targets	400	400
U.S. SIOP forces	2,302	2,302
French and British strategic nuclear forces	80	80
Theater nuclear forces capable of hitting the Soviet Union	250	250
U.S.–NATO conventional power projection forces	200	50
U.S.–NATO administrative-governmental targets	150	50
U.S.–NATO economic-industrial, war supporting, and economic recovery targets	1,250	200
Reserve warheads, including warheads allocated to targets in China	208	20

The U.S. notion that attacks should be withheld from command-and-control assets, at least to the extent that such assets are needed to control escalation and conduct negotiations, is not reflected in Soviet military doctrine. On the contrary, it appears to be Soviet policy to attack command-and-control systems at the outset of any strategic nuclear exchange in an effort to disrupt and degrade the enemy's military forces, political and administrative control, and industrial support capacity. As Major General Van C. Doubleday testified in 1979, "Soviet strategic doctrine indicates Soviet strategic targeting specifically includes U.S. C³I."[16] And Douglass and Hoeber concluded that "there would likely be an intensive, overt, active attack on reconnaissance, command and control, and communications assets at the very beginning of the war."[17] The destruction of U.S. national command-and-control facilities would disrupt U.S. attacks and would allow the Soviet Union to control the progress of the conflict and to conduct military and political reconstitution more effectively. Attacks on strategic and tactical command-and-control systems would be an integral part of the missions against the strategic nuclear and other military forces. As Colonel Shirikov wrote in 1966:

> Under conditions of a nuclear war, the system for controlling forces and weapons, especially strategic weapons, acquires exceptionally great significance. A disruption of the control over a country and its troops in a theater of military operations can seriously affect the course of events, and in difficult circumstances, can even lead to defeat in a war. Thus, areas deserving special attention are the following: knowing the coordinates of stationary operations control centers and the extent of their ability to survive; the presence of mobile command posts and automatic information processing centers; the communications lines' levels of development and, first of all, that of underground and underwater cable, radio-relay, ionospheric and tropospheric communication lines; field communications networks and duplicate communication lines; communication centers and the extent of their facilities, dispersion and vulnerability.[18]

The Soviet Union has evidently developed and deployed a wide range of forces designed specifically for operations against command-and-control apparatus. Some 380 KGB teams are reported to have been organized for operations against NATO C³I facilities.[19] Secretary Harold Brown expressed the opinion that "more than 200 SS-9 [ICBMs] were almost surely targeted against the one hundred Minuteman launch control complexes, two missiles to a complex."[20]

There is no serious consideration in the Soviet literature of such concepts as controlled escalation and limited nuclear war. The Soviet reaction to Robert McNamara declarations of 1962 regarding the "no cities" counterforce policy and James Schlesinger's statements of 1974 on limited and selective options were quite negative. In a critique of McNamara's speech that described the no cities strategy, Marshal Sokolovskii rejected what he termed "rules for waging a nuclear war."[21] And in response to Schlesinger's statement announcing the new U.S. strategic policy, G.A. Arbatov wrote, "In actual fact these proposals are a demagogic trap designed to lull public opinion and to make the prospect of nuclear war more acceptable or, if you like, more digestible. . . . The idea itself of introducing 'rules of the game' and of artificial limitations 'by agreement' is based on an illusion and is without foundation. It is hard to imagine that nuclear war, if launched, could be held within the framework of the 'rules' and not grow into general war."[22]

Similar declarations from Moscow followed the announcement that on July 25, 1980, President Carter had signed a presidential directive on U.S. nuclear strategy (PD 59) that the United States should develop the plans and capabilities for limited, selective, and possibly quite protracted nuclear exchanges. In August 1980, President Brezhnev said that "statements about alleged limited and partial use of nuclear weapons have nothing in common with reality."[23] Other Soviet spokesmen stated that the notion that nuclear attacks could be conducted against military targets while limiting civilian casualties was "absolute fantasy";[24] that any U.S. strike at targets in the Soviet Union would produce "a decisive swift response—[a] full-scale response";[25] and that "the logic of a nuclear war is inexorable. If it is unleashed, it is impossible to put it in some narrow limits or to somehow restrict it."[26]

Despite these statements, Western commentators in recent years have increasingly argued that the avowed doctrine and supportive pronouncements no longer reflect likely Soviet actions in the event of a conflict with the United States and its allies. Rather the Soviet declarations about the automaticity of escalation of any limited use of nuclear weapons to an all-out exchange are intended to engender doubts within NATO about the viability of the policy of flexible response and hence to induce NATO self-deterrence in any crisis. Some statements can be cited from the Soviet military literature to the effect that notions of control, selectivity, and restraint are not entirely absent from Soviet military thinking and that capabilities for exercising control and restraint that are embodied in the current Soviet strategic force posture and supportive command-and-control systems are undoubtedly greater than would be required for massive and indiscriminate operations.

The evidence that Soviet military doctrine now incorporates the possibility of control, selectivity, and restraint in a strategic nuclear conflict is actually very fragmentary, however. It derives principally from some statements that stand apart from the overwhelming thrust of Soviet military literature—and even these statements fall short of suggesting a Soviet willingness to engage in controlled escalation. And insofar as notions of control, selectivity, and restraint appear at all in the Soviet military literature, they have quite different connotations from those that form major elements of current U.S. strategic doctrine.

It is clear in the Soviet literature that military strategy is subservient to political objectives and that the scale and character of military operations are determined by the political leadership:

> Politics determines the priority and strength of the blows inflicted on the enemy, the measures taken to strengthen allied relations within the coalition, and the general strategic plan of the war, which is directed at the quickest possible rout of the enemy or at a drawn out struggle and the gradual exhaustion of the enemy's forces. At the same time, politics, by taking into account the strategic possibilities at its disposal, must determine the speed and the intensity of the military actions, and also the forces and means it is necessary to mobilize in order to attain the aims intended, etc. In doing so, politics takes into account not only the aims of the war but also those of the post-war settlement and subordinates the conduct of the war to the attainment of these aims.[27]

> The decision to employ such devastating implements as nuclear weapons has become the exclusive prerogative of the political leadership. It is primarily the political, not the military, leaders who determine the necessity of employing mass destruction weapons, who specify the principal targets, and when they are to be hit.[28]

However, to acknowledge that modern weapons have such "tremendous destructive capabilities" that they cannot remain "outside political control" is very different from suggesting that Soviet decision makers have a propensity for controlled response strategies.[29]

It is also clear that the Soviet Union exercises some selectivity in the choice of targets to be attacked in the event of a nuclear conflict. Colonel Shirokov has written that "the quantity of objectives, especially military-economic, located on the territory of warring states . . . is very great. Therefore, the belligerents will strive to *select* from the objectives *those which have the greatest influence on the outcome of the armed struggle.*"[30] However, to acknowledge that the Soviet strategic nuclear arsenal is inadequate to cover all possible military, political, and economic targets in the West and that it is considered more urgent to destroy some targets than others is very different from suggesting that the Soviet Union accepts any notion of selective options or selective response. In the Soviet context, the term *selective* should not be equated with "limited" or "few."[31]

It is also possible to find references in the Soviet literature to various notions of restraint—in terms of the types of weapons that might be used in a particular conflict, the targets to be attacked, and the collateral damage that might be attendant on certain operations. Moreover, Soviet military doctrine does not imply the all-out use of nuclear weapons in all situations in which Soviet armed forces or Soviet national interests are involved. For example, Soviet intervention in Yemen (1967), Somalia (1970), Iraq (1973), Angola (1975), and Afghanistan (1980) never envisaged nuclear operations. But to state that such activities "clearly suggest the evolution of a Soviet doctrine and posture of flexible response" is to put a quite unreasonable construction on the notion of flexible response.[32]

A far more interesting area of possible Soviet restraint is conventional military operations in the European theater. Soviet military planners have given some consideration to the possibility of nonnuclear operations in Europe, at least in the initial phases of a conflict. For example, Marshal Iakubovskii, then the commander in chief of the Warsaw Pact forces, argued in 1967 to the effect that "Soviet doctrine should increasingly direct its attention to the hitherto largely ignored requirements of waging not only nuclear war in the European theater but also using conventional weapons only."[33] And in 1970 Colonel Sidorenko wrote, "In spite of the fact that nuclear weapons will become the chief means of defeating the enemy, their role and capabilities cannot be made absolute, especially in the attainment of goals of combat actions by *podrazdeleniia* and *chasti* [regimental units and smaller]. In a number of cases *podrazdeleniia* and *chasti* will have to perform various combat actions, including the attack, without use of nuclear weapons, using only conventional organic 'classic' means of armament— artillery, tanks, small arms, etc."[34]

In 1967, Warsaw Pact exercises began for the first time to simulate conflict scenarios whose initiation and early phases remained confined to conventional military operations.[35] These exercises, however, invariably evolved into simulated exchanges, and Warsaw Pact commentators continued to assert that any war in Europe would be transformed into all-out nuclear conflict "from the very beginning or after a few days of conventional warfare."[36] That resort to the large-scale use of nuclear weapons would not necessarily be immediate or that some Warsaw Pact troops would have to fight without direct nuclear support in no sense implies acceptance of the notion of controlled escalation.

The same point can be made with respect to the notion of withholding strategies. Various Soviet commentators have declared that it is not necessary to destroy everything in either the homeland of the adversary or in a particular theater of operations. For example, Colonel M. Shirikov wrote in 1966 that "the objective is not to turn the large economic and industrial regions into a heap of ruins (although great destruction apparently is unavoidable), but to deliver strikes which will destroy strategic combat means, paralyze enemy military production, making it incapable of satisfying the priority needs of the front and rear areas and sharply reduce the enemy capability to conduct strikes."[37] And in 1968 he wrote that "political motives can force the abandonment of strikes against extremely important economic and military targets or their implementation with smaller forces and means and on a selective basis."[38]

The rationale for this is quite pragmatic: it is militarily more effective to concentrate attacks on particular vulnerable points, such as critical links in the economic infrastructure, than to target all the possible elements of a given target set;[39] preserving certain installations or regions allows them to be "used in the interests of strengthening the economic potential of our own country and for supplying the troops";[40] caution in attacking certain urban areas in Western Europe is required because the resultant rubble might impede Soviet military operations;[41] and, from a longer-term perspective, capture of the European production base would provide the Soviet Union with a major asset in postwar strategic relationships.[42] Again, there is nothing in this discussion of withholding to suggest any serious consideration of the notion of controlled escalation.

Soviet C³I Capabilities and the Control of Nuclear War

The Soviet Union has a very extensive network of C³I systems for the command, control, and support of its strategic nuclear forces. Although little is publicly known about some of its particular elements, especially the specific line of authority and other more procedural aspects, the physical elements are quite apparent. The construction of underground command-and-control centers takes at least a year and is easily noted by photographic reconnaissance satellites; communications facilities, navigation stations, and radar sites are mapped by a variety of signal intelligence (SIGINT) systems; and satellite launches and orbits are continuously monitored, although the precise mission must necessarily often be inferred.

C³ Survivability

Since the 1950s, the Soviet Union has placed great emphasis on ensuring the survivability during a nuclear exchange of the Soviet leadership—not just of the NCA and armed forces at the national level but also of the military, political, and economic leadership throughout the country. Shelters have been constructed for about 110,000 members of the leadership, made up of some 5,000 party and government officials at the national and republic level; 63,000 party and government leaders at *krai, oblast,* city, and urban *raion* level; 2,000 managers of key installations; and about 40,000 members of civil defense staffs.[43]

According to testimony of the chairman of the Joint Chiefs of Staff, General George S. Brown, "The first echelon command-control-communications centers of the Soviet government and armed forces at a national level are dispersed and hardened within an 80-mile radius of Moscow." This includes some seventy-five underground command posts within Moscow itself. Some of these structures are several hundred feet deep and are capable of withstanding 1,000 pounds per square inch (psi) of blast overpressure.[44]

According to testimony of the secretary of the U.S. Air Force in 1977, the Soviet Union has also built "thousands of hardened military command posts, communications antennae and associated control facilities,"[45] many of which are hardened to withstand overpressures greater than 600 psi.[46]

These ground-based command-and-control centers are backed up by a fleet of several airborne command posts operated by the Soviet air forces and regularly used during exercises and crises. However, the Soviet airborne system is rather more archaic than its U.S. counterpart.[47] It consists of several Il-62 Classic and Il-76 Candid four-engine turbojet transports and perhaps also ten Tu-20 Moss aircraft. It is more than simply an airborne communications link, but it is not comparable to the U.S. National Emergency Airborne Command Post (NEACP) in terms of maintaining fully equipped battle staffs with comprehensive intelligence data links.

Some further backup capability is provided by two Sverdlov-class light cruisers, *Zhdanov* and *Admiral Seniavin,* which have been extensively converted to the command ship role.[48] However, these are primarily alternate command posts to the navy headquarters in Moscow and would have only marginal capability of supporting national-level command and control; they must also be considered quite vulnerable in any nuclear exchange.

Surveillance, Warning, and Assessment

Early warning of U.S. ballistic missile attack is provided by satellites, three over the horizon (OTH) back-scatter radar systems (one near Nikolayevsk in the extreme eastern Soviet Union, another near Kiev, and a third in the Caucasus Mountains), and some twenty-five extremely large early warning and target-tracking phased array radars (PARs), including fifteen Hen House search-and-track radars with a range of about 3,200 nautical miles, seven Pechora-class radars (located at Pechora, Abalakov north of Krasnoyarsk, Lyaki near the Caspian Sea, Sary Shagan, Michelevka, just north of Mongolia, on the Kola Peninsula, and on Kamchatka Peninsula), and three PARs directly associated with the Moscow ballistic missile defense (BMD) system (one of which is located at Pushkino just northwest of Moscow and the other two to the southeast of the city). In addition to their early warning function, these radar would also have some attack characterization capability.[49]

Communications Systems

The Soviet Union has a military communications system incorporating a degree of redundancy similar to, if not greater than, that of the U.S. system. Links in the network are provided by various land line, airborne, satellite, troposcatter, microwave, and other radio systems. Because of the enormous distances to be covered and the inhospitable terrain of much of the Soviet Union, there is a relatively greater dependence on long-range high frequency (HF) and very low frequency (VLF) radio and satellite communications systems.

Until the mid-1970s, HF radio was the principal means of Soviet long-range military communications; however, HF transmissions are extremely susceptible to interruption by solar storms (which partially affect the northern regions of the Soviet Union) and to the effects of nuclear explosions, and HF signals have a propensity to travel around the globe, which makes secure communications somewhat difficult. Hence the Soviet Union has come to rely much more on satellites for military communications.

Three types of military communications satellites have been deployed. One involves extremely large numbers of small (100 centimeter diameter) satellites launched in groups of eight by a single rocket; they are launched into circular orbits of about 1,400 to 1,500 kilometers (km) and have an operational life of two to three years. A minimum of twenty-four such satellites is needed to provide global coverage, but Soviet military chiefs evidently prefer thirty-six to forty-eight to ensure plenty of redundancy and to make it impossible for the West to jam them all.[50] The second type is the *Molniia* series of communications satellites. These follow highly elliptical orbits, with apogees in the northern hemisphere of approximately 40,000 km, each satellite thus providing eight to ten hours per day of continuous communications throughout the Soviet Union and associated countries. (The Soviet contribution to the Moscow–Washington hot line uses *Molnii 2* satellites.) The third type of satellite is in geostationary orbit, and the first of these was launched on July 29, 1974.

An extensive network of *Orbita* ground receiving terminals has been deployed throughout the Soviet Union, and terminals are located near the headquarters of most of the military districts and near naval bases and missile fields. A mobile ground station with a 7 meter dish has also been developed for providing links with the *Molniia* and geostationary communications satellites; one was deployed at Termez in 1980 to support the Soviet invasion of Afghanistan.

VLF is both the principal means of communicating with Soviet ballistic missile submarines, as well as of transmitting long-range navigation signals for submarines, surface vessels, and aircraft. There are thirty VLF stations in the Soviet Union, including eleven with outputs of 500 kilowatts (kW) or more, giving them worldwide coverage, and another five with outputs of 100 to 500 kW.[51] Soviet VLF transmissions tend to be concentrated in the lower part of the VLF band, indicating perhaps an emphasis on maximizing underwater reception rather than the rate of data transmission. A backup capability for communicating with submarines is provided by HF, and possibly by satellites, but there is no evidence of any Soviet airborne systems having been developed for this purpose.[52] (See table 3-2.)

Operational Control

The Soviet strategic forces are generally maintained on much lower alert rates than their U.S. counterparts and have never demonstrated any significant surge capability. In the case of SLBMs, for example, the proportion of the Soviet submarines on alert at sea at any one time is currently about 15 percent, which would allow the deployment of about seven SSBNs in the Atlantic Ocean and perhaps two in the Pacific Ocean.[53] In the case of ICBMs, only a relatively small proportion are kept on a readiness alert comparable to that of the U.S. Minuteman missiles.[54] The principal reason for these relatively low alert rates is that the Soviet Union lacks the complex and expensive command systems required to combine a high state of launch readiness with adequate safeguards against unauthorized firing.[55] This is a particular problem in the Soviet Union since control of the nuclear warheads is evidently shared by the KGB and the strategic rocket forces. For about the first decade of the missile age, the warheads were reported to be kept physically separate from the ICBMs and under direct control of the KGB. With the development of improved safety devices, however, dual control could be exercised by electronic means from the missile launch control centers (LCCs).

The Soviet Union has dispersed about 300 hardened command-and-control centers for the strategic rocket forces throughout the ICBM and M/IRBM deployment areas.[56] These include the 100 3X command-and-control silos—the subject of great controversy in the mid-1970s—[57] which have antennas that provide a direct link with higher headquarters. The internal design of these LCCs, with consoles for two independent operators acting in concert, is similar to that of the Minuteman LCCs in the United States.[58]

General Assessment

Overall the Soviet command-and-control system for the strategic nuclear forces is at least as good as that of the United States. Indeed, former Secretary of the Navy J. William Middendorf once declared that "the Soviets have the best command-and-control one can imagine.[59] Some elements of the Soviet

Table 3–2
Soviet VLF Stations (3–30 KHz)

Station	Coordinates		Power (kW)	Frequency (KHz)	Year Operational
	Latitude North	Latitude East			
Komsomolskamur	50.34	136.58	500	11.905 12.5 12.649 13.281 14.881 15.625	1968
Krasnodar	45.02	38.39	500	11.905 12.5 12.649 13.281 14.881 15.625	1968
Novosibirsk	55.04	82.58	500	11.905 12.5 12.649 13.281 14.881 15.625	1968
Ostachkov	57.10	33.05	15	14.3	1945
Petropavlo Kam	52.55	158.39	500	14.3 17.9	1959
Piltun	53.20	143.25	1	14.3	1951
Preobrajenskoe	54.46	167.37	1	14.3	1946
Batumi	41.39	41.38	100	14.6	1959
Vladivostok	43.06	131.53	100	15 27.5	1959
Dikson Ostrov	73.00	80.25	200	15.3	1958
Odessa	46.29	30.44	1000	15.6	1959
Algazy	43.50	77.11	15	16.1	1945
Kaliningrad 1	54.42	20.30	500	16.2	1959
Kaliningrad 2	54.45	20.30	1000	30	1973
Moscow	55.49	37.18	1000	17.1 28.64	1959
Salair	54.10	85.47	1	17.9	1946
Matotchkinchar	73.16	56.24	100	18.1 23	1959
Murmansk	68.58	33.05	1000	18.1	1978
Rostov	57.14	39.48	1000	18.9	1959
Pereiezdnaia	48.54	38.08	15	19.3	1946
Panfilov	44.09	79.56	1	19.3	1946

Table 3-2 continued

Povorotnyi	42.55	133.06	15	19.3	1951
Arkhangelsk	64.33	40.32	150	19.7	1958
Darasun	51.00	115.00	1	20.6	1951
Lazo Khabarovs	43.20	134.00	1	23	1945
Millerovo 1	48.55	40.22	15	23	1946
Millerovo 2	48.55	40.27	50	23.2	1959
Sarpa	47.15	45.10	15	24.3	1946
Pioner Sovkhoz	53.11	49.46	25	25.7	1945
Rostov-on-Don	47.58	39.48	1000	27	1975

Source: *International Frequency List Drawn up by the International Frequency Registration Board* (International Telecommunications Union, Geneva).

strategic command-and-control capability, such as the airborne command posts and satellite early warning and intelligence systems, are technically much less capable than their U.S. counterparts. On the other hand, protection of the top political and military leadership is much more extensive, and Soviet communications links are much more dispersed and redundant. It would probably not be possible to isolate the Soviet NCA completely from the strategic forces or completely impair the Soviet strategic intelligence flow.

Perhaps the greatest weaknesses in the Soviet strategic command-and-control system are the extreme reliance on satellites for secure long-range military communications and the high degree of centralization in the command-and-control structure and procedures. Satellites systems—the satellites, the ground stations, and the communication links among them—are vulnerable. More important, however, the highly centralized procedures employed in Soviet command-and-control expose the whole system to disruption. Observation of Soviet military exercises gives the impression that ships, aircraft, and commands have carefully and specially planned roles and that operational communications flow directly between headquarters in Moscow and the individual units in the field. Local commanders seem to have relatively little scope to adapt general orders to field conditions or to use their own initiative if they do not receive central orders. This tendency could be even more pronounced in the strategic forces since Soviet leaders would be particularly loath to allow lower commanders much room for initiative where nuclear weapons were concerned. The temptation to exploit this characteristic is immense. As Admiral Murphy testified in 1976, the Soviet command and control "is highly centralized. . . . If we put enough effort into countering . . . their command and control system, we could find this could be the Achilles heel of the fighting forces of the Soviet Union in a war."[60]

This weakness of the Soviet C³I system adds critical support to the doctrinal predilections of Soviet strategic planners to react to any actual or seemingly imminent U.S. nuclear attack, no matter how limited or supposedly controlled, with a massive response, especially since it is known that U.S. strategic nuclear targeting plans include a wide range of Soviet leadership and C³I facilities.[61]

Conclusion

The Soviet Union in recent years has developed and deployed an extensive and redundant array of command-and-control capabilities, which could potentially be used to control escalation in a nuclear war, but this does not necessarily imply any Soviet propensity to engage in controlled escalation. Indeed, the Soviet command-and-control system is weakest in the capabilities required for controlled nuclear war fighting, such as timely intelligence, attack characterization, damage assessment, and targeting flexibility. Rather, the Soviet effort emphasizes the survivability of the leadership and a centralized control network emanating from that leadership so as to guarantee that the United States could not paralyze the Soviet strategic forces and to enable the leadership to maintain political control of the Soviet military, economy, and society during both the conflict and a period of restoration and recuperation.

There remains the possibility that in an actual nuclear exchange, the Soviet leadership might discard its avowed doctrinal predilections and use extant command-and-control capabilities to improvise some notions of limitation and escalation control. This was the possibility that McNamara grasped to rationalize his no cities doctrine. Although McNamara believed that any nuclear attack by the Soviet Union would include an attack on the major urban areas of the United States, he also reckoned that every incentive should be given to the Soviet Union to desist from attacking cities in the event that its leaders might reconsider their doctrine during a crisis.[62] However, the doctrine that once the nuclear threshold is passed, it is the task of the nuclear forces to terminate the war by achieving military victory through massive, crippling strikes, is deeply rooted in Soviet strategic culture, and the preferences and habits of the military bureaucracy would tend to rule out any possibility of improvisation in favor of "American-formulated rules of intra-war restraint."[63] To prepare for controlled nuclear exchanges on the basis of this possibility is therefore likely to be a fruitless exercise, reflecting wishful thinking rather than the realities of the strategic situation.

Notes

1. For a fuller discussion of the concept of controlled nuclear war, from which much of the material in this chapter is derived, see Desmond Ball, *Can Nuclear War*

be Controlled? Adelphi Paper No. 169 (London: International Institute for Strategic Studies [IISS], Autumn 1981).

2. See Desmond Ball, *Targeting for Strategic Deterrence*, Adelphi Paper No. 185 (London: IISS, Summer 1983), pp. 17–25.

3. Richard Nixon, National Security Decision Memorandum (NSDM) 242, January 17, 1974, cited by Jack Anderson, "Not-So-New Nuclear Strategy," *Washington Post*, October 12, 1980, p. C-7.

4. *Marxism-Leninism on War and Army*, trans. and pub. under the auspices of the U.S. Air Force (Washington, D.C.: Government Printing Office [GPO], 1972), pp. 9–10.

5. For fuller discussion of Soviet strategic doctrine, see Benjamin S. Lambeth, "The Sources of Soviet Military Doctrine," in F.B. Horton, A.C. Rogerson, and E.L. Warner, eds., *Comparative Defense Policy* (Baltimore: Johns Hopkins University Press, 1974), pp. 200–216, *Selective Nuclear Options in American and Soviet Strategic Policy* (Santa Monica: Rand R-2034-DDR & E, December 1976), and *The Elements of Soviet Strategic Policy* (Santa Monica: Rand P-6389, September 1979).

6. Cited by Joseph D. Douglass, Jr., and Amoretta M. Hoeber, *Soviet Strategy for Nuclear War* (Stanford: Hoover Institution Press, 1979), p. 36.

7. *Marxism-Leninism on War and Army*, p. 217 (emphasis added).

8. N.A. Lomov, ed., *Scientific-Technical Progress and the Revolution in Military Affairs*, trans. and pub. under the auspices of the U.S. Air Force (Washington, D.C.: GPO, 1974), p. 147.

9. I. Glagolov and V. Larionov, "Soviet Defense Might and Peaceful Coexistence," *International Affairs* (Moscow) (December 1963):32.

10. Marshal A.A. Grechko, cited by Leon Goure, Foy D. Kohler, and Mose L. Harvey, *The Role of Nuclear Forces in Current Soviet Strategy* (Miami: Center for Advanced International Studies, University of Miami, 1974), p. 107.

11. V. Zenskov, cited by Douglass and Hoeber, *Soviet Strategy*, p. 16.

12. M. Shirokov, cited by Leon Goure and Michael J. Deane, "The Soviet Strategic View," *Strategic Review* (Winter 1980) (emphasis added)

13. Cited by Douglass and Hoeber, *Soviet Strategy*, p. 75.

14. See Joseph D. Douglass, Jr., *Soviet Military Strategy in Europe* (Elmsford, N.Y.: Pergamon Press, 1980), p. 74.

15. Colonel Shirokov, cited in Goure and Deane, "Soviet Strategic View," pp. 81–83.

16. U.S. Congress, House, Appropriations Committee, *Department of Defense Appropriations for 1980* (Washington, D.C.: GPO April 1979), pt. 6, p. 98.

17. Douglass and Hoeber, *Soviet Strategy*, p. 45.

18. Cited by ibid., p. 78.

19. William Schneider, "Trends in Soviet Frontal Aviation," *Air Force Magazine* (March 1979):76.

20. Text of address to the U.S. Naval Academy, Annapolis, May 31, 1979, pp. 6–7.

21. Marshal Sokolovskii, "A Suicidal Strategy," *Krasnaia zvezda*, July 19, 1962.

22. G.A. Arbatov, "The American Strategic Debate: A Soviet View," *Survival* 16 (May–June 1974):133–134.

23. *Guardian*, August 30, 1980.

24. *International Herald Tribune*, August 28, 1980.

25. Ibid., August 15, 1980.

26. *London Times,* September 24, 1980.

27. *Marxism-Leninism on War and Army,* p. 17.

28. V.I. Zemskov, cited by Douglass, *Soviet Military Strategy,* p. 162.

29. Zemskov, cited by Goure, Kohler, and Harvey, *Role,* p. 112.

30. Cited by Goure and Deane, "Soviet Strategic View," p. 81 (emphasis added)

31. See Joseph D. Douglass, Jr., "Soviet Nuclear Strategy in Europe: A Selective Targeting Doctrine?" *Strategic Review* (Fall 1977):19.

32. C.G. Jacobsen, "The Emergence of Soviet Doctrine of Flexible Response?" *Atlantic Community Quarterly* 12(Summer 1972):236.

33. Lambeth, "Sources of Soviet Military Doctrine," p. 204.

34. A.A. Sidorenko, *The Offensive,* trans. and pub. under the auspices of the U.S. Air Force (Washington, D.C.: GPO, 1973) p. 222.

35. See Thomas A. Wolfe, *Soviet Power and Europe, 1945–1970* (Baltimore: Johns Hopkins University Press, 1970) pp. 477–482.

36. Ibid., p. 458.

37. Cited by Douglass, "Soviet Nuclear Strategy in Europe," p. 26.

38. Cited by Goure and Deane, "Soviet Strategic View," p. 83.

39. Ibid., p. 82.

40. Col. Shirokov, cited by Douglass, "Soviet Nuclear Strategy in Europe," p. 26.

41. Ibid., p. 22.

42. Ibid., p. 25.

43. Director of Central Intelligence, *Soviet Civil Defense,* CIA, N178–10003 (July 1978), p. 8.

44. Letter from General Brown to Senator William Proxmire, February 3, 1977, in *Survival* 19(March–April 1977):77.

45. Cited by Edgar Ulsamer, "The USSR's Military Shadow Is Lengthening," *Air Force Magazine* (March 1977):42.

46. U.S. Arms Control and Disarmament Agency (ACDA), *Effectiveness of Soviet Defense in Limiting Damage to Population,* ACDA Civil Defense Study Report No. 1 (Washington, D.C.: GPO, November 1977), p. 20.

47. *Department of Defense Appropriations for 1980,* pt. 6, p. 143.

48. Norman Polmar, "Thinking about Soviet C³," *NATO's Fifteen Nations* (October–November 1979):38.

49. U.S. Department of Defense, *Soviet Military Power 1984* (Washington, D.C.: GPO, 1984), pp. 32–35, and Ted Agres, "Soviets Building ABM Radar System," *Washington Times,* April 19, 1984, p. 1.

50. Reginald Turnill, *The Observer's Spaceflight Directory* (London: Warne, 1978), p. 253.

51. International Telecommunications Union, *International Frequency List Drawn Up by the International Frequency Registration Board* (Geneva: International Telecommunications Union, 1982), pp. 1–5.

52. Owen Wilkes, "Command and Control of the Sea-Based Nuclear Deterrent: The Possibility of a Counterforce Role," in Stockholm International Peace Research Institute, *SIPRI Yearbook 1979* (London: Raylor and Francis, 1979), p. 407.

53. George S. Brown, *United States Military Posture for Fiscal Year 1979,* January 20, 1978, p. 28.

54. U.S. Congress, Joint Economic Committee, *Allocation of Resources in the Soviet Union and China-1977* (Washington, D.C.: GPO, June–July 1977), p. 94.

55. Edward Luttwak, *The Strategic Balance 1972*, Washington Paper No. 3 (Washington, D.C.: Center for Strategic and International Studies, Georgetown University, 1972), pp. 16–17.

56. Colin S. Gray, "Strategic Rocket Forces: Military Capability, Strategic Utility," *Air Force Magazine* (March 1978):51.

57. Nicholas Daniloff, "How We Spy on the Russians and Monitor SALT," *Washington Post*, December 9, 1979.

58. *Aviation Week and Space Technology*, September 1, 1975, p. 16.

59. Cited by Polmar, "Thinking about Soviet C³," p. 36.

60. U.S. Congress, Senate, Armed Services Committee *Fiscal Year 1977 Authorization for Military Procurement, Research and Development and Active Duty, Selected Reserve and Civilian Personnel Strengths*, pt. 4 (December 1975–February 1976), p. 1971.

61. See Ball, *Targeting for Strategic Deterrence*, pp. 26, 31–32.

62. U.S. Congress, House, Armed Services Committee, *Hearings on Military Posture* (Washington, D.C.: GPO, 1963), p. 332: U.S. Congress, House, Appropriations Committee, *Department of Defense Appropriations for 1964* (Washington, D.C.: GPO, 1963), pt. 1, p. 234.

63. Jack L. Snyder, *The Soviet Strategic Culture: Implications for Limited Nuclear Operations* (Santa Monica: Rand R-2154-AF, September 1977).

4
Ballistic Missile Defense and Soviet Strategy

Jeffrey Richelson

D espite the signing and ratification of the ABM Treaty over ten years ago, both the United States and the Soviet Union have pursued vigorous research and development programs with respect to ballistic missile defense (BMD). Indeed, for several years many U.S. analysts have charged that the Soviet Union's BMD program has moved beyond the limitations set by the ABM Treaty and that they are preparing to break out of the treaty. Such charges have been echoed by Reagan administration officials and study groups. A senior intelligence official was quoted as stating that "the emerging pattern clearly shows the Soviets are upgrading their ABM capability and could be preparing for a breakout of the ABM Treaty."[1] The report of the General Advisory Committee on Arms Control and Disarmament concerning Soviet compliance practices charged the Soviet Union with violation of the prohibition on the development and deployment of nonpermanently fixed ABM radar on Kamchatka Peninsula in 1975.[2]

Beyond concern with Soviet BMD activities, the subject of BMD has been the focus of renewed interest in recent years due to improvements in conventional BMD technology, as well as the suggestions that laser and particle beam technology can be employed to provide a workable BMD system. The most visible manifestation of this interest was President Reagan's speech of March 23, 1983, advocating development of space-based BMD. Subsequently he signed NSDD 85, entitled "Eliminating the Threat of Ballistic Missiles," to accelerate R&D. NSDD 85 was followed by NSDD 6-83 setting up the Future Security Strategy Study Teams and the Defensive Technologies Study Team.[3]

The Defensive Technologies Study's principal finding was that "despite the uncertainties, new technologies hold great promise for achieving the President's goals of eliminating the threat of ballistic missiles to ourselves and our allies."[4] R&D concerning such technologies has been assigned by NSDD 119 of January 6, 1984, to the newly formed Strategic Defense Initiative Organization (SDIO).

Several of those who both fear Soviet breakout and are optimistic about the ability of the United States to develop a workable BMD program have advocated revision or abrogation of the ABM Treaty to allow for U.S. deployment of a significant defensive system. In the light of U.S. efforts in the BMD field and such attitudes, it would be useful to examine the present and possible future roles of BMD in Soviet strategy. Understanding these roles requires an examination of the history of Soviet BMD activity, the Soviet motivation for participating in the ABM Treaty, and developments in Soviet BMD activity since 1972.

Early Developments

The Soviet R&D program for BMD was authorized by Josef Stalin at the end of World War II as one of a series of strategic defense projects. The authorization was probably a response to several stimuli: the damage suffered by the Soviet Union in World War II air raids, the British experience with the V-1 and V-2 weapons, and the Soviet ICBM program.[5]

The first detailed information concerning the Soviet BMD program came in April 1960 as a result of a U-2 flight over Sary Shagan. The U-2 photos showed components of three systems that had eventual BMD possibilities. Within two years high Soviet officials were claiming to have solved the problem of BMD. At the Twenty-second Party Congress in October 1961, Defense Minister Marshal Rodion Malinovsky noted that "the problem of destroying enemy missiles in flight has been successfully resolved." And in July 1962 Premier Nikita Khrushchev stated that Soviet missile defenses could "hit a fly in space."[6]

The overall BMD program that emerged in the Khrushchev era involved several distinct interceptor missiles: Griffon, Galosh, and possibly the SA-5 Gammon.[7] Griffon was developed in the mid-1950s to early 1960s and tested in 1962.[8] Apparently it could reach an altitude of 25 to 30 miles, and it had a slant range of 100 miles and a speed between Mach 3 and Mach 5.[9] Deployment of the Griffon began in 1962 around Leningrad with thirty launcher structures but was halted in 1963 and dismantled in 1964.[10] It is not clear whether Griffon was intended for interception of strategic ballistic missiles; its probable mission was to defend against high altitude threats such as the planned B-70 bomber and Hound Dog tactical ballistic missile.[11] In either case the system was deployed with the intention not only of protecting Leningrad but also to cover flight paths into the western Soviet Union from the United States.[12]

At the same time that U.S. satellite reconnaissance revealed the halt in construction of Griffon launchers, it revealed new construction near Tallin in Estonia. The system being installed involved the SA-5 Gammon interceptor missile, with three batteries of six launchers each arranged around a single engagement radar.[13] The exact purpose of the Tallin line, as it was called, was a subject of dispute within the defense and intelligence establishment. The CIA, supported by the Navy and State departments, maintained that the Tallin line did not represent the beginnings of a BMD system but rather of an antiaircraft system. The army, supported by the air force and the Defense Intelligence Agency, drew the opposite conclusions. The dispute was settled by the CIA director, John McCone, in favor of the army, and the view that the Tallin line represented the beginnings of an ABM system was incorporated in national intelligence estimate 11-3-63 on Soviet strategic defensive forces.[14]

Development of the Galosh (ABM-1) interceptor overlapped that of both the SA-5 and Griffon. Galosh was first exhibited in Red Square in 1963 and became operational in the late 1960s.[15] The size of the missile indicated that it was armed with a nuclear warhead and capable of exoatmospheric interception at long range, making a shoot-look-shoot strategy feasible.[16] Additionally, it had the ability to stop and start its engines, a feature permitting land-based radars time to discriminate between actual warheads and chaff or decoys.[17]

In 1970 the Soviets activated the fourth Galosh complex, half of the planned number for the Moscow area.[18] Each complex consisted of sixteen launchers (two batteries of eight) and six Try Add guidance and engagement radars, the radars being mechanically steered.[19] The complex radars were fed information by the Hen House and Dog House phased array radars. Hen House radars were distributed along the periphery of the Soviet Union to provide early warning and missile acquisition information to the defenses around Moscow. The Dog House radar in the Moscow area is "believed to provide battle management for the totality of Moscow's defenses, assigning targets to the tracking radars and interceptors, and providing target acquisition information to the tracking radars."[20]

Although work on a fifth site was resumed in 1971, it was never finished, and no other sites were constructed. The Soviets did, however, replace the original version of Galosh with a more modern version (the ABM-2).[21] The range of the Galosh, along with the capabilities of the radars, enabled it to provide protection for an area of several thousand square miles, an area stretching to most of the western Soviet Union and including 300 ICBMs.[22]

The failure to complete the Moscow complexes and then expand it into a nationwide urban defense was presumably due to Soviet realization that the system had two serious flaws: an inability to distinguish between decoys and warheads and an inability (given the low speed of the associated data processing computers) to deal effectively with a large-scale attack.[23]

ABM Treaty

Soviet agreement to a treaty sharply limiting the deployment of ABM launchers and the employment of radars in an ABM mode represented a sharp reversal of the Soviet position. The Soviet position on BMD had always stressed the defensive and life-saving role of BMD as opposed to the offensive and life-threatening role of offensive missiles. To some, Soviet acceptance of BMD limitations indicated that Soviet strategists had finally recognized the value of mutual vulnerability in producing strategic stability.[24]

Others have suggested that the Soviet agreement represented a temporary surrender to technological and strategic reality—the technological reality being the striking inferiority of Soviet BMD technology in relation to that of the United States. In addition to the technological dilemma, the Soviet Union was also faced with a major reorientation of U.S. BMD plans. U.S. plans had progressed from visions of a thick urban defense to a light urban defense to the hard-point defense of ICBM silos under the Safeguard system. Such a reorientation, announced by the Nixon administration in March 1969, threatened to undercut a Soviet strategy that stressed the value of a (preemptive, if possible) counterforce attack, with U.S. silos and C^3 structures being the highest priority targets. The Safeguard system threatened to negate the future value of the hard-target killer ICBMs then under R&D: the SS-18 and SS-19.[25]

Thus the Soviet leadership was faced with an inability to obtain its most preferred outcome: damage limitation by means of preemptive counterforce and strategic defense, with the later method including urban BMD. Negotiation of the ABM Treaty in all likelihood gave the leadership its second most preferred option: damage limitation by means of counterforce and a temporary abstention from serious BMD deployment by both nations, during which time the Soviet Union might be able to close the BMD technology gap. Clearly, the least desirable option for the Soviet leadership would be a hard-point U.S. BMD system that could blunt a Soviet countersilo attack.

It took the Soviet Union only seven days to accept the U.S. proposal of April 1970 to limit BMD deployment to the location of each nation's national command authority (NCA), Washington and Moscow. However, U.S. decision makers soon concluded that Congress was unlikely to approve funds for any sort of urban defense, even of the nation's capital, in the face of public disapproval. Hence, the offer so readily accepted by Soviet negotiators was withdrawn, and several new offers were tabled. Ultimately, on May 22, 1972, it was agreed that each side could deploy two BMD complexes: one at the site of the NCA and the other an ICBM field not fewer than 1,300 kilometers from the NCA site.[26] A limitation of one hundred launchers and interceptors at each site was agreed to, as well as a variety of restrictions concerning the associated radar systems. A 1974 protocol to the treaty reduced the number of permitted sites to one each. Ultimately the United States dismantled the launchers from its own site at Grand Forks, North Dakota, although it has continued to operate the associated perimeter acquisition radar characterization system (PARCS) at Concrete, North Dakota, for space tracking and early warning purposes.

Although the Soviet Union agreed to continue the state of mutual vulnerability that existed in the absence of BMD systems, Soviet negotiators refused to consider any measure limiting defenses other than BMDs, such as air defenses against bomber attack.[27]

Developments Subsequent to the ABM Treaty

The ABM Treaty did not preclude R&D programs concerning BMD. As a result the United States and the Soviet Union have pursued vigorous R&D programs, programs that involve both conventional BMD technology, as well as laser and particle beam technology.

The major aspect of Soviet R&D BMD activities has apparently focused on overcoming serious deficiencies in the associated radar systems at the BMD complexes. The Soviet radar network includes fifteen Hen House and seven Pechora class radars, all of which are of the larger, phased array variety. The Hen House radars are primarily located along Soviet borders—for example, in Irkutsk along the Barents Sea and in Latvia—and can connect with OTH radar systems and satellites to distinguish the size of an attack and provide target tracking data for ABM deployments.[28]

The Pechora class radars were first spotted in 1980 and have a fan-shaped array 110 feet high and 300 feet long. Five of the seven Pechora class radars—those on or at Kamchatka, Lyakincar near the Caspian Sea, Pechora in the northwest Soviet Union, the Kola Peninsula and Michelevka just north of Mongolia—are on the Soviet periphery. The other two are located at the Sary Shagan BMD test site and at Abalakova, near Krasnoyarsk in central Siberia, some 400 miles north of Mongolia.[29]

The Abalakova radar has been described by the Defense Intelligence Agency as being "ideally suited for ballistic missile tracking and target acquisition."[30] Since its discovery by a U.S. reconnaissance satellite, the Abalakova radar has been pointed to by many as a certain or almost certain violation of the ABM Treaty.[31] According to article 6-b of the treaty, the United States and Soviet Union agreed "not to deploy in the future radars for early warning of strategic missile attack except at locations along the periphery of its national territory and oriented outward."

The Abalakova radar appears to be oriented outward to the northeast rather than the south, enabling it to detect Trident missiles launched from submarines in the Bering Sea or Gulf of Alaska. Its proximity to three SS-18 and one SS-11 ICBM fields, as well as its radar fan being totally within the Soviet Union, have led many to conclude that its primary purpose is early warning and BMD battle management rather than space tracking, which the Soviet Union claims as its purpose.[32] One official suggested that it was placed at Abalakova because "somebody decided it was too expensive to put it where the treaty requires."[33]

As part of the upgrading of the Moscow BMD system, new Pushkino class phased array radars are under various stages of construction. One completed site is north of Moscow (at Pushkino), and at least two others are under construction.[34] The Pushkino provides 360 degree strategic defense coverage from the phased array radars in its four-sided structure, which is 120 feet high and 500 feet wide. It assigns targets and ties together all of the elements of a BMD system. Although a recent addition to the system, it is apparently no more advanced than the U.S. missile site radar deployed at the now-closed Safeguard sites.[35]

Upgrading of the Moscow complexes revolve around development of the ABM-X-3 system, which consists of two types of radars and two types of interceptor missiles. The radars are the Flat Twin tracking radar and the Pawn Shop missile guidance radar. The interceptors are known as the SH-04 and SH-08.

Of the two radars, Flat Twin is considered the more essential element of the ABM-X-3 system, providing the final tracking of ballistic missiles at reentry.[36] Beginning in 1974, there were reports of the Flat Twin being developed in mobile form, in violation of the ABM Treaty. It was reported that the Flat Twin could be built around several trailers and activated within several months rather than the years required to construct large conventional radars. The system may also incorporate more advanced computer technology than the Soviets have previously possessed. However, it is also believed to have a relatively low power output, a limitation that would severely constrain its range and its ability to distinguish real from decoy targets.[37]

The SH-04 is an exoatmospheric interceptor, while the SH-08 is an hypersonic endoatmospheric interceptor, which together provide for a layered defensive similar to the Spartan-Sprint combination developed for the Safeguard system. The SH-04 and SH-08 are nuclear armed and will be deployed in underground silos to reduce their vulnerability to attack. It has been reported that the SH-08 has been tested in a rapid reload configuration at Sary Shagan, with two missiles being fired from the same silo within two hours.[38] The SH-04 has a maneuvering capability and can loiter as incoming reentry vehicles are sorted out from decoys. It can then restart its engines and head toward the intended target. It also apparently has an infrared homing system to allow it to separate a true warhead from a decoy.[39]

The ABM-X-3 is expected to reach fully operational status in the late 1980s.[40] So far the number of Galosh missiles have been reduced to thirty-two as part of a conversion program that involves the construction of five new launcher sites and the conversion of Galosh silos.[41] Apparently some SH-08 missiles have already been installed in the reconverted silos.[42]

In addition to developments in conventional BMD interceptor technology, developments in two other areas—air defense and directed energy weapons—are of relevance. Three surface-to-air missiles, two operational and the other in development, have caused concern—one as possibly having a capability against strategic ballistic missiles. The deployment of the SA-10 and SA-11 has been upgraded Soviet air defense capabilities.[43] The SA-10 is approximately equivalent to the U.S. Patriot which is considered to have a limited tactical BMD potential. When it first appeared, the SA-10 was considered as possibly having an ABM potential. The most recent view is that it is primarily a counter to low-altitude targets such as cruise missiles. Of more concern to the United States has been the SA-X-12 Gladiator, which has been flight tested and has a capability against aircraft and tactical ballistic missiles, including the Pershing II. Unlike the SA-10, the SA-12 is mobile, being transported on a large tracked vehicle. According to the Department of Defense, "These systems could, if properly supported, add significant point-target coverage to a widespread ABM deployment."[44] Additionally, as further improvements are made in their intercept capabilities against tactical missiles, they will become more capable against ICBM and SLBM warheads.[45]

At the other end of spectrum, Soviet developments in directed energy weapons—laser and particle beam technology—have also been a source of concern because there appears to be a substantial Soviet interest in these technologies as they apply to the problem of BMD.[46] According to one analyst:

> The potential advantage of laser and charged-particle beam technologies in a BMD role is their faster response time against RVs although there is a problem of radar vulnerability to saturation of the defenses by incoming MIRV RVs. A second advantage of [laser and charged particle beam] technologies over nuclear armed ABM interceptors, such as the Sprint, Spartan and Galosh is that there is no radar "blinding" as a result of the detonation of interceptors' warheads. A third possible advantage is its virtually limitless shot capacity within the restrictions of its energy sources; this could do away with the problem of Interceptor exhaustion which plagued designers of ballistic missile ABMs.[47]

At the same time, there are drawbacks involving line-of-sight limitations and the difficulty of hitting a small target with sufficient energy at a great distance.[48] Some scientists have suggested that development of such weapons would face "insurmountable obstacles." At the very least, according to the Department of Defense, a ground-based laser BMD system is not likely until at least 2001, and ground- and space-based particle beam BMD systems will be even more difficult to develop.[49]

Ballistic Missile Defense and Soviet Strategy

The history of the Soviet BMD program is one that involves a continuing and vigorous research, development, testing, and evaluation program with conventional and more exotic technologies. At the same time, that history also reveals a series of stops, starts, and reversals concerning the actual deployment of BMD systems. At no time have the Soviets actually deployed as many as one hundred interceptor missiles.

The U.S. intelligence community, however, projected a large-scale deployment of a BMD system throughout the 1960s. In the early 1960s the intelligence community estimated that the Soviets might deploy about 2,000 exoatmospheric and 6,000 to 8,000 endoatmospheric interceptors.[50] National intelligence estimate (NIE) 11-3-63 on Soviet strategic defensive forces predicted that the Moscow BMD system under construction would be expanded by 1975 to provide coverage for every major city—with 500 to 1,500 interceptors per city.[51]

NIE 11-3-63 advanced the proposition that the Soviet Union was beginning to deploy a BMD system "in earnest."[52] In 1966 congressional testimony, Defense Secretary Robert McNamara estimated that by 1968 the Soviets could have a defense capability against U.S. ICBMs passing through the "threat corridor" to Moscow with a similar capability against Polaris SLBMs by 1970.[53] Even after construction of the Moscow system was halted in 1967, there were still projections of large-scale future BMD deployment. One issue that was debated was whether the SA-5 missile in the Tallin system (agreed by then not to be a BMD system) could be upgraded to have a BMD capability. The deputy director for research and engineering for the Department of Defense argued that it could be, and his views were shared by the Joint Chiefs of Staff and the Defense Intelligence Agency.[54] And in 1969–1970 "one service was projecting as many as 7,000 to 9,000 Soviet ABMs within a few years while even the NIE carried a figure that was far greater than the number of ABMs."[55]

An examination of the record of U.S. intelligence estimates concerning Soviet BMD has led one observer to write, "Why was U.S. intelligence so eager to detect a Soviet ABM system that never did materialize? Part of this misjudgement was founded on an assessment of Soviet strategic doctrine. The Soviets were greatly concerned about strategic defense. They had an extensive air defense network to intercept bombers, and they had something of a civil defense program. Many intelligence analysts logically concluded that they would construct a comprehensive ABM system as well."[56]

What the intelligence analysts apparently ignored, incorrectly assessed the impact of, or simply lacked the information on were the other factors that would influence a Soviet decision on BMD deployment. These factors included the state of Soviet BMD technology, the state of U.S. BMD technology, and the objective and nature of the U.S. Safeguard system (something that analysts in the mid-1960s could hardly be expected to know). All three factors mitigated against Soviet BMD deployment and in favor of Soviet participation in the ABM Treaty. All three factors need to be considered in assessing the role of BMD in current Soviet strategy, as well as the present Soviet attitude toward strategic defense, the implications of changes in U.S. targeting policy and force structure, and larger foreign policy questions.

The Soviet commitment to strategic defense does not seem to have waned in the years since the signing of the ABM Treaty. In addition to R&D in the BMD field, the Soviets have continued to upgrade their air defense capability with missiles such as the SA-10, SA-11, and eventually the SA-X-12. There has been improvement in the radars associated with air defense and development of the SUAWACS (Soviet Union airborne warning and control system), to give the Soviet Union a "look-down–shoot-down" capability.[57] The commitment to this area is likely to grow even greater as U.S. development and deployment of systems such as the air-launched cruise missile (ALCM), advanced cruise missile, B-1B, B-1C, and advanced technology bomber (ATB) advances.

This predilection for strategic defense follows from Soviet military strategy and doctrine, which holds that in the event of nuclear war, the Soviet Union must have two objectives: elimination of the United States as an effective opponent and preservation of the Soviet Union as a viable state, a state with "resources and power adequate to effect restoration and to maintain dominance in the post-war environment."[58] These two objectives, if attained, constitute victory.

Thus, in the Soviet view, victory requires an integrated offensive and defensive posture, a posture that preempts to the greatest extent possible the enemy attack and limits the damage that can be done by offensive forces that survive or cannot be preempted. Damage limitation is to be attained by a combination of passive (civil defense, hardening) and active (strategic defense) systems. Hence, deployment of an effective BMD system would be a natural outgrowth of this attitude. A BMD system, even an urban-oriented system, would not have to be totally effective to be judged useful; rather, if it was able to make a significant marginal contribution to victory, it would be considered a worthwhile undertaking.

But as shown by past events, the Soviets do not ignore technological reality or U.S. programs in making such a commitment. Whether the Soviets are on the verge of attaining an effective BMD capability, have already attained one, or will attain one is hardly apparent from the unclassified literature. Nor may the classified literature hold the answers. It is possible that the Soviets themselves do not know how close or how far they are from developing an effective BMD technology—that events six months or a year from now in a research institute will provide a definitive answer. Although it is clear that there has been substantial progress in BMD technology by the United States and the Soviet Union, it is not clear that either side has made or will make sufficient progress to deploy an effective BMD system.

One can, however, make an assessment of the impact of the other factors that are likely to affect Soviet attitudes toward BMD deployment and treaty revision. Since 1972 there have been several significant changes in U.S. strategic nuclear targeting policy, as manifested in NSDM 242, "Planning the Employment of Nuclear Weapons"; PD 59, "Nuclear Weapons Employment Policy"; and most recently NSDD 13. One consequence of these directives has been the shift in emphasis from destruction of Soviet economic recovery capability to the targeting of Soviet military (strategic and conventional) and political control assets. The second result has been the formulation of a significant number of selective attack options (SAOs), which allow for the use, if the situation warrants, of tens or hundreds of warheads against the Soviet target base rather than thousands.[59]

The first consequence, in combination with several other factors, is unlikely to have a significant positive impact on Soviet attitudes in favor of BMD and particularly treaty revision to allow for hard-point defenses. Given a Soviet preference for preemption or launch-on warning, hard-point defense would be valuable only if U.S. warheads—specifically for the MX and Trident D-5—had significant capabilities against SS-18 and SS-19 silos and the Soviets feared not being able to launch before U.S. warheads landed.

According to air force testimony before Congress, "The yield and CEP combination of Peacekeeper [MX] is sufficient to achieve acceptable damage against the current generation of SS-18 and SS-19 ICBM complexes."[60] Even presuming the Trident D-5 warhead was assessed by the Soviets as having an equivalent hard target kill capability and being deliverable in a much shorter period of time than MX, it would not be clear that BMD would be the most effective Soviet countermeasure.

BMD can be defeated by penetration aids and saturation. Given the fear of Soviet breakout from the ABM Treaty, it appears that plans have been considered to upgrade the effectiveness of such aids, as well as to increase their availability in the event of Soviet breakout.[61] Sufficient attention has been devoted to the subject to produce NSDD 91 on Penaids and MARVS of April 1983.[62] On the other hand the air force testimony noted that "If the Soviets choose to upgrade these facilities [SS-18, SS-19 silos] using the U.S. superhard technology, it would be necessary to either reduce the CEP or increased the warhead yield (or both)."[63] However, it is not clear given the already low CEPs and high yield being assumed for MX and D-5 warheads that such a goal would be obtainable if the Soviets deployed missiles in superhard silos of 25,000 to 50,000, the number now being cited as quite attainable by U.S. defense officials.[64]

Thus, as was the case in 1969, a hard-point-only system would probably be to the net disadvantage of Soviet strategy, sharply reducing counterforce potential while not being the way to attain maximum survivability for Soviet ICBMs.[65] At the same time, the targets that need to be protected for Soviet survival and recovery would be destroyed by any U.S. attack that explicitly sought to destroy these targets or urban-industrial-economic recovery targets. Hence, the perception of the threat to the vast majority of these targets is unlikely to have changed since 1972 because of changes in doctrine.

On the other hand, the second consequence of the changes provides a rationale for a system that might have only limited effectiveness. A BMD system that could not function effectively against a large-scale attack—whether due to leakage or data processing shortcomings—could cause severe problems for U.S. implementation of selective attack options. Such a system would, at the very least, greatly increase the warheads required for a limited attack. Calculations by Kevin Lewis indicate that with a 0.8 single shot kill probability for each warhead and a 0.6 kill probability for the defensive system, six warheads would be required to achieve a 0.9 actual kill probability. If the initial kill probabilities were 0.8 and 0.8, then sixteen warheads would be required to achieve a 0.9 actual kill probability.[66] Under such conditions, the notions of an effective and limited strike might become an internal contradiction.

But beyond the advantage to be gained in complicating U.S. selective attack plans, there may be a Soviet rationale for accepting or negotiating treaty revision for a limited defense, especially one that could be employed around cities. A limited Soviet BMD system could deprive the United States of a credible extended nuclear deterrent short of large-scale war to be employed on behalf of NATO.

Hence simply the negotiation of revisions that would allow such a situation to exist could create serious rifts in the Atlantic Alliance, being perceived as a U.S. attempt to reduce its vulnerability at the expense of increasing Western Europe's jeopardy. Sharply increasing the resentment would be the realization that a limited but substantial Soviet BMD capability would not only negate the credibility of U.S. selective attack options but of the entire British and French nuclear forces.[67]

European reaction to the strategic defense initiative (SDI) certainly supports this scenario. Subsequent to the April 1984 meeting of the NATO Nuclear Planning Group, various Western European leaders expressed the fear that the SDI would help create a "fortress America" mentality—with U.S. leaders perceiving U.S. security as being separate from the security of Western Europe.[68] Concern among West German officials has been particularly high. On April 11, 1984, West German Defense Minister Manfred Woerner stated, "It is in the interest of all mankind that [the SDI] does not open up a new dimension in the arms race." Other West German officials, including Foreign Minister Hans-Dietrich Genscher and Franz Josef Strauss, head of the Christian Social Union, have indicated their belief that European security interests would be harmed by any deployment of space-based missile defense systems.[69]

The same perceptions are probably shared by the leadership of the People's Republic of China (PRC). Indeed the Chinese leadership might be even more sensitive concerning limited BMD systems; such a Soviet system could negate the Chinese nuclear threat against Soviet urban and industrial targets. Since the Chinese leaders may see a much greater need to deter the Soviet Union than do European leaders, a U.S. and Soviet agreement to revise the ABM Treaty to permit more extensive deployments would severely undercut Chinese strategy, exacerbating the latent Chinese fear of U.S.-Soviet collaboration at the expense of others and increasing the value to the PRC of an accommodation with the Soviet Union.

Thus, in considering BMD breakout or treaty revision, the Soviet leadership has two basic concerns: the impact on the U.S.–Soviet strategic balance and the impact on third parties. The present state of U.S. and Soviet doctrine, BMD technology, U.S. offensive capabilities, and potential countermeasures would seem to mitigate against, or at least not strongly in favor of, BMD breakout or treaty revision permitting limited defenses. On the other hand, the potential impact of assenting to U.S.-inspired treaty revision allowing limited BMD may quite favorable for the Soviet Union with respect to its positions regarding China and Western nations such as France and England.

Notes

1. "Soviet BMD Moves," *Aviation Week and Space Technology*, November 14, 1983, p. 23.

2. General Advisory Committee on Arms Control and Disarmament, *A Quarter Century of Soviet Compliance Practices under Arms Control Commitments*

1958–1983, (Summary) (Washington, D.C.: U.S. Arms Control and Disarmament Agency, 1984), p. 9.

3. Senate Armed Services Committee, *Department of Defense Authorization for Appropriations for Fiscal Year 1985, Part 6 (Strategic Defense Initiative)* (Washington: Government Printing Office 1984), p. 2949.

4. Ibid., p. 2993.

5. Sayre Stevens, "The Soviet BMD Program," in Ashton Carter and David Schwartz, eds., *Ballistic Missile Defense* (Washington, D.C.: Brookings, 1984), p. 191.

6. Ibid., pp. 191, 194, 195; Theodore Shabad, "Khrushchev Says Missile Can 'Hit a Fly in Space,' " *New York Times*, July 17, 1962, p. 18.

7. Mark E. Miller, *Soviet Strategic Power and Doctrine: The Quest for Superiority* (Washington, D.C.: Advanced International Studies Institute, 1982), pp. 99–100.

8. Robert Berman and John Baker, *Soviet Strategic Forces: Requirement and Responses* (Washington, D.C.: Brookings, 1982), p. 148.

9. Michael J. Deane, *Strategic Defense in Soviet Strategy* (Washington, D.C.: Advanced International Studies Institute, 1980), p. 27.

10. Berman and Baker, *Soviet Strategic Forces*, p. 148.

11. Miller, *Soviet Strategic Power and Doctrine*, p. 100.

12. Stevens, "Soviet BMD Program," p. 195.

13. John Prados, *The Soviet Estimate: U.S. Intelligence Analysis and Russian Military Strength* (New York: Dial Press, 1982), p. 157.

14. Victoria S. Price, *The DCI's Role in Producing Strategic Intelligence Estimates* (Newport, R.I.: Naval War College 1980), p. 81.

15. Thomas K. Longstreth and John E. Pike, *A Report on the Impact of U.S. and Soviet Ballistic Missile Defense Programs on the AMB Treaty* (Washington, D.C.: National Campaign to Save the ABM Treaty, 1984), p. 12.

16. Stevens, "Soviet BMD Program," pp. 198–199.

17. Berman and Baker, *Soviet Strategic Forces*, p. 148.

18. Prados, *The Soviet Estimate*, pp. 168–169.

19. Stevens, "The Soviet BMD Program," p. 198; Department of Defense, *Soviet Military Power—1984* (Washington, D.C.: Government Printing Office, 1984), p. 33.

20. Stevens, "Soviet BMD Program," p. 197.

21. Prados, *Soviet Estimate*, pp. 168–169.

22. Stevens, "Soviet BMD Program," p. 199; Miller, *Soviet Strategic Power and Doctrine*, p. 100.

23. Berman and Baker, *Soviet Strategic Forces*, p. 148; Miller, *Soviet Strategic Power and Doctrine*, p. 100.

24. Raymond Garthoff, "Mutual Deterrence and Strategic Arms Limitation in Soviet Policy," *International Security* (1978):112–147.

25. Miller, *Soviet Strategic Power and Doctrine*, p. 100.

26. Deane, *Strategic Defense in Soviet Strategy*, pp. 50–51.

27. Sidney Graybeal and Daniel Goure, "Soviet Ballistic Missile Defense (BMD) Objectives: Past, Present and Future," in *U.S. Arms Control Objectives and Implications for Ballistic Missile Defense* (Cambridge: Center for Science and International Affairs, Harvard University, 1979), p. 75.

28. Ted Agres, "Soviets Building ABM Radar System," *Washington Times*, April 20, 1984, pp. 1A, 12A.

29. Longstreth and Pike, *Report on the Impact*, p. 32; Jim Bussert, "Soviet Air Defense Systems Show Increasing Sophistication," *Defense Electronics* (May 1984): 75–86.

30. Agres, "Soviets Building ABM Radar System."

31. Department of Defense, *Soviet Military Power*, p. 34; Philip J. Klass, "U.S. Scrutinizing New Soviet Radar," *Aviation Week and Space Technology*, August 22, 1983 pp. 19–20.

32. Longstreth and Pike, *Report on the Impact*, p. 32.

33. Walter Pincus, "U.S. Eyes Soviet Rate of Making Bombers," *Washington Post*, December 22, 1984, p. A18.

34. Clarence A. Robinson, Jr., "Soviets Accelerate Missile Defense," *Aviation Week and Space Technology*, January 16, 1984, pp. 14–16; Agres, "Soviets Building ABM Radar System."

35. Department of Defense *Soviet Military Power*, 2d ed. (Washington, D.C.: Government Printing Office, 1983), p. 5.

36. Robinson, "Soviets Accelerate Missile Defense."

37. Prados, *Soviet Estimate*, p. 170.

38. Robinson, "Soviets Accelerate Missile Defense."

39. Miller, *Soviet Strategic Power and Doctrine*, p. 242.

40. Department of Defense, *Soviet Military Power—1984*, p. 33.

41. Longstreth and Pike, *Report on the Impact*, p. 12.

42. "Soviet BMD Moves."

43. John Pike, "Is There an ABM Gap?" *Arms Control Today* 14(July–August 1984):2–3.

44. Department of Defense, *Soviet Military Power—1984*, p. 34.

45. Longstreth and Pike, *Report on the Impact*, p. 13.

46. Ibid.

47. Leon Goure, "Developments in Soviet Ballistic Missile Systems: Offensive and Defensive Capabilities," in Leon Goure, William G. Hyland, and Colin S. Gray, *The Emerging Strategic Environment: Implications for Ballistic Missile Defense* (Cambridge, Mass.: Institute for Foreign Policy Analysis, 1979), p. 24.

48. Ibid.; Paul Nahin, "The Laser BMD and Other Radiant Energy Weapons: Some Thoughts," *IEEE Transactions on Aerospace and Electronic Systems* (March 1977):100; William J. Beane, "Strategic Policy Implications of the High-Energy Laser," *Strategic Review* (Winter 1977):100–107.

49. For example, Kosta Tsipis, "Laser Weapons," *Scientific American* 246(1981): 51–57; Department of Defense, *Soviet Military Power—1984*, p. 34.

50. Les Aspin, "Debate over U.S. Strategic Forecasts: A Mixed Record," *Strategic Review* (Summer 1980):29–43.

51. Ibid.

52. Lawrence Freedman, *U.S. Intelligence and the Soviet Strategic Threat* (London: Macmillan 1977), p. 87.

53. Ibid.

54. Prados, *Soviet Estimate*, p. 164.

55. Ibid., pp. 168–169.

56. Aspin, "Debate over U.S. Strategic Forecasts."

57. Berman and Baker, *Soviet Strategic Forces*, p. 148.

58. Deane, *Strategic Defense in Soviet Strategy*, p. 180.

59. See Desmond Ball, "Developments in U.S. Nuclear Policy under the Carter Administration," *ACIS Working Paper* No. 20 (Los Angeles: Center for International and Stratetic Affairs, 1980); Jeffrey Richelson, "PD-59, NSDD-13 and the Reagan Strategic Modernization Program," *Journal of Strategic Studies* 6(1983).

60. Senate, Armed Services Committee, *Department of Defense Authorization for Appropriations for Fiscal Year 1985, Part 7* (Washington, D.C.: Government Printing Office, 1984), p. 3290.

61. Ibid., pp. 3285, 3289.

62. House, Armed Services Committee, *Department of Defense Authorization of Appropriations for Fiscal Year 1985, Part 2* (Washington: U.S. Government Printing Office 1984), p. 300.

63. Senate, Armed Services Committee, *Department of Defense Authorization*, p. 3290.

64. Ibid., p. 3272.

65. Richard Garwin, "Effective Military Technology for the 1980s," *International Security* 7(1982):143–174.

66. Kevin Lewis, "BMD and U.S. Limited Strategic Employment Policy," *Journal of Strategic Studies* (forthcoming).

67. See David Yost, "Ballistic Missile Defense and the Atlantic Alliance," *International Security* 7(1982):1.

68. Longstreth and Pike, *Report on the Impact*, p. 35.

69. Ibid.

5

Soviet Arms Control Decision Making since Brezhnev

Rose E. Gottemoeller

A hallmark of Soviet arms control decision making in Brezhnev's last years was an ever greater concern among Soviet leaders for the impact of their arms control policy on public opinion. This trend applied especially to Western audiences, although it also had an effect at home in the Soviet Union. Of course, the Kremlin had long placed emphasis on the public impact of its proposals for propaganda purposes. Khrushchev was a master at this game, proposing agreements that were unnegotiable but attractive in their deep-seated emotional appeal.[1] But the Brezhnev years brought something different. They found the Soviet leadership engaged in serious discussions to control offensive nuclear weapons. These strategic arms limitation talks (SALT) were negotiations that the Soviets evidently wanted to see brought to a successful close with an agreement to limit the pace and direction of nuclear force deployments on both sides.

The leadership's quest for public support in the negotiations was one apparent result of this more serious commitment. The Soviets seemingly decided that if they could make their case on its own merit to a broad cross-section of Western opinion, public acceptance of their position would work to their advantage in the negotiations.

This new-found concern for the political impact of its arms control policies was probably best symbolized by the creation of the Central Committee's International Information Department in 1978. The need for this department, which by virtue of its creation became an influential element of the Central Committee apparatus, was stated forthrightly in a speech by Leonid Brezhnev. At a Central Committee Plenum in November of that year, Brezhnev took to task the propaganda and general media organs of the Soviet Union:

> It is high time to make reporting on international affairs prompter, more understandable, and more concrete. International commentaries should

I would like to thank Matthew Gallagher, William Garner, Werner Hahn, and Ellen Jones for their thoughtful comments and assistance with the research reported in this chapter.

following hot on the heels of events, and sum them up. What we need is not a repetition of accepted truths but an in-depth and well-argued analysis of facts of international life.[2]

Brezhnev noted in the same speech that the Politburo had set up a special commission to consider all these questions. The International Information Department (IID) might have been one product of this commission's work.

Created during a campaign to improve the overall credibility of the Soviet media, the IID most clearly—to foreign observers—focused its attention on influencing opinion abroad.[3] The department sent spokesmen on extended trips to Europe, both West and East, and to the United States. Far from the propaganda mouthpieces of old, these individuals were generally well informed and willing to deal directly with Western correspondents.

By virtue of their intense contacts in the West, the IID representatives also apparently widened the circle of those involved in Soviet arms control decision making. As Western opinion became a factor in Soviet efforts to achieve arms control agreements, those best versed in its quirks were evidently admitted to Kremlin deliberations on arms control policy.

As one facet of this politicization, the Soviet military began to articulate its position more openly and clearly, not only in the arms control negotiating arena but also before Soviet and Western audiences. Probably the prime illustration of this trend was Marshal Ogarkov's brilliant performance at a live press conference in November 1983, immediately after the Soviets had walked out of the intermediate-range nuclear force (INF) negotiations and the strategic arms reduction talks (START). Ogarkov, then chief of the Soviet General Staff, provided a clear military rationale for the Soviets' protest against the NATO deployment of new nuclear weapons in Western Europe. Although accompanied on the podium by Zamyatin and Georgiy Korniyenko, first deputy minister of the Ministry of Foreign Affairs, Ogarkov dominated the press conference with his forceful presentation of the Soviet viewpoint. His performance was impressive on this occasion, but it was not unique. The Soviet military had gradually been opening up to public discussions of its position throughout the later SALT years.

Thus, both the political and military actors in Soviet national security decision making became attuned to the influence of public opinion on the outcome of policy.

Against the backdrop of this evolution, the Soviet Union entered a major period of leadership succession. Between Leonid Brezhnev's death in November 1982 and Mikhail Gorbachev's assumption of power in March 1985, two interim leaders presided over a fitful but persistent move toward change. The generation that the succession brought to power injected new actors and ideas into the Soviet policy process. Their arrival, in turn, raised an important issue for observers of Kremlin politics: to what extent did the forces that acted on Soviet arms control decision making in the late 1970s become a constant element in that process?

This question is the subject of the research presented in this chapter. In examining the issue, the analysis concentrates on evidence that the Soviet decision process born of the later SALT years has become routine, not subject to rapid change in the face of policy reversals or leadership turnover. It concludes with a suggestion of how this decision-making system might bear on the future of Soviet arms control policy. If certain changes will remain in force no matter who occupies the offices in the Kremlin, the effect on Soviet policy might be a positive one for the West.

Soviet Arms Control Bureaucracy

The extreme secretiveness of the Soviet decision-making process clearly emerges in any attempt to probe or study it. A pungent example of this phenomenon is Leslie Gelb's attempt to question his counterpart at the close of negotiations on conventional arms sales in 1968. Gelb reports that chief Soviet negotiator Lev Mendelevich, when questioned about how the Soviets had put together their negotiating position, abruptly closed off the conversation:

> You don't expect me to answer that, do you? We know so much about how you make decisions. Americans are talking about this and writing about this all the time. It is more than we can swallow. But you know little of how we make decisions and we are not going to tell you. Because we do know, we have some chance of influencing your decisions. Because you don't know, your chances of influencing ours are limited and we intend to keep it that way.[4]

Despite this resistance, Westerners have been able to reach a fair degree of consensus on the Soviet policy process by observing Soviet activities during the arms control negotiations of the past decade and a half. Perhaps the richest record emerged from the ten-year history of SALT. This study reflects the first-hand observations of astute U.S. participants in the negotiations.[5] It also reflects the knowledge of Soviet participants in Kremlin decision making, some as official commentators from within, others as émigré sources.[6]

The Politburo, the top decision-making body in the Soviet Union, is the seat of important national security decisions. Valentin Falin, a senior figure in the Central Committee's IID, has commented publicly on the Politburo's role: "In our case, all foreign policy and national security decisions must be discussed and decided in the Politburo."[7] Falin's statement may be an exaggeration given the role of the Central Committee Secretariat; nevertheless, Falin does focus attention on the Politburo's intimate role in arms control decision making. In effect, the top Soviet leadership may be much more involved in day-to-day negotiating guidance than the U.S. president and even his cabinet officers.

Because the Politburo must address so many issues, it seems to depend a great deal on the Central Committee secretariat. Officially subordinate to the Politburo, the secretariat is also a powerful policymaking body in its own right. "The Secretariat frames policy decisions," according to a senior Soviet official. "By the time an issue reaches the Politburo, the framework for decision is usually already there."[8] The Politburo and Secretariat actually appear to be an interlocking policy directorate where lines dividing responsibilities are unclear. The most powerful members of the Kremlin hierarchy are members of both bodies.[9]

A practical result of the Politburo's monopoly over decision making is that the secretariat and its staffing apparatus, some twenty-three departments, become a filter through which only processed analysis will pass. As Michael Voslensky describes the process, the Central Committee staff pares an ocean of information down to a trickle for the Politburo.[10] Voslensky reports that all material submitted to the Politburo is prepared according to strict rules. The proposed decision must take up no more than two typed pages, and background information is limited to five. This short dossier then goes to the leaders' aides, who abbreviate it further. By thus controlling information, Voslensky states, the secretariat can exercise as much power as the Politburo.[11]

The Central Committee departments thus gain enormous importance as the mechanism that selects information for presentation to the top leadership. The General Department is the most powerful of these, for it is the gatekeeping entity that manages the final flow of policy papers to the Politburo. Those who work there are reportedly men of great experience who, knowing the dislikes of a Central Committee secretary, can hold up action on an issue by submitting it to him for his approval.[12] As long as a secretary refuses to sign off, an issue will normally not be submitted to the full Politburo for consideration.

Of the other Central Committee departments, probably only a few are directly concerned with arms control issues. The likeliest candidates are the International Affairs Department, headed by Boris Ponomarev; the IID, headed by Leonid M. Zamyatin; and the Defense Industry Department, headed by Igor Dmitriyev.

The International Affairs Department, officially responsible for relations with nonruling communist parties, actually addresses a wide range of foreign policy problems related to capitalist countries and the Third

World.[13] Arkady Shevchenko seems to indicate that the International Affairs Department has sustained a greater overall emphasis on Third World issues, while the Ministry of Foreign Affairs has emphasized U.S.–Soviet relations. According to his account, Minister of Foreign Affairs Andrei Gromyko was the impetus for this division of labor since he maintained an abiding interest in the United States and acquired the authority under Brezhnev to control policy in this area.[14] Zagladin, Shevchenko reports, once criticized Gromyko for his stress on great power politics. "You Foreign Ministry people," Zagladin said, "don't understand the power of communist ideas in the world and ways to exploit them."[15] Whatever his personal preferences, however, Zagladin's public involvement in arms control issues is unmistakable.

The IID was established in February 1978, apparently to remedy weaknesses in the presentation of Soviet foreign policy to foreign and domestic audiences.[16] In the early 1980s, as preparations unfolded for U.S.–Soviet negotiations on European-based intermediate-range nuclear forces (INF), the IID also acquired a specific role in the Soviet arms control bureaucracy. The department's chief, Leonid Zamyatin, and his first deputy, Valentin Falin, became extremely active in selling Soviet INF positions to audiences in Western Europe and the United States. Zamyatin, who was said to enjoy Brezhnev's confidence, accompanied the general secretary on several foreign trips to serve as his spokesman.[17]

Zamyatin's role as a high-level Kremlin spokesman continued in the immediate post-Brezhnev era. He and his department in fact became associated with the trappings and events usually associated with official media spokesmen in the West. For example, the department began to produce press briefs in a format familiar to Western journalists. During the INF negotiations, such briefings included discussions of Soviet military doctrine, weapon programs, and arms control proposals.[18] In addition, Zamyatin and his colleagues participated in numerous press conferences, taking questions from foreign correspondents extemporaneously. The most important of these followed the downing of Korean Air Lines flight 007 in September 1983 and the Soviet Union's walkout from the INF negotiations in November 1983. On both occasions, Zamyatin was joined by Marshal Nikolai Ogarkov, then chief of the Soviet General Staff, and Georgiy Korniyenko, first deputy minister of foreign affairs. Ogarkov's performance on these occasions was especially impressive.[19]

Ogarkov's highly visible participation in these events seems to point to an important political–military agreement that Soviet policy, to gain credibility, must be explained in a sophisticated manner to the general public, whether Soviet or foreign. The colorful but simple propaganda statements so beloved of Khrushchev are evidently no longer deemed adequate, at least in many circumstances. Instead expert military spokesmen provide detailed explanations of Soviet positions on arms issues. In addition to Ogarkov, these people have included long-time General Staff figures such as General Nikolai Chervov.[20] Nonmilitary figures have also explained Soviet arms control initiatives in a manner calculated to sound plausible to Western audiences. Besides Zamyatin and Zagladin, these have included Georgiy Arbatov, head of the USSR Academy of Sciences' Institute of the USA and Canada.[21]

The IID seemed to be a locus of planning and organization for these activities. Because the department thus played a role in laying the ground-work for Soviet arms control initiatives, it doubtless remained in close contact with the upper layers of the arms control bureaucracy in Moscow. Although it evidently advised that bureaucracy on how to make initiatives acceptable to Western public opinion, its influence may have extended further. The department, along with the International Affairs Department, may have provided an important political input to Soviet arms control policymaking.

Evidence on this point is scant, although the conclusion might be logically drawn from the overwhelming visibility that Zamyatin and Zagladin enjoyed in the early 1980s. In addition, an important U.S. partici-pant in the process has suggested off the record that the Soviet military was unwilling to walk out of the INF negotiations in November 1983, hoping to constrain U.S. deployments in Europe to a minimum number. However, Zamyatin and Zagladin, the "Z-Z" axis as this source termed them, insisted that no U.S. deployments should occur. With the creation of such a politi-cal imperative, the Soviets ultimately had to walk out of the negotiations when U.S. deployments began on schedule. The walkout did not buy them any long-term benefits, however, since Soviet hopes that public protest in Western Europe would stop the deployments also were not borne out. The Soviets eventually agreed in January 1985 to return to negotiations with the United States on INF, central strategic weapons, and space-based systems.

Despite the evident failure of their INF strategy, Zamyatin and Zagladin and their departments continued to play a visible role in the Soviet arms control policy process. In mid-1985, however, rumors began to circulate that the IID was being disbanded and Leonid Zamyatin removed from his job.[22] These rumors were unconfirmed at the time of this writing, but such action would make sense in the light of the department's inability to achieve results in the INF campaign.

A fall from grace for Zamyatin would not necessarily signal that other individuals had ceased to perform similar functions. Soviet spokesmen continued to grant interviews and hold press conferences on arms control issues important to the Kremlin.[23] The lesson of these activities seemed clear.

Whether they advise the leadership on the best ways to influence Western public opinion or insist on certain policy positions, Soviet media figures have apparently provided an important impetus for the politicization of Soviet arms control decision making. Whereas top-level political and military figures formerly produced and negotiated serious arms control initiatives in private, now the Soviets seem to have decided that their initiatives will be more successful if they are effectively advertised abroad.

The Defense Industry Department is the third Central Committee entity that seems to have an important arms control role. Responsible for implementing weapons research, development, and production policies,[24] the department reportedly has authority to request information from the General Staff of the Armed Forces, Central Committee departments responsible for individual military industries, the Military Directorate of the State Planning Commission (GOSPLAN), and deputy defense ministers.[25] It is therefore in an excellent position to know development and deployment stages for individual weapon systems and where those systems fit into overall Soviet military plans.

In addition, the Defense Industry Department apparently keeps track of production potential in individual military industries.[26] Because of this knowledge, it would be aware of some of the constraints that may prevent full production of a weapon system. The information available to the Defense Industry Department therefore would be indispensable for formulating arms control negotiating strategies.

The International Affairs Department, the IID, and the Defense Industry Department have independent authority to request information from government agencies at lower levels. Such agencies are part of the Soviet government hierarchy, not the Communist party apparatus, and they are generally considered to be less influential than the Central Committee departments. Individual agencies, however, are centers of expertise that have not been duplicated elsewhere in the Soviet system. Two such are the General Staff of the Soviet Armed Forces and the Ministry of Foreign Affairs.

Ministry of Defense and General Staff

In the arms control arena, the working relationship between the Ministry of Defense and the General Staff is obscure. The General Staff is officially subordinate to the Ministry of Defense but maintains a special position as the source of Soviet military doctrine and strategy. At the same time, although the Ministry of Defense has formed a separate office to handle arms control issues, little is known about its personnel, position in the hierarchy, or responsiblities.[27] U.S. negotiators noted that during the SALT talks, Soviet Defense Ministry representatives reported to Moscow through channels separate from those used by the General Staff representatives. The Americans were unable to discern whether the two groups performed different functions, however.[28] The General Staff, because it has provided the chief military delegates to SALT, seems to be the military organization most actively involved in arms control.[29]

On the other hand, the Ministry of Defense contains organizational entities that may be very important to Soviet arms control decision making. The armaments directorate, created in 1970, is a likely example. Arthur Alexander suggests that the armaments directorate is responsible for major new weapons programs, those "characterized by high levels of priority, uncertainty and costs."[30] The directorate may also, according to Alexander, provide a link between force planning and weapons procurement. These roles could place the directorate in a position to represent Defense Ministry interests during negotiations, bureaucratic or otherwise, on arms control. The fact that General Nikolay Alekseyev, an early delegate to the SALT negotiations, returned to Moscow to head the directorate bears out this supposition. In his new job, Alekseyev reportedly continued to be involved with SALT problems.[31]

But the General Staff remains the main source of Soviet military doctrine and strategy. The Soviet leadership has thus far not attempted to intrude on the General Staff bailiwick by setting up competing centers of expertise on military affairs. Civilian analysts in the Soviet Union concentrate on Western strategic doctrine. They do not comment on Soviet doctrine or posture.[32] The General Staff thus seems to enjoy a virtual monopoly on the information that underlies the training and equipping of the Soviet armed forces, including strategic forces.[33]

In a staffing role for arms control negotiations, the General Staff reportedly interacts with the Central Committee Secretariat. Probably its most important inputs, however, go through the Defense Council, the high-level decision-making body that addresses national security issues. As Michael Checinski points out, "The most effective kind of pressure on the Defense Council takes the form of military strategy and doctrine prepared by the Soviet General Staff."[34] The General Staff would thus provide the background for any unified military position on a negotiation. Nonmilitary members of the Defense Council would lack alternative sources of information to assess the military's position.[35]

Depending on the stature of the defense minister, the chief of the General Staff might be the main spokesman for the professional military on the Defense Council. Marshal Ogarkov, chief of the General Staff through the Brezhnev transition years, was a forceful spokesman for military requirements and doubtless an effective influence on Defense Council decisions.

Ogarkov, however, was removed from office for "unpartylike" behavior in September 1984.[36] Although the Soviets have not explained his demise, Ogarkov clearly seems to have collided with important party priorities for defense planning and resource expenditure. These priorities perhaps had a strong supporter in Minister of Defense Dmitry Ustinov, a man whose career as a defense industrialist had probably sensitized him to the upheavals that major resource reallocations create.

Ustinov's death in December 1984 deprived the Soviet military of a voice on the ruling Politburo.[37] Following as it did on Ogarkov's demotion, this event seemed to leave the armed forces in a relatively weak position in Kremlin decision-making circles. General Sergey Sokolov, Ustinov's successor, became a candidate member of the Politburo in April 1985, several months after taking office. This position granted him access to leadership discussions but not a vote on policy.

Sokolov remained a candidate member through an important party plenum in June 1985 at which a number of individuals were raised to Politburo status.[38] That Sokolov was passed over in these promotions seemed to signal a near-term unwillingness to grant the military a direct vote on Soviet defense policy.

The permanence of the military's weaker position was unknown in this period. Sokolov was clearly a transitional figure, one of the older generation chosen at a time when the predicted successor, Ogarkov, had landed in disfavor. As Gorbachev gained power, rumors began to circulate that Ogarkov was reemerging to prominence with the titles of first deputy minister of defense and commander in chief of Warsaw Pact forces.[39]

Gorbachev's commitment to economic reform would possibly have made him a natural ally for Ogarkov, who even following his departure from the General Staff continued to espouse conventional force improvements.[40] Gorbachev's urge to revitalize the Soviet industrial base corresponded to Ogarkov's call for defense industrial modernizations that would enable his conventional buildup. The two men may thus have become partners in breaking down bureaucratic barriers to their similar goals.

This development would account for an Ogarkov return to grace in Moscow. It would not ensure a military vote on defense policy in decision-making circles, however. Such a guarantee would emerge only from the appointment of a prominent military leader—almost certainly the Minister of Defense—to full membership on the Politburo.

Ministry of Foreign Affairs

The Ministry of Foreign Affairs (MFA) is a natural participant in the arms control arena, although in the past its effectiveness may have been hampered by excessive compartmentalization. Compartments seemed to limit the flow of facts and analysis both within the ministry and in the interagency policy arena.[41] U.S. SALT negotiators provide the best-known example of the latter instance. They have recounted how, during SALT I, MFA representatives on the Soviet delegation were denied access to information under the purview of Soviet military representatives.[42]

This segregation of the MFA role has often led Western observers to conclude that the ministry is at a significant disadvantage when compared to military players in the Soviet policy process.[43] The disadvantage may have been especially significant in the early years of SALT, when for the first time the Soviet military was playing a direct and major role in arms control negotiations.[44] Because the military was evidently concerned about restraining a U.S. reactive buildup just as the Soviet Union was approaching parity, the General Staff and Ministry of Defense may have dominated Soviet arms control policymaking during that period.[45]

At the same time, however, Raymond Garthoff reports that the strong preference of the Soviet military for caution in disclosing military interests clearly contributed to a passive and reactive Soviet stance at the negotiations. The fact that the United States took most of the initiative to raise new proposals, Garthoff further states, probably worked to U.S. advantage.[46]

Realization of this outcome may have been an important reason behind the Soviets' decision to open up their policy process in an effort to gain support for Soviet initiatives among Western publics. Soviet spokesmen have been advertising Soviet proposals and even providing detailed arguments to back them up. In addition to the Central Committee's International Affairs Department and IID, the MFA also has played a part in pursuing this course. The effort may ultimately have been to its benefit.

The MFA has in fact always had its own special expertise as an actor familiar with the negotiating partners and the international negotiations arena. The chief Soviet SALT negotiators have been senior MFA officials.[47] Thus, like the General Staff, the ministry has a monopoly on expertise that it can exploit to its advantage. The activities of Anatoliy Dobrynin, the Soviet Union's long-time ambassador to the United States, illustrates its unique utility.

Although Dobrynin has had no full-time place in the Soviet arms control bureaucracy, he has frequently used his position to contribute to the negotiating process. He can thus be considered an important part of Soviet arms control decision making involving the United States. During SALT I, for example, Dobrynin and Henry Kissinger opened secret discussions to resolve deadlocks that had developed during the negotiations in Vienna and Helsinki. Kissinger has recounted that Dobrynin, acting on behalf of the Politburo, could informally explore options that would be impossible to raise formally through the delegations. According to Kissinger, he also performed the function of providing the Politburo with a "sophisticated assessment of conditions" in the United States.[48]

However important Dobrynin was to the SALT process, his role is difficult to generalize to other men and other negotiations. It is unclear, for example, that a replacement would be able to enjoy Dobrynin's wide access to Washington policymakers, at least in the early stages of an appointment. Indeed after the Nixon and Ford presidencies, question arose about the ease of Dobrynin's entrée to the White House and the State Department, especially in the light of the U.S. ambassador's perennial access problems in Moscow.[49] Furthermore, Soviet ambassadors are often moved to new assignments every few years. They do not always remain in one place for lengthy periods, as Dobrynin has. Thus, in many cases they would not have the contacts and information necessary to conduct secret discussions.

Nevertheless, Dobrynin's pivotal role in SALT I can serve as a symbol of the wider importance attained by the MFA in the arms control negotiations of later years. While military concerns were foremost in driving Soviet arms control policy, military technical expertise may have dominated the policy process. Once political methods became a way to achieve military goals, political expertise may have gained new status in Soviet arms control decision making. By virtue of its mission in the diplomatic world, the MFA represents one type of political expertise: it has the background and experience to communicate effectively with foreigners.

The experience of negotiating with the West in the 1970s and 1980s is another possible factor in the MFA's expanding role. As the Soviet arms control bureaucracy absorbs that experience, the result may spell greater interagency communication. A rigidly compartmented, vertically oriented system that would work to the Foreign Ministry's disadvantage would also tend to perform poorly when faced with the demands of a busy negotiating calendar. As a result, the volume of cooperation between the ministries of Defense and Foreign Affairs may have expanded considerably in the 1970s. Some Western observers have posited the post-SALT I addition of a Defense-Foreign Affairs group to coordinate work and provide support for negotiations.[50] Such a group would symbolize breakdown in the lateral rigidity of the system and presumably an improved position for the MFA.

A final major factor in the MFA's improved position was doubtless the growth in Minister of Foreign Affairs Andrei Gromyko's influence under Brezhnev and its continuation under his immediate successors, Andropov and Chernenko. According to Arkady Shevchenko, Gromyko early recognized Brezhnev's potential as a national leader and decided to cultivate him. He became Brezhnev's mentor on foreign policy issues and eventually, in Shevchenko's words, "achieved genuine authority over Soviet foreign policy."[51]

This authority was perhaps stated most directly by Gromyko's rise to the Politburo in 1973. He, along with Minister of Defense Grechko and KGB Chief Andropov, thus achieved the right to participate in Politburo meetings on a regular basis. Since Central Committee department heads evidently do not enjoy this right, Gromyko also thus acquired the right to present his ministry's position to the Politburo without the interference of the Central Committee apparatus. He has apparently used this right well. Shevchenko reports that even as a newcomer to the Politburo in 1973, Gromyko presented his proposals with such force and precision that few would dare object to them.[52] His power was no doubt greatly expanded during the upheaval of the Brezhnev succession years.

Gromyko's status was radically altered, however, by the transition to a younger generation of Soviet leaders. Konstantin Chernenko died in March 1985 at the age of seventy-three. Into his place stepped Mikhail Gorbachev, a man in his fifties with strong ideas about the steps that the Soviet Union should take to propel itself into the next century. Gromyko continued to reign over Soviet foreign policy in the early months of Gorbachev's tenure.

Then, in the summer of 1985, Gorbachev took radical action to consolidate his power. At a meeting of the USSR Supreme Soviet on July 2, he nominated Andrei Gromyko to become chairman of the presidium of the Supreme Soviet, the titular Soviet head of state. Gorbachev simultaneously proposed a resolution "relieving Andrei Gromyko of the duties of ... Foreign Minister of the USSR."[53]

With this move, Gromyko was accorded the honor of a graceful retirement in a country where top leaders usually die in office or are toppled from power. Gromyko's new job preserved his position on the ruling Politburo, a seat from which he doubtless would continue to influence the formulation of Soviet foreign policy. At the same time, it removed him from access to the day-to-day workings of the MFA, the organization that he had forged into his own instrument in over twenty-eight years at its head. The ministry's daily operations provided Gromyko with his most important resource, information on which to base important foreign policy initiatives. Once that information was denied to him, he no longer controlled the means to develop unique, fully supported proposals to present to his colleagues in the Politburo.

Instead, those means came under the purview of Eduard Shevardnadze, Gromyko's successor as minister of foreign affairs.[54] Shevardnadze probably arrived in his new position tasked with two complex but related problems. The first was to break up the monopoly that Gromyko had maintained over information necessary to the formulation of Soviet foreign policy. The second was to reinstate a direct channel for that information between the ministry and the top leadership in the Kremlin.

Brezhnev opened such channels in 1973 by promoting the ministers of defense and foreign affairs and the head of the KGB to full membership on the Politburo. For Brezhnev, this step was probably a way to loosen the grip of the Central Committee staff on the foreign policy agenda. Gromyko evidently seized upon his Politburo status to advance policy proposals well honed from his ministry's inputs. Brezhnev's action in effect ensconced a new agenda setter for Soviet foreign policy, Andrei Gromyko.

Gorbachev, the new Soviet leader, doubtless intended to set his own agenda. He clearly recognized before the July 2 Supreme Soviet session that Gromyko was in a position to impede that course. Viktor Afanas'yev, an informal Gorbachev spokesman and the chief editor of *Pravda*, provided evidence of that recognition in an interview in early April 1985:

> [Question] Some analysts say, and you yourself have mentioned it, that Gorbachev has not been much concerned with foreign policy, and the conclusion is drawn on that basis that foreign policy will continue to be pretty much Andrei Gromyko's "responsibility."
>
> [Afanas'yev] I don't think so. In our country foreign policy is not Gromyko's affair, it is the affair of the party, of the Politburo, of the Central Committee. We have collective leadership. I did say that in the past Gorbachev has not been sufficiently involved with foreign policy. Nevertheless, during Chernenko's funeral, he received 27 statesmen in 2 days. Those were all important meetings in which an evaluation was made of mutual relations. No one wrote out what he was supposed to say, he had no notes to go on, he spoke freely. We must not let foreign policy take a back seat.[55]

Gorbachev thus advertised his intent to involve himself closely in Soviet foreign policy. That close involvement could not emerge as long as Gromyko maintained tight control over the MFA.

The decision to remove Andrei Gromyko to higher office certainly related to the personal management style of Mikhail Gorbachev. Dynamic and reform minded, Gorbachev was evidently unwilling to leave foreign affairs to the established regime in the MFA. Thus, the principal decision maker in the Kremlin once again placed his stamp on the process of policy formulation. At the same time, the change repeated past practice sufficiently to signal long-term implications for the Soviet decision process.

Eduard Shevardnadze became a full voting member of the Politburo one day before he assumed the post of minister of foreign affairs. His promotion continued the trend begun by Brezhnev in 1973 but with a significant difference; its occurrence one day before Shevardnadze became foreign minister emphasized an apparent conviction in the Kremlin that important ministerial bureaucracies should have a direct voice in Politburo decisions.[56]

The leadership's urge to maintain a channel of communication into the MFA thus seems to have become a constant factor in the Soviet decision process. How Shevardnadze uses that channel remains to be seen. Since his initial task is doubtless to open the ministry to Kremlin access, he will probably provide a fairly free flow of information and policy options to the top leadership. In the long term, however, he may develop the authority to use the channel as Gromyko did: as a means to push preferred options through the Politburo.

Defense Research and Production

Soviet scientists, engineers, and production managers made significant contributions to achieving the SALT agreements. Their exact roles in Soviet arms control decision making are difficult to define, however, because the extreme secrecy that cloisters the defense sector also prevents Western observers from developing a clear idea of how scientists and production managers contribute to the policy process. Certain organizations have been clearly identified with it, but the exact nature of their roles is uncertain. For example, the Military-Industrial Commission caught the attention of U.S. SALT participants when its chairman, L.V. Smirnov, emerged from the background to negotiate some unresolved SALT I issues during the final hours of the Moscow Summit in May 1972.[57] The commission is evidently a high-level body with authority to coordinate defense research and production for projects where multiple ministries are involved. Some analysts conclude that the commission may, in addition, be involved in economic planning and setting priorities for the defense industry sector.[58] If so, Smirnov would not only have an intimate knowledge of weapons programs, he would also be in a position to advance SALT trade-offs involving them.

Other analysts assert, however, that the Military-Industrial Commission's responsibility does not extend beyond directing and coordinating the huge military-industrial bureaucracy.[59] Its focus, they say, is policy implementation, not formulation.[60] If this analysis is correct, Smirnov may not have owed his starring role in the SALT I finale to the policymaking functions of his commission but rather to his close association with the top leadership.

The Military-Industrial Commission is an important force in Soviet defense procurement. It is less clear that it has a formal, constant place in arms control matters. Smirnov's role in SALT I may well have been related to a personal tie to Dmitry Ustinov, who was then party secretary (in the Central Committee Secretariat) in charge of defense research and production.[61] Such relationships are common in the Soviet system and are often an important source of an individual's power and influence.

Whether similar relationships exist today is an interesting question. Grigory Romanov, who succeeded Ustinov as Central Committee secretary for defense industries, was also a Politburo member and leading contender (in Western eyes) to succeed Konstantin Chernenko.[62] He thus possessed credentials at least equal to Ustinov's at the height of his power as Soviet defense industry czar.[63] Unknown, however, was how well Romanov would be able to translate those credentials into cooperation with powerful and influential figures such as Smirnov. Their interests would of course coincide significantly. Romanov needed information in order to influence the policy process, while his sources needed a channel for their own proposals to the Politburo.

Nevertheless, Romanov had built his power base as a party leader and military industrialist in Leningrad. When he became defense industry secretary, a lack of long-standing ties in Moscow may have prevented him from succeeding with the military-industrial establishment there. It is also possible that a weak Moscow power base was a factor in Romanov's failure in the post-Brezhnev Kremlin. He was removed from his Politburo and Central Committee posts in July 1985.[64]

The extent of Romanov's success or failure in building personel contacts during his time in Moscow will probably remain a mystery. Comparing his tenure with Ustinov's lengthy reign, however, serves as a reminder of the importance of *svyazi* (contacts) to the Soviet policy process. As powerful relationships vanish with the deaths of leading figures, the impact on Soviet decision making must be considerable.

Other entities in Soviet defense research and production also seem to participate in the policy process through highly placed individuals. Aleksandr Shchukin, the USSR Academy of Sciences representative at the SALT negotiations, is a good example. Shchukin had worked on missile guidance systems and continued to direct a Moscow staff researching guidance during his tenure on the Soviet delegation.[65] Prior to SALT I, Shchukin also apparently chaired an academy study group devoted to preparing recommendations on arms control proposals.[66] His delegation and study group roles probably gave him considerable influence on Soviet SALT policymaking.

Like Shchukin, other prominent Soviet scientists seem to have played important roles. Their influence is apparently felt most often through the consulting relationships that they develop with top Soviet leaders who are seeking information outside the regular Kremlin staff channels.[67] In addition, since the academy's head, Anatoly Aleksandrov, reportedly attends Politburo meetings frequently, he can presumably present the academy's views to the top leadership.[68] Whatever the access enjoyed by individual scientists, however, the academy as a whole—especially its civilian sector—does not seem to contribute technical information for arms control decisions through a well-established institutional staff structure.

Other defense production and management entities probably have at least a periodic role in Soviet arms control decision making. Among the management agencies are the Military Department of GOSPLAN, the State Planning Commission, and the State Committee for Science and Technology. The production side is represented by nine full-time defense ministries that are supplemented by others that produce goods, such as automobiles, for both the civilian and defense sectors.[69] Although the management agencies may make routine inputs to arms control policy, the production ministries probably do not.[70] They doubtless provide information on the status of research and production programs when called on by entities such as the Central Committee's Defense Industry Department. But unlike the Defense and Foreign Affairs ministries, the defense production ministries have not had their own representatives in the Politburo. Their location in the bureaucratic hierarchy suggests therefore that their access to top leaders is somewhat limited.

Intelligence Agencies

The Committee for State Security (KGB) and the Main Intelligence Directorate (GRU, or military intelligence) are organizations whose place in the arms control bureaucracy is not clearly understood. Both undoubtedly serve as sources of raw intelligence data on U.S. and NATO weapon systems, but they also probably produce analysis on the directions of U.S. military R&D and on political issues affecting arms control.[71] How their research reaches top policymakers, however, is largely unknown. One Soviet official has noted that on urgent foreign policy problems, the KGB and GRU may or may not be called upon to report to the Politburo but that Politburo-level figures, such as former KGB chief Yuri Andropov, would be "virtually automatic participants" in the process.[72]

In the Gorbachev regime, the head of the KGB has also become a full member of the Politburo. Viktor Chebrikov, the current head, was promoted to full membership in April 1985.[73] Like Andropov, Chebrikov had many years of party service before joining the KGB in 1967.[74] As a result, Chebrikov's participation in policymaking at the top level is probably somewhat comparable to Andropov's during the years when the latter enjoyed full Politburo status as the KGB chief.

Chebrikov is distinguished from Andropov, however, by a much shorter period of service in the powerful KGB slot. Andropov's fifteen-year chairmanship of the KGB was marked by significant successes at home and abroad.[75] This record presumably provided Andropov a certain authority in national security affairs. By contrast, Chebrikov's voice on the ruling Politburo might be considerably weaker.

But even should Chebrikov be in a weaker position, the KGB represents a type of special expertise in the Soviet system. Its chief was probably admitted to full membership in the Politburo in 1973 to allow direct leadership access to that expertise for policymaking purposes. The fact that the current KGB chief has been admitted doubtless means that he can still have a major effect on Soviet national security decisions.

Like the KGB, the GRU seems to have fairly easy access to the Soviet leadership. Officially subordinate to the General Staff, it apparently can be called on to provide information and analysis to the Central Committee departments, perhaps in conjunction with the Main Operations Directorate, site of the staff's major arms control support group.[76] In addition, the chief of the general staff might also be called on to present GRU findings directly to the top leadership, thus bypassing the Central Committee apparatus.

Social Science Institutes

The Institute of the USA and Canada (IUSAC) and the Institute of World Economy and International Relations (IMEIMO) are social science institutes that the USSR Academy of Sciences oversees in addition to research facilities addressing technical issues. Some Western observers argue vigorously that these institutes have a vital role in Soviet foreign policymaking; others argue with equal vigor that they are ignored by the top leadership and are used only to co-opt foreign visitors. Still others assert that the true role of the institutes lies between these two extremes. The issue remains unresolved, but it may be too much to place the institutes themselves in the midst of the policy process.

Instead, their most direct influence on Soviet leaders seems to come from individuals at the top of the institute hierarchy. A prime example is Georgiy Arbatov, IUSAC's director. Specialists like Arbatov, as one source states, "retain frequent enough contact with men of at least [Central Committee] Secretariat level to make an important contribution to the policy machine."[77] Michael Voslensky reports that Arbatov could telephone Konstantin Chernenko directly when the latter was serving as head of the Central Committee's General Department, the powerful entity that manages the final flow of policy papers to the top leadership. According to Voslensky, Chernenko readily agreed on one occasion to distribute an Arbatov paper to the full Politburo.[78]

As important foreign policy specialists, high-level institute figures apparently participate in formulating foreign policy decisions on a fairly regular basis. Either they are asked to serve as consultants to the Central Committee departments or are invited to advise the Secretariat or Politburo directly.[79] In the first case, they may be asked to prepare a written assessment of a particular situation. If called into a Politburo session, they could express their opinions in person.

The high-level institute contributions reportedly tend to be of a longer-range nature than those intended to answer a specific diplomatic initiative from the other side.[80] On arms control matters, this long-range orientation may mean that institute specialists have less to do with day-to-day negotiating tactics than with helping to advise Soviet leaders throughout the course of a negotiation by providing important insights into the other side's style and possible motives. In any case, since the specialists lack regular access to information on Soviet weapon systems and military policy, their ability to contribute to specific Soviet negotiating positions would be limited.

Institute personnel at lower levels probably participate in arms control policymaking only through the demands for staff support that their superiors place upon them. In general, the arms control sections of the institutes do not appear to participate routinely in formulating arms control policy, although they undoubtedly would supply information on Western positions and constraints if called upon directly by the Central Committee apparatus or MFA. Thus, the academy's social science institutes seem to play a role through knowledgeable, high-level individuals who are admitted to the policy process.[81]

Soviet Decision-Making Process

These agencies and personalities must come together at the highest level to formulate decisions on Soviet arms control policy. Traditionally, the Soviet system was regarded as a strict pyramid up which information flowed to a small group of leaders who maintained tight control over decision-making authority. Information from the ministerial bureaucracies, according to this model, had to pass through the Central Committee apparatus before it could reach the Politburo. In the Central Committee it would be abbreviated until it perhaps bore little resemblance to the original ministry product. It might also languish in the hands of a powerful Central Committee staff member with reason to see that it did not reach the top leadership. Once out of the Central Committee, it would pass into the hands of the leaders' aides. These important individuals might abbreviate and polish the information further, until at last it arrived on the desks of Politburo members. By this time, the ministry that produced the information might have had difficulty recognizing it.

Evidence of the late Brezhnev era indicated that the actual Soviet model did not operate according to these simple rules. It seemed clear that Brezhnev and his Politburo colleagues had taken steps to ensure access to information outside Central Committee channels. The Central Committee staff remains the main means to route information to the Politburo, but other roads are possible as well. Thus, under the revised version of the model, the leadership still maintains strict authority over decisions, and the Central Committee staff still exercises a powerful influence over what information reaches them. At the same time, individuals and institutions that represent unique expertise can be heard directly at the very highest level. Sometimes, as in the case of Andrei Gromyko, they become powerful influences on the leadership by joining its ranks.

How does this revised model perform in practice? In the national security field, it revolves around the operations of the Defense Council. The Defense Council brings together Politburo members, senior military officers, and party and government representatives to formulate policy on defense and arms control.[82] It seems to provide a forum where the political leadership's policy commitments can be reconciled with the concerns of the professional military. The subgroup of Politburo members responsible for defense and foreign policy probably also includes those who serve on the Defense Council.

When an issue, perhaps a negotiating strategy, is coming up for consideration in the council, the Central Committee apparatus might begin to ask various government agencies to produce position papers on it. The Central Committee staff would receive these and begin to modify them according to standards of brevity or perhaps political necessity. From the staff they would pass into the General Department, the powerful gatekeeping organization that decides who within the top leadership should receive them. Only then would they be handed to the leaders' personal aides, the influential men who ultimately decide what issues and background information should appear on the desks of Politburo members.[83]

Each Politburo member and doubtless each Central Committee secretary has such a personal secretariat. They are made up of long-time close associates of the leader, as well as experts on international affairs and other issue areas.[84] Some of these experts become permanent fixtures in the high-level staff arena. For example, former Brezhnev foreign policy adviser Andrei Aleksandrov-Agentov also served successive general secretaries Yury Andropov and Konstantin Chernenko.[85] These individuals, because of their control over the information that reaches top leaders, are actually influential decision makers in their own right. As position papers arrive on their desks from the Central Committee apparatus, they might decide to call upon top experts to present their views directly to the Politburo. In this way scientists and academics, who can be termed consultants to the Politburo, either prepare written analyses to submit to the top aides or appear in person to present their views at Defense Council sessions. These consulting relationships are a means to circumvent normal staff channels; as such, they are probably the closest that Soviet leaders have come to seeking alternative advice on touchy matters such as weapon development programs.[86]

After a long process of policy formulation by the high-level staffs, an arms control proposal would be placed on the roster for a Defense Council meeting. If all sides had agreed by the time the meeting convened, the proposal would presumably be voted on quickly and passed forward for Politburo approval. Since the Politburo members of the Defense Council are likely also the subgroup of the full body responsible for national security issues, a proposal approved in the Defense Council would probably be approved by the Politburo without further discussion. It is possible, however, that more expert opinion would be brought to bear and discussion would occur, especially regarding issues that concern both foreign and domestic policy.

This revised model of Kremlin decision making permits a number of paths to the top leadership in addition to the Central Committee channels. But at the same time, the limits on the system's flexibility are profound. Because the Politburo retains ultimate responsibility for many decisions that leaders elsewhere would delegate, its agenda is perennially crowded. As Michael Voslensky puts it, the Kremlin hierarchy thus becomes a decision-making machine or a machine "for rubberstamping decisions that have already been made."[87] The Brezhnev Politburo seemed to recognize this limitation, for it built up the system of consulting relationships, most prominently (to Western eyes) in the national security field. Such specialists, however, are hobbled by controls on their access to information. Information unique to an organization is likely to remain so; the monopoly maintained by the Soviet military is the clearest example. Because General Staff–Defense Ministry expertise is still accepted as sufficient to generate advice on military matters, the military's requirements probably tend to escape question. As a result, the Soviet leadership must enter its political concerns into the decision-making process in the face of military requirements at least somewhat immune to alteration. No matter how effective a political or foreign policy adviser, he faces a formidable barrier in this immunity.

Impact of the Post-Brezhnev Succession

The picture that emerges is one of a process highly dependent on personalities and the relationships among them. Individuals have had major impacts on Soviet arms control decision making in the years since the beginning of the SALT negotiations. A strong leader, Leonid Brezhnev, was first in this regard, but others such as Foreign Minister Andrei Gromyko and Marshal Nikolai Ogarkov, former chief of the General Staff, have also clearly put their marks on Soviet arms control policy. These individuals are associated with certain staff aides and outside experts. In essence, a network of close personal advisers supports each decision maker. But what happens when the strong leader disappears or shakeups occur in the ruling hierarchy? Death and personnel changes have been the rule rather than the exception since the Brezhnev succession began at the start of the 1980s. Several effects of this have been visible to Western observers.

Continuation of staffing arrangements has clearly been viewed as a necessity by the Kremlin hierarchy. Proud of maintaining policy uninterrupted no matter what changes occur in the regime, Soviet leaders have evidently not been willing or able to discard eminent foreign policy advisers such as Aleksandrov-Agentov. As a result, they have the same policy but perhaps not the same policymaking arrangement. Brezhnev apparently had the authority to impose his will in issue areas such as arms control that were important to him. He therefore could set at least general directions for his personal secretariat. With each Politburo member now seeking such authority for himself, probably no one can impose his will in the same way. As a result, high-level staff members are probably in a good position to provide the needed impetus through institutional memory and long-established influence.

The flux within the Politburo may also be having an impact on the locus of Kremlin decision making. The balance of power in that body was apparently well established during Brezhnev's tenure, and its members probably understood how the balance would play out in the decision process. Hence, although Brezhnev at the height of his power clearly dominated Kremlin decision making on SALT, his authority did not excuse him from seeking agreement with other top leaders. They could evidently override him if he went too far.[88]

Brezhnev's "exclusive authority" seemed in fact to be limited by his incomplete grasp of technical issues. Since heads of state are not supposed to be caught up in the details of silo dimensions, this gap is entirely proper. At the same time, technical expertise was represented by other Politburo and Defense Council members whose organizations were responsible for military policy and weapon development programs. Brezhnev was a strong enough leader to impose his will on general issue areas such as arms control, but the details of how his policy was accomplished were still subject to tight scrutiny by his fellows and their expert staffs. In this way, bureaucratic structure and procedure remain an important check on the power of any one member of the collective leadership.

Since Brezhnev's demise, expertise has continued to reside in party and government organizations, and these have continued to be represented on the Politburo. With no strong leader to impose his will on policy, however, the decision-making behavior of that body is perhaps a good deal less predictable to its members. Certain established actors such as Andrei Gromyko probably have wielded unusual influence because they have long been associated with important national policies. They in essence embody policy continuity.[89] Other leadership figures, the comparative newcomers, are doubtless searching for ways to balance such influence. For that, they must turn to building relationships not only within their staffs but also within the bureaucracies that feed them information and analyses. Such influence building may account for Gorbachev's move to appoint Eduard Shevardnadze to succeed Gromyko as foreign minister.[90]

If individuals such as Gorbachev broach a new proposal to the Politburo, they presumably have strong behind-the-scenes support to bring to bear on remaining Politburo members. Nevertheless, the guarantees they can exercise that their proposals will be accepted are probably somewhat limited. Before Gromyko's promotion, for example, the MFA perspective that he represented was probably a better predictor of the outcome of policy in the national security arena. Hence, for a time the locus of Soviet arms control decision making may have shifted from the Kremlin to one of the organizations that traditionally supported it.

The shift was almost certain to be temporary, however. Andrei Gromyko's lengthy tenure and the power that accrued to him as a result were unusual even by Soviet standards. Gromyko and Minister of Defense Ustinov before his death apparently served as moorings for the regime's legitimacy in a longer succession than the Soviets probably intended. Their roles could not automatically be assumed by those who follow them. Thus their organizations would not always have controlling influence on Soviet policy.

At the same time, Brezhnev's attempts to diversify the sources of information available to the top leadership have evidently acquired a significant permanency in the Soviet decision process. KGB chief Chebrikov, for example, rather quickly acquired a voting seat on the Politburo. Brezhnev's successors have seemingly concluded that direct access to expertise in government ministries and other specialized organizations is an important aspect of decision making.

Thus, the innovations of the Brezhnev years will probably continue. By admitting a range of actors and considering the issues that they raise, the Soviet leadership perhaps hopes to improve its overall success in implementing policies worldwide. Certainly the leaders turned their attention in the 1970s to the importance of public opinion in achieving serious arms control agreements. The same actors who provided that link for the Kremlin in the Brezhnev era have been active since his death. They are an established symbol of the breadth of issues that impact on Soviet arms control decision making.

A wider range of expertise applied to the Soviet policy process does not necessarily foretell positive changes in U.S.–Soviet relations, however. In fact, a major reason for the Soviets' urge to diversify actors was evident in their eagerness to influence Western Europe against NATO. This overall goal of Kremlin policy is bound to place the Soviets on at least an intermittent collision course with the United States.

But if these developments are not entirely positive for U.S.–Soviet relations, neither are they wholly negative. Greater public access to Soviet military and political positions in the arms control arena improves the predictability of the policy process in Moscow. Although in some cases proposals broached in the media are clearly calculated to affect public opinion alone, in others they create major political imperatives for Soviet arms control negotiators.

Perhaps the prime example of this phenomenon was the Soviet promise to walk out of the INF negotiations should NATO proceed with Pershing-2 and GLCM deployments in December 1983. When the deployments went forward, the Soviets had no choice but to abandon the negotiations, a move that isolated them in Europe and colored their arms control policy for the remainder of the post-Brezhnev transition.

Political imperatives of this type create opportunities for the United States to predict better the outcomes of Soviet policy. Such foreknowledge, aids in the formation of long-term strategies for negotiating with the Soviets. In this sense, the Soviet arms control decision-making process as it exists today is a positive force in Soviet–U.S. relations.

Notes

1. Arkady Shevchenko presents a convincing picture of Khrushchev's views with regard to the value of propaganda proposals. See *Breaking with Moscow* (New York: Alfred A. Knopf, 1985), p. 101.

2. Leonid Brezhnev speech, *Pravda*, November 28, 1978; translated in Foreign Broadcast Information Service, Soviet Union *Daily Report* (hereafter FBIS), November 30, 1978, p. R10.

3. At the same time, Soviet audiences are receiving more information through their own media, and the IID probably has played a role in this area. For an interesting discussion of the enriched information content, see the Jonathan Sanders interview on Columbia University's study of Soviet television, MacNeil-Lehrer Newshour Transcript, Public Broadcasting System, Washington, D.C., February 8, 1985.

4. Leslie H. Gelb, "What We Really Know about Russia," *New York Times Magazine*, October 28, 1984, p. 67. Despite his seeming confidence in Soviet ability to influence the U.S. process, Mendelevich's comment that the flood of information "is more than we can swallow" suggests that the Soviets have the opposite problem but suffer the same result. Overburdened with information, they may not be able to make the best use of it.

5. The recollections of delegation members and other U.S. officials involved in SALT have appeared in John Newhouse, *Cold Dawn: The Story of SALT* (New York: Holt, Rinehart and Winston, 1973); Mason Willrich and John B. Rhinelander, (eds.), *SALT: The Moscow Agreements and Beyond* (New York: Free Press, 1974); Gerard Smith, *Doubletalk: The Story of the First Strategic Arms Limitation Talks* (Garden City, N.Y.: Doubleday, 1980); Henry Kissinger, *White House Years* (Boston: Little, Brown, 1979); Raymond L. Garthoff, "Negotiating with the Russians: Some Lessons from SALT," *International Security* 2(Spring 1977):3–24; Raymond L. Garthoff, "SALT I: An Evaluation," *World Politics* 32(October 1978):1–25; Raymond L. Garthoff, "Negotiating SALT," *Wilson Quarterly* 1(Autumn 1977):76–85; Thomas W. Wolfe, *The SALT Experience* (Cambridge, Mass.: Ballinger, 1979); Strobe Talbott, *Endgame: The Inside Story of SALT II* (New York, Harper & Row, 1979); U.S. Congress, House of Representatives, Committee on Foreign Affairs, *Soviet Diplomacy and Negotiations Behavior: Emerging New Context for U.S. Diplomacy,* Special Studies Series on Foreign Affairs Issues, vol. 1 (Washington, D.C.: GPO, 1979); Strobe Talbott, *Deadly Gambits* (New York: Alfred A. Knopf, 1984).

6. Problems may arise with each of these types of sources. Western observers are subject to misperceptions, or they may simply forget details. Official Soviets may have other goals in mind in revealing information, such as misleading curious Westerners. In turn, émigrés may have their own agendas and may also be subject to faulty memory. Despite these limitations, when taken together the sources represent a useful record.

7. Henry Brandon, "How Decisions Are Made in the Highest Soviet Circles," *Washington Star,* July 15, 1979.

8. Ned Temko, "Who Pulls the Levers of Power in the Soviet Machine," *Christian Science Monitor,* February 23, 1982.

9. Michael Voslensky, *Nomenklatura* (Garden City, N.Y.: Doubleday, 1984), pp. 247, 266.

10. Ibid., p. 274.

11. Ibid., pp. 267, 274.

12. Ibid.

13. Emigré accounts have highlighted this wider responsiblity. See, for example, Vladimir Sakharov, *High Treason* (New York: G.P. Putnam's Sons, 1980), pp. 248–250; Nicolas Polianski, *M.I.D.* (Paris, Pierre Belfond, 1984), pp. 241–242; Shevchenko, *Breaking with Moscow,* pp. 189–191.

14. Shevchenko, *Breaking with Moscow,* pp. 147, 149.

15. Ibid., p. 190.

16. Herwig Kraus, *The International Information Department of the Central Committee of the CPSU,* Radio Liberty Research Bulletin No. RL 95/80, Radio Free Europe-Radio Liberty, Washington, D.C., March 4, 1980, p. 4; and Elizabeth Teague, *The Foreign Departments of the Central Committee of the CPSU,* Supplement to the Radio Liberty Research Bulletin, Radio Free Europe-Radio Liberty (Washington, D.C., October 27, 1980), p. 5.

17. Kraus, *International Information Department,* p. 2; "A Tribute to a Spry Brezhnev Brings an Edgy Soviet Reply," *New York Times,* November 25, 1981, p. A14.

18. See, for example, Hamburg DPA in German, October 29, 1981, translated in FBIS, October 30, 1981; and Josef Riedmueller dispatch, *Sueddeutsche Zeitung* in German, October 30, 1981, translated in FBIS, November 2, 1981.

19. See, for example, "Text of 5 Dec Foreign Ministry Press Conference," Moscow World Service in English, December 5, 1983, in FBIS, December 6, 1983, pp. AA1–AA17.

20. See, for example, Chervov's comments in Don Oberdorfer and Walter Pincus, " 'Star Wars' Will Trigger Arms Buildup, Soviet Warns," *Washington Post*, March 6, 1985, p. A1.

21. Shevchenko calls these three individuals the Kremlin's most important troika of spokesmen for influencing Western public opinion. See *Breaking with Moscow*, p. 110.

22. Paris AFP in English, June 20, 1985, in FBIS, June 21, 1985, p. R4. One day later, TASS reported that Zamyatin was still on the job. See Moscow TASS in English, June 21, 1985, in FBIS, June 21, 1985, p. R4.

23. See, for example, Vladimir Lomeyko interview for Prague television, June 26, 1985, in FBIS, June 27, 1985, pp. A1–A2.

24. Arthur J. Alexander, *Decision-Making in Soviet Weapons Procurement* (London: International Institute for Strategic Studies, 1978–1979), p. 11.

25. Michael Checinski, *A Comparison of the Polish and Soviet Armaments Decisionmaking Systems* (Santa Monica: Rand Corporation, R-2662-AF, January 1981), pp. 67–68.

26. Ibid., p. 68.

27. Edward L. Warner III, *The Military in Contemporary Soviet Politics: An Institutional Analysis* (New York: Praeger, 1977), p. 243.

28. Kenneth A. Myers and Dimitri Simes, *Soviet Decision Making, Strategic Policy, and SALT* (Washington, D.C.: Georgetown University Center for Strategic and International Studies, 1974) pp. 27–28, 31.

29. Warner, *Military in Contemporary Soviet Politics*, p. 240.

30. Alexander, *Decision-Making in Soviet Weapons Procurement*, p. 17.

31. Smith, *Doubletalk*, p. 48. For more on Alekseyev, see John Erickson, *Soviet Military Power* (London: Royal United Services Institute, 1971), pp. 16, 24.

32. A fascinating exception to this rule may be a group of sociologists attached to the Soviet Ministry of Defense. According to an émigré source, this group was called upon in 1971 to study the social problems of war. The results of this study reportedly "called into question the conviction of military specialists that they could limit human suffering in nuclear conflict so as to prolong military play to some (decisive) conclusion." These results evidently attracted enough attention in the Soviet leadership that a commission of party, military, and government figures was formed to study General Staff concepts. In this way, according to the source, the sociologists had a profound effect, for they "concluded that the USSR must subordinate military tactics to politics." See Il'ya Zemtsov, "Istoriya razvitiya sovetskoy sotsiologii" (History of the Development of Soviet Sociology), *Grani* (Frankfurt/ Main, Verlagsort, January-March 1977), pp. 269–271. I am grateful to Matthew Gallagher for this citation.

33. For more on the General Staff, see Alexander, *Decision-Making in Soviet*

Weapons Procurement, pp. 17–18; Wolfe, *SALT Experience,* pp. 62–64; Warner, *Military in Contemporary Soviet Politics,* pp. 24–26, 240–241, 243. Erickson, *Soviet Military Power,* pp. 16, 21. For the Soviet description of the General Staff, see *Sovetskaia voennaia entsiklopediia* (Moscow: Voenizdat, 1976), 2:511–513.

34. Checinski, *Comparison of the Polish and Soviet Armaments Decision-making Systems,* p. 69.

35. For a discussion of the General Staff's arms control support work, see Warner, *Military in Contemporary Soviet Politics,* p. 243; Raymond L. Garthoff, "The Soviet Military and SALT," in Jiri Valenta and William Potter, eds., *Soviet Decisionmaking for National Security* (London: George Allen & Unwin, 1984), p. 143.

36. For commentaries on Ogarkov's demise, see Rose Gottemoeller, "Ogarkov's mistake," *Christian Science Monitor,* October 4, 1984, p. 16; Richard Owen, "Dismissal of Outspoken Military Chief Signals Soviet Power Upheaval," *London Times,* September 8, 1984, p. 5; Bernard Gwertzman, "Ogarkov's Views on Defense Seen as Clue in Soviet Shake-Up," *International Herald Tribune,* September 9, 1984, p. 1; "USSR—the Riddle of Marshal Ogarkov," Radio Liberty Research Memorandum, RL 41/84, Munich, October 26, 1984.

37. For leadership speeches at Ustinov's funeral and obituary information, see FBIS, December 26, 1984, pp. R1–R8.

38. See Dusko Doder, "Gorbachev Tightens Hold on Leadership, Promotes Associates," *Washington Post,* April 24, 1985, p. A1.

39. These rumors could not be confirmed at the time of this writing. See Dusko Doder, "Soviets Restore Ogarkov to Military Leadership," *Washington Post,* July 18, 1985, p. A1; Mark Frankland, "Marshal Ogarkov Plans a High-Tech Warsaw Pact," *London Observer,* July 21, 1985, p. 15.

40. See N. Ogarkov, "Nemerknushchaya slava sovetskogo oruzhiva" (Unfading Glory of Soviet Arms), *Kommunist vooruzhennykh sil,* no. 21 (November 1984): 16–26; N.V. Ogarkov, "Istoriya uchit bditel'nosti" (History Teaches Vigilance) (Moscow: Voyenizdat, 1985).

41. Arkady Shevchenko's account of Foreign Ministry operations contains numerous examples of intraministry compartmentalization. See *Breaking with Moscow,* esp. pp. 83, 116, 141, 229.

42. Committee on Foreign Affairs, *Soviet Diplomacy and Negotiating Behavior,* p. 455. Raymond Garthoff has clarified the record on this event, which previously held that MFA representatives were being denied access to military hardware information. Garthoff states that they actually were being denied participation in discussions of military concepts. See "Soviet Military and SALT," p. 153.

43. See, for example, Wolfe, *SALT Experience,* pp. 60–61.

44. Garthoff, "Soviet Military and SALT," p. 142.

45. Ibid., p. 140.

46. Ibid., p. 142.

47. Myers and Simes, *Soviet Decision Making, Strategic Policy, and SALT,* p. 24; Glagolev, "Soviet Decision-making Process in Arms-Control Negotiations," p. 771; Shulman, in *SALT,* p. 111.

48. Kissinger, *White House Years,* pp. 139–140.

49. For discussion of this issue, see Gelman, *Politburo's Management of Its America Problem*, pp. 69–70.

50. Wolfe, *SALT Experience*, p. 61. Raymond Garthoff claims that as early as 1968, steps were taken to coordinate the arms control work of the Defense and Foreign Affairs ministries. See Raymond L. Garthoff, "SALT and the Soviet Military," *Problems of Communism* (January–February 1975):29; Arkady Shevchenko describes such interagency cooperation taking place as early as 1957. See *Breaking with Moscow*, p. 83.

51. Breaking with Moscow, p. 149.

52. Ibid., p. 150. See also pp. 151–153.

53. "Excerpts From Nominating Speech," *New York Times*, July 3, 1985, p. A4.

54. Shevardnadze assumed his new post without previous experience in international relations. See Serge Schmemann, "Gromyko Made Soviet President by Gorbachev," *New York Times*, July 3, 1985, p. A1; Celestine Bohlen, "Gromyko's Successor Seen as New Broom," *Washington Post*, July 3, 1985, p. A24; Gary Lee, "Tough but Green, Shevardnadze 'Very Much a Break with the Old,' " *Washington Post*, July 3, 1985, p. A25.

55. Pero Rakocevic, "Gorbachev's Selection Was Not Accidental," Interview with Viktor Afanas'yev, *Kommunist* (Belgrade), April 5, 1985, pp. 18–19. Afanas'yev went on to say that Gorbachev would not emphasize relations with the Third World at the expense of the Soviet Union's other international partners: "We cannot set up any firm priorities, since the problem of relations with the socialist countries and . . . with the capitalist countries are not less important than relations with the Third World."

56. It also reemphasized the Soviet military's current disadvantage, which may well prove short term.

57. John Newhouse, *Cold Dawn*, pp. 250–260; Kissinger, *White House Years*, pp. 1233–1238, 1241.

58. Wolfe, *SALT Experience*, p. 59.

59. Checinski, *Comparison of the Polish and Soviet Armaments Decision-making Systems*, p. 71.

60. Alexander, *Decision-Making in Soviet Weapons Procurement*, p. 21.

61. Ustinov died while serving as minister of defense in December 1984. The role of personal contacts has in some ways been institutionalized through the party's *nomenklatura* system. According to Leonard Schapiro, "The right to participate in the appointment of personnel depends on a series of documents to which the term *nomenklatura* applies. These set out the appointments to be filled and the particular officials at different levels, both party and state, who are entitled to be consulted and to decide on the appointments listed. These lists cover virtually all responsible appointments in the country. Nothing is known of the method in use for solving any cases of conflict in the selection of personnel. It is fairly certain that the weight of the party decision will tend to predominate in most cases." Leonard Schapiro, *The Government and Politics of the Soviet Union* (New York: Vintage, 1967), p. 127. Recent émigré accounts have clarified the importance of the *nomenklatura* system. See, for example, Voslensky, *Nomenklatura*.

62. For more on Romanov, see Ellen Jones, "The Defense Council in Soviet

Leadership Decisionmaking" (paper presented at colloquium on Soviet National Security Decisionmaking, Kennan Institute for Advanced Russian Studies, May 3, 1984), p. 42; "Potential Successors to Andropov and Some Who Will Help Decide," *New York Times*, February 11, 1984; "Don't Overlook Romanov," *Economist*, November 24, 1984, p. 50.

63. After his appointment as Central Committee secretary, Romanov was increasingly active in the military sphere overall. Some analysts took this activity as a sign of strengthened party oversight of the military. See Marc D. Zlotnik, "Chernenko Succeeds," *Problems of Communism* (March–April 1984):26–27.

64. According to some reports, Romanov tried to block Gorbachev's bid to become general secretary of the party at the time of Chernenko's death in March 1985. See Dusko Doder, "Gorbachev Rival Loses Party Posts," *Washington Post*, July 2, 1985, p. A9; Serge Schmemann, "Romanov, a Gorbachev Rival, Is Out," *New York Times*, July 2, 1985, p. A10.

65. Smith, *Doubletalk*, p. 47.

66. Shulman, in *SALT*, pp. 111–112. According to Wolfe, there was some question as to the study group's continued existence after SALT I. See *SALT Experience*, p. 66.

67. Wolfe, *SALT Experience*, p. 66.

68. Temko, "Who Pulls the Levers."

69. For a full listing, see Alexander, *Decision-Making in Soviet Weapons Procurement*, p. 22.

70. For more on GOSPLAN's Military Department, see Michael Checinski, *A Comparison of the Polish and Soviet Armaments Decisionmaking Systems* (Santa Monica: Rand, January 1981), pp. 67–68. For more on the State Committee for Science and Technology, see Louvan E. Nolting, *The Structure and Functions of the U.S.S.R. State Committee for Science and Technology,* Foreign Economic Report No. 16 (Washington, D.C.: U.S. Department of Commerce, Bureau of the Census, November 1979). The arms control role of these organizations is discussed in detail in Rose E. Gottemoeller, "Decisionmaking for Arms Limitation in the Soviet Union," in Hans Guenter Brauch and Duncan L. Clarke, eds., *Decisionmaking for Arms Limitation: Assessments and Prospects* (Cambridge, Mass.: Ballinger, 1983).

71. John Barron, *KGB: The Secret Work of Soviet Secret Agents* (New York: Reader's Digest Press, 1974), pp. 76, 102. Policy analysis, however, may not be the KGB's forte. Arkady Shevchenko reports that he soon learned to regard KGB political reporting with derision. See *Breaking with Moscow*, p. 238.

72. Ned Temko, "It's Not 'Democracy' But Many Soviets Have a Say," *Christian Science Monitor*, February 24, 1982.

73. Doder, "Gorbachev Tightens Hold on Leadership". Celestine Bohlen, "New Men All Were Andropov's," *Washington Post*, April 24, 1985, p. A30. Chebrikov had been a candidate member of the Politburo since 1983. See Marc D. Zlotnik, "Chernenko Succeeds," p. 22.

74. Amy W. Knight, "Soviet Politics and the KGB–MVD Relationship," *Soviet Union* 11(1984):169.

75. Amy W. Knight, "Andropov: Myths and Realities," *Survey* 28(Spring 1984):43.

76. Warner, *Military in Contemporary Soviet Politics*, p. 243.

77. Temko, "It's Not 'Democracy.' "

78. Voslensky, *Nomenklatura*, p. 384.

79. Temko, "It's Not 'Democracy.'"

80. Ibid.

81. For more on the academy's social institutes, see Blair A. Ruble, *Soviet Research Institutes Project*, vol. 2: *The Social Sciences* (Washington, D.C.: U.S. International Communication Agency, January 1981); Rose E. Gottemoeller and Paul F. Langer, *Foreign Area Specialists in the USSR: Training and Employment of Specialists* (Santa Monica: Rand Corporation, R-2967-RC, January 1983).

82. Wolfe, *SALT Experience*, pp. 52, 57–58. See also Alexander, *Decision-Making in Soviet Weapons Procurement*, pp. 14–16; Marshall D. Shulman, "SALT and the Soviet Union," in Willrich and Rhinelander, *SALT: The Moscow Agreements and Beyond*, p. 112; Edward L. Warner, III, *The Military in Contemporary Soviet Politics: An Institutional Analysis* (New York: Praeger, 1977), p. 46. In the 1970s, participation in the Defense Council by Central Committee secretaries may have been determined by the personal power of those who occupied those positions. For example, ideology secretary Mikhail Suslov, until his death in January 1982, was evidently an extremely powerful figure in Kremlin politics. See also Jones, "Defense Council in Soviet Leadership Decisonmaking."

83. Michael Voslensky has described how information passes through the Central Committee apparatus. See *Nomenklatura*, pp. 272–275.

84. Alexander, *Decision-Making in Soviet Weapons Procurement*, p. 13; Wolfe, *SALT Experience*, p. 53; Kenneth A. Myers and Dimitri Simes, *Soviet Decision Making, Strategic Policy, and SALT* (Washington, D.C.: Georgetown University Center for Strategic and International Studies, December 1974), pp. 14–17. Arkady Shevchenko reports that after Andrei Gromyko became a member of the Politburo, his small group of personal aides was expanded to include a doctor, military adjutant, and KGB guards. Shevchenko also describes the important role of Vasily Makarov as Gromyko's personal gatekeeper. See *Breaking with Moscow*, pp. 144–145, 160.

85. Alexander Rahr, "Chernenko's Aides," Radio Liberty Research Brief, RL 426/84, November 9, 1984. Rahr reports that Chernenko actually inherited several of Brezhnev's and Andropov's personal aides.

86. The Central Committee apparatus itself also calls upon specialists directly. Its roster of consultants presumably permits it to circumvent bureaucratic limits placed on the information flow from government ministries.

87. Voslensky, *Nomenklatura*, p. 105. Shevchenko also comments on the Politburo's heavy agenda. See *Breaking with Moscow*, pp. 175–181.

88. Henry Kissinger, *White House Years*, pp. 1220–1222.

89. Arkady Shevchenko advances this view in *Breaking with Moscow*. See p. 150.

90. It may also account for reports that Gorbachev has preferred his office in the Central Committee building to his Politburo office in the Kremlin. See George Russell, "The Succession Problem," *Time Magazine*, February 11, 1985, p. 40.

6

Soviet Positions on Strategic Arms Control and Arms Policy: A Perspective Outside the Military Establishment

Anne T. Sloan

S ince the late 1970s, little has been accomplished in Soviet–U.S. relations. There is no aspect of the relationship where this lack of
accomplishment is more evident than arms control. Responsibility
for the deterioration that has occurred in Soviet–U.S. relations in general
and arms control in particular may be attributed to a variety of events and
perceptions. Neither nation is solely responsible for the failures in the
relationship nor is either blameless.

Arms control has suffered from failures in other aspects of Soviet–U.S.
relations, but it has also fallen victim to the exigencies of U.S. politics.
Defense issues and arms control positions are, along with economic issues,
the most salient elements in national electoral politics in the United States.
In the last decade, discussions on defense and arms control have been
increasingly dominated by academic and policy specialists who believe the
Soviets have a policy bent on world domination and that one of the corner-
stones of that policy is a strategic doctrine and force posture that will
enable them to wage and win a nuclear war against the United States.

Their views are based to some extent on studies of Soviet positions on
arms control and Soviet strategic doctrine that have been based primarily
on the views espoused by Soviet military writers. Reliance on military
literature in this area of research is the logical outgrowth of two Western
perceptions: Soviet strategic doctrine is either synonymous with or so
closely intertwined with Soviet arms control attitudes that they can and
should be treated synonymously, and the military is the source of strategic
doctrine and, therefore, is also the source of arms control positions. The
fallacy in this line of reasoning is that those who make these assumptions
have never legitimized them by disqualifying other possible inputs into
Soviet arms policy. Other sources, largely academic and political in nature,
are necessary to elaborate on past studies based primarily on military
materials.

Several justifications can be made for this type of approach. Not least among the justifications is the nature of the Soviet regime. Dennis Ross notes that "the post-Khrushchev period has been characterized by a growing routinization of function, heightened sense of bureaucratic order, greater leadership stability, and general normalization of the decision-making process."[1] He continues to describe the Brezhnev regime as "a system where the country's major interests (as embodied in the central institutional actors) meet at the apex of the regime, to be mediated and minimally satisfied."[2] Ross's argument seems to have been strengthened by events in the post-Brezhnev era. Despite not only the rather rapid turnover in the post of Communist Party of the Soviet Union general secretary but also the loss of several key people in the Politburo since 1980, the Soviet regime has been marked by the same sense of stability and continuity that was a trademark of Brezhnev's leadership. If this is indeed the case and Ross's contention that the major interests are "mediated and minimally satisfied" at the Politburo level, it would imply that, although the military espouses certain ideas and sets certain criteria necessary for the defense and preservation of the Soviet Union, other areas of concern also compete for a limited number of resources. Those who must mediate among these competing areas of concern might seek out alternative sources of information and suggestions in an attempt to satisfy minimally all the elements with which they must deal. Although it is not the purpose here to support such ideas as institutional interest groups, incrementalism, and decision making by bargaining, the possibility that this is the reality of Soviet policymaking should not be desregarded out of hand.

A second justification of the approach advocated here is that past studies based on articles, books, and speeches produced by the Soviet military have been inconclusive. There are basically two diametrically opposed Western schools of thought based on research on Soviet military strategic thought and arms policy attitudes.[3] It is doubtful that the disagreement between these schools will be resolved by an additional interpretation of Soviet military thinking. Rather than add another voice to those advocating one of these positions or the other, the time has come to look for corroboration from other elements in Soviet policy circles. Some such corroborative elements are included among the analysts writing for *U.S.A.: Economics, Politics, and Ideology (SShA)*, *Mirovaia ekonomika i mezhdunarodnye otnosheniia (MEMO)*, and *International Affairs*.

These sources have been largely ignored by most scholars with the exception of such people as Raymond Garthoff[4] who used them on a limited basis to counter arguments supporting the singlemindedness of Soviet strategic thinking.[5] Garthoff, along with Thomas Wolfe[6] and Karl Spielmann,[7] offer persuasive arguments for research on Soviet arms positions beyond those of the military. Spielmann maintains that the defense industry sector of the economy is intimately involved with arms limitation decision making. It might be argued that the defense industry is simply an extension of the military;[8] however, Spielmann makes some convincing arguments that the defense industries interests differ to some degree from those of the military in general. Roman Kolkowicz carries this argument even further by suggesting that there may be groups within the military advocating different points of view and that some of these groups cut across institutional boundaries with the inclusion of nonmilitary personnel like defense industry planners.[9]

Thomas Wolfe argues that numerous organizations are in some way concerned with and to some degree able to influence the decision process. Wolfe points out that the Ministry of Foreign Affairs includes a section under the International Organizations Division called the Disarmament Section that approximates the function of the Arms Control and Disarmament Agency (ACDA) in the United States, but it is not an actual counterpart to ACDA.[10] The Disarmament Section, although staffed by arms control specialists, is smaller than ACDA and has traditionally been in a much more subordinate position than ACDA. Both the head of the Foreign Ministry, A.A. Gromyko, and deputy foreign minister, V.S. Semenov, have been actively involved in the SALT process. Semenov was the chief Russian negotiator, and Gromyko has played a prominent role since the 1974 Vladivostok Agreement. However, it is necessary to note that inputs from the Ministry of Foreign Affairs have been largely political and diplomatic in nature and that its representatives have shown a general lack of sophistication concerning strategic and technical problems that have arisen in past arms negotiations.[11] Nevertheless, there have been indications that this phenomenon has become less prevalent over time. Given Gromyko's prominent role in the post-Brezhnev leadership, a continued increase in Foreign Ministry participation in future arms negotiations and decisions concerning those negotiations is likely.

In addition to the Ministry of Foreign Affairs, both the Institute of the USA (SShA) and the Institution of World Economy and International Relations (IMEMO) have Disarmament Sections. Roman Kolkowicz calls these two subsections of the Academy of Sciences the Americanologists.[12] Both Garthoff and Kolkowicz acknowledge that these academicians do contribute to the arms control decision-making process. Kolkowicz describes the role of the Americanologists: "They provide inputs into policy framing and offer policy makers a greater sense of the nuances, complexities, and realities of American politics. They seek to enhance the effectiveness of Soviet policy framing by relating it to certain American values and perceived intentions."[13] G.A. Arbatov, SShA director, describes their role as a resource arm for the policymakers in the various ministries, the Central Committee, and even the Politburo, providing reports much like the working papers found in Western decision-making units.[14] An additional clue to the importance of the academicians may be found in the advancement of both Arbatov (1976) and IMEMO director N.N. Inozemtsev (1971) to membership on the Central Committee. This is not only a reflection of an individual's prestige but also an indicator of the importance of his institutional affiliation.[15]

Additional evidence supporting the incorporation of nonmilitary attitudes into the study of overall Soviet arms control perspectives comes from two more recent studies. Jerry Hough notes the increase of well-trained specialists in the Ministry of Foreign Affairs and the upsurge of academic institutes in the past three decades.[16] Various new institutes for the training of undergraduates were founded after World War II, including the Moscow State Institute of International Relations (MGIMO). According to Hough, MGMIO has had a close relationship with the Ministry of Foreign Affairs, and its "legendary class of 1949 (including Inozemtsev and Arbatov) produced an unusually high proportion of the top advisors of the Brezhnev period."[17] Graduates of MGIMO and the other undergraduate institutes pursue three main career paths: they go directly into the Ministry of Foreign Affairs or other ministries with international foci, they become *zhurnalist-mezhdunarodniki* (international journalists), or they become scholarly researchers.

Many of these researchers enter one of the institutes under the Academy of Sciences, the most prestigious of the IMEMO. Established shortly after the Twentieth Party Congress, IMEMO was under the directorship of Anushavan A. Arzumanian, a wartime colleague of Brezhev. Upon his death in 1966, Arzumanian was succeeded by Nikolai Inozemtsev. By 1974, IMEMO was staffed by 572 research associates and had given birth to a minimum of four independent institutes, including SShA.[18] The importance of these institutes and their staffs is described by Hough:

> These men . . . were not simply engaging in academic research. The Ministry of Foreign Affairs has had little research staff, and this apparently is also true of the KGB. The Scholarly Community working on contemporary problems—and there are some 2,000 to 3,000 of them in Moscow—are supposed to fill the gap . . . those doing policy-revelant work—and there is great pressure to do so—can spend 25 percent of their time or more on classified work usually called "the director's assignments" [the institute director]. These assignments, which themselves reflect demands or requests from higher authorities, can range from the preparation of a short informational memorandum to a prediction of future developments in the area of their specialization or even to participate in a group working out different policy options for consideration by the Politburo.[19]

According to Hough, there has also been some direct co-optation of scholars into posts directly involved in policymaking.

Samuel Payne also argues for the importance of Soviet foreign affairs specialists represented by foreign affairs journalists and academic specialists as contributors to Soviet arms control policymaking.[20] "The supreme leadership apparently does listen to the advice of Soviet foreign affairs specialists and accept some of it; ideas first expressed in scholarly articles in 1969 and 1970 often appeared in Brezhnev's speeches in 1972 and 1973."[21] Payne looks at two groups: the militarists and the arms controllers. He maintains that "Soviet policy toward strategic arms limitation evolves from the interaction of . . . three elements, the arms controllers and the militarists offering alternative policies and the supreme leadership choosing between them."[22] Payne also notes that this choice is more likely to be some sort of compromise or synthesis of the two extremes.

There are enough indicators of nonmilitary input to warrant further research into the role of the Ministry of Foreign Affairs and the Americanologists or arms controllers in arms policymaking. On hypothesis that may be drawn is that although the Soviet military may have preeminent influence over strategic policymaking, including arms control policies, it does not operate in a vacuum. There are inputs into the process from other elements that at a minimum have the potential of influencing the policies selected by the top leadership.

Payne is the only author who has attempted a rigorous examination of the militarists and the arms controllers. He maintains that there are two major areas of agreement between these elements: the U.S. government is hostile to the Soviet Union, prone to aggressiveness, and tends to be dominated by an oligarchy commonly known as the "military-industrial complex"; and the power relationship between the United States and the Soviet Union has changed considerably, with the Soviet Union becoming more militarily and economically powerful while the United States has been growing weaker. Nevertheless, within the framework of these two commonly held beliefs, there is quite a bit of disagreement.[23] The militarists tend to have a much darker view of the United States and to give a much more negative assessment. According to Payne, the militarists as a group express or have expressed the following: (1) until the SALT I agreement, they described the United States as becoming more aggressive and hostile to the Soviet Union; (2) from the time of SALT 1, they have sometimes described the United States as seeking military superiority; (3) U.S. strategic weapons systems under development have a first-strike capability; (4) until 1972, there were no serious differences of opinion among the U.S. ruling elite and that elite as a body was hostile, aggressive, against arms control, and anti-Soviet; (5) the U.S. government is hostile to arms control and determined to build up a strategic nuclear force regardless of the outcome of SALT negotiations and to continue the arms race; and (6) because of the nature of the U.S. ruling elite, nuclear war remains a real possibility and the Soviet Union should be prepared to fight and win or, at a minimum, be able to survive a nuclear war. Additionally, the militarists believed, at least through the mid-1970s, that preemption was one possible way of surviving and winning such a war.[24]

On the other hand, the arms controllers have maintained that (1) U.S. defeats and internal crises are driving its leaders to accept détente; (2) neither country can attain nuclear superiority, and it would not be very useful if they did; (3) the development of new weapons threatens SALT; (4) many members of the U.S. ruling elite are sober minded and realize the arms race does not serve U.S. interests (such as economic problems and domestic opposition to policies), and SALT I marked the ascendancy of those who are sober minded; (5) there is strong and steadily increasing popular opposition to the arms race and military spending in the United States, and this can force the ruling elite to change their policies; and (6) the probability of a deliberate attack by the United States is very low, and it is almost impossible to fight and survive a nuclear war.[25]

Payne also points to the possibility that silence on a topic may be an indicator of dissent in Soviet policy discussion. He notes that prior to the initiation of SALT negotiations, there was active opposition to such talks on the part of the militarists; however, after the negotiations were underway and throughout the SALT I period (1969–1972), "the Soviet military press maintained almost complete silence on the subject of SALT."[26] Since SALT I, the militarists have endorsed the agreements but temper their endorsements with assessments of the aggressive nature of the Soviet Union's enemies.

A recent book by David Holloway, *The Soviet Union and the Arms Race,* reinforces the importance of looking at the broader picture of Soviet arms positions. He argues that there is a military and a political aspect of Soviet doctrine and that the political is intended to be the dominant component.[27] Only by understanding the interface between the two aspects can one truly grasp Soviet positions on arms policy and strategic doctrine.

Despite these strong and cogent arguments, the predominant voices in the area of Soviet arms policy analysis, many of whom occupy key positions in the current U.S. administration's policy circles, have relied on the writings of the Soviet military. Many of them have judged Soviet policy and doctrine harshly and largely denigrated Soviet sincerity in the pursuit of arms control and disarmament. They argue that the Soviet Union's policies are based on an unchanging doctrine promulgated solely by the military, which advocates a counterforce strategy predicated on the ability to fight and win, or at least survive, a nuclear war.[28] This differs considerably from the literature that argues that there are voices, some within the military and some outside the military establishment, advocating various stances on strategic arms policy and that they do not believe that a nuclear war can be won. Additionally, according to the second group of analysts, Soviet arms policy positions have not changed across time. The real point of debate, however, is whether the Soviet Union can be depended upon to negotiate and implement strategic arms limitation agreements in good faith.[29] Those analysts who take a negative, distrustful point of view regarding Soviet strategic doctrine are arguing implicitly, and at times explicitly, against strategic arms agreements with the Soviets. This antinegotiation stance has been prevalent among many of the security advisers, especially those in the Pentagon, in the Reagan administration.

Soviet Positions outside the Military Establishment

Before discussing various areas of disagreement over Soviet arms policy found among Western analysts, it is necessary to review briefly positions taken by Soviet writers in *MEMO, SShA,* and *International Affairs* during the 1970s.[30] Writers in these journals, especially those writing in *SShA,* take several specific positions of interest. One of these is the opinions expressed about mutual assured destruction and deterrence. Soviet analysts tended to view the basic assumptions upon which these elements of U.S. strategic policy have been based as rather naive and illogical in their conceptualization. Nevertheless, they accepted them as the best alternative given the nature of strategic arms competition. However, Soviet analysts have little faith in the ability of deterrence in the form of mutual assured destruction to persevere in the long run. Given the inevitability, from this perspective, of the breakdown of this concept, Soviet analysts also advocated continued readiness of Soviet defensive capabilities. The general premise of these analysts was that since deterrence seemed to work, it should be supported; however, when it eventually failed, the Soviet Union should not find itself in a position where it could not defend itself by fighting and hoping to survive a nuclear war.

This perspective on deterrence in the form of mutual assured destruction led Soviet analysts to certain other conclusions. One was that the very delicately balanced mechanism of deterrence was extremely vulnerable. This vulnerability, according to Soviet analysts, was evident in some of the policies that the United States had incorporated into its overall perspective on deterrence. For instance, they found U.S. ideas concerning the utility of local wars, limited wars outside the territory of either major power (whether those wars were conventional or nuclear), and limited or contained nuclear strikes inside the home territory of either the United States or Soviet Union as artificial and dangerous distinctions. They feared that any war, especially one where nuclear weapons were used, would escalate into all-out nuclear war. At least some Soviet analysts expressed the belief that this escalation could not be controlled.

They also criticized the idea of preemptive first strikes on the basis that such use of nuclear weapons had a high probability of failure because there was little guarantee that such a strike would be successful enough to destroy the other side's retaliatory capability. This implicitly supports the contention that Soviet analysts who are not part of the military bureaucracy support the idea of mutual assured destruction since they believe in the utility of a survivable second strike capability. Additionally, given the nature of nuclear weapons and the fact that they exist in such large numbers and have such destructive capability, the chances of either side's surviving a nuclear war was fairly slim in the view of several analysts. This is, of course, a gross oversimplification of the positions found in *International Affairs, SShA,* and *MEMO* concerning the questions of surviving and winning a nuclear war. In fact, there were a variety of assessments concerning these questions ranging from the suicidal nature of nuclear war for the United States to the catastrophic nature of nuclear war for both countries.[31]

Additionally, some Soviet analysts, evidently in response to U.S. critics who argued that Soviet strategic doctrine was based on a war-winning perspective that relied on a first strike, stressed the point that the Soviet Union had no intention of attacking anyone. This opinion was expressed explicitly in *SShA* a few times during a period when Soviet doctrine was coming under especially intense attack.[32]

Analysts in all three journals also took a hard line on the arms race. They uniformly agreed that a continued arms race greatly increased the threat of nuclear war. Much of the thrust of their arguments against the arms race was based on the futility of either side's attempts to achieve superiority or a one-sided advantage over the other. Most discussions of the arms race were couched in terms critical of the United States for its attempts to preserve or reestablish strategic superiority over the Soviet Union; however, implicitly, and in some instances explicitly, the arguments used applied to both the United States and the Soviet Union. They argued that neither side would allow any advantages by the other to persist but instead would meet any new weapons development with another that would neutralize the advantage, thus creating a spiraling of the arms race. Additionally the technological revolution increased the importance of the arms race because qualitative escalations were much more dangerous than quantitative ones.

The issue of qualitative improvements received serious attention from these Soviet analysts. They saw qualitative developments as potentially more destablizing than quantitative ones. Eventually, qualitative developments might lead to a situation where a preemptive first strike or a deliberate nuclear attack would become attractive as a way of taking advantage of a short-term inequality created by qualitative improvements. Use of this qualitative edge would short-circuit the seesaw effects of the arms race and allow one side or the other to sustain their advantage. Despite this scenario, all the analysts who discussed the arms race from this perspective leave the impression that any attempt to truncate the arms race in this fashion would not result in neutralization of the enemy but in nuclear war.

Concomitant to the belief that the arms race was the chief danger to peace was the opinion, expressed in all three journals, that the United States was responsible for the arms race. U.S. pursuit of new weapons systems like ABMs and MIRVs forces the Soviet Union into the position of having to develop its own systems to meet the challenge of U.S. weapons development.

An interesting sidelight to discussions of new weapons systems was that there were some indications that careful attention to these discussions might help illuminate Soviet sensitivity to negotiations on certain types of systems. The Soviet analysts were apparently prone to attacking weapons systems that they feared would leave Soviet defenses most vulnerable. For instance, during he early 1970s, there were what might be termed vitriolic attacks on certain U.S. systems like MIRVed ICBMs and SLBMs; however, by 1973, when Soviet "heavies" (heavy missiles) were being deployed, such discussions took on a much more conciliatory tone. In the mid-1970s, the Soviet analysts began to talk more and more about the escalative danger of qualitative developments and linked this, at least implicitly, to the need to negotiate qualitative strategic reductions. Between 1976 and 1978, the same reaction occurred in regard to neutron bombs, cruise missiles, Trident submarines, and the B-1 bomber. This is in contrast to the failure to discuss established U.S. systems where equivalent systems had already been developed by the Soviet Union.

These qualitative weapons development surges by the United States combined with changes in strategic doctrine, such as advocating limited nuclear war and counterforce targeting (a move which was viewed as an attempt to prepare for a preemptive strike), resulted in a cyclical reaction pattern on the part of Soviet analysts during the 1970s. There is a strong indication that in this area the analysts were responsive in the sense that they reacted to U.S. policy.

Another important element of Soviet arms policy positions concerns strategic equality or parity. Soviet journals quickly established that the appropriate way of conceptualizing parity was to think in terms of equal or identical security. The result was to shift the emphasis from strategic parity or numerical equality to the idea that equivalent numbers were less important than equivalent defensive capabilities. In regard to arms negotiations, this meant that all agreements must conform with the goal of limiting arms in such a way not to endanger the security of either side. The peculiar vulnerabilities of each side made the simple calculating of equal numbers impossible. This argument was pursued rather forcefully in 1973 when the strategic asymmetries of the two sides became a key concern, especially in the eyes of *SShA* analysts.[33] Probably one of the most important aspects of this concept of equal security was the unacceptability of either side's being able to gain a unilateral advantage.

This concept of equal security has been an intergral part of Soviet attitudes on arms control and disarmament. It is only on the basis of equal security that any efforts at arms control and disarmament are possible and support for arms control negotiations rests.

Before SALT I this support appeared gradually. In general, SALT did not become a real topical focus, however, until 1971, and by then support seemed relatively cohesive among most analysts. This support was focused primarily on the need to stop the arms race. There was a brief flurry of praise for the concept of strategic arms limitation and then a period of silence until after the first SALT agreement was signed. Following the signing of SALT I, strategic arms limitation was mentioned much more frequently and from an extremely positive perspective.

In 1973, all three journals demonstrated positive orientations toward further efforts along these lines. These journals also began to discuss the directions that future agreements might take. Primary among these was was the need to begin reducing nuclear arms. From the Soviet perspective, this meant moving from quantitative to qualitative limits. Qualitative limitations meant that agreements would move beyond simple numerical limits on types of launchers to the qualitative aspects of what types of payloads those launchers would carry—for instance, limitations on MIRVed systems. An interesting aspect of this was that Soviet analysts began to discuss qualitative limits only after the Soviets began to deploy MIRVed "heavies." This is an indication of the strong sense one gets from Soviet analysts that negotiations are possible only on the basis of equal security.

This positive trend persisted until mid-1976 when Soviet positions on SALT began to reflect the general deterioration of Soviet–U.S. relations. Soviet analysts still supported SALT; however, references to the SALT process decreased while the tone of those references became more defensive. Most references focused on the adequacy of verification by national technical means and on arguments defending SALT against charges that the agreements favored one side over the other. Emphasis was placed on the dangers of the arms race. The argument was made that people who advocated increasing security by building more weapons might have failed to realize that, given the nature of modern weapons, a war would lead to no victors.[34]

In 1978, the journals returned to promoting more extensive strategic arms limitation agreements. They also castigated the United States for its responsibility in delaying the successful conclusion of a second SALT agreement. Additionally new weapons systems were criticized, and proposals were renewed that such systems should fall within the purview of arms control before they were developed and deployed.

Between the end of 1978 and the signing of SALT II, the journals were silent on the issue of agreements, as they had been before SALT I was signed. After the signing, all three journals stressed the extreme importance of the agreement for reducing the arms race and decreasing the threat of nuclear war. They also emphasized the mutual benefits of the treaty, its basis in the principle of equal security, and the adequacy of the prescribed verification techniques.

Throughout the entire SALT negotiating period, it appears that all three journals may have been addressing at least two primary audiences: policymakers in the United States and some elements in the policy process in the Soviet Union. That some of the discussions were aimed at the United States is fairly obvious; however, there are several indicators that some arguments may have been aimed at decision makers closer to home. One instance of this is the apparent *SShA* efforts to sell SALT I. There also may have been a domestic audience in mind when the analysts began urging qualitative limits, as well as quantitative ones, in 1973 and 1974 and for their urgency about the importance of new arms agreements in 1975 and early 1976. Arguments urging curtailment of the arms race because of its contribution to the danger of nuclear war also may have been aimed at domestic elements as well as elements in the United States. The strongest indicator, however, of a domestic audience for the discussions in *International Affairs, SShA,* and *MEMO* was the emphasis given to equal security and the reassurances that arms agreements had not adversely affected the defensive capability of the Soviet Union. There is little reason, especially during the SALT II period, to direct such messages toward the United States.

Another indicator that these journals may indeed be a forum in which Soviet decision influencers air some of their opinions and concerns over strategic arms limitation agreements and arms policy is the diversity of positions found in the journals. Although the overall tenor of all three journals is supportive, at times even enthusiastic, over SALT, there are some dissenting voices. There is certainly not the wide range of opinions and the open debate found in similar sources in the United States, but there does appear to be some variation. Although no one in the three journals examined here overtly opposed SALT, there were people who did not mention arms limitation, disarmament, or détente. This silence on these subjects combined with an attitude toward the United States that was fairly hostile and had an antagonistic tone may be an indicator of unvoiced opposition. Their tone is certainly different from that of the articles overtly supportive of SALT and/or disarmament.[35]

Assessing Western Analysis

One of the most important points of controversy in understanding the Soviet positions is the question of the existence of opinion variations or policy divisions. This study's findings support Western analysts like Garthoff and Payne who argue that there are divisions over arms policy positions in the Soviet Union.[36] Even if we make the assumption for argument's sake that the Soviet military speaks with a single voice and that it advocates fighting a nuclear war based on developing a first strike capability, we see numerous instances in *MEMO, SShA,* and *International Affairs* that are in opposition to this. Shevchenko, Shatalov, Zhilin, Rybkin, Karenin, Sanakoev, Stepanov, Arbatov, Berezhkov, Petrovskii, and Tomashevskii all speak out against nuclear war, and Berezhkov explicitly attacks the principle of a first strike.[37]

Another indicator of possible divisions over arms policy challenges the premise that the military is monolithic in its advocacy of a war-fighting posture. Several of the analysts included in this study are present or former military personnel. Included among these are E. Rubkin (colonel), M.A Mil'shtein (general lieutenant, retired), L.S. Semeiko (colonel, retired), P. Zhilin (general lieutenant), and R.G. Simonian (general major). Although these writers share a military background, they do not write from a single perspective. Additionally, Rybkin, Zhilin, and Simonian deviate rather obviously from the policies purportedly advocated by the military. This is especially true in regard to their attitudes toward the consequences of nuclear war.[38]

Many Western analysts would dismiss this entire discussion on the grounds that the differences noted, at least in the literature designed primarily for a civilian audience, are not manifestations of policy discussions but are positions expressed for propaganda purposes. There is no way to disprove this contention. Undoubtedly there is a large propaganda element in these articles. Nevertheless, the same arguments also may be made about all material published by the Soviets, including that written by the military.[39]

This brings us to the second issue of this study: the question of changes in Soviet arms policy positions over time. Some analysts, Richard Pipes, for example, express the belief that there has been no change in Soviet positions since the 1950s, while others like Garthoff, Payne, and Simes have argued that there have been modifications in Soviet positions on arms policy over the last two decades. This study supports the contention of the latter group. Soviet analysts have modified their assessments of the United States, their perceptions concerning détente and peaceful coexistence, their assessments of weapons systems (a change in emphasis to qualitative limits for example), their perceptions of equal security, and their reactions to strategic arms limitations. Nevertheless, the changes are very subtle in some instances, and most of the indicators included here are only indicators of strategic policy positions. Additionally some of the changes are evidently in response to the United States in the sense that they are apparently reactions to changes in U.S. policy and/or rhetoric. On the other hand, however, it is of interest that there seems to have been some change by individuals over the 1970s. Some of this apparent change is undoubtedly in response to outside stimuli, but other instances appear to be reflections of opinions modified across time. Trofimenko may be an example of this type of change.

The third issue involves the question of Soviet positions on deterrence. Richard Pipes and Paul Nitze are representatives of the perspective held by several analysts that the Soviets reject mutual assured destruction, and possibly any other deterrent theory, and are determined to achieve quantitative superiority and a first strike capability designed to fight and win a nuclear war.[40] Garthoff and Payne are exponents of the opposite view.[41] Again the findings of this study support Garthoff and Payne. There are several instances, especially in *International Affairs* and *SShA*, where the analysts give grudging credence to policies of deterrence such as mutual assured destruction; however, their support is based largely on the pragmatic position that it seems to work rather than on any commitment to the philosophical soundness of such policies.[42] Nevertheless, they tend to argue that negotiated strategic arms agreements ultimately resulting in disarmament are highly preferable to a policy based on a precarious balance that may well result in world catastrophe if it ever fails. Additionally, they leave little doubt that they find deterrence so fragile that the Soviet Union should be prepared to pursue another policy if and when deterrence fails.

In general, Soviet analysts examined here show little faith in any policy predicated on fighting and surviving, much less winning, a nuclear war. This is evident in much of their writing. First, they question the validity of the concept of controlled nuclear confrontation (limited war).[43] Instead there is the often expressed belief that once nuclear weapons are used, the result would be all-out nuclear war. Second, they doubt that a first strike capability is feasible. Several authors express the belief that neither side would allow the other to achieve the advantage necessary to make such a strike feasible, and even if it were, modern weapons systems and technology are such that the other side might still survive an initial strike with the ability to retaliate.[44] Third, they believe a nuclear war would be so destructive that even if one side survived the other, there would be no victor. There is also evidence that, contrary to Pipes's evaluation, there are people in the Soviet Union who do not believe war is an extension of policy in the Clausewitzian sense.[45]

The fourth and fifth issues deal with the role that personnel outside the military establishment play in the arms policy process in the Soviet Union. We can never definitely determine what that role is. At best we can make postulations that are unverifiable because so little is known about the Soviet policy process, especially in the area of defense policy, that our findings cannot be confirmed. However, we may be able to lend some strength to arguments made by other analysts.

The fourth issue is whether the Soviet military are the sole source of Soviet arms policy. In general, analysts like Pipes and Ermarth argue that this contention is correct.[46] The opposite view is held by Garthoff, Wolfe, Payne, and Simes.[47] There are indications that in the late 1960s, the military, or at least some of the military, opposed strategic arms negotiations.[48] This contention is supported by Payne's study on Soviet attitudes about SALT.[49] Nevertheless, the Soviet Union has negotiated three agreements on strategic arms, including the ABM Treaty. If the military was opposed to the negotiations, who supported taking part in them?

Several analysts, Payne foremost among them, have suggested that this military versus nonmilitary dichotomy in the Soviet policymaking process is artificial.[50] This is probably correct; nevertheless, there were certainly powerful opponents of negotiations. On the other hand, this study has found elements that were supporters of SALT. All three sources show strong support for SALT by 1971, and *SShA* featured analysts supportive of negotiations beginning with its first issue in January 1970.

Beyond this simplistic pro and con position on SALT in general, there are differences about which we may speculate over some of the basic elements of SALT. These include ABMs, MIRVs, and forward-based systems (FBS). Because there is virtually no discussion of Soviet weapons systems in Soviet publications, there is no clear juxtaposition of views on these systems, but it would logically follow that the military position would be to develop, preserve, and possibly even extend systems such as MIRVed missiles. This especially should be true since Soviet missiles are of such a size that they have a greater throw weight than U.S. missiles do. This allowed the Soviets to develop the MLBM (modern large ballistic missiles, or "heavies"), which gives the Soviets the advantage of deploying more warheads of greater megatonnage. This in turn potentially gives them the technological edge that might make a first strike feasible, which, according to Western analysts, is essential for a war-winning posture. Therefore positions in oppositions to such weapons logically would be in opposition to the military. However, the Soviet Union developed ABM and MIRV systems, so one would assume that they were promoted by some element or group of elements within the policymaking process. Nevertheless, the findings in this study indicate that some analysts were opposed to such systems.[51]

During SALT I negotiations, the primary aspects under discussion were ABMs and quantitative limits on ICBMs. Specifics about numerical limits are not discussed in nonmilitary sources; however, both ABMs and MIRVed systems are. Analysts, especially those writing in *SShA*, are generally opposed to both because of their adverse effects on the arms race. This is an intriguing position for two reasons. First, the Soviets had opposed discussing ABMs as part of any arms limitation negotiations at Glassboro, New Jersey, in 1967.[52] By November 1969, they were interested in including such systems in negotiations. There may be many reasons why the Soviets changed their position on ABM negotiations. Possibly they may no longer have felt that such negotiations might leave them at a disadvantage, in contrast with what they could have believed two years earlier. On the other hand, they might have felt that U.S. ABM developments would leave them in a less advantageous position. Regardless of the reasons behind the Soviet decision to negotiate on the ABM systems, some Soviet analysts were arguing against ABMs in the early 1970s, and it may have been that they opposed them much earlier than this.[53] The most obvious explanation for their opposition to ABMs in the early 1970s would have been to support the negotiating posture that had already been determined; however, their concomitant opposition to MIRVs seems to belie this explanation.

At the same time that some Soviet analysts were opposing ABMs, they were also attacking MIRVs. According to John Newhouse, restrictions on MIRVs were not part of the Soviet negotiating stance during the early part of SALT I.[54] In fact, negotiations on qualitative developments, like MIRV, would have threatened to leave the Soviets in a technologically inferior position in relation to the United States, and, in 1970, the Soviets were opposed to any ban on production or deployment of MIRVs.[55] Regardless of this policy position, some Soviet analysts were opposed to MIRVed systems. Indeed, some of their arguments resembled those taking place in the United States concerning the destabilizing effects MIRVs were having on the arms race.[56] It may be that rather than echoing accepted policy, the analysts were trying to create greater understanding about the nature and danger of the arms race and the links between defensive and offensive systems.

After SALT I and the ABM Treaty were signed, MIRVed systems were still under attack. By the middle of 1973, however, the emphasis shifted to the necessity of extending limits to qualitative systems:[57]

> The aims of the second stage, as the "basic principles" point out, consist of the more complete quantitative and qualitative limitations of strategic

offensive arms and their subsequent reduction. The task is set of determining definitely and for the long term a mutually agreed number for the two sides' offensive arms, a number which would take into account the interests of their equal security. This is a difficult task if one takes into account the fact that under conditions of scientific and technical progress and the quantitative aspect of strategic arms is linked more closely than ever before with their qualitative aspect. And the fact that the USSR and the United States have now agreed to examine simultaneously complex questions of qualitative limitations, signifies not only the broadening of the range of questions under discussion but also a serious and exceptionally important advance in the talks themselves.

In accordance with the agreement reached, measures must also be elaborated for a subsequent reduction in strategic arms. The transition from arms limitation to their reduction would symbolize the beginning of general disarmament.[58]

The need for qualitative limitations was an argument that appeared often during the remainder of the 1970s. Again, the timing of arguments in favor of qualitative limits is of interest. It corresponded with Soviet deployment of MIRVed heavies. This achievement did much to put the Soviets on a technological, as well as numerical, par with the United States. MIRVed Soviet missiles meant that Soviet systems were closer to equaling those of the United States. Although they still lacked the accuracy of U.S. MIRVed systems, Soviet missiles were more destructive because they had a larger throw weight. This created an environment in which negotiated limits on qualitative elements would not lock the Soviets into a technologically inferior position. The time was ripe for advocating qualitative limits.

An even more intriguing aspect of this shift is that nonmilitary analysts may have been advocating not only the limitation of MIRVed systems but also other qualitative aspects (for instance, throw weights). The extensiveness of the qualitative limitations advocated by nonmilitary writers can only be a matter of speculation; however, their opposition to MIRVs is quite evident. In this instance, a stronger link can be established between nonmilitary positions and negotiating stances. Although accounts of negotiations in the early stages of SALT II reflect Soviet intransigence on the subject of MIRVed systems, by November 1974 the Soviets were willing to agree to limits on those systems.[59]

Another instance where there may be some link between arguments made by nonmilitary analysts and a Soviet negotiating position concerns forward-based systems (FBS). Admittedly Soviet analysts normally do not talk about FBS except to chastise the United States over the existence of these systems. The general policy stance in the Soviet Union has been to attack the FBS of the United States. In 1973 and 1974, however, Soviet analysts discussed strategic asymmetries and geographic asymmetries.[60]

This discussion implicitly emphasizes that U.S. FBS have strategic counterparts in the Soviet Union. One element of these asymmetries is that isolation of the United States from and proximity of the Soviet Union to enemy nuclear weapons have created differences in perspectives. The Soviets are not only vulnerable to United States FBS but also to Chinese, British, and French nuclear arsenals. This presented them with a type of threat that was of no concern to the United States, especially in the period when decisions on research and development of current systems were being made. The Soviets, lacking an FBS of their own, created a strategic weapons system, MIRVed mobile-launched ballistic missiles (MLBMs), that helped offset what they perceived to be a U.S. advantage. In the early 1970s, before this system was in place, FBS was a prime target in attempts to increase Soviet security. It was also something that the United States was unwilling to classify as part of its strategic capability, thus removing it from the purview of strategic arms negotiations. It is impossible to gauge how much, if any, influence discussions by nonmilitary analysts about asymmetries had on the Soviet position; however, following the Vladivostok meeting, a trade-off of asymmetries took place with the signing of an aide-memoire that allowed Soviet retention of heavy ICBMs in return for U.S. retention of its FBS.[61] That there were analysts advocating, at least implicitly, sensitivity to the asymmetry question during a period when FBS was generally under attack and that the asymmetries were then accommodated in the SALT process may be an indicator of the ability of people outside the military establishment to influence policy or negotiating stances.

There is also evidence that the agreements reached at Vladivostok had some opposition within the Soviet Union. According to Strobe Talbott, one of the underlying reasons that the Soviets reacted so adversely to what they considered to be attempts by the Carter administration in 1977 to scrap the Vladivostok agreement was the potential political cost for Brezhnev. When Cyrus Vance visited Moscow in March of that year, he brought with him a set of proposals that would have revised the agreement on MIRVed systems and reopened heavy ICBMs as a topic for negotiation.[62] This brought about a sharp rebuff from Brezhnev and Gromyko. The impact of these proposals was quite severe:

"What are you trying to do—kill SALT?" asked one Soviet official in private conversation with his American counterpart. Gromyko's deputy, George Kornienko, took Paul Warnke aside and admonished him. "You shouldn't have disregarded the fact that Brezhnev had to spill political blood to get the Vladivostok accords." Kornienko said that the Soviet leader had been especially incensed by the American attempt to cut the heavy missile force and by the across-the-board 2,500-kilometer range limit on cruise missiles."[63]

This demonstrates that Soviet policy stances have been aligned on occasion with positions taken by analysts other than military analysts and reinforces earlier arguments that there are divisions of opinion among Soviet elites and subelites within the policy process. In the remainder of the 1970s, no easily recognizable policy suggestions were made by the journal analysts; however, the fact that by the end of the SALT II negotiations, these analysts were advocating a third round of arms limitation agreements may be a policy suggestion itself.[64]

The fifth issue addressed in this study is a corollary to the fourth: can Soviet strategic doctrine be taken at face value and equated with Soviet strategic arms policy and negotiating stances? This question arises because of the propensity of some Western analysts to equate Soviet strategic doctrine with Soviet strategic arms policy while other Western analysts believe that they are separate policy areas. Evidence has been offered here that certain subelites in the policy process in the Soviet Union counter the typical perspective associated with Soviet strategic doctrine as interpreted by many Western analysts. These alternative Soviet spokesmen vary from this strategic doctrine perspective in such areas as the alleged adherence of that doctrine to Clausewitzian principles proclaiming war as an extension of policy, the feasibility of a first strike, the acceptance of deterrence theory in the form of mutual assured destruction, and the consequences of nuclear war. Support for the different set of views held by some Soviet analysts is reinforced by the work of Robert Arnett. He found that in the area of doctrinal questions concerning the utility of nuclear war as an instrument of policy, the possibility of victory in a nuclear war, and the consequences of nuclear war. Soviet spokesmen do not support nuclear war as a policy tool nor do they believe victory is possible or the consequences acceptable.[65]

> What Soviet spokesmen have been saying about nuclear war does not support claims of various Western analysts who argue that the Soviets believe they can win and survive a nuclear war—especially the notion that they can survive such a war with fewer losses than they incurred in World War II. The Soviet usage of the dictum "war is a continuation of politics" is a basic tenet of Marxist-Leninist theory explaining the causes of war. Soviet statements proclaiming that victory is possible in such a war seem to tell us little about actual Soviet thinking on the subject. This conclusion is based upon the fact that these statements are necessary to keep up morale and are required by Marxists-Leninist ideology. In addition, these declarations about victory are contradicted by their statements made on the usefulness of war as a practical instrument of policy, and by their estimates of the probable consequences of such a conflict.
>
> Soviet spokemen in publications written for internal consumption contend that nuclear war cannot serve as a practical instrument of policy and they continually talk about the dire consequences of such a war.

Spokesmen at all levels, in different forms, generally agree that nuclear war would cause unprecedented damage. Thus, the Soviets seem to be acutely aware of the destructive capability of the U.S. nuclear arsenal and there seems to be little doubt that the U.S. has the capability to inflict unacceptable damage upon the Soviet Union.[66]

Arnett also found that these views, especially on the consequences of nuclear war, often prevail at the Politburo level. Among other things, Arnett notes Brezhnev's recognition of the reality of mutual assured destruction.[67]

There is also some indication that positions expressed by some analysts concerning certain weapons systems, and potentially the whole concept of strategic arms limitations, were in opposition to others within the policy process. If this is indeed the case, analysts often have been in accord with the interests that prevailed in the formulation of policy. At best, they may have helped in shaping policy. Given the positions taken in Soviet strategic doctrine, as it has been interpreted by several Western analysts, on war as an extension of policy, on the acceptance of mutal assured destruction, and on the consequences of a nuclear war, the support of Politburo members for concepts that differ from that doctrine and coincide with some of the views expressed by analysts examined here would indicate that strategic doctrine presented by the military and Soviet strategic arms policies are not necessarily identical and should not be treated as though they are.

This brings us to the sixth and final issue concerning the relationship between Soviet strategic arms policy and other foreign policy goals. If Soviet strategic arms policy is essentially an area of policy solely controlled by military strategic decision makers, Soviet arms policy is an independent policy area concerned only with the security and war-fighting capability of the Soviet state. If it is intertwined with other foreign policy goals, it is open to influence from nonmilitary decision makers. The previous discussions of influences on arms policies suggest that there are considerations that go beyond military policy, especially in the area of détente and in domestic economic and foreign aid policies. Although this link may be attacked as tenuous, some analysts certainly think that arms policy should be part of broader foreign policy concerns. This is evident from several opinions found in the journals, including emphasis on linking military détente with peaceful coexistence; belief that the correlation of forces goes beyond a balance of military strength to include social, political, and economic forces; arguments that resources invested in the arms race might be put to better use elsewhere, both at home and abroad; linking of strategic arms limitation to broader bilateral and multilateral disarmament proposals; discussions of the mutual advantages of cooperation between the United States and Soviet Union beyond arms control; and belief that modern weapons systems are so destructive that conflict must be resolved by political rather than military means.

David Holloway gives an eloquent explication of the apparent contradiction between Soviet strategic doctrine and Soviet arms control positions. These contradictions arise out of the bifurcation between political and military aspects of strategic thinking in the Soviet Union.

> Since the mid-1970s the Party leaders have laid more stress on the political side of military doctrine, in an apparent attempt to adapt the doctrine to the relationship of strategic parity with the United States.
>   ... The military stress on preparing to fight and win a nuclear war has been reinforced by the ideological belief that, if nuclear war did take place, it would be the decisive contest between capitalism and socialism and socialism would emerge victorious. As the Soviet leaders made clear in the polemics with the Chinese Party, however, the chief aim of their military preparations have been to prevent such a war. Party and military leaders alike have pointed to the terrible destruction it would bring. This does not mean, however, that all preparations to survive a nuclear war should be abandoned, for such a war might take place.[68]

Holloway argues that both aspects are part of Soviet strategic arms policy and that what appear to be contradictions are actually a single policy that in some ways is a Soviet version of mutual assured destruction. Prevention of war comes about through preparation for war.[69]

Although this helps to explain the Soviet perspective, it does not mean that there is a perfect meshing of the political and military aspects of Soviet thinking. Indeed, at a minimum, there are the perennial questions of how much preparation is enough, how arms control agreements interface with strategic doctrine, and what the utility is of an arms race. Thus the tension exists between the purely military perspective and that of those policy elites who must also deal with the political aspects.

Role of Arms Policy Positions Found in *International Affairs*, *SShA*, and *MEMO*

Because we are limited to indirect measures in the study of Soviet policy-making, it is impossible to give a definitive answer to the question of how the positions and opinions of personnel outside the military establishment are integrated into the arms policy process in the Soviet Union or to know if they are integrated at all. The evidence presented here indicates that these analysts may have some influence in the arms policy area, but this cannot go beyond well-informed, logical conjecture. Even with the support given this conjecture by the appearance of positions in negotiating stances that had been advocated earlier in journal articles, there is no proof that these positions originated with the analysts advocating them. They may only be presenting positions advocated by elites at higher decision-making levels. However, this does indicate that the analysts, at a minimum, articulate arms policy issues. Additionally, this articulation may provide a forum for circumscribed debates within the journals themselves and almost certainly provides a vehicle by which views that appear to be in some opposition to traditional military positions are voiced.

From the tenor of many of the articles, another potential role seems to exist for these analysts in the policy implementation phase of Soviet arms policy: the role of consensus builder. It may be that this is the aim of articles presenting positive view of SALT and Soviet–U.S. cooperation. This may also be the function of the many negative references to the arms race. Given the purported strength of the military, and concomitantly heavy industry, in the Soviet policy process, it is interesting that attacks on the arms race are usually tied either to the economic benefits that would accrue if the arms race did not exist or to the dangerous consequences that would result from the use of these accumulated arms. The possibility that consensus building is one of the roles played by nonmilitary analysts is reinforced by the efforts to sell SALT at a time when it seemed doomed by the deterioration of Soviet–U.S. relations. Although the Soviet government was committed to arms limitation negotiations and détente, there are indications that there was some opposition to these policies. Building and maintaining a consensus on the importance of SALT and détente might have been an extremely important function, especially as many of the advantages of such policies began to disappear with the deterioration of Soviet–U.S. relations. This may also have been the motivation behind the stress placed on elements like the inadmissibility of a unilateral advantage, the importance of equal security, and the maintenance of Soviet defensive capabilities. It may be that SALT provoked the same type of criticism in the Soviet Union that it did in the United States and that frequent references to the importance given to security concerns in the negotiations were to counter this criticism and allay fears in both the Soviet Union and among its East European allies.

Nonmilitary analysts may have another policy implementation role as purveyors of propaganda concerning Soviet arms policy. Many articles, especially in the early 1970s in *International Affairs* and *MEMO,* use arms policy, especially weapons developments, to portray the United States as an aggressive, imperialist warmonger. This message seems to be aimed at the Third World, as does the opposite picture of the Soviet Union as a nation continually striving for peace and the good of humanity. This is almost certainly part of the underlying reason for the emphasis on general and complete disarmament.

Another role that may fall into the policy implementation category is that of facilitator. It may be that nonmilitary analysts are part of an effort to help create and maintain a dialogue between the United States and the Soviet Union. Quite often this is also labeled as propaganda largely because messsages are couched in terms that are an attack on U.S. strategic policy; however, a careful reading of the journals suggests that these analysts are trying to communicate with elites and subelites in the United States about Soviet preferences in arms control negotiations. This might certainly be the case with strategic weapons. Attacks on ABMs coincided with a willingness to negotiate on these systems. Discussions of quantitative limitations and strategic asymmetries preceded movement on negotiations on limiting MIRVs and exchanging FBS for heavy ICBMs. On the negative side, intransigence on subjects such as equal security may indicate that there is extreme sensitivity to any threat to defensive capabilities. The possibility that this is a facilitating role played by the nonmilitary analysts is reinforced by the reactive nature of the journals. Occurrences in the United States and changes in U.S. policy stances that have negative connotations for the Soviets usually evoke hostile reactions in these journals. On the other hand, positive developments, like the appearance of sober-minded forces in U.S. policy circles, are reinforced.

It is highly probable that these analysts are involved in all the roles discussed here, including some level of participation in policymaking in the Soviet Union. Regretfully, the nonmilitary analysts and their roles in Soviet policy decisions and policy implementation have too often been ignored or disregarded by Western analysts. At a minimum, their writings help to illuminate aspects of Soviet arms policy. It is apparent that relying on military positions alone presents Western analysts with a distorted view of Soviet arms policy and that a better understanding is gained by combining military and elements from outside the military establishment in an analysis.

At best, greater attention to these commentators might give Western analysts, whether they are involved in the policy process or scholarly research, greater insight into Soviet perspectives on arms policy and arms control. For the policymaker, this would potentially create a greater sensitivity to the most fruitful avenues to pursue in future negotiations and a better understanding of the potential implications of Soviet strategic doctrine. The FBS–heavy missile trade is an example of the type of understanding such sensitivity could promote. Failure to appreciate essential elements has led to one of the most troublesome issues in arms control efforts: the tension between the equal security–parity question.[70] For the scholar, this provides new avenues of research in an attempt to gain a better understanding of Soviet politics and eventually may lead to a better understanding of the process by which policies are formulated and how the collective leadership arrangement in the Soviet Union operates.

Notes

1. Dennis Ross, "Coalition Maintenance in the Soviet Union," *World Politics*, 32, No. 2 (Jan. 1980), 264.

2. *Ibid.*, p. 268.

3. Anne T. Sloan, "Soviet Non-Military Arms Policy Attitudes: Do They Make a Difference?," paper presented at the twenty-second annual meeting of the International Studies Association, Philadelphia, 18-21 March 1981.

4. Raymond L. Garthoff, "Mutual Deterrence and Strategic Arms Limitation in Soviet Policy," *International Studies*, 3, No. 1 (Summer 1978), 112-47.

5. Richard Pipes, "Why the Soviet Union Thinks It Could Fight and Win a Nuclear War," *Commentary*, 64, No. 1 (July 1977). Reprinted by the National Strategy Information Center, Inc.

6. Thomas D. Wolfe, *The SALT Experience: Its Impact on U.S. and Soviet Strategic Policy and Decision-Making* (Santa Monica, Calif.: RAND R-1686-PR, Sept. 1975).

7. Karl Spielmann, "Defense Industrialists in the USSR," *Problems of Communism*, 25, No. 5 (Sept.-Oct. 1976), 52-69; and *idem, Analyzing Soviet Strategies Arms Decisions* (Boulder, Colo.: Westview Press, 1978).

8. Vernon V. Aspaturian, "The Soviet Military-Industrial Complex—Does It Exist?," *Journal of International Affairs*, 26, No. 1 (1972), 1-28

9. Roman Kolkowicz, "Strategic Elites and the Politics of Superpower," *ibid.*, pp. 40-59.

10. Wolfe, pp. 37-38.

11. *Ibid.*, p. 39; and John Newhouse, *Cold Dawn: The Story of SALT* (New York: Holt, Rinehart and Winston, 1973).

12. Kolkowicz, "Strategic Elites," p. 52.

13. *Ibid.*

14. Conversation with G. Arbatov at the University of South Carolina, 22 May 1979.

15. Ross, "Coalition Maintenance," pp. 265-66.

16. Jerry F. Hough, *Soviet Leadership in Transition* (Washington, D.C.: Brookings Institution, 1980), pp. 118-30.

17. *Ibid.*, p. 119.

18. *Ibid.*, pp. 121-22, IMEMO is a revival of the old Varga Institute.

19. *Ibid.*, p. 123.

20. Samuel B. Payne, Jr., *The Soviet Union and SALT* (Cambridge, Mass.: MIT Press, 1980).

21. *Ibid.*, p. 7.

22. *Ibid.*, p. 9.

23. *Ibid.*, pp. 21-28.

24. *Ibid.*, pp. 29-35 and pp. 49-56.

25. *Ibid.*, pp. 36-48 and pp. 57-61.

26. *Ibid.*, p. 64.

27. David Holloway, *The Soviet Union and the Arms Race* (New Haven, Conn.: Yale Univ. Press, 1983), pp. 29-64.

28. Pipes, "Why the Soviet Union"; Benjamin S. Lambeth, "How to Think about Soviet Military Doctrine," *The RAND Paper Series*, P-5939 (Feb. 1978), pp. 3-4; Paul H. Nitze, "Deterring Our Deterrent," *Foreign Policy*, 25 (Winter 1976-77), 195-210; Benjamin S. Lambeth, "The Political Potential of Soviet Equivalence," *International Security*, 4, No. 2 (Fall 1979), 27; Fritz W. Ermarth, "Contrasts in American and Soviet Strategic Thought," *ibid.*, 3, No. 2 (Fall 1978), 140; Colin S. Gray, "Nuclear Strategy: The Case for a Theory of Victory, *ibid.*, 4 No. 1 (Summer 1979), 54-87; and Stanley Sienkiewicz, "SALT and Soviet Nuclear Doctrine," *ibid.*, 2, No. 4 (Spring 1978), 91.

29. Garthoff, "Mutual Deterrence"; and Dmitri K. Simes, "Deterrence and Coercion in Soviet Policy," *ibid.*, No. 3 (Winter 1980-81), 85-88.

30. This discussion is based on a qualitative content analysis of *Soedinennye Shtaty Ameriki* [*SShA*], *Mirovaia ekonomika i mezhdunarodnye otnosheniia* [*MEMO*], and *International Affairs* articles appearing between 1970 and 1979. The findings are presented in Anne T. Sloan, "Positions of Strategic Arms Control Issues in Three Major Soviet Journals: The Decade of the 1970s," unpublished Ph.D. dissertation, Ohio State Univ., 1982.

31. A. Karenin, "The Soviet Union in the Struggle for Disarmament," *International Affairs* (Sept. 1975), p. 15; G.A. Arbatov, "Outlook for Soviet-American Detente," *SShA* (Feb. 1972), p. 33; V. Shestov, "Razoruzhenie ideal sotsializma," *MEMO* (Oct. 1971), pp. 3-8; D. Tomashevskii, "Nalputi k korennoi perestroike mezhdunarodnykh otnoshenii," *ibid.* (Jan. 1975), p. 11; G. Trofimenko, "Na sterzhnevom napravlenii," *ibid.* (Feb. 1975), p. 3; and E. Primakov, "Politicheskaia razriadka i problem razorusheniia," *ibid.* (Oct. 1975), pp. 8-9. [Unless otherwise noted, all *International Affairs* articles are titled as they appeared in the original English-language Moscow publication; *MEMO* articles are in Russian; and English-titled *SShA* articles are *Joint Publication Research Service* translations.] See also Sidney D. Drell, Philip J. Farley, and David Holloway, "Preserving the ABM Treaty: A Critique of the Reagan Strategic Defense Initiative," *International Security*, 9, No. 2 (Fall 1984), 59-63.

32. V.M. Berezhkov, "Basic Principles of Soviet-US Relations," *SShA* (April 1977), p. 3.

33. M.A. Mil'shteyn and L.S. Semeyko, "SALT: Problems and Prospects," *ibid.* (Dec. 1973), pp. 3-10; G.A. Trofimenko, "USSR-US Peaceful Coexistence as the Norm," *ibid.* (Feb. 1974), p. 9; and M.D. Kolosov, "On the Evening of the New Summit Meeting," *ibid.* (May 1974), p. 65.

34. V. Karavaev, "Appetity Pentagona," *MEMO* (April 1974), pp. 85-86; V. Zhurkin, "Krupnyi vklad v uprochenie mira," *ibid.* (Aug. 1974), pp. 6-7; A. Kaliadin, "Bor'ba za razoruzhenie: novye prospektivy," *ibid.* (Nov. 1974), pp. 6-14; Tomashevskii, "Nalputi k korennoi," pp. 7-11; Trofimenko, "Na sterzhnevom," p. 3; Primakov, "Politicheskaia raziadka," pp. 3-12; E. Khesin, "Militarizm i uglublinie obshego krizisa kapitalizma," *MEMO* (Dec. 1975), pp. 57-68; D. Tomashevskii, "Shirokie gorizonty leninskoi politiki mira," *ibid.* (June 1976), pp. 6-11; A Svetlov, "Razorushenie—nasuschenaia zadacha bor'by za mir," *ibid.* (July 1976), pp. 3-16; N. Inozemstev, "XXV s 'ezd KPSS i problemy sovremennogo mirovogo razvitiia," *ibid.* (Nov. 1976), pp. 3-20; I. Ivanov, "Razriadka mezhdunarodnoi napiazhnosti i al'ternativy voennoi ekonomike," *ibid.* (Nov. 1976), pp. 51-63; O. Bykov, "SShA i

real'nosti mezhdunarodnoi razriadki" *ibid.* (Aug. 1976), pp. 28-38; R. Faramzian, "Voenno-promyshlennye kompleksy i ganka vooruzhenii," *ibid.* (Dec. 1976), pp. 13-20; Iu Tomilin, "Razorushenie—kliuchevaia problema mirovoi politiki," *ibid.* (Feb. 1977) pp. 3-12; V. Kelin, "Razriadka—put'k prochnomu miru," *ibid.* (March 1977), pp. 4-13; and V. Fedorov, "Neprimenenie sily—global'naia problema," *ibid.* (May 1977), pp. 3-12.

35. Payne, p. 5; Robert Conquest, *Russia after Khrushchev* (New York: Praeger, 1965); Carl Linden, *Khrushchev and the Soviet Leadership* (Baltimore: Johns Hopkins Univ. Press, 1966); and Michael Tatu, *Power in the Kremlin* (New York: Viking, 1970).

36. Garthoff, "Mutual Deterrence"; Payne, pp. 7-64; and Simes, "Deterrence and Coercion," pp. 81-92.

37. V. Berezhkov, "Detente Prospects and Soviet-American Relations," *SShA* (Dec. 1977), p. 14.

38. Robert L. Arnett, "Soviet Attitudes towards Nuclear War: Do They Really Think They Can Win?," *The Journal of Strategic Studies*, 2, No. 2 (Sept. 1979), 172-91.

39. Payne, p. 50.

40. Pipes, "Why the Soviet Union", Nitze, "Deterring Our Deterrent," pp. 195-210; and Ermarth, "Contrasts," p. 140.

41. Payne, pp. 7-64.

42. L. Zavialov, "Who Formulates Policy in America Today?," *International Affairs* (May 1970), p. 56; A. Shevchenko, "Disarmament: A Problem That Can be Solved," *ibid.* (May 1971), pp. 30-32; I. Shatalov, "The Scientific and Technical Revolution and International Relations," *ibid.* (Aug. 1971), pp. 30-31; M. Kudrin, "An Important Step Toward Strengthening Peace," *ibid.* (Oct. 1973), p. 10; P. Zhilin and Y. Rubkin, "Militarism and Contemporary International Relations," *ibid.* (Oct. 1973), pp. 23-28; N. Kapchenko, "Socialist Foreign Policy and Restructuring of International Relations," *ibid.* (April 1975), p. 11; A. Svetlov, "The Soviet Union's Struggle for Military Detente," *ibid.* (Feb. 1976), p. 94; N. Doronina and D. Nikolayev, "Disarmament: A Solution in Sight?," *ibid.* (Nov. 1978), p. 51; Y. Kashlev, "Imperialist Foreign Policy: An Ideological Breakdown," *ibid.* (Jan. 1979), p. 63; P. Zhilin, "On Guard for Peace and Socialism," *ibid.* (March 1978), pp. 19-22; Y. Tomilin, "Eliminating the Nuclear Menace—An Urgent Task," *ibid.* (Jan. 1978), pp. 70-71; Sh. Sanakoyev, "The Most Pressing Problem of Our Day," *ibid.* (Aug. 1978), p. 9; R. Simonyan, "Curbing the Arms Race—A Key Problem of Our Time," *ibid.* (Jan. 1979), pp. 72-73; V. Israelyan, "The Soviet Union Works for Nuclear Disarmament," *ibid.* (Feb. 1979), p. 77; V. Ustinov, "New Weapons Threaten Peace," *ibid.* (Jan. 1979), p. 67; V. Shestov, "Disarmament—Key Problems of World Politics," *ibid.* (March 1979), p. 94; G. Arbatov, "American Foreign Policy at the Threshold of the 1970s," *SShA* (Jan. 1970), pp. 15-24; "A Current Topic: Between Helsinki and Vienna," *ibid.* (Jan. 1970), p. 76; V.V. Larionov, "The Strategic Debates," *ibid.* (March 1970), pp. 35-38; B.G. Dostupov, "Arms Race Trends," *ibid.* (Aug. 1970), pp. 136-43; G.A. Trofimenko, "Some Aspects of U.S. Military and Political Strategy," *ibid.* (Oct. 1970), pp. 16-21; B.L. Teplinsky, "What Is New in the Building of U.S. Armed Forces," *ibid.* (Feb. 1970), pp. 19-40; M.V. Belousov, "The MIRV System," *ibid.* (Sept. 1971), pp. 165-68; G.A. Arbatov, "A Step in the

Interest of Peace," *ibid.* (Nov. 1971), pp. 81–84; V.V. Larionov, "Transformation of the 'Strategic Sufficiency' Concept," *ibid.* (Nov. 1971), p. 42; G.A. Trofimenko, "U.S. Military-Political Strategies," *ibid.* (Dec. 1971), pp. 1–17, "Report of Discussion at the Institute of U.S. Studies of the Academy of Sciences of the USSR," *ibid.* (Feb. 1971), pp. 34–35; G.A. Arbatov, "Outlook for Soviet-American Detente," *ibid.* (Feb. 1972), pp. 33–34; "A Base for Developing Soviet-American Relations," *ibid.* (July 1972), p. 2; G.A. Trofimenko, "The Soviet–U.S. SALT Agreements," *ibid.* (Sept. 1972), pp. 7–13; "Soviet-American Summit Talks," *ibid.* (Aug. 1973), pp. 1–2; G.A. Arbatov, "U.S. Foreign Policy and the Scientific and Technical Revolution," *ibid.* (Oct. 1973), p. 7; *idem*, "Soviet-American Relations in the 1970s," *ibid.* (May 1974), pp. 11–16; Trofimenko, "USSR-U.S. Peaceful Coexistence," pp. 1–19; M.A. Mil'shteyn and L.S. Semeyko, "The Problem of the Inadmissibility of a Nuclear Conflict (On New Approaches to the United States)," *ibid.* (Nov. 1974), pp. 3–11; V.M. Berezhkov, "Soviet-American Relations and the Modern World," *ibid.* (Sept. 1975), pp. 1–15; Yu. F. Oleshchuk, "On the 'Limited Detente' Theory," *ibid.* (April 1975), pp. 1–13; M.V. Valerianov, "The USSR-United States: Results, Difficulties, and Prospects," *ibid.* (Jan. 1976), trans. in *Foreign Broadcast Information Service* [hereafter *FBIS*], 30 Jan. 1976, pp. B5–B6; K.M. Georgiev, "Razriadka—formula i protsess. Voprosy razriadki v sovetsko-amerikanskikh otnosheniiakh," *ibid.* (Aug. 1976), pp. 4–12; D.P. Iur'ev, "Chto stoit za'nifom o 'sovetskoi ugroze'," *ibid.* (Sept. 1976), pp. 62–68; Berezhkov, "Basic Principles," pp. 1–6; S.I. Baronovskiy, "The Arms Race Budget," *ibid.* (Oct. 1977), pp. 63–69; V.M. Berzhkov, "Detente Prospects and Soviet-American Relations," *ibid.* (Dec. 1977), pp. 12–14; G.A. Trofimenko, "American Approaches to Peaceful Coexistence with the Soviet Union (History and Perspectives)," *ibid.* (June 1978), pp. 21–38; Ernst Henry, "Plot against Detente," *ibid.* (June 1978), pp. 39–53; V.P. Konobeyev, and A.A. Poduzov, "Some Economic Effects of the Arms Race," *ibid.* (June 1978), pp. 1–19; V.V. Larionov, "The 'Nuclear Threshold' Debate," *ibid.* (July 1978), pp. 19–29; V.P. Abarenkov, "Soviet Disarmament Program," *ibid.* (Aug. 1978), p. 7; V.V. Zhurkin, "U.S.-NATO Arms Build-up Resulting from 'Soviet Threat'," *ibid.* (Aug. 1978), pp. 13–16; and V.F. Petrovsky, "Evolution of Doctrine of 'National Security'," *ibid.* (Nov. 1978), pp. 12–18.

43. *Ibid.*

44. *Ibid.*

45. V.M. Berezhkov, "Detente Prospects and Soviet-American Relations," *ibid.* (Sept. 1975), trans. in *FBIS*, 9 Oct. 1975, pp. A5–A8.

46. See Sloan, "Positions," pp. 20–26 for a full discussion.

47. *Ibid.*, pp. 26–29, 36–40.

48. *Ibid.*, p. 15.

49. Payne, *loc. cit.*

50. *Ibid.*

51. D. Proektor, "Military Detente: Primary Task," *International Affairs* (June 1976) pp. 38–39; "A Current Topic," p. 76; Trofimenko, "USSR-U.S. Peaceful Coexistence," p. 14; Mil'shteyn and Semeyko, "SALT," pp. 2–3; Arbatov, "Soviet-American Relations in the 1970s," p. 27; Zhurkin, "Krupnyi vklad," pp. 6–7; and Kaliadin, "Bor'ba za razorushenie," pp. 6–7.

52. Newhouse, p. 173.

53. Proektor, "Military Detente"; "A Current Topic"; Mil'shteyn and Semeyko, "SALT"; Arbatov, "Soviet-American Relations in the 1970s"; Zhurkin, "Krupnyi vklad"; and Kaliadin, "Bor'ba za razorushenie."

54. Newhouse, p. 183.

55. *Ibid.*, p. 165.

56. *Ibid.*, pp. 166–92.

57. Mil'shteyn and Semeyko, "SALT," pp. 2–10; Trofimenko, "USSR-U.S. Peaceful Coexistence," pp. 9, 14; Kolosov, "On the Eve," p. 65; Arbatov, "Soviet-American Relations in the 1970s," pp. 19–20; "Summit Meetings," *SShA* (June 1974), p. 4; G.A. Trofimenko, "Problems of Peace and Security in Soviet-American Relations," *ibid.* (Sept. 1974), p. 10; N.D. Turkatenko, "An Important Stage in the Development of Soviet-American Relations," *ibid.* (Jan. 1975), p. 10; "In the Interest of Lasting Peace," *ibid.* (July 1974), p. 3; "Life Itself Is on the Side of Detente," *ibid.* (Aug. 1974), pp. 1–2; K.P. Borisov, "In the Interests of Consolidating Universal Security," *ibid.* (Jan. 1975), pp. 66–68; S.V. Vaganian, "Doklad agenstva po razoruzheniiu i kontrol'iu nad vooruzheniem," *ibid.* (July 1975), pp. 60–62; Ye. I. Popova, "The Senate and Strategic Arms Limitations," *ibid.* (May 1975), pp. 14–27; Valerianov, "USSR-United States," pp. B3, B9; Berezhkov, "Basic Principles," p. 7; Abarenkov, "Soviet Disarmament Program," pp. 7, 11; Zhurkin, "U.S.-NATO Arms Build-up," p. 25; Petrovsky, "Evolution of Doctrine," pp. 24–25; "Imperative of Detente," *ibid.* (July 1979), p. 6; A.A. Platonov, "Major Arms Limitation Achievement (SALT II Treaty)," *ibid.* (Sept. 1979), pp. 18–25; M.M. Petrovsky, "United States Public Opinion and SALT II," *ibid.* (Oct. 1979), pp. 76–79; P.T. Podlesny, "The SALT II Debate," *ibid.* (Nov. 1979), pp. 85–90; and V.F. Davydov, "Banning of Nuclear Weapons Tests—Urgent Problem Concerning Disarmament," *ibid.* (Dec. 1979), p. 1. See Sloan, "Positions," pp. 251–54, 273–79, for a discussion of this subject.

58. Mil'shteyn and Semeyko, "SALT."

59. Strobe Talbot, *Endgame: The Inside Story of SALT II* (New York: Harper and Row, 1979), pp. 100–03.

60. Mil'shteyn and Semeyko, "SALT," pp. 2–10; Trofimenko, "USSR-U.S. Peaceful Coexistence," p. 9; Kolosov, "On the Eve," p. 65; Arbatov, "Soviet-American Relations in the 1970s," pp. 19–20; "Summit Meeting," p. 4; Trofimenko, "Problems of Peace," p. 10; and Turkatenko, "An Important Stage," p. 10.

61. Talbot, p. 63.

62. *Ibid.*, pp. 46–73.

63. *Ibid.*, p. 73.

64. Doronina and Nikolayev, "Disarmament," pp. 52–57.

65. Arnett, "Soviet Attitudes," pp. 173–81. See also Drell, "Preserving," pp. 59–63.

66. *Ibid.*, pp. 190–91.

67. *Ibid.*, pp. 177–78.

68. Holloway, p. 57.

69. *Ibid.*, p. 56.

70. See Sidney D. Drell, *Facing the Threat of Nuclear Weapons* (Seattle: University of Washington Press, 1983), p. 51.

7
Negotiating with the Soviets and Prospects for Arms Control Negotiations

Harold Brown
Ralph Earle II
Gerard C. Smith
Helmut Sonnenfeldt

Ambassador Smith: I have been asked to talk about political objectives and SALT I, military doctrine, domestic political restraints, differences in negotiating styles, and differences between the agencies of government. It seems clear to me that the Soviets' main interest in SALT I was to get a registration of parity—that they are the equivalent of the United States—and they constantly harped on this question of equal security and equivalence. Secondary to that was their intention, their hope to abort a race in defensive ballistic missile systems. We persuaded them over some years (not we in the delegation—this was largely done before the negotiations started) that an ABM, contrary to the original impression, was not a benign instrument but a rather dangerous thing to introduce into the arms competition. Also I think the Soviets aimed to split us from our allies. They constantly were talking about forward-based systems, which they knew were anathema to our allies, and this is still going on. It is one of the roots of the so-called INF (intermediate nuclear forces) problem. Our main motivation was to stop the resurgent Soviet buildup. After the Cuban missile crisis, the Soviets were determined not to get themselves in that sort of a jam again, and they built up their forces radically. At a time when we were building no launchers at all, they were adding to their forces substantial numbers each year, and it was very unpleasant to look at pictures of Soviet submarines introduced (we watched them carefully) and new Soviet ICBMs each year coming on-stream.

On May 31, 1984, the Carter Center of Emory University sponsored a symposium on arms control negotiations. Chaired by former President Jimmy Carter, it was the first part of a three-stage conference on international security and arms control. The editors of this book defined the central issues and asked each participant to consider a set of questions. This chapter is an edited version of that day-long session.

At least from my point of view, this was a main motivation: how do you choke this off? We had no idea of any terminal point to the Soviet deployments. They knew about our deployments by reading budget figures and other open literature. Until SALT we did not have any idea whether there was going to be any end, and that was one of the main products of SALT: we knew pretty well (at least in terms of major elements like launchers and submarines) what they were going to build. That was a great help for our planners. We also wanted to avoid an ABM race and to cultivate an easing in relations because all of us felt (and Henry Kissinger especially) that arms controls by themselves were good but not sufficient; unless they lead to an improvement in political relations, they would not fulfill their main function.

On military doctrine, I confess that neither Soviet nor American military doctrine is crystal-clear to me, except to deter war. But once you get beyond that, I think most of this discussion is more appropriate for intellectual academic circles than it is for practitioners in the field. I remember President Eisenhower saying to me once, "War plans are wonderful things as long as you throw them away the first day war is declared." I suspect that something like that would happen if deterrence failed. A lot of these elaborate schemes for surgical strikes or massive spasms or other schemes are not in the cards. What drove us much more was, "What could be verified?" I remember hearing that a thousand times, and I don't remember ever hearing people say, "Well what can we afford to limit that would still permit us to carry out a plan?" My view (and this may seem a little heretical) is that doctrinal efforts are hopeless attempts to figure out a rational way to use irrational explosive power and give it some color of a claim of morality.

In negotiating style, the United States tends to take the initiative. We tend to be rather specific. We proposed almost the first week something called "illustrative elements" in order to give concreteness to our approach, and strangely enough most of those illustrative elements found their way, after two and a half years, into the final product. We tend to be impatient and changeable. Our record on ABM proposals was scandalous and confusing, but it reflected domestic considerations, most of which I was not clearly aware of. The Soviets, on the other hand, tended to be reactive. They spoke mostly in general terms. They were repetitive almost to a state of brainwashing us. They were consistent. They liked to get agreement on principles first. For instance, on the question of equal security, they hammered away at that hundreds of times.

The domestic political restraints that exist in the Soviet Union are terra incognita as far as I am concerned. We assumed their military programs were pinching their civilian economy, but we also assumed that in extremis they could always find the resources to deploy what they thought was militarily necessary. There is a great asymmetry here in that U.S. popular pressures have an effect on controlling our weapons. We have seen in the last two years a substantial upswing in popular interest, and President Reagan has been leaning with that punch and becoming much more a convert to arms control. Now there's a counterpressure of disillusion about arms control and the feeling that we must find some other approach; arms control may even be counter-productive and generate arms races. I am aware of that. I hope it is not widespread.

In our country we have to use arms control as a lever to get appropriations for weapons, the so-called bargaining chip. I never recall the Soviets using the term *bargaining chip*. Their military systems represent what they think they need for the defense of their motherland, and I think that we gave them a good psychological advantage in talking to us; where we were constantly reading (in newspapers at least) that we had weapons to give away, the Soviets never talked in those terms.

Differences among the Soviets are also terra incognita for me. On our side, I was surprised to find that the general lineup in the agency discussions would find the Department of State and ACDA and CIA and the Joint Chiefs pretty much in agreement; the dissenter was the Office of the Secretary Department of Defense (OSD). Even then the OSD was trying to use arms control to reconstruct the Soviets' missilery. They wanted to get the Soviets to agree to sharp reductions in ICBMs, especially the heavy ICBMs. To give an example, against all of my protests one day I was forced to propose to the Soviets the ridiculous idea that we would destroy one B-52 if the Soviets would destroy one heavy ICBM, and the people in the Defense Department, most of whom had never had any international experience at all, thought that was a going proposition. Well, the Soviets didn't take thirty seconds to turn that one down. There was some degree of indiscipline in the American delegation and it was entirely on the part of the people from OSD. I don't think this was owing to the efforts of their leader, Paul Nitze, for whom I have respect, but some of his underlings deliberately tried to generate suspicion of the delegation in Washington, with the secretary of defense, and it got so bad that in the middle of negotiation I had to meet with Melvin Laird and tell him what the facts were. After that we never heard anything more about it. But this is a danger that you don't usually associate with American delegations operating abroad.

I think the JCS views were quite enlightened although too simple to my mind. They wanted to keep the first agreement clear and simple, without interrupting the flow of technology—and that is one of the reasons that led them to stay away from any MIRV banning. The Arms Control and Disarmament Agency, as you might suspect, was always on the side of the angels: always progressive and not always successful. We proposed a ban on MIRVs;

we proposed a total ban on ABMs; and I thought for a moment we might have President Nixon on our side, but finally he wrote me a letter and said, "Tell the Soviets that will be a main object of SALT II." Well it wasn't and has never been since then; it's been forgotten.

One advantage we had in the American delegation was that most of us had known each other before, had worked with each other, and on the whole were on a friendly basis. Semenov, the head of the Soviet delegation, told me early on that he had never seen other members of his delegation; they had not known each other before assembling just a few weeks earlier to start preparing for this negotiation. I think it is important not only to have good people but to have people who work well together, especially where there are a number of different agencies. I like to think that the main prize of SALT I was the ABM Treaty. The question of the relation between the offensive part of SALT I and the defensive part was very important. We started with the principle that the two would have to go together; an agreement could not be made to limit defenses while offenses ran completely without control. The Soviets saw the possibility of a quick ABM treaty and pressed very hard in 1970 and 1971 for having just an ABM treaty and then looking at possibilities for offensive systems to be reduced substantially. We constantly said we had to have something in both respects. Henry Kissinger in May 1971 worked out an arrangement where the Soviets said they could work out something. It was very indefinite, but that's what led to the 1972 agreement where there was a treaty on ABM control and an executive agreement, approved by both houses of Congress, on a so-called freeze of offensive launchers, which limited the number of submarines they could have if they reduced some of their older ICBMs and older submarines. It was a mushy sort of freeze but certainly better than nothing.

Harold Brown: I have one question to ask Gerry. I wonder whether he meant to convey the impression that he sees everything the Soviets do in terms of weapons deployment as vital to their Soviet security: that the SS-18s and SS-19s are understandable as a Soviet need for a sufficient force to deter the United States. The Soviets don't justify what they do as bargaining chips, but that's not the same as saying that the Soviets have no military forces beyond what is needed for self-defense.

Ambassador Smith: That's quite right. I'm talking about Soviet rhetoric. I'm not talking about their real intention.

Helmut Sonnenfeldt: What I want to ask Gerry Smith about relates to negotiating procedures and style. As he knows only too well and has written about at length, in the negotiations leading up to the ABM Treaty and SALT I, there operated in our government something called the front channel and the back channel—a separate channel used by the president and by his national security adviser, Mr. Kissinger, in direct dealings with the Soviets. I wanted to get Gerry's further reflections on this manner of doing business: the question of how he feels, now with ten to twelve years' distance from that negotiation, about the use of somewhat unconventional and extraordinary ways of breaking deadlocks and getting into the meat of some of the issues, which, in the more cumbersome and formal negotiations in the front channel, may be deadlocked and difficult to approach.

Ambassador Smith: The president should have every right at all times to use any techniques he thinks will be effective. The question in my mind is, How effective were they in the case of SALT I? I mentioned the 1971 agreement where the president succeeded, through the instrument of Henry Kissinger, in getting an agreement to combine the offensive and defensive limits. My recollection is that this proposal, announced in May, had been proposed to the delegation in December of the previous year, and we spent months spinning our wheels while it was being worked out in a second channel. I think, by the same token, that the use of a separate channel in the spring of 1972 probably was necessary. There's nothing like a summit to stimulate the juices of chief magistrates to get on and button up an agreement, and that was useful in this case. I think the way it was done was imperfect. If the White House had let the delegation go ahead with the negotiation, with people like Harold Brown and Paul Nitze, they would have come to the same, if not a better, solution for one or two of the technical points. Nothing resolved at the summit was an essential plank in the final agreement, but some incidentals may be important.

Harold Brown: With respect to the unity of the Soviet delegation, clearly you did not get the kind of open disagreement that pervades all levels of the U.S. government in every administration and is made public. You did get different perspectives from the academicians in the Soviet delegation—the R&D people—than you got from the military. I think that at the beginning, there were considerable bureaucratic differences between the Foreign Ministry and the Soviet military, but it is my impression that, through the SALT I negotiations at least, the General Staff had essentially a complete veto on Soviet positions. I also think that the Soviets are better than we at floating an idea in a semiformal way and seeing whether it's attractive to the other side without making any commitment. There was no sign of fundamental disagreement among those who have authority in the Soviet delegation.

Helmut Sonnenfeldt: We have a very pluralistic system of government, and many different attitudes surface, but we have managed more or less through most of these disarmament negotiations eventually to get some decisions, which then constitute our formal negotiating position. It hasn't meant that those who were overruled didn't on occasion take their earlier views to the public or to their friends in the Congress; the system is not the most disciplined. In the Soviet case, there is a good deal of discipline and secretiveness so that possible differences don't surface. Our kremlinologists who read the Soviet literature very carefully and look at the pronouncements of Soviet leaders and generals can from time to time detect differences in emphasis and position. I can give two examples in my own experience involving meetings with Brezhnev that suggested that there was controversy before Brezhnev was able to make his own decision stick. This was to some extent a function of the fact that he was meeting directly with his American counterpart and was negotiating and haggling. In 1972, on the secret trip that Henry Kissinger and a group of us took to Moscow to prepare for the summit meeting of 1972, there was worked out a formula whereby the Soviets could go above the ceiling in submarines negotiated in the treaty by destroying some older land-based missiles, SS-7s and SS-8s. The principle was worked out but not the details. It was a breakthrough; however, it was a painful breakthrough for the Soviets, as we could tell from a number of telephone calls that Brezhnev actually made at the table, thinking, evidently, that none of us knew any Russian. He was obviously talking to someone who we thought might have been Grechko, then the uniformed head of the Soviet military establishment, explaining to him what a good deal this was and how sooner or later they were going to have to get rid of these old weapons anyway. Soviet generals don't like to get rid of weapons; they like to keep them. That was a fairly heated conversation on the telephone. The meeting itself was recessed then for several hours and resumed later. Evidently Brezhnev had to do some calling to the Politburo to get this one straightened out. The second was at Vladivostok, involving President Ford and Brezhnev. There too we worked out the outlines of what later became SALT II, after a number of byways and delays. But it did involve the Soviets' postponing once more their often-advanced proposals regarding the forwardbased systems that Gerry Smith referred to earlier. There was a break in the negotiations, and Brezhnev went off to make a telephone call to Moscow. At least judging from the intensity of his voice and the loudness of his voice, he seemed to be talking over 6,000 kilometers. He was obviously persuading somebody that if we were going to get an agreement with this new president, who was clearly eager to start his career with an agreement, this was a good thing to hold up on and come back to later. There was a very heated conversation for about twenty minutes with somebody in Moscow. Eventually that principle was worked out. I cite these examples only to say that while Brezhnev, at that time at the height of his power, was able to get things he wanted, he couldn't get them entirely without doing some politicking. I don't know what the payoffs were to the people who finally agreed with what he was doing.

Ambassador Earle: One of the most important objectives the Soviets had at SALT II—and I would presume the same applied at SALT I—was recording that the mere fact of the negotiations constituted a recognition by the United States of the Soviet Union as the other superpower. In spite of the rhetoric of the last few years, I think now (and was almost certain then when I was seeing them on a daily basis) that they were insecure regarding the world's view as to whether they were a superpower; I think they were even a bit insecure as to their own confidence in that status. Anecdotally, I tried hard to be polite to my counterpart, Minister Semenov (who was also Ambassador Smith's counterpart), but on several occasions—only two or three—I spoke what for me was fairly harshly to him and each time he responded with, "Don't talk to me as if I represent a small African republic." I thought to myself after the first (and indeed after the second and third) time that I could not imagine a representative of the United States feeling that he had to remind the Soviet negotiator that the United States was not a small African republic.

It's forgotten how important what happened at Vladivostok was; with the SALT I agreements in May 1972, the defensive systems had been put behind us, in effect, with a treaty of indefinite duration, and we were to concentrate on offensive weapons. The Soviets had been maintaining and continued to maintain that the so-called forward-based systems—the U.S. aircraft in Europe, the carriers in the Mediterranean, and the submarines based at Rota, Spain—constituted strategic weapons and should be put into the mix. We agreed that the submarines were such weapons, whether they were based in Charleston or in Rota, but we resisted, including forward-based systems. The Soviets asserted that they were strategic because they could hit their homeland. We rejected this. But in 1974 at Vladivostok, the Soviets in effect withdrew or agreed to withdraw their continuing complaints or assertions about forward-based systems. But at the same meeting—and this was hard to make clear to the Senate five years later—we also agreed that the Soviets could maintain their 300-plus launchers of heavy ICBMs. It did make it easier for the negotiators to be rid of that forward-based system issue, but it has now arisen again as an issue in a different guise with the reappearance of the French and the British missiles. At one point—the Soviets had always complained about the French and the British missiles—they began to complain about the Chinese missiles as if they too were U.S. allies but we noted that it was they who had a treaty with the Chinese and not we.

On the point of the monolithic delegation, I can say that only twice in my experience did there appear to be any cracks in it; on two occasions Minister Semenov reversed a decision or an agreement he had given us, and on one of those two occasions he noted to Alex Johnson (Ambassador Smith's successor) that his military wouldn't go along with him on it. But those were two in six and one-half years, so I can't say that the cracks I perceived were very large.

With respect to the manner of negotiation on the part of the Soviets, I couldn't disagree with anything Ambassador Smith has said. I felt that the civilians on their delegation, at least those from the Foreign Ministry, had a far lower knowledge of the weapon systems we were discussing than their military or anybody else on the U.S. delegation.

On the back channel question, my biggest complaint—and I would refer much more, in fact almost entirely, to the pre-Carter period—was the failure of those participating in it to keep the delegates in Geneva informed. I remember when Malcolm Toon was going off to be ambassador to the Soviet Union he said, "How much do you know about the back channel?" I said: "Well, when Henry Kissinger comes to Geneva he meets at the Intercontinental with Gromyko. Nobody from the delegation is present. Then he sends one of his staff down here to brief Alex Johnson, the head of our delegation, but not the delegation as a group. I think he tells Alex 60 percent of what happens, and I think Alex tells us 60 percent of what he's been told, so I figure we know about 36 percent of what's going on. And that wasn't the back channel; that was the high-level front channel. Secretary Vance and President Carter made a great effort, and a successful one, to keep the delegation advised of what was going on in the conversations in Washington. It was very important because it was clear to me that the Soviets knew what was going on, and it was not only disadvantageous to us as negotiators for the other fellow to know more than we did, but it was just downright embarrassing. Happily that embarrassment was removed.

On the Soviet side, I observed that Andrei Gromyko very seldom added anything to the proposals, but sometimes he accepted proposals of ours. The first time I went to a meeting between the foreign ministers I thought, "Well, finally I am going to see some real negotiation because we were disciplined in Geneva. The Soviets read from their piece of paper, and we read from our piece of paper, and we keep our instructions in mind throughout." But Gromyko behaved exactly like Semenov: he had his piece of paper to read from, and he didn't go beyond it, and it was a disappointment in several respects. However, meetings at the highest level are important. If you are going to make a concession or if you're going to take a big step toward the other side's position, you want to give it importance, and therefore periodic meetings between the foreign ministers play a useful role, as long as we negotiators are told what they're doing.

Harold Brown: In Washington in the cabinet room, when Gromyko agreed on the counting rules for Soviet missiles at Pervomaisk and Derazhnya (which was something that had not all surfaced before then, I think), he had a piece of paper in front of him, but my impression was that he had the choice as to whether he would read that piece of paper, and the purpose of that was to make a concession available to him as a negotiator.

Helmut Sonnenfeldt: Until he bacame a member of the Politburo, Gromyko was a victim of the high degree of compartmentalization in the Soviet governmental system. I don't think he had access to highly classified military data of the Soviet Union. He was basically an instructed individual, a very disciplined individual, but no doubt he contributed to writing his own instructions (having even then been foreign minister for a very long time). After he became a member of the Politburo in 1973, together with Andropov and Grechko, he apparently got access to much more information and participated in Politburo meetings in which decisions on weapons and budgets were taken. While I don't think that even after that he ever spoke extemporaneously or ever ventured beyond what he clearly knew was the position of the Politburo, he did acquire a certain confidence in dealing with foreigners—confidence in the sense of being able to go into greater depth in probing and explaining than he had previously. It transmitted itself to some extent to one or two of his key people in the Foreign Ministry, particularly Georgy Kornienko, who is now the number two man and also a member of the Central Committee (although not of the Politburo).

Ambassador Earle: Considering the question of instructions and their constraints, I would say that floating a new idea that goes beyond instruction is problematic. In an ideal situation with one person sitting in Washington and one sitting in Geneva, they could coordinate the floats, and Geneva could tell Washington, "I'm going to float an idea if that's all right with you," and Washington would say, "Fine." It doesn't work that way because those opposed to the issue in substance would be opposed to floating it; then you have the same fight over whether to float it. Therefore it won't happen. But that would be the ideal way to do it. As far as the Soviets are concerned, in the example of the walk in the woods in which Kvitsinksii and Nitze were talking, it is inconceivable to me that Kvitsinksii had that discussion, or any other similar discussion, without the authority of a lot of people in Moscow.

Harold Brown: So Nitze says, and I would agree. But the example that you gave, the walk in the woods, is widely regarded in the United States as the single most hopeful activity in arms control over the past three years. Whatever the details of that encounter, it seems clear that it was not a fully authorized activity on the part of the U.S. negotiator.

Helmut Sonnenfeldt: The circumstances of the walk in the woods proposal were, as I understand it from the press and Paul Nitze's accounts of it, which the Soviets have by and large repudiated, that after a period of fencing about the possibilities of some sort of a compromise on the INF, the two negotiators, the American and the Soviet, did meet in the woods near Geneva. There appears to have been a piece of paper of somewhat unclear provenance in which a compromise arrangement was outlined involving the nondeployment on the American side of Pershing IIs and the deployment of ninety SS-20s with three warheads each, and of seventy-five cruise missile launchers, each of which carries four cruise missiles. That was the essence of the arrangement, with also some limitations on what the Soviets could put in Asia and what in Europe. Supposedly that document was accepted by Kvitsinskii, the Soviet negotiator, for referral to Moscow and by Nitze on the same basis for referral to Washington; they were to be in touch further (this was shortly before recess of the meetings in Geneva) during the summer while the formal talks were in recess. I think it was left that the Soviet negotiator would get in touch with Mr. Nitze if, as, and when he had some reaction from his own government. Nitze took the paper back home, and it caused a fair amount of heartburn in Washington by all accounts. After a lot of back and forth in the American government, what Nitze was left with was that he should listen to what the Soviets had to say in response but that he should not pursue it. The Soviets never had anything to say in response, and when the talks resumed, they totally repudiated it as unacceptable. There are further complications because the Europeans weren't completely briefed on what happened, and while some of them were told what was going on, subsequently the Germans in particular felt that an important opportunity to make progress had been missed. What that tells you about the question of getting beyond one's own government's position is that it's probably not a healthy thing to do. Individuals who are in delegations or in contact with the Soviets ought to have some scope for probing if it is done in a disciplined and controlled fashion—not for putting forward pieces of paper that then become a potential agreement but trying out some ideas to see the reaction. It's a very tricky business, and it's got to be controlled carefully by the head of the delegation. Washington's got to know about it so that when it comes floating back through the Soviets, you don't suddenly get blindsided by something somebody may have said in Geneva or Vienna or Helsinki.

Ambassador Earle: Concerning the participation of Congress, in the beginning the problem was that the Soviets seemed to be grossly ignorant of the U.S. system of government. They thought that if a Democratic senator came over, it must be at President Jimmy Carter's bidding and under his instructions and the senator would therefore comply with whatever the president told him to do. It took the Soviets about six months to be disabused of that impression. After that it really didn't matter if our visitors strayed from the reservation because the Soviets were well aware of who they were and their relationship (or lack of one) to the executive branch.

Ambassador Smith: Let me return to a consideration of the ABM negotiations. I did not sense that the Soviets were especially concerned about the relative position of research and development between the two systems. They had deployed the so-called Galosh system around Moscow, which was clearly a primitive system that didn't give us any concern about being able to penetrate it. I think they saw the Spartan and Sprint missiles as a subsequent generation, but they must have known that they were not going to be effective. One of the most curious events in the whole ABM discussion occurred in 1971. For many months one of our ABM facilities was struck by construction workers, and the Soviet satellites going over must have seen this complete suspension of work. There was nothing in the major papers about it. The Soviets must have concluded, "Well, the Americans are sending us a signal that they are willing to have a moratorium." The delegation didn't know anything about this; the Joint Chiefs or the Department of Defense never told us anything about it. If it ever existed, it was a false signal. I think the Soviets were not so much concerned about competition for ABMs, because they might be technologically a little backward (because they have always overcome that backwardness in the past), but rather because they thought to enter a new dimension of weaponry was bound to sharpen the overall competition.

Harold Brown: Maybe that's too benign an interpretation, Gerry. Especially given the position that Kosygin took in 1967 at Glassboro, I find it hard to believe that there was such a complete conversion in two years. I think that it's a combination of two things. The Soviets did have a more nearly operational system; they saw us as having a more advanced system, but it was still in development, and that (combined with the question of whether at that time they wanted to get into an additional massive program) created a good environment for an arms control agreement. When the forces of the two sides differ but there may be balancing advantages on each side, that may be a good time to try to reach an agreement not to do anything more on either side or to limit it somehow. It worked quite well for ABM, but how much of a lesson it is for other cases I'm not sure. I think, then and subsequently, that there was never a prospect that those systems would be more than slightly effective. The point is that when you are defending populations, you have to be nearly 100 percent effective the first time—the first time you employ an incredibly complicated system. Probably both sides recognized that. Now there are alternative purposes for ABM systems that raise more complicated questions. But I don't think that there were any illusions at that time, in the late 1960s or early 1970s, on the part of senior people on either side, that an antiballistic missile system would substantially change the outcome of a nuclear exchange in terms of casualties. There would have been a hundred million on each side. The Soviets have maintained their system, and they are updating it but only around Moscow. It has about sixty-four interceptors; that doesn't do much, except perhaps against an accidental launch. It may or may not have some value against a Chinese attack. I doubt it because I think it unlikely that these things would work the first time, but what psychological effect it has on the Chinese or Soviet leadership is harder to say.

Helmut Sonnenfeldt: They have spent quite a bit of money on the Moscow system to modernize it and replace the launchers and do various things to it with radars.

Ambassador Smith   This raises again the issue of using new systems as bargaining chips. It is not an effective strategy. My judgment is that no weapon system should be started just for the purpose of bargaining it away. I think that there should be a clear military purpose for any weapon system we begin. Later, if you find you can get a substantial concession for giving up such a weapon system, you might call it a bargaining chip, but it ought to be a bargaining chip in retrospect and not in prospect. On several occasions we have come close to using the weapon system just for the purpose of throwing it away. The cruise missile may fall into that category. Soon it gains a life of its own, and the original motivation is lost, and it becomes an indispensable part of the arsenal.

Harold Brown: I would agree in general with Gerry's approach that these things should not be started as bargaining chips but that they might well be curtailed or eliminated for good and sufficient return. The cruise missile, I think, Henry Kissinger almost did bargain away, but he was not allowed to do so. Whether that was a good outcome I don't know; it's a complicated question. These systems do gain a life of their own, and they tend to be overvalued as time goes on. I think Gerry's approach in general is the right one. Concerning the MX, I think the momentum has already gone far enough so that if it is cancelled, it will have some negative consequences. There's a separate issue about the details of how good a system it is and how much it depends on how it is based. My own judgment is that the big problem there happened when the Reagan administration abandoned a relatively survivable system; what to do after that became much more complicated.

Helmut Sonnenfeldt: As a matter of historical fact, we have never acquired weapons as bargaining chips. In practice it's very difficult to get the Congress and sensible secretaries of defense and the Office of Management and Budget to approve programs for the specific purpose of getting rid of them the following year.

Harold Brown: I thought I would speak briefly about the goals of arms control because in trying to decide how it interacts with military force structuring and defense postures, you have to ask what's the purpose of each of them. Arms control has the following goals in contributing to national security. Both the United States and Soviet Union share these to some degree, although the emphasis is quite different. One is predictability: that is, improving the predictability of the forces on the other side so that you know what to plan for. To some extent the Soviets need this as much as we because the U.S. program is not all that predictable even though it's arrived at quite publicly. Second, each side would like to limit the threat to its own forces, partly as a way of improving stability. The less you have to worry about the vulnerability of your own forces, the more you are able to carry out a posture of deterrence. A third possible goal is to ensure parity. Early on in the negotiations, the Soviet Union saw them as a way of asserting parity with the United States. Now that most people think that the Soviet Union enjoys at least parity (and some people think that the Soviet Union enjoys superiority, for whatever value that may have) a goal of the United States in arms control—certainly a goal of U.S. negotiators in terms of achieving public acceptance of any arms control agreement—has to be that the United States has parity in some sense under such an agreement. Next I would say a possible goal of arms control is to avoid the exacerbation of political differences that can occur through arms deployments. In my judgment, it's not solely or even principally the existence of nuclear arms or deployment of nuclear forces that creates political differences between the Soviet Union and the United States. There are historical reasons, differences of system, somewhat different norms of behavior. All of these produce an adversarial relationship that can be exacerbated by suspicions and fears that the other side is about to gain or might gain a decisive military advantage through deployment of nuclear weapons. To the degree that arms control agreements can dampen that, such dampening can be a useful product of arms control. A fifth and somewhat different sort of goal is that in the West at least, arms control negotiations (and some evidence of progress therein) have become in practical terms a political condition for the deployment of nuclear arms. That's perhaps a more restrained way of saying what others have said: arms control negotiations have become an excuse for the deployment of nuclear weapons. I don't accept that formulation, but you can see how the formulation I made could be stretched that far. It is a fact that major segments of public opinion in the West—in the United States and in Western Europe as well—believe that unless there are arms control negotiations and proposals from the United States that are seen as equitable, they should not support arms programs—that is, nuclear force deployments. And finally, arms control might save money. Arms control can do these things only to a limited, often marginal, extent, but in some cases these goals, if they can be achieved to a significant degree, can be very important. I would class the ABM Treaty in that category because it saved us from a substantial chance of a less stable condition in which each side deployed major antiballistic systems for the defense of populations—systems of unknown capability but probably of a very low real capability—which in a crisis could have led to misjudgments of the outcome of a nuclear war and thus increased the chance of a nuclear war. I would put in the same category the proposal to prevent deployment of space-based antiballistic missile systems. What can't arms control be expected to do? It can't be expected to end the threat of nuclear weapons. They can't be uninvented even if the stockpiles were destroyed. The type of verification needed to verify the destruction of nuclear weapons stockpiles down to a zero level would be very intrusive and would require quite a different relationship between nation-states than now exists.

Second, nuclear strategic arms control can't save very large percentages of present expenditures on weapons, on defense establishments because strategic arms are only 10 to 15 percent of that amount now. Given what arms control can't do and what it might be able to do, there clearly is a history of overblown expectations. I believe that arms control and armaments are complementary parts of national security; that neither is a substitute for the other; that you have to base national security policies on a combination of elements. In terms of armaments, you have to base them on force deployments, but if you don't have an adequate arms control component, in the West, at least, you will be lacking the political underpinning for an adequate military program and a way of stabilizing, moderating, and limiting, however marginally, the dangers of competition. There are a lot of other arms control negotiations that deserve attention in addition to the strategic arms negotiations: intermediate-range nuclear forces; conventional forces (particularly in Europe); limitations on potential attacks on satellites; limitations on space-based antiballistic missile systems; progress toward limitations of nuclear tests; and finally some that don't belong quite with the others, the so-called confidence-building measures: to exchange information and reduce the chances of surprise attack or misinterpretation of moves on either side, one superpower or another.

Verification presents two problems. One relates to verification and one to response to issues of noncompliance. Verification is, in part at least, a technical problem; in part it's a matter of how you define agreements so as to be clear about what is allowed and what is not allowed. There will always be limits on what unilateral detection means or verification means can do, and there will always be certain ambiguities about agreements. Both need to be made much clearer in the future than they have been in the past. With respect to strategic arms limitations, verification history divides into two parts. Before 1981 or 1982, there had been no clear violations on either side. There had been ambiguities, and the Soviets certainly pushed these ambiguities quite far, although on occasion the United States also did things that brought into question verification and compliance. They are not quite so well publicized in this country; an example is the shelters over the Minuteman silos, which (depending on how you read the agreements) were at least pushing fairly close to the edge of a possible problem. Soviet testing of radars—air defense radars in an antiballistic missile mode—was certainly a problem. These were all resolved satisfactorily, if not perfectly, through the procedure of the Standing Consultative Commission, set up for this purpose. Lately there have been bigger problems. Soviet encryption—that is, coding of test data upon which the United States has been relying for verification—has become more of a problem. Again, one can argue how much this was a matter of ambiguity in the agreement. Certainly the Soviets have pushed right up against any possible ambiguity of interpretation. Furthermore, the Soviets have installed near Novosibirsk a radar that in my judgment is likely—unless adequately explained—to be a violation of the ABM Treaty, which forbids having early warning radars, let alone antiballistic missile radars, except on the periphery—and Novosibirsk is not on the periphery. The Soviets have offered unsatisfactory explanations. There is a separate question about whether the Soviets are testing a second new ballistic missile, when the SALT II agreement—which of course isn't ratified but which both sides have said they would observe—allows only one. I don't think they have given satisfactory answers. While there may not yet be unambiguous violations, these trouble me more than what has happened before. The same thing goes for some biological and chemical warfare activities. There was an anthrax outbreak at Sverdlovsk that appeared to be associated with a biological warfare factory or laboratory, and there are unanswered questions of possible use of chemical agents in Southeast Asia and Afghanistan, or of toxins that are either chemical or biological agents. Let's not set these aside but go on to the next question.

What do you do about noncompliance, especially if the agreements, as we judge them, remain in the U.S. interest? Does the United States denounce the treaty and thereby free the Soviets to do anything they want? To me that doesn't make much sense. It depends on the nature of the violation. Abandoning the ABM Treaty is not a sensible response to an unsatisfactory explanation of Soviet behavior that we think may be a violation. Nor is it sensible to build a system in response that would otherwise not be cost-effective. I'm not sure what the right answer is. Perhaps the best course would be to build more of what we would build anyway within the agreement so as to show that unsatisfactory Soviet compliance will be followed by actions of our own that redress the balance in some way. How best to do that is a case-by-case matter. Given the U.S. decision process, it is difficult to make a measured response to almost anything, and a reaction that the Soviets need to be countered with a massive program is a more likely response. This poses a real problem for political leaders, one that is unlikely to be solved in an atmosphere where negotiations aren't proceeding and where the usual and historic adversarial position is replaced by a completely defiant attitude on the Soviet part or a U.S. attitude that says, "You just can't deal with the Soviets."

Helmut Sonnenfeldt: Secretary Brown's listing of what one can expect from arms control is a sober and reasonable one, although even that very modest listing is one about which one could raise questions insofar as the history of arms control to date is concerned. It is not in prospect that negotiated arms control agreements between ourselves and the Soviet Union are going to relieve us of the risk of nuclear war or war of any kind—at least not in any future that I can foresee. Historically, if we look back over the last forty years of post–World War II history, the crises that we have had with the Soviet Union, the situations in which it appeared that we might be on the brink of conflict, have not been abstract crises over arms issues, over the vulnerability of weapons and things of that sort. They have been crises over some particular interest in some particular place in the world: in Berlin, Korea, Vietnam, the Middle East, Cuba, on occasion (although not quite as acutely) Africa. These kinds of problems will continue, depending on how governments in Washington and Moscow judge the risks and depending on the behavior of third and fourth and fifth countries. If we are able to sign another SALT or START agreement, or some agreement on antisatellite warfare or the various other subjects that have been under negotiation over the years, it is conceivable that such agreements can contribute to a political climate in which governments here and on the other side will see incentives to conduct themselves with restraint. But history on that score is not particularly helpful. Unfortunately, the few agreements that we have been able to make with the Soviets in arms control have almost invariably been followed by a new outbreak of crises or confrontation. Sometimes a confrontation has been followed in fairly short order by an agreement in the arms control area, as was the case after the Cuban missile crisis.

Moreover, the Limited Test Ban Treaty in 1963 could get through the Senate of the United States only because the Kennedy administration promised to increase underground testing and not to permit that treaty to hinder necessary weapons developments. In his remarks, Harold mentioned this perhaps paradoxical and bizarre role of arms control, but it is all too true. The aborted—so far—SALT II agreement was another one in which the price that was being paid in an effort to get ratification involved the firmest commitments to Congress by President Carter's administration that nothing in that treaty would preclude the United States from building the MX missile, and nothing in that treaty, even its protocol, would preclude the United States, after the lapse of those protocols, from proceeding with the agreements that we were then negotiating with the NATO allies to deploy in Europe the Pershing IIs and the cruise missiles, which were restricted for a limited period of time in the SALT II agreement. Arms control up to this point has been negotiated by both sides, Soviets and Americans, in such a way that it would not significantly impede military dispositions that either side judges to be important to its security.

There are some exceptions where perhaps the arms control agreements have produced certain restraints or at least certain modifications of previous planning and previous requirements. Perhaps the Soviets intended at some point to militarize their sector of the Antarctic. Perhaps we did too. This may in fact be the most successful arms control agreement that we have ever made: the Antarctic Treaty, which has kept that part of the world demilitarized. Generally the negotiations are conducted in such a way as not to impede doing what one judges to be necessary for one's security.

The agonizing fact is that every arms control proposal, even the most ambitious ones—President Carter's of March 1977, President Reagan's in the early part of his administration—would by its nature result in only a limited agreement. Even those that are relatively comprehensive and tackle a whole series of issues are still limited in their scope. Since the relationship between the United States and the Soviet Union is inherently antagonistic, the overwhelming impulse on both sides when they are restricted in one or another category is to compensate themselves and to fill your military requirements by going to another category that is not restricted by the treaty. Thus, in SALT I the limits that were placed on launchers of intercontinental land-based ballistic missiles and on numbers of submarines were compensated for by MIRVing and thus increasing the numbers of warheads per missile. Bombers were excluded altogether, and the United States, because of the aging of the B-52s and for various other reasons, looked for ways to maintain that leg of the American strategic deterrent. So did the Soviets, with their Backfires and another bomber, the Blackjack, and the various cruise missiles programs.

This pattern suggests a fundamental truth about arms control in this era: if we make it the central issue in the U.S.–Soviet relationship, dissociating it from the other issues that divide us, it will draw all the lightning produced by that relationship and sooner or later will land us where we did—with the SALT II agreement. That agreement could not be ratified in the Senate, principally because of the surrounding circumstances that did not make it politically feasible. There are other similar episodes: President Johnson was ready to start the SALT I talks with the Soviets; the Soviets invaded Czechoslovakia; he had to cancel the meeting.

How is arms control related to military programs and military strategy? Harold says that arms control and defense policies are two sides of the national security coin. I think that is accurate enough. But we in this country have had a special problem with nuclear arms control. The heart of the matter is the special geopolitical position in which we have found ourselves vis-à-vis our principal adversary since World War II. We cannot possibly protect the interests we have in many areas of the world or the commitments that we have made in every administration since World War II with our own forces. Therefore we have relied to the extent possible on local forces, on our nuclear weapons, and on the mobility provided by our navy and our air force. But since we had a monopoly in nuclear weapons at the beginning of the postwar era and a great advantage in these weapons for several more years after that, we have come to rely, even to this day, on nuclear deterrence, not only of a possible nuclear attack upon us but to preserve other interests both adjacent to the Soviet Union and sometimes more remote from it.

The concept of extended deterrence is the subject of much debate. On the one hand, we depend on a strong nuclear weapons posture to protect our security interests; on the other, we seek to do what we can through the arms control process to reduce the danger of nuclear war; to reduce the possibility of nuclear accidents; to reduce the growth of nuclear weapons stockpiles. The Soviets, on their own periphery, have been able to rely on other ways to protect and advance their interests and sometimes even to break out of their frontiers.

We have not resolved the manner in which we protect our distant interests militarily. How do we deter attacks or pressures on these interests while negotiating with the Soviets about the means with which we seek to protect them? What are our security needs, and do the kinds of agreements we are striving for in the end derogate from what we have long held to be our absolutely essential military requirements? That's a national problem. There is an underlying incoherence in our approach.

On the question of treaty violations, my own view is that if there is to be any future to arms control, it is extremely important that we not ignore even trivial violations. The Standing Consultative Commission that Gerard Smith negotiated in the first SALT agreement provides a means for quietly raising political issues or real issues of ambiguity and violation, but it is an extremely cumbersome mechanism. It is, on our side, bureaucratized; it meets at fixed periods during the year; it's very difficult to call a special meeting; it is attended by low-level officials who themselves are at the end of a long line of instructions and know nothing about what is actually going on in their own forces (perhaps our people do but the Soviets don't) and therefore it will take them months (since the Soviets are slow anyway) to come back and give explanations. But there is a utility. Still, I believe that in areas where there is more sensitivity, it may be better to approach the Soviets in very private diplomatic channels, even back channels, if you will. We have the additional problem of leaks in our government and it is difficult to maintain confidentiality. If on the ambiguous issues one can talk to the Soviets quietly, one may on occasion get them to stop the ambiguous behavior or give the kind of detailed explanation that will provide reassurance that no violation occurred. Once it leaks, once it becomes a headline issue, it becomes a matter of prestige.

One final observation on nonproliferation: we have made some agreements with the Soviet Union and with others concerning the supply of nuclear materials and expertise. We have agreed to arrangements under the International Atomic Energy Agency in Vienna, another one of the more successful arms control arrangements that we have made with the Soviets, going back to the Eisenhower administration. Through that mechanism, we have established a system of safeguards on peaceful nuclear activities designed to prevent diversion of nuclear materials to military purposes. The basic issue is that people who want to keep the option to become nuclear powers will not submit to this kind of a regime, and that includes a number of countries around the world that feel threatened either by a nuclear power or by a collection of enemies who they believe may be so powerful some day that only a nuclear capacity will keep them at bay. That may be the case with South Africa, Israel, Taiwan, South Korea, and Pakistan. We have done better in the relatively simpler area of getting those who don't want to proliferate to subscribe to a regime of safeguards and to the Non-Proliferation Treaty. I would argue that the hard-core issue of nonproliferation in some important measure comes back to the basic American–Soviet antagonism, albeit not exclusively to that. Some of the potential proliferees want to keep the nuclear option open because the Soviet Union is allied or associated with their enemies. That's been true of Israel, Pakistan, and South Africa. (There are different motivations in Argentina and Brazil connected with great power status and perhaps their own enmities in the hemisphere.) I don't think we have made a great deal of progress on that political aspect of proliferation.

To sum up, arms control has to be woven into a broader agenda of relations with the Soviets. Although we should continue to try to negotiate broader agreements involving levels of forces and a variety of systems, along the lines of SALT II or START, this will remain a slow and cumbersome process that will have virtually no (or at least only a very modest) effect on actual nuclear forces. Therefore, a concurrent series of negotiations with the Soviets on some specific, precise, and concrete measures that would not cap the arms race or produce a millennium but could have some useful, modest effect would be highly desirable. I would include in such an agenda that part of SALT II that puts limits on the number of warheads per missile. I would pull it out of SALT II. Second, I would pull out of the SALT II agreement and of past negotiations the prohibition on fractional-orbital tests of sea-based missiles—that is, an effort to cut the flight times and to stay under the radars. This won't prevent nuclear preemption if a government decides on it, but it could inhibit one method. An agreement would make a marginal contribution. I would pursue the hot-line issues and some of the crisis management propositions, although if Moscow wants a crisis, or Washington feels sufficiently challenged, no hot line will stop it. The hot line has been used in the past, I am afraid, to mislead as much as to reassure at various times of crisis. Nevertheless, it's good to have rapid communications if necessary. The prohibition of antisatellite weapons may be beyond us; it may not be definable; I don't think it's verifiable. I think it would probably create more tension and uncertainty than assurance. Still, there may be certain aspects or parts of that problem that we can still get a grip on and that may be in our interest. I cannot subscribe, unfortunately, to the comprehensive test ban. I have never approved of it. I believe we need to retain the option to test nuclear weapons as long as we rely on them. And I wish our administrations would start being honest with our people and not use verification as an excuse for not getting an agreement. We have been through this for five administrations, and every one of them in the end has come to the point where it will not proceed. I believe that we cannot avoid testing—at least proof testing—weapons. I do think that the Threshold Test Ban Treaty and the accompanying treaty on peaceful explosions was a good one; it fits into my concept of what we ought to be doing. I regret that they were not ratified. Now they have become a political football.

Harold Brown: My general comment on Hal's approach is that if you start off with so little, you are likely to end up with very much less. There is the other risk that you promise too much and leave people disappointed, but I believe that there is something in between: promise little and seek a variety of things and seek somewhat more than you hope or expect to get. On strategic nuclear arms, it is useful to try to hold down payloads. On the antisatellite side, I agree that there are lots of problems with definitions and that you can't be sure of verifying all kinds of antisatellite actions, but you can still limit the more extreme things, and I think it's worth trying. About Star Wars I feel much more strongly. I think that an antiballistic missile system from space is a road down which we should not begin walking. It is easier to stop some things before both sides get caught up in them; it is easier not to do something in which you do not have a big investment. And I think that is an area of arms control agreements that can be fairly ambitious. Arms talks are now organized into separate intermediate and strategic meetings; having a single delegation and a single venue for both sets of discussions makes sense. There is a separate issue as to whether you should have a single ceiling for both kinds of systems, and there I come down on the other side. Indeed the Soviets regard anything that can hit them as strategic, but they don't regard anything that can hit our Western European allies from their territory as strategic, and that's a distinction that we cannot afford to accept. If there were to be a single ceiling to include both long-range and medium-range systems, it would have to include quite a few Soviet systems from our point of view that the Soviets would not like to count under that ceiling. Under those circumstances you present the Soviets with a real problem: they would either have to reduce their intermediate-range forces so that the relative advantage becomes much less to them than it is now, or else they would have to use part of their strategic ceiling to give them intermediate-range forces and then the United States would have the opportunity to have the advantage in strategic forces. Probably there will have to be separate ceilings or some rather high combined ceilings. One would have to find a way to consider the British and French forces but without including them because they are not U.S. forces. The United States cannot accept the British and French forces in our ceiling, and I think the British and French won't agree with that either. To carry it to an absurdity, suppose the British and French decide to build up to the Soviet numbers together. That means that the United States would be left with zero. What is possible is a side agreement that sets a limit on the British and French forces as a fraction of U.S. or Soviet or—as happened during the Kissinger era—tacit compensation to the Soviets. The Soviets by and large will probably have more launchers than the United States, and that could be tacit compensation.

Helmut Sonnenfeldt: On combining the talks, Harold has stated the issue correctly. It will reemerge in the same form whether you have it under one roof or not. What we cannot do, and what the Soviets in fact one day may propose when they get ready to come back, is to trade intercontinental forces for the INF forces. If so, we would have to come back and say, "But no, you've got to count the SS-20"—and we'd be right back in the same negotiation. On the British and French, the reason that that's a problem is that SALT and START have been bean-counting negotiations for the last fifteen years. We have a unit of account, and the British and French forces make a difference because you add them to the numbers. The fact of the matter is that the

Soviets for years—since the 1950s—have targeted Britain and France with their existing forces—strategic forces—and they continue to do so today (even more so today) with the SS-22, which they are deploying forward, as well as the SS-20. Soviet security interests and military requirements are amply met under existing force dispositions. I see no military reason to compensate the Soviets for the British and the French.

Ambassador Smith: It seems that this merger of INF and START is inevitable. One can think seriously about a two-stage scheme where Harold's problem about counting both types under ceilings would be avoided, at least for a time. There could be some arrangement that recognized that one of our main aims is to reduce the Soviet heavy missiles, and the price would be in some sort of coin that would involve our Pershing missiles and perhaps the deferment of the ground-launched cruise missiles (GLCMs). Then, in a second stage, there could be an overall ceiling, with both parties being able to deploy some systems in the continental United States and the Soviet Union or forward in Czechoslovakia or Germany. That still leaves the French and British problem, but if Henry Kissinger was clever enough to solve that problem in 1972, I don't see why it's beyond our ingenuity to do the same in the years to come.

Harold Brown: The one thing we must not accept is a situation in which U.S. systems that can reach our allies from the Soviet Union but can't reach the United States are not counted. That would amount to accepting the Soviet position, which is that Western European security is a matter regarding only Western Europe and the Soviet Union, in which the United States plays no part.

Ambassador Smith: Haven't we already been guilty of that cardinal sin in taking account of the British and French forces in 1972 in figuring out how many submarines we would be allowed to have?

Harold Brown: There's a difference between what is in an agreement and what rationale is given for it in an explanation afterward. Codifying such an agreement by counting British and French systems or counting U.S. systems that can reach the Soviet Union but not vice-versa sets on this an unacceptable seal. Let me address the strategic defense initiative. There are two big problems with it. One is the feasibility—and it has to go beyond the technical feasibility. You can write on a blackboard some numbers that tell you that you are halfway there and that you should go ahead with the system. But even if you've done that, there remains the problem of going to engineering feasibility and then going to economic feasibility. We are talking here about a system that might well be the first trillion-dollar military system. And finally, you are left with the problem of countermeasures. These defensive systems would be up in space would be subject to attack. It's much easier to destroy a satellite in space than to destroy a ballistic missile. There are some compensating factors, but you get into a measure–countermeasure business and are left with the question of how feasible it really is even if it's scientifically possible, and I conclude it is unlikely to be.

If everything that I've said is wildly pessimistic and you eventually have something that shoots down half the incoming ballistic missiles, is that satisfactory from a policy point of view? It clearly is not good enough to save the population because 5,000 incoming warheads will kill almost as many people as 10,000 incoming warheads because of the saturation effect. You have not taken care of the other means of delivery: the cruise missile and bombers. The trouble is that populations are much more vulnerable than military forces and specifically than strategic military forces, whether the latter are deployed in the ground, on the ocean, or in the air. You are fighting a losing game, and indeed, to some extent, the administration appears to appreciate this because they have said, "Well, as a partial measure we may not be able to defend populations right away; what we'll do is defend ballistic missiles, and technically that's much more feasible and even under some circumstances justifiable." If you let arms control go by the board, you may have to defend ballistic missiles. But what seems to have been overlooked in this course correction is that as soon as you say you are going to defend your ballistic missiles, which is much more feasible because if you knock 50 percent of the incoming attacking forces, that's a very cost-effective defense of ballistic missiles, you are now talking about defending ballistic missiles. Well, for what purpose? Answer: for deterrence and retaliation. You are right back where you were, and the high moral purpose is down the drain, at least for the time being.

Finally, you've got the question of how you get there from here. And when this question is posed to some advocates of the strategic defense initiative, they say, "Well, you get there a little at the time; you share the information with the Soviets; you don't send them any Apple computers because that is destabilizing and gives them technology, but you do share the strategic defense initiative technology with them so that both sides can be protected from ballistic missiles." But the prospects for deceit and misreading of a situation where one side thinks it has a temporary advantage over the other become enormous under those circumstances. The worst scenario that I can envisage is one where each side thinks it has 95 percent capable ballistic missile defense but what it actually has is 10 or 5 or 50 percent capability. If you then get into a crisis, the thought arises, "Well, if we don't strike first and defend against the ragged retaliation with our defensive system, we are going to come out very badly, and what we have to lose if we back down is greater than what we may lose if we accept a ragged retaliatory strike." In other words, a clever military briefer may persuade a political leader—I don't think it's likely but it's conceivable—to take an action that is catastrophic to everybody, based on the existence of a nonworking defensive system. It's not the road I think we should start down.

Helmut Sonnenfeldt: Never before in history has the defense of one's people and territory been judged to be futile, silly, destabilizing, and dangerous. Historically, people have built walls around their cities and ditches and tank traps. It is the utter perversity of the nuclear age that defense is bad, offense is good; attacking weapons is bad, attacking people is good. That's what supposedly gives you stability. Presidents have suffered under the corrosive effects of having to live with those kinds of military and security options. Therefore I think the quest for defending your people and your territory will go on regardless of what the defense intellectuals say about the destabilizing character, the dangers, the technical infeasibilities, and the costs. And I think that's among the motivations in this case. On the technical side, I have no idea what the prospects are. I tend to agree that there could be destabilizing effects. But the possibilities of defending missiles should not be simply written off as futile or as no more than the kind of deterrence we already have. If the plans of a potential attacker—whether a preemptive attacker under enormous pressure or a planned premeditated attacker—are complicated by calculations about how much damage he will do to the other side's retalitatory capability, it seems a desirable addition to deterrence, potentially. This would be so whether that's accomplished by superhardening, shuttling missiles around in tunnels, or by active defense, if that proved feasible. I do think it has some merit, and if the technology enables us to consider it as a valid possibility, then with due debate and consideration, it is something we should consider. The submarines we defend in other ways: by concealment, quietness, secure communications, unless Soviet satellites cripple them. The question of the future of the land-based missile force is a legitimate one, and many times over the years it has been asked whether it is worth continued investment. On the whole, I have been in favor of maintaining the triad in order to complicate any possibility of attack by the Soviet Union or some other source.

Harold Brown: Our submarine-launched ballistic missiles are now the most secure that we have in the way of retaliatory capability. If we are relying on our deterrent forces, it makes sense to put in different systems that have different vulnerabilities. To the extent that that can be afforded and done in a politically acceptable way, it argues for increasing the survivability of land-based ICBMs (or the bomber forces, although they are much more difficult to defend this way) with active defenses. To the extent that one can limit a potential attack on them, (for example, by arms control agreements), active defense becomes less necessary. I would still not rule out possible active defense of strategic forces as one element, but one must then remember that if we follow this path, the president and the rest of us continue to live with deterrence as a doctrine, and the alleged great moral imperative favoring defense is certainly much weaker—actually nonexistent—in this case. The other thing that has always made me regard active defense as, if not the last resort then fairly far down the list, is something that Hal hinted at: how would we behave if there were such an agreement and the Soviets started defending their ballistic missiles? The distinction between a hard-point defense system (defense of strategic missiles) and defense of a wide area (defense of population) could be seen by a technologist, but I can assure you there would still be ambiguities. If the Soviets began, by agreement, defending their ballistic missile sites, there would be an enormous uproar about cheating—about Soviets using this not only for potential breakout but as a force in being to defend their cities. In other words, the distinction may be hard to draw as to what is actually being done. There would be an enormous distinction in effectiveness as missile defender and as city defender, but the political repercussions in our country of a suspected Soviet population defense program would be very grave.

If the strategic arms reduction talks are reengaged, it seems to me there are three general paths that can be followed. One is to try to extend or modify SALT II. The Soviets have actually proposed the modification. As always with Soviet negotiating proposals, there are some hooks in it that have to be extracted before we can consider it, but that, it seems to me, is a sort of minimum possibility. It is desirable to try to improve the survivability of our systems and thus improve the stability of our systems by reducing numbers of warheads. If SALT were to lapse and the sides were to build up, they'd probably build up to about 15,000 ballistic warheads by 1990. If you extend SALT, you would build up to a somewhat higher level than the present 8,000—to maybe 10,000. It would be desirable to try to hold it down to 6,500 or 7,000 to improve stability and survivability. You can do that by restructuring the forces, which is the general nature of the original Reagan administration proposals, the freeze, and the build-down. Now why do I say the freeze is restructuring? It's a restructuring of the prospective force of the freeze. If you look at what the forces would be in 1990, they would not be the same with a freeze nor would they be the same with a build-down or with the Reagan proposal. Because of the differences to which Hal referred—of the present state of development and progress in replacement of systems—in other words, the cycle of weapons improvement for sea-based systems and land-based systems—the restructurings tend to affect the Soviet Union more than the United States in many of these proposals. They tend to affect the United

States more than the Soviet Union in the freeze proposals because a larger fraction of the U.S. land-based systems is supposed to be changed over the next five or six years than is the case with the Soviets. The reverse is actually true on the sea-based systems. If you look at these from the Soviet perspective, by and large they don't offer very much because they do tend to restructure the Soviets more than the United States. One possible alternative is to follow what the SALT II and SALT I approach was, which was to have balancing asymmetries in effect. In the case of SALT I, the bombers were not constrained. In the case of SALT II, again, the United States took account of the fact that it had some advantages that were to balance the Soviet advantages in large missile systems. The environment has changed, however, It will be much more difficult to sustain politically in the United States an agreement that doesn't allow parity of the United States with the Soviet Union in some of the subceilings or submeasures in which the Soviets have had, in the past, an advantage. The Soviets are not going to agree to be equal in some things and inferior in others. And because of the difference in the forces ...

Helmut Sonnenfeldt: ... except in air defense ...

Harold Brown: Well, that's not a matter of agreement. We could build air defense if we were profligate enough. The only way around this is for us to be ahead in some things and they in others and to allow each side the choice to move its force structure in the direction of the other's balance of forces. I don't think either side will do that. In the end we are going to come to something that allows each side to pick whether it's going to modernize its sea-based forces, for example, but not allow one side to modernize everything and the other to modernize only something. There are an infinite number of ways that you can structure this. But I think that by the Reagan administration's saying that it is willing to trade off bomber advantages against missile advantages, it leaves open the possibility of such a balancing asymmetries approach. This is still fairly ambitious in terms of what Sonnenfeldt is proposing. It's not just picking up here and there; it's an attempt to reduce the number substantially from what they would otherwise be but allowing each side to pick what sorts of forces it will have within those numbers. I don't know that that will fly with the Soviets. I think it would fly within the United States, but that's something that one would have to try to negotiate.

Helmut Sonnenfeldt: One of the reasons why I have been attracted to the idea of proceeding in very small, separable steps is that this may be relatively less dependent on the total political climate. Basically this is a hostile relationship, which makes arms control extremely difficult. But I believe that arms control itself has to be embedded in a broader political modus vivendi of some sort, or else it will not be negotiable at all, even apart from the technical reasons; and if it is, it will be frustrated by the continuation of military competition in other avenues that have not been covered by the arms control agreement. I wish I could give you a more hopeful answer, but I'm afraid that's what I think.

Ambassador Smith: I would like to make one or two observations about Hal's point of view. It seems to me that he has been too pessimistic about the past and too optimistic about the future. I think, for instance, that in describing the ABM Treaty as a marginal achievement, he is discounting its importance. I thought that it was a very useful achievement from the point of view of reducing costs and risks and having something to do with setting up a little easement in political relations between the two parties. The two-stage outline that I suggested is a reasonable approach, wherein we would have a merger of the INF talks and the START talks, and I would hope that some administration, whether in 1985 or 1989, will come around to tailoring such an approach and then there is some prospect we can make some more progress.

Ambassador Earle: In spite of some of the things I have heard this afternoon, I still believe that arms control can and should play a vital role in our national security policy. And sometimes I wonder—when we have conferences and seminars of this sort—if we shouldn't either drop the phrase *arms control* from the title or make it a subset of the title *national security* because sometimes we, and thereby the audience and the public at large, concentrate on it as a single, isolated policy or group of policies. It has to be integrated into defense policy, if that's a separable item in the whole national security spectrum. It has to go forward incrementally. We made great strides in SALT I and then SALT II; the boiler plate was created there for a lot of future arms control agreements. One of the problems is that those who negotiate good arms control agreements have difficulty getting them ratified, and vice-versa. We should go forward with the process. But we have to bring this into the overall spectrum of national security considerations and the reduction of the risk of nuclear war. We've got to find something beyond arms control. Arms control is essential and necessary, but it is not going to save the world by itself. I am not sure what the solution is. Perhaps Senator Nunn's idea is a start. I would like to see it followed up.

We must have a bilateral discussion with the Soviets in an effort to reduce not necessarily the tensions that naturally arise from our adversary relationship—which I agree exists—but to direct ourselves to the elimination or near elimination of the possibility of a nuclear conflict arising through stupidity, arrogance, rhetoric, or simple misunderstanding.

8

Sitting on Bayonets: The Soviet Defense Burden and the Slowdown of Soviet Defense Spending

Abraham S. Becker

Talleyrand is supposed to have told Napoleon, "You can do everything with bayonets, sire, except sit on them."[1] Neither can they be eaten, of course, or clothe a family. But if the society sees the development of bayonet skills as its highest purpose, the provision of food, clothing, and shelter to the population will be slighted, and the subordination will be justified by ideology. There have always been castes or classes in civilized societies that have attached the highest value to military pursuits. But for most people in the contemporary world, the essential purpose of the military is to provide the security necessary to pursue other goals. This is the first condition under which military expenditure may be said to impose a burden on the society: that defense be seen as an instrument to unrelated ends.

The second condition is that military activities use resources that would otherwise be employed in the civil economy, thereby reducing the potential level of other end uses of the national product. The existence of substantial unemployment and underutilized capacity (or the availability of gifts from an external source) might permit an expansion in military production without sacrificing civilian output. But with near full employment, the use of resources in the military sector involves a cost: the value of production forgone by not using these resources in the civil sector. The necessity for sacrifice is the essence of the second requirement for deeming defense a burden on the society.

Whether the first condition is satisfied in the Soviet Union may depend on whose perspective—that of the leaders or the led—is taken as guide. Elsewhere I have argued that "the role of military preparedness in the leaders' 'utility functions' is much more than that of an instrument to achieve other social ends."[2] Few observers doubt, however, that Soviet citizens see the goals of day-to-day living in much the same light as their counterparts in the West. For the ordinary Soviet, defense unquestionably constitutes a burden—a necessary one, to be sure, but clearly a burden. To that extent, therefore, the idea of defense burden must also have meaning for the most militaristic of Soviet leaders.

Not too many years ago, the burden of Soviet defense seemed a secondary issue. The conventional estimates of the size of the burden were low, and the Soviet economy was growing rapidly. Now the era of rapid growth seems to have come to an end, and the Western estimates of the burden are much higher. Moreover, there appears to have been a substantial cut in the growth rate of Soviet military expenditure after 1976. The conjunction generates intense interest in the relation among these developments. To what extent was the size or growth of the burden a factor in the apparent slowdown of the Soviet military buildup in the mid-1970s? Especially important is the role of the defense burden in shaping future growth prospects. How serious a drag on the economy does the Soviet military budget represent? Is cutting defense spending the solution to current Soviet economic problems? Will the military budget nevertheless continue to grow? These questions are the focus of this chapter, although they will hardly be resolved here. It is hoped that the issues can at least be clarified.

How Large Is The Soviet Defense Burden?

The defense burden is conventionally measured as the share of total output—most often GNP, sometimes gross domestic product or national income—allocated to defense. It is generally known that there has been sharp controversy over the level and growth of Soviet military expenditure; there is less argument about Soviet GNP growth rates. The controversy on Soviet military expenditure has tended to produce a diffused skepticism about all such estimates among those who have neither the specialized knowledge to judge who is right nor a penchant toward one or another ideological pole in the public debate. No attempt will be made here to resolve that controversy. At least a small monograph would have to be devoted to that subject, and as a public document that effort would be incomplete because of the barrier of classification of U.S. government estimates. Moreover, it is doubtful that the controversy can be resolved by ordinary debate. Much of the conflict results from different perceptions of the nature of the Soviet Union and different views of the desired direction of change in U.S. defense spending; these are not easily swayed by arguments about the evidence of Soviet outlays.[3] For these reasons, the discussion to follow will attempt only to sketch out the range of available estimates and to comment briefly on the major differences of estimating methodology.

Level and Growth of Soviet Military Outlays

The controversy arises because of the unreliability of the Soviet government's official annual series of outlays on defense (column 1 of table 8–1). No breakdown of these single figures has been published since the 1940s, and very little information is provided on their meaning. Doubts about the reliability of this series as an indicator of the total Soviet defense effort are long-standing in the West, but the pattern of the 1970s has effectively settled the matter. There are few Western observers who are prepared to waive the physical evidence of Soviet force buildup or modernization during this period, in every category of armament and in every theater of operations, in favor of official assertions that the growing Soviet military establishment was being purchased with a declining budget, equivalent at official exchange rates to roughly $25 billion. If the Soviet figures refer to some real budget category—if they are not simply arbitrary extensions of an earlier reality or perhaps mere political artifacts—the clue has not yet been discovered in the West.[4]

The alternative to acceptance of the official figure is independent estimation. A number of individuals and institutions have tried to decipher the mysteries of Soviet statistics and come up with estimates of the true total or of major components. The most frequently attempted route to estimating aggregate military outlays is analysis of the Soviet state budget. There is a minimum agreement among Western observers that in addition to the official defense figure, military outlays are probably contained in the allocations to science (military R&D). Many writers have argued that military spending is concealed in additional budget categories, especially weapons procurement in the so-called national economy allocations. Still others believe there are extrabudgetary sources of defense spending.[5]

Among the developers of independent estimates based on analysis of the budget, only the Stockholm International Peace Research Institute (SIPRI) and U.S. Defense Intelligence Agency (DIA) are perhaps still actively engaged in the effort. The word *perhaps* is used because SIPRI's current methodology has not been revealed. For a while, SIPRI was virtually the lone Western organization relying essentially on official Soviet defense figures.[6] In 1979, SIPRI changed its ruble estimates but provided no explanation of its revised methodology. The sole clue was a cryptic reference to a " 'compromise' . . . which corresponds neither with the official figures nor with the CIA estimates."[7] The same formula backs up the revised figures of the 1980–1983 yearbooks, which are also declared to be "imputed values with a high degree of uncertainty."[8] SIPRI was apparently content to move its 1979 series, in current ruble prices, parallel to the official claim for the 1960s, although on a path almost twice as high as the official. The SIPRI yearbooks of 1980–1983 provide a further revision but only in the level of outlays. The relative changes between 1960 and 1970 and again between 1970 and 1978 are virtually the same in the two series, 92–93 and 13 percent, respectively. The entries for the 1970s in the 1980s series show constant annual differences of 0.6 billion or 0.7 billion rubles.[9] SIPRI apparently believes there was no

Table 8-1
Soviet Military Expenditure, Various Estimates, 1955–1983
(billion rubles)

	Soviet Official Defense	1979 SIPRI	1980s SIPRI	Lee Current Prices	Lee 1970 Prices[b]	Rosefielde 1970 Prices	DIA Reconstructed Current Prices	CIA 1970 Prices
	current prices							
1955	10.7		23.3	14.0				30
1956	9.7			12.5				29
1957	9.1			12.5				26
1958	9.4	17.0		13.5(14.0)				26
1959	9.4	18.4		15.0				26
1960	9.3	18.3	21.8	16.0(16.5)		14.3(22.5)		27
1961	11.6	22.8		18.5		15.5		30
1962	12.6	24.9		21.0		16.9		34
1963	13.9	27.3		23.0		18.3		35
1964	13.3	26.1		24.5		19.8		38
1965	12.8	25.1	30.0	26.0(26.5)		21.7		39
1966	13.4	26.3		28.0	29.2	23.7		40
1967	14.5	28.5		32.5	33.0	26		43
1968	16.7	32.4		38.5(41.0)	38.5	28.7		46
1969	17.7	34.6		42.0	42.2	31.6		48
1970	17.9	35.2	42.0	46.0(49.0)	46.5	43.5	50	49
1971	17.9	35.7	42.7		52.0	46.7	53	50
1972	17.9	36.3	43.3		56.5	50.2	56	51
1973	17.9	36.9	44.0		63.5	55	60	53
1974	17.7	37.4	44.7		69.0	59.7	64	57
1975	17.4	38.0	45.4	71.5[a]	77.0	64.7	70	59
1976	17.4	38.5	46.0		83.5	70.3	74	63
1977	17.2	39.1	46.7		89.0	75.4	79	63
1978	17.2	39.7	47.4		98.0	82.5	85	65(64)
1979	17.2		48.0		107.0	91	90	67(66)
1980	17.1		48.7		117.0		96	71(67)
1981	17.1		49.5				100	(68)

1982	17.1			
1983	17.1	50.2		(70)

Sources: Official "defense" 1955–1980: Ministerstvo finansov SSSR, *Gosudarstvennyi biudzhet SSSR i biudzhety soiuznykh respublik*, (Gosfinizdat, 1962); "Finansy" 1966, 1972, 1976; "Finansy i statistika," 1982. 1981–1983. TsSU, *Narodnoe khoziaistvo SSSR v 1983 g.* (Moscow: Finansy i statistika, 1984), p. 547.

SIPRI: 1979: *World Armaments and Disarmament SIPRI Yearbook 1979* (New York: Crane Russak, 1979), pp. 38–39. SIPRI Yearbooks: 1980, p. 25; 1981, p. 102; 1982, p. 146; 1983, p. 167. The 1980 yearbook was published in the United States by Crane Russak, the 1981–1982 Yearbooks by Oelgeschlager, Gunn and Hain in Cambridge, Mass., the 1983 by International Publication Service, Taylor and Francis, New York.

Lee, Current Prices: William T. Lee, *The Estimation of Soviet Defense Expenditures 1955–1975. An Unconventional Approach* (New York: Praeger, 1977). p. 97. These are midpoints of ranges, rounded. The estimates in this source refer to national security expenditures, but in later work Lee reverted to the more conventional term *defense expenditures*. Figures in parentheses are from Lee's submission in *CIA Estimates of Soviet Defense Spending*, Hearings before the Subcommittee on Oversight of the Permanent Select Committee on Intelligence, House of Representatives, Washington, D.C., 1980, p. 21.

Lee, 1970 prices: *CIA Estimates of Soviet Defense Spending*, p. 22. The figures in the table are midpoints of ranges presented in the source.

Rosefielde: Steven Rosefielde, *False Science: Underestimating the Soviet Arms Buildup* (New Brunswick, N.J.: Transaction Books, 1982), p. 186.

CIA: *USSR: Measures of Economic Growth and Development, 1950–80*, Studies Prepared for the Use of the Joint Economic Committee, U.S. Congress, (Washington D.C., December 8, 1982), p. 123. The figures are midpoints of ranges presented in the source. The figures in parentheses are my crude estimates of the revised CIA figures, assuming a constant 2 percent per year growth rate. CIA has stated that this was the average annual rate of increase in the late 1970s and early 1980s. *Allocation of Resources in the Soviet Union and China—1983*; Hearings before the Subcommittee on International Trade, Finance, and Security Economics of the Joint Economic Committee, Congress of the United States, pt. 9, Washington, D.C., 1984, p. 230; Statement by Robert Gates, deputy director for intelligence, CIA, on the Allocation of Resources in the Soviet Union and China—1984, before the Subcommittee on International Trade, Finance and Security Economics of the Joint Economic Committee, U.S. Congress, November 21, 1984, pp. 11–12.

DIA reconstructed: DIA's estimates assume "that defense has absorbed a constant share of the state budget since 1970. Based on this assumption and other evidence, Soviet military spending in current rubles rose from about 50 billion in 1970 to roughly 100 billion in 1981 or at a nominal rate of 6 to 7 percent annually." DIA, *USSR: Military Economic Trends and Resource Allocation—1983*, DDB-1900-59-83 (August 1983), p. 12. (This statement is repeated verbatim in the written submission by Major General Schuyler Bissell, deputy director, DIA, in *Allocation of Resources in the Soviet Union and China—1983*, p. 94.) These figures correspond to about a third of state budget expenditure. According to "Soviet Defense Trends: A Staff Study Prepared for the Use of the Subcommittee on International Trade, Finance, and Security Economics of the Joint Economic Committee, Congress of the United States," September 1983, the share is that reported "by knowledgeable sources" for the 1960s and 1970s—31–34 percent. The DIA estimating procedure is therefore taken to be multiplication of state government expenditures by 0.325, with the results rounded to the nearest billion rubles. For total budget expenditures, see the sources already cited for the official defense series.

ᵃProjection.

ᵇ". . . as the Soviets reckon constant prices"; however, "R&D estimates are mostly in current prices because a satisfactory method of converting R&D outlays to constant prices is lacking."

change in the Soviet price level over the decade because its constant price dollar series grows at the same rate (no constant ruble series is presented).[10]

The other major nongovernment institution relied on for estimates of Soviet activity is the London-based International Institute of Strategic Studies (IISS). The IISS now abstains from providing its own estimate of Soviet military expenditure or the defense–GNP ratio, citing insufficient information and Soviet pricing practices. Instead, estimates by others are presented, ranging from the official Soviet claim to a Chinese estimate.[11]

The U.S. DIA believes that military expenditure, concealed in several state budget categories apart from defense, absorbed a roughly constant one-third of budget outlays in the 1970s, and it is on that basis that a DIA series is reconstructed in table 8–1. The notion of a constant budgetary share for the military is troubling. In an economy where commodity planning is paramount, one might rationalize constant shares of various real aggregates—machinery production, for example—but shares of (current price) budget outlays could be expected to fluctuate. However, since DIA has not released the details of its methodology, little further can be said.

A less popular path to replicating total outlays is through analysis of Soviet national income (net material product) statements on the end use side. The Soviet descriptive literature on its national income accounting theory and practice permits some speculation but little informed estimation.[12]

Much attention has been focused on procedures for estimating military hardware procurement through analysis of Soviet data on the output of machine building. This is the core of William Lee's approach to estimating total Soviet military expenditure. The methodology is inherently difficult because procurement is obtained as a residual after a series of judgmental, sometimes even speculative, deductions from totals that are not known with precision.[13]

All of these approaches have in common an effort to extract information on Soviet military outlays believed to be concealed in Soviet economic and financial statistics. The CIA, however, believes that these procedures are unreliable because of Soviet secrecy and Moscow's success in manipulating the statistical information it publishes. Even if these efforts were successful, they would not provide estimates in the detail and distribution required for intelligence purposes. Therefore, the CIA estimates outlays on Soviet forces (military expenditures less R&D) by the so-called building block or direct costing method, essentially building up detailed estimates of quantities and then valuing the quantities at 1970 prices and costs.[14] Security considerations have severely limited the information published on either the methodology of these estimates or the actual results.

Rosefielde's estimate of military outlays depends on an elaborate critique of CIA procedures and on an interpretation of the basis for and meaning of the CIA's 1976 revision of its ruble estimates that CIA continues to deny.[15]

It is apparent that all the Western estimates belie the official Soviet claim as to level of output in all years—the Western estimates for 1970, for example, are two to three times the Soviet claim—and with regard to both direction and annual rate of change in the 1970s and 1980s. There is a consensus that Soviet military expenditure rose continually in the 1960s and 1970s; however, there is a substantial divergence among the various Western estimates of the rate of growth. For the 1970s, Lee and Rosefielde estimate the highest growth—130 and 109 percent, or 9.7 and 8.5 percent per year, respectively; SIPRI the lowest; CIA's series is in between. DIA accepts the CIA series; however, DIA's own estimates of outlays at current prices show more rapid annual increases and imply considerable change in the price level. This conclusion is accepted by the CIA: current price data "would show higher growth than our constant price estimates because of the inflation that characterizes the Soviet economy generally," declared the deputy director for intelligence of the CIA before the Proxmire subcommittee.[16] However, the CIA has not presented any current price estimates or data on the rate of inflation in the military sector.

In 1982–1983 the CIA cut in half its previous estimate of Soviet outlay growth in the last half of the 1970s, from about 4 to about 2 percent per year. This change is reflected in the five entries in parentheses in column 8 of table 8–1. Again, DIA appears to concur in that estimate, although it maintains that outlays at current prices continued to increase at a rapid pace. Nevertheless, newspaper stories in the past few years have reported continuing disagreements between the CIA and DIA regarding the rate of growth of Soviet military spending. In June 1983 the DIA was said to claim on the basis of "an examination of only half the procurement budget," that the dollar cost of Soviet procurement rose 5 to 10 percent in 1983 over the previous year and the overall military budget increased 3 or 4 percent.[17] In early 1985, the DIA revised its 1983 procurement growth estimate slightly to an increase of 5 to 8 percent (apparently again, in terms of dollar costs), while the CIA is supposed to have estimated an increase of only 1 to 2 percent in the same year. On the other hand, a DIA analyst is quoted as saying that "we really don't take issue with" CIA estimates that after 1976 overall military expenditure grew in real terms by 2 percent annually.[18]

The DIA's official position in mid-1983 included the following separate estimates:

1. The dollar cost of all Soviet defense programs (at constant prices) increased at an average annual rate of 3 percent from 1970 to 1981, but there was a marked slowdown after 1976 to about 2 percent.

2. Soviet military spending in current rubles rose at a steady nominal rate of 6 or 7 percent annually between 1970 and 1981.

3. Military machinery output increased more rapidly in 1982 than the 5 percent attained by the machinery industry as a whole.[19]

The first estimate is consistent with CIA calculations at 1970 ruble prices. The second would be consistent with the CIA's if the military price level rose some 40 percent between 1970 and 1981, or about 3.5 percent per year. This seems high but is not beyond consideration.[20] The DIA's claim for a better than 5 percent increase in military machinery output in 1982 needs to be reconciled with the CIA estimate of a more or less zero real procurement growth in that year.[21] Moreover, the DIA apparently believed that military machinery output grew at an average rate of 11 percent per year between 1970 and 1982.[22]

The most recent official statement of the DIA position is circumspect but still unreconciled with CIA calculations. The growth of machinery output is estimated to have declined to an annual average rate of 5 to 8 percent during 1980-1983 compared to 8.6 percent in the previous four years; in the former period apparently, military machinery output outpaced that of civilian machinery, 6.3 percent to 5.0 percent; however, nothing is said about the relation to the trends in procurement.[23] As for the CIA, it apparently believes that the period of zero growth in procurement extended at least through 1982 and perhaps into 1983. If procurement increased in 1983, the growth was moderate.[24] These estimates are derived from direct costing of Soviet military weapons acquisition in dollars and 1970 rubles. DIA's 1983 claim of more rapid (real) procurement growth is also based on direct costing, done entirely in dollars. It is not clear whether the divergence between the two organizations is explained by differences in the unit prices used or in the estimates of physical quantities or both.

Defense Share of GNP

Table 8-2 displays the burden ratios—defense divided by GNP—that correspond to the outlay estimates of table 8-1. The official Soviet defense figures have been divided by figures of GNP at current prices, estimated from Western sources; the DIA burden ratios for years between the initial and terminal points of the series are similarly constructed; for the CIA ratios, the GNP denominator is a CIA estimate.[25]

The absurdity of the official Soviet claim, already apparent in the absolute figures of table 8-1, is underscored when defense is divided by GNP at current prices. These figures would indicate a burden diminishing to insignificance. In contrast, the minimum level in Western estimates is the 8 percent for 1977 presented by the 1979 SIPRI yearbook, and SIPRI subsequently revised that figure upward. By 1980, the SIPRI figure is about a third below the CIA estimate.[26]

SIPRI continues to believe that the Soviet burden is declining, mono-tonically.[27] In the CIA estimates, the ratio at 1970 factor cost has remained more or less constant over more than two decades. Lee and Rosefielde have charged the CIA with sharply underestimating the recent level and rate of growth of Soviet military outlays, and they picture increasing defense–GNP ratios. As compared with CIA, Lee and Rosefielde estimate considerably lower burden ratios in 1960 and 1965 and higher ones after 1970; Lee's figures also fall more slowly in the late 1950s because he estimates an 18 percent increase in military outlays, 1955–1960, whereas CIA believes real expendi-ture declined in that interval. After 1965, CIA's GNP and military outlay series increase more slowly than do those estimated by Lee or Rosefielde. DIA's burden estimate in current prices rises from 13 percent in 1970 to 15 percent in 1981. The most recent DIA statement declares that there took place an increase from 14 to 16 percent in 1980 to 15 to 17 percent "now in the mid-1980s."[28]

Lee's estimation of military outlays depends on the calculation of mili-tary procurement by the method of machinery residuals, a difficult and controversial procedure. Lee's GNP series is said to be "the result of a very modest effort—about 50 man days."[29] Rosefielde's GNP series is derived crudely by inflating official Soviet figures of net material product by 17 percent in all years.[30] It was also noted previously that the CIA denies the validity or relevance of Rosefielde's critique of the agency's expenditure estimates.

Igor Birman is another critic of the CIA estimates who believes the level of total Soviet military expenditure and the burden on the Soviet economy is much greater than the CIA reports. Birman has made no independent estimates of his own, and his dissent is based on two apparently unreconciled arguments.[31] First, a back-of-the-envelope calculation leads to the conclu-sion that military expenditure in 1970 must have considerably exceeded the CIA figure.[32] Second, distortions in Soviet prices and the favored position of the military sector mean that calculations of actual outlays understate their true level. These arguments are apparently not additive, for Birman concludes:

> In other words, the CIA is possibly right in estimating the share of [Soviet military expenditure] at 11–14 percent of GNP: according to Soviet book-keeping, these figures may be more or less correct (though the Soviets do not calculate GNP). But bookkeeping procedures do not reflect the realities of the Soviet economy, the actual economic burden of the military. If we take into account this factor, our estimate of the military share of GNP will skyrocket. How much? Hard to say, but I will risk suggesting that it will be not less than 20 percent of GNP, or even higher.[33]

The first argument is flimsy but the second, although not novel, involves a more substantial issue.

Table 8-2
Defense-GNP Ratio, Various Estimates, 1955–1983
(percentage)

	Soviet Official Defense[a]	SIPRI 1979	SIPRI 1980–1981	SIPRI 1982–1983	Lee Current Prices	Lee 1970 Prices[b]	Rosefielde 1970 Prices	DIA	CIA 1970 Factor Cost
1955	9.0				11.5				17
1956	7.6				9.5				15
1957	6.5				8.7				13
1958	5.9	11.0			8.6				12
1959	5.5	11.2			8.7				11
1960	5.1	10.4	12.4		8.9		10		12
1961	6.2	12.3			9.7				12
1962	6.3	12.5			10.2				13
1963	6.3	13.4			10.4				14
1964	5.8	11.9			10.2				14
1965	5.1	10.7	12.8		10.2				13
1966	5.0	10.5			10.0	11.0	10.1		13
1967	5	10.5			10.5	11.5			13
1968	5	11.0			11.4	12.3			13
1969	5	10.9			11.8	12.8			13
1970	4.7	10.0	12.0		11.7	12.9	14	13	13
1971	4	9.7	9.7			13.6		13	12
1972	4	9.6	9.6	11.4		13.7		13	13
1973	4	9.0	9.0	10.8		14.5		13	12
1974	4	8.7	8.7	10.4		14.8		13	13
1975	4	8.6	10.3	10.3	14.5[c]	15.5	15.3	14	13
1976	3	8.3	9.9	9.9				14	13
1977	3	8.0	9.6	9.5			16.5	14	13
1978	3		9.4	9.2				15	13
1979	3			9.0				15	13
1980	3			8.8		19.4[d]		15	14(13)
1981	3			8.7				15	13-14

13-14

| 1982 | 2 |
| 1983 | 2 |

Sources: Soviet official defense: Defense figures from table 8-1 divided by GNP estimates as follows: 1955 from Abram Bergson, *The Real National Income of Soviet Russia since 1928*, (Cambridge: Harvard University Press, 1961), p. 300; 1956–1957 from Nancy Nimitz, *Soviet National Income and Product, 1956–1958*, RM-3112-PR (Santa Monica: Rand, June 1962), p. 6; 1958–1964 from Abraham S. Becker, *Soviet National Income and Product, 1958–1964*, (Berkeley and Los Angeles: University of California Press, 1969), p. 23; 1965–1966 from Sally Anderson, *Soviet National Income 1964–1966, in Established Prices, RM-5705-PR*, (Santa Monica: Rand, September 1968), p. 7; *1970, 1976, and 1980, from CIA, Soviet Gross National Product in Current Prices, 1960–1980*, SOV 83-10037, (March 1983), p. 2; 1967–1969, 1971–1975, 1977–1979, and 1981–1983 estimated from Soviet reported NMP inflated by the ratio of GNP to NMP (assumed to grow linearly from 1.30 for 1966 to 1.32 for 1970 and 1.38 for 1976, and to remain stable at 1.38, as implied by the available GNP estimates compared to NMP in these years). NMP figures are taken from various issues of *Narkhoz* (the Soviet statistical yearbooks, *Narodnoe khoziaistvo SSSR*): 1958–1964, *Narkhoz 1965*, p. 589; 1965–1978, *Narkhoz 1978*, p. 385; 1979, *Narkhoz 1980*, p. 379; 1980, 1983, *Narkhoz 1983*, p. 407; 1981, 1982, *Narkhoz 1982*, p. 378.

SIPRI 1979: *SIPRI Yearbook 1979*, pp. 38–39; *1980–1981: SIPRI Yearbook 1980*, p. 29, 1981, p. 166. *1982–1983: SIPRI Yearbook 1982*, p. 150 and 1983, p. 171. While the SIPRI tables declare that the denominator of the ratio is gross domestic product, the notes following the tables indicate that GNP was used for Warsaw Treaty Organization countries. For the three SIPRI series, GNP is computed by converting a 1975 figure in dollars, estimated from data provided by Ruth Sivard (*World Military and Social Expenditure* [Leesburg, Va.: WMSE Publications, March 1978], p. 21), and moving that figure by Soviet reported changes in net material product.

Lee, current prices: *The Estimation of Soviet Defense Expenditures*, p. 97. I have calculated the percentages from Lee's data. On p. 98, Lee presents the percentages directly, but for unknown reasons they diverge from the figures implied by the values for numerator and denominator of the ratio supplied on p. 97.

Lee, 1970 prices: *CIA Estimates of Soviet Defense Spending*, p. 22, table 3. These percentages would be somewhat lower if the defense expenditure numerators were taken from the midpoints of ranges given in table 2 of the same source page. However, Lee prefers the upper end of the range and cited these figures in his table 3.

Rosefielde, 1970 prices. Rosefielde, *False Science*, p. 201. Rosefielde computes the GNP denominator from Soviet NMP using the inflation ratio 1.17 (ibid., p. 198), citing Rush Greenslade, "The Real Gross National Product of the USSR, 1950–1975," in *Soviet Economy in a New Perspective*, Joint Economic Committee, U.S. Congress, Washington, D.C., 1976.

DIA: 1970 and 1981: *Allocation of Resources in the Soviet Union and China—1983*, p. 23. Other years: outlays from table 8-1 divided by GNP at current prices as derived for the official defense figures.

CIA: 1955–1980: Table 8-1 figures divided by GNP at 1970 factor cost from *USSR: Measures of Economic Growth*, pp. 52–54. 1981–1982: *Allocation of Resources in the Soviet Union and China—1983*, pp. 214, 231.

[a]The denominator is GNP, Western estimates.

[b]See note b to table 8-1 with respect to the defense numerator; nothing is said about the prices of GNP.

[c]"Projection."

[d]"Forecast."

Apart from the possibilities of estimating error, the CIA series has the important drawback of using 1970 prices. The burden of defense in any year is best measured in terms of the then-relevant trade-offs: usually this would be the prices of the same year or perhaps those of a closely neighboring year—assuming that relative prices correspond approximately to real relative costs. If the defense–GNP ratio cannot be measured in prices of each given year, second best would be a calculation in a linked set of constant prices, with the links as short as the data allow.[34]

In the absence of such calculations, what can be said about the likely trend of the burden? The change over time in the ratio of defense to GNP can be viewed as the product of the change in the physical volume of burden multiplied by the change in the relative price of defense.[35] If we may take the former to be represented by CIA's 1970 factor-cost calculations, which show a virtually stable trend, the trend in the burden ratio will depend largely on the change in price of defense relative to that of GNP. The economic theory of index numbers suggests that the relative price of defense, or at least that of defense procurement, should decline. Presumably the pace of technological change is more rapid in military industry than in the rest of the economy, which should be reflected in relatively larger reductions of average cost over time as production of new products is mastered.[36] This does not necessarily mean a decline in the average price level of military procurement—it seems highly likely that procurement prices rose on the average over the decade—only that military prices rose less rapidly than the average price of nonmilitary GNP.[37]

The converse is possible, however, and may even be likely. If DIA accepts the CIA's estimates of military outlays at 1970 factor cost, DIA's own current price estimates of the burden, which rise from 13 to 15 percent over the 1970s, imply an increase in the military price level of some 40 percent during that period, or approximately 3.5 percent per year. Comparison of the change in CIA estimates of GNP, 1970–1980, valued at current and constant prices implies an overall price level increase of about 21 percent, or roughly 2 percent per year.[38] If these estimates hold up on detailed reexamination, they indicate that the burden expressed in 1980 prices is higher than that calculated in 1970 prices. Assuming that price movement in military procurement is the most significant element in the change of the relative price of military outlays, it would be hypothesized that the Soviet military bought relatively more of the hardware whose average production costs were declining slowly and relatively less of the weaponry whose costs were moving rapidly down the production learning curve. Such behavior might be self-defeating in a market but could be rational in an arms competition where one's adversary was more technologically sophisticated and was seeking to convert that advantage into higher-quality armaments.

With these inconclusive judgments in mind, it is therefore prudent to minimize the interpretive weight placed on the CIA figures in table 8-2. It appears probable that the burden of defense as measured by the defense-GNP ratio was reduced after the death of Stalin. According to CIA, military expenditure began a monotonic climb in 1960, which has not yet reached an end. Over the next two decades, military expenditure increased about two and a half times and GNP somewhat less,[39] thus resulting in a rough stabilization of the burden. The absolute level of the defense-GNP ratio may be altered when CIA estimates are updated to a new price base.

Whatever the updated numbers may turn out to be, there is no question that the share of GNP allocated to military spending in the Soviet Union far exceeds that of the United States and by a wider margin still that of any of its NATO allies. At the height of the Vietnam war, the U.S. defense-GNP ratio was less than 10 percent, and it fell almost continuously until 1979, reaching a low of 5 percent. Even under current spending programs of the Reagan administration, the U.S. ratio is not likely to rise above 7 to 9 percent at most. To match the Soviet ratio, one must look to the countries engaged in Middle East arms races, but the Soviet ratio has been maintained for more than two decades, an unprecedented duration even in the Middle East.[40] Assuming that something like 13 to 15 percent is an acceptable reading of the current ratio of Soviet military outlays to GNP, is this the true measure of Soviet defense burden? The CIA estimates have been criticized as too low by some and too high by others. For the most part, these criticisms judge the estimates within their own definitional framework, but is that framework itself appropriate? Two sets of considerations apply.

First, to weigh the social costs of military activity requires a comprehensive measure of what is military. Conventional measures of military expenditure are generally limited in scope, defined largely by the functions of the institutions identified with the military (ministries or departments of defense). This results in both overestimation and underestimation of total military outlays, the former through inclusion of military agency expenditure primarily benefiting the civil economy (such as, civil construction) and the latter through exclusion of outlays by civil agencies that are primarily military in character (such as civil defense, industrial hardening, and emergency preparedness planning). In the case of the Soviet Union, the exclusions seem to be much more significant than the inclusions because the economy is more highly militarized relative to Western societies. The major examples of uncounted military outlays relate to the cost of maintaining reserve facilities for expansion of military output and other elements of mobilization potential, including strategic reserves.

Conventionally, also, burden is associated with military expenditure. But the opportunity costs of a state's international stance with respect to a major adversary (or set of adversaries) may encompass much more than outlays in the military sector. Should one include the effect of Soviet autarkic trade policies—whether the near-total autarky of mature Stalinism or the more limited policies, centered primarily on agriculture, of the Brezhnev period—or the costs of developing and maintaining the Soviet empire (such as subsidies to Eastern Europe or Cuba)?[41] Similarly, should the U.S. burden incorporate the costs of maintaining national and alliance-wide trade controls or the costs of U.S. international involvement that form part of and are traceable to the global competition with the Soviet Union? Most analysts have concluded that there is more merit in restricting the concept of defense burden to outlays that are identifiably military.

Second, to measure the sacrifice of civil output forgone, resources devoted to military (and nonmilitary) uses should be valued at opportunity cost.[42] Ordinarily this is understood in Western economic theory as the marginal factor cost of the military good or service—that is, the cost of the factors of production that must be diverted from other uses to produce one additional unit of the particular military good or service. Observed prices may understate the true social cost of that marginal reallocation because of such pricing practices as paying military labor less than the wage it could earn in civilian employment or government subsidies to manufacturers of military equipment. On the other hand, social opportunity costs may be overstated by prevailing prices if draftees are being trained in a skill that will increase their productivity in civilian production or if technology developed in military industry and paid for through military procurement spills over to civilian industry without charge.

These or similar divergences between actual prices and true social opportunity cost are to be found in many developed Western countries. On the whole, however, because these states are market economies, a rough approximation to opportunity cost can be obtained from prevailing prices, perhaps with suitable discounts or supplements to allow for the divergences observed. Such a correspondence cannot be assumed for the Soviet Union because it is a centrally directed economy where prices are largely administered. The very meaning of price as a measure of opportunity cost must be questioned.

To allow for the major distortions inherent in Soviet prices, CIA estimates of the burden are obtained by adjusting ruble values of defense and GNP to a factor cost basis. However, it has been argued that the true opportunity cost of Soviet defense is understated by the estimates employing adjusted factor costs because they do not reflect the costs imposed on the civilian economy by the military-favoring priority system that is one of the essential operating mechanisms of the Soviet economy. For example, military industry is supplied with scarce, high-quality resources often unavailable to civilian industry; the pick of production in dual-line plants may be taken for military needs, leaving the inferior product for civil use; in the event of shortages, military programs tend to be protected, leaving civil activities to cope as they can. In addition, the walls of insulation that for so long separated civil and military economies and that still today are only partly permeated have hindered spillovers of usable military innovation in products, processes or, to a lesser extent, organization.[43]

There is probably considerable merit in these critiques, and it would be useful to develop a broader measure of the Soviet burden, taking the elements of greater Soviet militarization and the opportunity costs of military priority into account.[44] However, three qualifications might be borne in mind. First, any comparative analysis of burden would have to consider the uncounted elements of U.S. (or other NATO) military expenditures. Outlays for mobilization planning, for example, are probably much lower in the West than in the East, but they are not now included in defense outlays. Other types of military-related outlays can also be found in the West. Second, some Soviet expenditures now counted by CIA do not burden the civil economy or do so only partially because they benefit civilian activities. Examples are education and health outlays on the armed forces that raise the productivity of demobilized recruits, use of troops and transport to help bring in the harvest, and use of construction troops to build civilian facilities. Thus, any effort to calculate the true burden must subtract from as well as add to the CIA estimates. Third, the scale of the opportunity costs of Soviet defense depends on one's reference point. If these costs are to be measured in terms of the production potential of the economy's resource endowment and the state of technical knowledge, they will be very large indeed. However, it would require a radical reorganization of the Soviet economy to attain that potential. The concept of opportunity costs in the Soviet Union should be related to the set of output possibilities that allows for the structural inefficiencies of the Soviet bureaucratized and centrally managed economy. If opportunity is considered in terms of what the economy realistically may be capable of achieving, given its systemic inefficiences, those costs will be smaller.

These considerations should not obscure several important conclusions that emerge from the data:

1. The Soviet Union allocates a share of its GNP to military expenditure (as it is conventionally viewed) that is far higher than counterparts in the West. By and large, this conclusion is not seriously disputed outside the Soviet Union.

2. The measured defense–GNP ratio understates the actual proportion of Soviet aggregate output that is devoted to military security requirements. This is probably true in the West as well, but the gap is surely larger in the Soviet Union.

3. More than likely, the proportional defense drain on national resources is less now than at Stalin's demise, although this is controversial. But the

impressive growth of the economy that took place in the three decades post-Stalin was paralleled by a military development effort, building on the foundations of economic modernization, that brought the Soviet Union superpower status.

Burden and the Slowdown

Had the Kremlin persisted in the rate of military buildup and modernization of the first Brezhnev decade, the defense share of Soviet GNP would have increased sharply in the late 1970s and early 1980s. If the post-1976 slowdown, largely the result of the flattening of procurement growth, is real and not an artifact of CIA's methodology, is the explanation that the Politburo decided to avoid increasing an already heavy burden?[45]

In its initial efforts to explain the change in its estimates, the agency attributed the prolonged slowdown "to a complex combination of factors, including technical problems, economic bottlenecks, and perhaps even policy decisions."[46] This language implies greater stress on the objective factors than on conscious policy acts. The deputy director of CIA made this explicit: "it is my judgment . . . that the decline in the rate of growth of procurement is tied principally to forces beyond [Soviet] control at this point."[47] DIA went further, maintaining that the Soviet "military retains top priority with regard to resources" and denying that the flattening of procurement growth was evidence of a "change or shift in priorities away from defense." Rather, "it is an attempt to try to cope with their food problem that they have had in the last three years."[48] A DIA analyst demurred at the argument "that if Soviet officials did not plan the slower defense production growth rate they at least did not take steps to assure continuation of the earlier faster rate," countering, "I do not think it is a question of accepting it, sir. I think it is the result of the conditions in the economy, having to cope with the transportation and agricultural problems."[49]

With the defense expenditure slowdown extending into 1982 or 1983, however, CIA in 1984 acknowledged that "this plateau arguably lasted too long to be the result exclusively of bottlenecks or technological problems." A policy decision had to be postulated, and now the bottlenecks and mastering difficulties are downgraded to a "supporting role."[50] If the retardation was in fact a matter of policy, why did Soviet leaders make such an unexpected decision?

One possible category of explanation is that Soviet leaders at last found their own answer to the classic question, How much is enough? Thus, some U.S. analysts are tempted to associate the defense spending slowdown with the development of the "Tula line" in Soviet military doctrine. Beginning with a speech in Tula in January 1977, Brezhnev (and other political and military leaders) on a number of occasions denied that the Soviet Union was seeking superiority, declared nuclear war unwinnable, and claimed that Moscow's goal was parity and reduction of armament levels. The tight restraint on procurement after 1976 would then be a proof of the reality of that doctrinal change.[51] In a related fashion, the slowdown might be viewed as a policy decision flowing from the logic of SALT I:

> Since the principles of the agreement were quite explicitly made the centerpiece of Soviet security policy, it is a reasonable inference that both the commitment to maintaining an evolving balance of forces and the detailed restrictions designed to preserve it were incorporated into Soviet defense plans and that the overall moderation of Soviet military procurement and the reallocation of investment are the consequences of implementing these restrictions.[52]

James McConnell, finding that doctrinal emphasis shifted to conventional forces, links reductions in investment and military expenditure growth after 1975 to the Soviet Union's "shift to a much longer conventional phase [in the canonical scenario of central war] and then to an independent protracted conventional option."[53]

Richard Kaufman, in the first serious analysis of the revised CIA estimates, analyzes DIA time series on numbers of Soviet weapons produced and deployed and finds declines in most strategic offensive systems but an upward trend in conventional systems. He offers the hypothesis that "there was a deliberate change in military investment priorities to reduce the emphasis on strategic offensive systems while continuing to emphasize theater nuclear and most categories of conventional forces."[54] Considering lead times involved in system development, Kaufman suggests that the decision was taken in the late 1960s or early 1970s in connection with the formulation of the Ninth Five Year Plan and on the eve of the SALT I agreements.[55] The Kaufman hypothesis seems consistent with the category of policy explanations one might call "so much is enough," although Kaufman refrains from making links to doctrinal change and remains explicitly agnostic on the relative weight of technical, economic, or policy factors in the ultimate explanation of the slowdown.

It would require a much more detailed examination of the interrelations among many factors—external threat perception, military doctrine, deployments, R&D patterns, production links, military outlay structure, and general economic policy—than can be attempted here or that the available data possibly allow to venture a firmer judgment on the role of military policy change in the slowdown. But one additional piece of evidence is intriguing. The CIA's deputy director for intelligence has stated that "the most striking feature of service spending is that all services shared in the reduced growth in spending ... the rate of growth of total spending in all the services decreased substantially," although the strategic rocket forces (SRF) and the air defense forces were particularly hard hit, suffering absolute declines in outlays.[56] If the slowdown was related only to Soviet strategic restraint and the SALT I agreements, one might have forecast compensating increases in theater nuclear and conventional forces, but apparently these branches too had their weapons acquisition plans cut back. Whether doctrinal changes underlay the sharp pruning of outlays on the SRF and the PVO, it seems difficult to make the same argument for the reduction in the rate of growth of outlays on the other services. Bearing in mind the long duration of the retardation, the inference seems strong that economic issues were also at stake.

Kaufman declares that the prolonged slowdown casts doubt on the assertions "that the Kremlin fails to consider costs as a major factor in its decision about the military or that the defense sector is impervious to problems in the economy." The latter assertion is indeed an oversimplification often encountered and rarely challenged, but the former was untenable long before the slowdown. After all, Soviet military expenditure before 1976 was increasing at 4, not 8 or 16, percent per year, and it could not have been entirely by accident that this rate of defense spending was roughly within the bounds of the growth of the economy. As Holloway notes, the issue is not cost consciousness but policy priorities.[57] In the late 1970s and early 1980s, the CIA continued to forecast a trend rate of growth because it presumed a high level of Soviet concern about the U.S. and NATO military threat, foresaw cost escalation due to the increasing complexity of new weapons, believed that there was a strong momentum in the Soviet weapons development-production-procurement cycle, with a large number of programs under development or near deployment, and credited the Soviet military decision makers with both unwillingness to slow the Soviet military effort and the power to secure their wishes.[58] The first three factors may well have been true, but the leadership's weighing of the trade-offs was apparently misread. It is plain that considerably more research is needed on the political economics of the resource allocation decisions underlying the Ninth, Tenth, and Eleventh Five Year Plans (FYPs). No definitive judgments can be rendered in advance of such study, but a few comments can be ventured.

It is a commonplace in the West to point to a major political-economic policy dilemma faced by Soviet leaders in the 1980s. During the first decade of the Brezhnev period, the economy was growing rapidly enough (although at a slower pace than in the 1950s) to allow for moderate rates of increase of consumption, investment, and defense. All the chief claimants on the national output were being satisfied with rising absolute allocations. But in the second decade, that became increasingly difficult to accomplish as aggregate growth rates slowed alarmingly. Indeed, the Tenth FYP, covering

1976-1980, provided for a sharp cut in the rate of growth of investment. The cutback was partly linked with the regime's desire to protect the claim of consumption, but as long as it was believed that Soviet military expenditures were continuing to grow at the trend rate of 4 or 5 percent per year, the Tenth FYP also appeared to be reallocating investment resources to defense.[59] If in fact procurement leveled off after 1976 and as a conscious government act, was the decision partly necessitated by the planned cutback in investment growth? Only partly, if at all, because investment resources would still increase, although at a much reduced rate, and the deceleration effect would damp down the growth rate of military production capacity only with a considerable time lag.

The Tenth FYP cutback in the rate of investment growth appears to have been a decision without much relation to the military budget. Its main rationale was the alarming rise in capital output ratios and the hope that change in the structure of investment and concentration on commissioning new assets would reverse that trend. The planners expected—at least publicly—only small further drops in the aggregate growth rate and in per capita consumption.[60] Moreover, machinery and metalworking production was scheduled for a 53 percent increase, whereas the equipment component of fixed investment was to grow by a considerably smaller margin.[61] Hence, there seems little reason to believe that military outlay plans were trimmed then as a necessary consequence of the investment decision.

The basic assumption of the Tenth FYP's investment-consumption trade-off was hollow. Reduction of the rate of growth of investment did not stimulate an increase in productivity but may have in fact contributed to the sharp downturn in industrial production growth in the late 1970s.[62] Investment rose more rapidly than planned, but output growth declined sharply. Curiously, however, the 1975-1976 investment cutback decision was reconfirmed in the Eleventh Plan (1981-1986) when the five-year investment increase was set at the lowest level since World War II (about 10 percent); state sector capital investment in each of the last three years of the plan was to be no greater than 5 to 7 percent over the 1980 level. Even so, real income per head was scheduled to increase at 3.1 percent per year compared to the 3.3 percent claimed as achieved in 1976-1980.[63]

Whatever the explanation of the military expenditure slowdown in 1977-1978—technical problems, particular bottlenecks, or a policy decision—one might speculate that the severe difficulties the economy experienced in 1979-1982 would have given the Politburo pause if it intended at that time to get back to the trend line of military procurement growth. Over those four years GNP increased only 1.5 percent in aggregate, while new fixed investment rose about 8 percent. Maintenance of the military outlay slowdown probably enabled the regime to provide some consumption growth, a maximum of about 1 to 1.5 percent per year per capita.[64] Several Western studies of

Soviet resource allocation trade-offs imply relatively large opportunity cost penalties for accelerating Soviet military spending under conditions of sluggish productivity growth. Perhaps these were among the arguments that Brezhnev made two weeks before his death when he apparently defended himself against his generals' complaints.[65]

Current Economic Prospects

The Eleventh FYP has produced mixed results in the official perception. Among the selected indicators in table 8-3, targets for utilized national income, industrial output, and agricultural production were missed in two of the four years, while industrial labor productivity failed to meet its target in any year. On the other hand, investment plans were consistently exceeded. The plan intended to keep investment within severe constraints, allowing an overall five year increase of only 10.4 percent; instead total investment increased more than 16 percent by 1984. The average annual rate of growth through 1984 is a percentage point below target for industrial production, industrial labor productivity, and real income per head, more than two

Table 8-3
Selected Major Indicators of Economic Change in the Eleventh FYP
(1985 annual percentage increases)

	1981–1985 Plan Average Annual[a] Increase	1981 FYP	1981 Actual	1982 FYP	1982 Actual	1983 FYP	1983 Actual	1984 FYP	1984 Actual
National income utilized	3.4	3.4	3.2	2.6	3.5	3.5	3.6	3.1	2.6
Industrial production	4.7	4.1	4.0	3.9	2.3	4.3	4.2	5.1	4.2
Industrial labor productivity	4.2	3.6	2.6	3.3	2.5	4.1	3.6	4.6	3.8
Agricultural production	4.8[b]	n.a.	-1.0	n.a.	5.5	n.a.	6.1	n.a.	0
Freight turnover, all transport	3.6	4.0	3.5	2.1	1.5	3.5	4.8	4.1	2.9
Total fixed investment	2.0	n.a.	4.2	n.a.	3.3	n.a.	6.0	n.a.	2.0
State fixed investment	1.1[c]	4.0	4.2	-0.7	3.5	2.2	5.4	1.2	n.a.
Real income per head	3.1	2.9	3.4	2.8	0	3.4	2.0	2.7	3.0

Source: FYP: *Izvestiia*, November 18, 20, 1981. Actual: *Narkhoz 1983*, pp. 39, 41–42, 212, 314, 355, 408; *Pravda*, 26 January 1985.

[a]Implied by terminal year index number or stated in plan announcement.

[b]Implied by the 1976–1980 value sum (*Narkhoz 1980*, p. 202) and the target of a 13 percent increase in the average annual volume of production compared with 1976–1980.

[c]Average of five-year sum of percentage changes.

points below for agricultural output. Presumably the better showing of freight transportation and the overfulfillment of investment targets are the main reasons why utilized national income shows an average annual growth rate only slightly below the FYP goal (3.2 versus 3.4 percent).[66]

The actual growth of the indicators in table 8-3 is probably tangibly less than shown because of the distortions of Soviet economic statistics. The CIA estimates GNP growth as only 2.1 percent in 1981, 2.6 percent in 1982, 3.2 percent in 1983, and back down to 2 percent in 1984. Industrial production is estimated to have gone up by only a little over 2 percent annually in 1981-1982 and consumption by less than 3 percent in the two years combined (thus allowing only a 1.3 percent increase in per capita consumption, compared to the claimed 3.4 percent growth in real income per head). However, the CIA estimates a recovery of industrial production in the last two years to about 3.5 percent annually.[67]

Prior to Gorbachev's accession, most Western observers agreed that the Soviet economy was not likely to show much better results during the rest of the decade. Traditional extensive growth was hindered by the sharp decline in rate of new entrants to the labor force and the problems of increasing capital investment. The intensive growth that Soviet leaders had been seeking for more than a decade eluded them because of the difficulty of raising productivity. Capital productivity has fallen almost continuously over the past thirty years, and labor productivity is growing much more slowly than anticipated. Up to 1984, the combined (factor) productivity of inputs of land, labor, and capital had been negative by CIA measure in every year but one since 1973.[68] Because the stagnation of productivity was so clearly related to the structural rigidities of the Soviet economy, it seemed apparent that the economic growth record would not turn much brighter without substantial policy change. Neither of Brezhnev's immediate successors seemed interested in or capable of carrying through such a change.

With the arrival of the younger, studiedly vigorous Gorbachev at the party helm, the question of Soviet economic prospects is raised anew. How much growth mileage can Gorbachev get out of discipline campaigns—against corruption, drunkenness, and sloth? How much change in the economic mechanism will he attempt and with what effect? The answers to such questions remain obscure, but it seems likely that the former category of issues—the exploitation of the economy's reserves—is more a matter of short-term relief than longer-term solution to the growth problem. The latter would require major "improvements in the economic mechanism," to use the Soviets' preferred replacement term for economic "reform."

In a study of Soviet resource allocation trade-offs using an optimal control model, Hopkins and Kennedy concluded that growth prospects in the 1980s were bound to be worse than in the 1970s unless productivity turned sharply upward.[69] If in the 1970s the economy managed a 3 percent per annum growth rate of consumption while increasing military expenditure at 4.5 percent (the conventional view at the date of publication), the same pace of military expansion would bring total consumption growth down to 2.5 percent; alternatively, a 3 percent growth rate of consumption in the 1980s would allow only a 2 percent increase of military expenditure.[70] Wharton Econometric Forecasting Associates has developed an econometric model of the Soviet economy (SOVMOD), and several of its earlier analyses were discussed elsewhere.[71] A more recent paper from this organization indicates baseline results similar to those of Hopkins–Kennedy: with defense outlays growing at 4.5 percent per year in the 1980s, total consumption and consumption per capita are limited to 2.5 and 1.6 percent, respectively. This scenario assumes "hesitant and only moderate growth in trade with the West." The key assumption clearly is the size of total factor productivity growth. It increases at an average rate of 1.1 percent, derived from the 1968–1978 estimated average for major sectors.[72] This rate seems high relative to Soviet experience during most of the 1970s as calculated by the CIA.

Another simulation of Soviet trade-offs, using a different type of model, was more pessimistic for the Soviet latitude of choice. Hildebrandt found that a 4.5 percent per year growth in military expenditure during the 1980s would allow a per capita consumption increase of only 0.3 percent per year—hence, total consumption growth of little more than 1 percent per year.[73]

For present purposes, the interest in the three studies cited is not which is correct. The interpretation of the results of model simulations depends on the nature of the model: its assumptions, form of the functions, and values of key parameters. All three, however, point up the serious choice problems imposed on the Soviet leadership by the combination of objective factors— primarily the decline in the rate of growth of labor inputs (to which one might also add the increasing cost of the changing geography of raw material production)—and the sharp decline in system productivity. If the economy is to escape its fundamental growth dilemma in the next decade, it will be only by attacking the productivity problem.

The importance of this conclusion is underscored by considering the significance of the help resulting from cutting back on defense costs. The various simulation studies have generally agreed that the overall growth benefits derived just from trimming military expenditure growth are limited. Although the defense budget is sizable, the changes postulated in these studies and the magnitude of the actual spending slowdown are small relative to the very large volume of fixed capital in the society. Referring back to table 8–1, the difference between military expenditure maintained after 1976 at an assumed rate of 4.5 percent and the actual constrained series would have amounted to about 37 billion (1970) rubles by 1982. If this sum consisted entirely of forgone hardware acquisition, painlessly translatable into investment resources, and ignoring the differences in prices between the various data sets, it would have augmented industrial investment over the period by 13 percent, but it would have added only about 6 percent to the value of the industrial capital stock at the end of 1981.[74]

Thus the cutbacks would have to be more substantial and prolonged to have a significant effect on the growth rate of GNP. Depending on how the savings were reallocated, the effect on consumption could be more apparent.[75] Assuming that savings in military procurement are allocated to capital formation, Hildebrandt was most pessimistic among the studies cited, estimating only a 0.5 percent increase per year in per capita consumption when the defense budget was frozen at the assumed 1980 level. Hopkins and Kennedy were most optimistic. In their base case, freezing the defense budget yielded an increase in the per capita consumption growth rate of 1 percent. Only if the defense outlay change was accompanied by other measures that raised the productivity of resources in use—economic reform and increased imports of Western technology, for example—would the effects become substantial, even in the medium term.

These results assume that the same resources are equally productive in different uses. If defense resources are considerably more productive than civilian resources, there should be a boost to growth prospects over the long run.[76] But according to Hildebrandt, this is a very long run, for the effects on productive capacity and consumption even during a decade will be miniscule.[77] To the extent that the defense freeze contributes to elimination of bottlenecks and shortages, some additional relief in the civil production sector may be anticipated.

Thus, it is hardly surprising that the six- or seven-year military procurement freeze has not rejuvenated the Soviet economic growth rate, although the record probably would have been worse without the spending constraint. What are the prospects for the near future? Continuation of the slowdown would mean further slow accretion of transferable resources for the civilian economy. Deeper cuts, involving actual and substantial reductions in the absolute level of spending, seem improbable, given the Kremlin's view of the U.S. military threat and of the political costs of such a response to the militant foreign policy of the Reagan administration. Among the restrictive options, a more interesting alternative would be to curb the military priority system.[78] The latter's effects on the civil economy are difficult to measure, but they may have become increasingly important in the Brezhnev period.

The growth of Soviet military power, along with the growth of the economic foundations on which it rested, were the prime goals of the economic system implanted on the Soviet Union by Stalin. With its organizational apparatus and central directive mechanisms, the economic system was geared to the promotion of these goals by a strategy of mobilization of resources. Mobilization processes tended to ignore considerations of initiative, innovation, and productivity. But resource constraints have forced the leaders to recognize the need to move from extensive to intensive growth strategies. At this point there has emerged an embarrassing contradiction between the requirements for future growth and the system of production. The chief structural deficiencies of the system are perverse incentives, overcentralization, and bureaucratization, but the dead hand of the military priority system is an important contributor. Once, the priority system was essential to ensuring the implementation of regime goals, which involved, among other things, the subordination of consumer interests. In recent years, the priority system has helped to undermine the limited efforts to raise civil-sector productivity. This problem significantly complicates the economic policy choices of the last half of the 1980s.

It is an important conclusion of the various simulation studies that the effects of accelerating Soviet military spending can be considerably more marked than those of freezing the budget. If the annual increase in the defense budget is raised from a hypothesized 4.5 to 7.5 percent, per capita consumption stagnates in the Hopkins-Kennedy model and turns negative in the Hildebrandt and SOVMOD models.[79] Additional production bottlenecks and shortages that might result from increasing the pace of defense spending would inflict heavier penalties on consumption and overall growth.

Accelerated defense spending poses grave dangers for the economy and the society unless productivity is sharply raised; even if military budget growth is cut to zero, the short-run economic effects will be small without additional help from improvements in productivity. Productivity is the key to unlocking the Soviet growth dilemma. Each of the Brezhnev successors has seemed to appreciate, at least in principle, that simple but fundamental reality. On acceding to the general secretaryship, Gorbachev demanded "a decisive turn in transferring the national economy onto the tracks of intensive development." But coming to grips with the bedrock causes of Soviet productivity lag will be a challenging task.

Implications for Future Defense Spending

Gorbachev's dilemma is essentially Brezhnev's dilemma. Personality differences lead to different styles of leadership and to different approaches to management, but the nature of the Soviet economic problem has not changed in the brief Andropov–Chernenko interregnum, and neither have the costs of either radical action of temporizing. Both options risk significant political dangers, the one through high-level group conflict or direct loss of control and the other through the indirect effects or rampant alienation or possibly increasing popular unrest. It is not surprising that the likely effects on the near- or mid-term course of the Soviet defense budget seem much as they appeared before Brezhnev's demise.[80]

For more than a decade, the Brezhnev regime's view of Soviet security requirements had seemed poorly connected to the real spending behavior of its major adversaries. The Soviet Union's propensity to expand its military expenditure from year to year appeared rooted in security concepts that posed almost open-ended demands for military resources; it was anchored in a political structure that fused party and military in unchallenged control of policy formation and implementation on security issues. There was considerable momentum behind the Soviet military buildup and reason to believe that any rationale for changing course would be strongly resisted. Nonetheless, it is now believed that the real rate of growth of Soviet military outlays was cut in half beginning in 1977. The full explanation of the slowdown remains to be worked out, but, assuming the phenomenon is real, one fact stands out as a beacon in the fog: the Kremlin allowed it to continue. However concerned it may have been about U.S. intentions and actions in the late 1970s and early 1980s, the Brezhnev Politburo decided not to attempt to intensify its national military effort. It is hard to avoid the conclusion that the country's economic condition worried the leadership even more. To avert the strains of accelerating military spending, Moscow attempted to degrade the security threat by political and diplomatic action. That apparently continued to be the main Kremlin strategy in the interregnum, assuming the defense budget slowdown was maintained into 1983.

Soviet growth retardation may be an even more palpable concern to Gorbachev than it was to Brezhnev. There is, too, some prospect of slowing the U.S. military drive through U.S. domestic economic and political pressures, especially now that arms control negotiations have been resumed in Geneva. Under these conditions, the strategy of political erosion of the Western security threat while holding the line on defense spending still seems the Politburo's best bet.

Such a judgment should not inspire Western complacency. Economic difficulties would not prevent a vigorous Kremlin response to perceived intensification of the external threat beyond some threshold. In that event, the domestic economic and political costs would be faced squarely, with results that could cast Soviet society back into its dark age. The challenge for Western policy is to retain a balance between pressure and promise, one that exploits the Soviet economic dilemma without inadvertently pushing Moscow into a resolution threatening world peace and any possibility of domestic liberalization.

Notes

1. *Bartlett's Quotations* cites a variant attributed to William Ralph Inge: "A man may build himself a throne of bayonets, but he cannot sit on it."
2. A.S. Becker, *The Burden of Soviet Defense. A Political-Economic Essay* (Santa Monica: Rand Corporation, R02752-AF, October 1981), p. 35.

3. See my testimony in *CIA Estimates of Soviet Defense Spending*, Hearings before the Subcommittee on Oversight of the Permanent Select Committee on Intelligence, House of Representatives, Washington, D.C., 1980, pp. 32–42.

4. For a discussion of the possible meaning of these numbers, see Robert Leggett and Sheldon T. Rabin, "A Note on the Meaning of the Soviet Defense Budget," *Soviet Studies* 30 (October 1978).

5. See the sources cited in Becker, *Burden of Soviet Defense*, pp. 13, 15; see also Leggett and Rabin, "Note on the Meaning."

6. Between 1974 and 1979, SIPRI'S estimates represented a 30 percent inflation of the official figures. See *World Armaments and Disarmament, SIPRI Yearbook 1974* (Cambridge: MIT Press, 1974), p. 190. (The yearbook titles vary only in the year of reference; hereafter, they are cited as *SIPRI* and the year.)

7. *SIPRI 1979* (London and New York: Crane Russak, 1979), p. 60. This formula has been repeated in each of the subsequent yearbooks.

8. *SIPRI 1982* (London and Cambridge: Oelgeschlager, Gunn and Hain, 1982), pp. 153, 156, and *SIPRI 1983* (New York: International Publication Service, Taylor and Francis, 1983), pp. 174, 177. According to Franz Walter of the Federal Republic of Germany's Ministry of Defense, from the 1979 yearbook on SIPRI estimates for years after 1970 are obtained by the addition of $1 billion in 1973 prices annually. The series is moved to a 1978, 1979 and 1980 dollar-price base in subsequent yearbooks by various inflation factors. Translation to rubles involves adjustments of a 1970 ruble-dollar ratio derived in the 1974 yearbook, but the method and rationale of these adjustments is not clear to me. Personal communication from Dr. Walter.

9. SIPRI provides no explanation for the differences between the two series. *SIPRI 1984* (London and Philadelphia: Taylor and Francis, 1984), repeats the formula for the derivation of its estimates but presents no figures in current prices or shares of GNP, as was the case in previous volumes. There is no explanation of the omissions.

10. The level of the dollar series increases in the 1981, 1982, and 1983 yearbooks because of a change in the price base but there is no change in the rate of growth of the series. *SIPRI 1979*, pp. 36–37; *SIPRI 1980* (New York: Crane Russak, 1980), p. 20; *SIPRI 1981* (Cambridge: Oelgeschlager, Gunn and Hain, 1981), p. 157; *SIPRI 1982*, p. 141; *SIPRI 1983*, p. 162; *SIPRI 1984*, p. 118. SIPRI believes U.S. military expenditures exceed the dollar cost of Soviet programs and have done so throughout the past decade. The margin narrows in the mid- and late 1970s to a low of 7 percent in 1979 but then jumps to 25 percent in 1982. *SIPRI 1983*, p. 161.

11. IISS, *The Military Balance: 1984–1985* (London: IISS, 1984), pp. 15–17; *1983–1984* (London, 1983), pp. 13–14; *1982–1983* (London: IISS, 1982), pp. 12–13, 124. The IISS also refers the reader back to *The Military Balance 1973–1974*, pp. 8–9, and *The Military Balance 1976–1977*, pp. 109–110. In the latter, the CIA method is compared to that of "academics," particularly William Lee. After the difference in results is noted, the editors conclude that "it is perhaps wise to suspend judgment for the moment."

12. On Soviet national income accounting and the place of defense expenditure therein, see A.S. Becker, *Soviet National Income and Product 1958–1964* (Berkeley and Los Angeles, 1969), chap. 7; A.S. Becker, "National Income Accounting in the

USSR" in V.G. Treml and J.P. Hardt, *Soviet Economic Statistics* (Durham, N.C.: Duke University Press, 1972), chap. 4, esp. pp. 90–91; and CIA, *USSR: Toward a Reconciliation of Marxist and Western Measures of National Income,* ER-78-10505 (October 1978). A very recent paper that uses primarily a national income approach is Peter Wiles, "Soviet Military Finance," pt. 1 of Peter Wiles and Moshe Efret, *The Economics of Soviet Arms* (London: STICERD, London School of Economics and Political Science, 1985).

13. For a critique and alternative set of calculations of procurement, see Daniel L. Bond and Herbert S. Levine, "The Soviet Machinery Balance and Military Durables in SOVMOD," in *Soviet Economy in the 1980's: Problems and Prospects,* Joint Economic Committee, U.S. Congress, pt. 1, (Washington, D.C.: GPO, 1982), pp. 296–318, which also cites the work of Stanley Cohn in this area.

Lee's estimates of the other components of military expenditure may also have sizable margins of error owing to the use of third-best procedures. For example, personnel costs are derived by multiplying an estimated manpower series by average rates of pay and allowances for 1958, extended by indexes of civilian wages and the official wholesale price index for the light and food industry. Other operating outlays and construction are generally assumed to be equal to the annual official defense figure less personnel costs, except in 1961–1964 and 1971–1975, when rules of thumb are applied to this residual.

14. The building block, direct costing approach is also used by the U.K. government, which concludes, much like the CIA, that the annual rate of growth of Soviet military expenditure was about 4 percent "up to the mid-1970s" but that was "more than halved" subsequently, "mainly as a result of a reduction in the rate of procurement growth." *Statement on the Defence Estimates 1984,* I, Cmnd. 9227-I (London: HMSO, 1984), p. 41. Evidently the British Ministry of Defence also computes value of expenditure in current prices. *Statement on the Defence Estimates 1981,* I (Cmnd 8212-I, 1981, p. 4) cites totals of 73 billion to 78 billion rubles for 1978, 76 billion to 81 billion for 1979, and 81 billion to 86 billion for 1980. However, at that point, the MOD also believed that the real rate of growth of Soviet outlays was a steady 4 percent per year in the 1970s.

15. See *CIA Estimates of Soviet Defense Spending,* pp. 77ff, and the review essay by Donald F. Burton, formerly chief of the CIA's Military-Economic Analysis Center, "Estimating Soviet Defense Spending," *Problems of Communism* (March–April 1983):85–93. For rebuttals by Lee and Rosefielde as well as a response by Burton, see *Problems of Communism* (March–April 1985), "Correspondence: Soviet Defense Spending," pp. 126–132.

16. Statement by Robert Gates, Deputy Director for Intelligence, CIA, on the Allocation of Resources in the Soviet Union and China—1984, Before the Subcommittee on International Trade, Finance and Security Economics of the Joint Economic Committee, U.S. Congress, November 21, 1984.

17. Fred Hiatt, "Soviets Sped Rate of Military Spending in '83, Pentagon Says," *Washington Post,* June 14, 1984; Robert S. Greenberger, "Pentagon Study Says Soviet Defense Costs Spurted after Several Flat Growth Years," *Wall Street Journal,* June 14, 1984.

18. Bill Keller, "CIA and Pentagon Report Rise in Soviet Arms Budget," *New*

York Times, February 26, 1985. See also George C. Wilson, "Intelligence Units Agree They Disagree," *Washington Post,* February 26, 1985.

19. *Allocation of Resources in the Soviet Union and China—1983;* Hearings before the Subcommittee on International Trade, Finance, and Security Economics of the Joint Economic Committee, Congress of the United States, pt. 9, Washington, D.C., 1984, pp. 23-24, 77, 94, 100-101.

20. See n. 38 below.

21. DIA disputes CIA somewhat on this point: "Mr. Michaud. We feel there is positive growth in the procurement line still, whereas CIA says it is [security deletion], very little growth.

"Senator Proxmire. You think it is a little higher than the CIA? Mr. Michaud. We think it is a little higher." Ibid., p. 45.

22. Ibid., p. 7. Is this DIA estimate one of real growth or of nominal increase at current prices? The question is raised by comparison with an alternative calculation of the growth of military durables output in current prices that yields an increase of 12 percent per year for the period 1965-1980 and 15 percent for 1972-1980. See Bond and Levine, "Soviet Machinery Balance and Military Durables in SOVMOD," esp. pp. 300, 306.

23. DIA, *USSR: Military Economic Resource Allocations—1984,* DDB-1900-88-85 (n.d.), p. 2. This is essentially the DIA testimony on the Soviet economy to the Proxmire subcommittee, presented on January 15, 1985. The CIA's testimony was heard by the subcommittee on November 21, 1984.

24. In his November 1984 testimony, Gates stated that "since reporting to you last year, we have noted evidence of some acceleration in the rate of increase in defense spending." Statement by Robert Gates, p. 9. The chart on defense spending and procurement attached to the statement does suggest a slight increase in procurement in 1983, but it appears to bring the absolute level to approximate parity with that achieved in 1976. See also the press articles cited in note 18.

25. Military expenditure is not separately identified in the agency's GNP estimates by end use, in part because a number of military outlay components are believed to be included with consumption and investment. GNP is computed by sector of origin. A share of military outlays is part of an end use residual, after allowing for consumption, fixed capital investment, R&D, and various other government expenditures. The CIA calculates burden by converting military outlays at 1970 prices to 1970 factor costs and dividing by GNP in the same valuation. While the expenditure estimates of table 8-1 are at 1970 prices, the differences from 1970 factor costs should not be significant for the calculation in table 8-2.

26. The SIPRI series implies an increase of 50 percent in GDP at current prices between 1972 and 1981 and an average annual growth rate of 4.6 percent. CIA's GNP series at 1970 prices grows only 32 percent in the same interval, thus at 3.1 percent per year. *USSR: Measures of Economic Growth and Development, 1950–80,* Studies Prepared for the Use of the Joint Economic Committee, U.S. Congress (Washington, D.C.: GPO, December 1982), p. 54, and *CIA Handbook of Economic Statistics 1982,* CPAS 82-10006 (September 1982), p. 68. SIPRI apparently regards its current price military outlay estimates as equivalent to constant price volume series.

27. At least this was true through the 1983 yearbook. The 1984 yearbook is silent on this issue.

28. DIA, *USSR: Military Economic Resource Allocations—1984*, p. 12. The U.K. Ministry of Defence currently estimates 14 to 16 percent but does not specify the price weights. *Statement on the Defence Estimates 1984*, I:41.

29. W.T. Lee, "USSR Gross National Product in Established Prices, 1955–1975," in Franz-Lothar Altmann, ed., *Jahrbuch der Wirtschaft Osteuropas* (Munich-Vienna: Guenter Olzog Verlag, 1979), p. 400.

30. Rosefielde, *False Science*, p. 198. Rosefielde cites Rush Greenslade, "The Real Gross National Product of the USSR, 1950-1975," in *Soviet Economy in a New Perspective*, Joint Economic Committee, U.S. Congress (Washington, D.C.: GPO, 1976) (but from p. 284, not p. 278 as Rosefielde states). While 17 percent is indeed the margin between Greenslade's 1970 GNP estimate and NMP (net material product) in that year, Greenslade's GNP series grows more slowly in every subperiod of the interval 1950-1975 than does NMP. Thus the ratio of GNP to NMP would have been higher than 1.17 before 1970 and lower after that date. It is not clear why Rosefielde did not use the Greenslade series instead of inflating Soviet NMP values by a constant coefficient; he does not explicitly reject Greenslade's indexes. Had he used the series, his GNP denominators would have been higher in 1960 and 1965 and lower in 1975, thereby lowering the defense-GNP ratio in the earlier years and raising it in the later year. Thus, the pattern he perceives of a sharp rise over time in the burden would have been accentuated. However, the validity of his defense numerator is a much more serious issue than the accuracy of the GNP denominator. On the former problem, the authoritative CIA view is given by Burton "Estimating Soviet Defense Spending" (note 15 above).

31. Igor Birman, "Professor Holzman, the CIA, Soviet Military Expenditures and American Security," *Russia*, no. 10 (1984):35–56; the main arguments on Soviet ruble expenditure and the burden of defense appear on pp. 46–49.

32. He sums the 18 billion rubles of official defense, 60 percent of total expenditures for science, or 7 billion, and 16 billion out of 22 billion rubles of allocations from the All-Union budget for industry and construction, to arrive at a subtotal of 41 billion rubles. He then argues that this must be augmented by some portion of nonbudget outlays on science, civil defense expenses of enterprises, bank credits, and so on. Ibid., p. 49. Birman outlined but did not develop a thesis of extrabudgetary financing of military outlays in his book, *Secret Incomes of the Soviet State Budget* (Boston: Martinus Nijhoff Publishers, 1981).

33. Ibid.

34. Because Soviet prices tend to depart from real costs between major price revisions, CIA has preferred 1970 prices (close to the reform period 1967-1968) to those of later years. The price revision of 1982 makes that year a possible choice for a new set of price weights.

35. If Q_D, Q_G are quantities of the composite goods, defense and GNP, and P_D, P_G are prices of these composites, then

$$B^{70} = \frac{P_D^{70} Q_D^{70}}{P_G^{70} Q_G^{70}}$$

is the 1970 burden ratio, and the index of burden in year t in current prices is

$$I_B = \frac{B^t}{B^{70}} = \frac{P_D{}^t Q_D{}^t}{P_G{}^t Q_G{}^t} \Big/ \frac{P_D{}^{70} Q_D{}^{70}}{P_G{}^{70} Q_G{}^{70}}$$

$$= \frac{P_D{}^t}{P_G{}^t} \cdot \frac{Q_D{}^t}{Q_G{}^t} \Big/ \frac{P_D{}^{70}}{P_G{}^{70}} \cdot \frac{Q_D{}^{70}}{Q_G{}^{70}} \; .$$

Setting the 1970 price and quantity ratios equal to 100,

$$I_B = \frac{P_D{}^t}{P_G{}^t} \cdot \frac{Q_D{}^t}{Q_G{}^t} \; .$$

I am indebted to Gur Ofer for suggesting this mode of approaching the problem of change in the defense burden.

36. This is the basis for Holzman's criticism of the CIA ruble series. Franklyn D. Holzman, "Soviet Military Spending: Assessing the Numbers Game," *International Security* 6(Spring 1982):95. Holzman believes that the error involved in using 1970 prices to measure the 1980 burden is reduced by the CIA procedure of estimating procurement first in dollars and then translating to rubles. He argues that 1970 dollar prices "representing scarcity relationships of a more advanced economy, probably reflect more closely Soviet 1980 scarcity relationships . . . than do 1970 ruble prices." However, Holzman continues, the more 1970 dollar price patterns diverge from the 1980 ruble price patterns, the smaller the correction applied to the initial error (pp. 95–96).

37. Although the official Soviet index of wholesale prices of machinery shows a monotonic decline after 1970 (*Narkhoz 1974*, p. 211; *Vestnik statistiki*, 1981, no. 9, p. 78, and 1983, no. 9, p. 67), there is weighty evidence that the index is unreliable even as to direction of change. See Morris Bornstein, "Soviet Price Statistics," in Treml and Hardt, *Soviet Economic Statistics*, pp. 357–362; Abraham S. Becker, "The Price Level of Soviet Machinery in the 1960s," *Soviet Studies* 26(July 1974):363–379; James Steiner, *Inflation in Soviet Industry and Machine-Building and Metalworking (MBMW) 1960–1975*, CIA, OSR, MEAC, SRM 78–10142 (July 1978); Fyodor Kushnirsky, *Price Inflation in the Soviet Machine-Building and Metalworking Sector*, Delphic Associates Monograph Series (n.p., January 1983). These conclusions by analysts in the West are based largely on the criticisms of various Soviet writers. One of them, G.I. Khanin, estimates a rate of inflation in machinery and metalworking of about 3.5 to 4.5 percent per year in the 1970s, cited by Philip Hanson, "The CIA, the TsSU and the Real Growth of Soviet Investment," *Soviet Studies* 36(October 1984): 577. Soviet writers identify price inflation in new products as the major factor in the rise of the machinery price level. Presumably, this should be true in military industry too, where change in the product mix is especially rapid.

38. CIA, *Soviet Gross National Product in Current Prices, 1960–1980*, SOV 83–10037 (March 1983), p. 7.

39. Linking CIA estimates of GNP growth in 1981–1982, from CIA's *Handbook of Economic Statistics, 1984,* CPAS 84–10002 (September 1984), p. 65, to those for the period 1960–1980, from *USSR: Measures of Economic Growth.*

40. Defense–GNP ratios for a large number of countries over the past decade are provided by the annual of the U.S. Arms Control and Disarmament Agency, *World Military Expenditures and Arms Transfers,* and by the annual SIPRI yearbooks. Comparisons in a few benchmark years are given in the IISS annual, *The Military Balance.*

41. See Charles Wolf, Jr., et al., *The Costs of the Soviet Empire,* R-3073/1–NA (Santa Monica: Rand Corporation, September 1983). The costs considered in that study include trade subsidies, trade credits, economic and military aid deliveries, covert operations, and military operations of Soviet forces in Afghanistan.

42. The next few paragraphs are developed in greater detail in Becker, *Burden of Soviet Defense,* pp. 4–10.

43. Gur Ofer, *The Opportunity Cost of the Nonmonetary Advantages of the Soviet Military R&D Effort,* R-1741–DDRE (Rand Corporation, August 1975), and *The Relative Efficiency of Military Research and Development in the Soviet Union: A Systems Approach,* R-2522–AF (Santa Monica: Rand Corporation, November 1980); William Odom, "The Riddle of Soviet Military Spending," *Russia* (1981):55. On organizational spillovers, see Robert W. Campbell, "Management Spillovers from Soviet Space and Military Programmes," *Soviet Studies* 23(April 1972): 586–607.

44. CIA now acknowledges the validity of many of these criticisms in principle but has not attempted to quantify the effect of taking them into account. Statement by Robert Gates, pp. 10–11.

45. Gates declares that the CIA audited its results for three possible sources of errors—physical estimates of military production, unit costs of new, sophisticated weapons systems, and change in defense industry productivity—and maintains "reasonable confidence" in the estimates of procurement growth. Statement by Robert Gates, p. 13.

46. *Allocation of Resources in the Soviet Union and China—1983,* p. 270.

47. Ibid., p. 278.

48. Ibid., p. 45.

49. Ibid., p. 46.

50. Statement by Robert Gates, pp. 14–15. Perhaps DIA still believes that at current prices, Soviet military spending continued to rise steadily at the rate of 6 or 7 percent. But if zero procurement growth at 1970 ruble factor cost has a near counterpart compiled in some inner sanctum of the Soviet Central Statistical Administration, it is still the case that the Soviet Defense Council could have allocated additional resources to retrieve the pre-1977 real rate of growth. DIA now speaks of possible planned delays or reduction in the levels of production "in anticipation of more technologically advanced systems." DIA, *USSR: Military-Economic Resource Allocations—1984,* p. 3.

51. David Holloway, "Comments on Richard Kaufman's Article," *Soviet Economy* 1(January–March 1985):37–38.

52. John Steinbrunner, "Comments on Richard Kaufman's Article," *Soviet Economy* 1(January–March 1985):33.

53. James M. McConnell, "Shifts in Soviet Views on the Proper Focus of Military Development," *World Politics* 37(April 1985):336. This is not the place to discuss the credibility or reality of this picture of Soviet military doctrine in the last years of the Brezhnev period. There is a considerable polemical literature on this subject, which is thoughtfully discussed in Benjamin S. Lambeth, *The State of Western Research on Soviet Military Strategy and Policy*, N-2230-AF (Santa Monica: Rand Corporation, October 1984).

54. Richard F. Kaufman, "Causes of the Slowdown in Soviet Defense," *Soviet Economy* 1(January–March 1985):22.

55. Ibid., pp. 28–29.

56. Statement by Robert Gates, pp. 12–13. It is not clear whether this statement alters Gates's 1983 view that "we have not seen a transition from weapons production capabilities from SALT to civilian purposes or to nondefense purposes, but rather a swing toward other defense areas." *Allocation of Resources in the Soviet Union and China—1983*, p. 277.

57. Holloway, "Comments on Richard Kaufman's Article," p. 39. So it was always, even under Stalin, as the following anecdote about his approach to the issue of resource allocation tradeoffs attests. Before World War II, the question arose of importing large, expensive machine tools to manufacture large propeller shafts and heavy artillery tubes. The Commissariat of Trade complained that one of those machines alone was equivalent in value to the amount of wheat that would fill the hold of a large freighter. Stalin was reportedly shaken by the comparison. "Grain is gold," he said. "We'd better think it over." Nevertheless, Stalin decided against the Commissariat of Trade, and the machine tools were ordered. The decision turned out to be an error because naval shipbuilding was curtailed during the war, and there was no need for the heavy guns that were produced with the aid of the imported tools. The point is, however, that Stalin weighed the trade-off and decided according to his priorities. B.L. Vannikov, "Oboronnaia promyshlennost' SSSR nakanune voiny," *Voprosy istorii* (1969):131.

58. See Kaufman, "Causes of the Slowdown in Soviet Defense," pp. 11–12.

59. See my "Overview" to part 3, "Military Allocations and Burden," and Myron Rush, "The Soviet Policy Favoring Arms over Investment since 1975," in *Soviet Economy in the 1980's*, pp. 287–295 and 319–330, respectively.

60. Cf. 1971–1975 claimed growth of 29 percent and 24 percent in utilized national income and real income per capita, respectively, (*Narkhoz za 60 let*, pp. 18–19) with 1976–1980 targets of 26 and 21 percent, respectively (*Izvestiia*, October 30, 1976).

61. *Izvestiia*, October 28, 30, 1976; *Narkhoz za 60 let*, p. 433.

62. Gertrude E. Schroeder, "The Slowdown in Soviet Industry, 1976–1982," *Soviet Economy* 1(January–March 1985):42–74, esp. 51–52.

63. *Pravda*, November 18, 20, 1981. The CIA estimates the growth of per capita consumption at only 2.2 percent per year in 1976–1980. Gertrude E. Schroeder and M. Elizabeth Denton, "An Index of Consumption in the USSR," in *USSR: Measures of Economic Growth and Development, 1950–80*, p. 326.

64. CIA, *Handbook of Economic Statistics, 1984*, p. 64 and population statistics in the *Narodnoe khoziaistvo SSSR* yearbooks.

65. *Pravda*, October 28, 1982.

66. There are often substantial differences between the realized percentage changes reported in the *Narodnoe khoziaistvo* yearbooks and those given in the plan fulfillment reports (PFR) published in the central press each January:

	1981		1982		1983	
	PFR	*Narkhoz*	*PFR*	*Narkhoz*	*PFR*	*Narkhoz*
Utilized national income	3.2	3.2	2.6	3.5	3.1	3.6
Industrial production	3.4	4.0	2.8	2.3	4.0	4.2
Industrial labor productivity	2.7	2.6	2.1	2.5	3.5	3.6
Agricultural production	–2.0	–1.0	4.0	5.5	5.0	6.1
All freight turnover	2.3	3.5	1.2	1.5	4.8	4.8
Total investment	3.0	4.2	2.0	3.3	5.0	6.0
Real income per head	3.3	3.4	0.1	0	2.0	2.0

On the whole, the plan fulfillment reports provide an even less optimistic picture of the fulfillment of the Eleventh FYP.

67. CIA, *Handbook of Economic Statistics 1984*, and Statement by Robert Gates.

68. CIA, *Handbook of Economic Statistics*, various annual issues.

69. Mark M. Hopkins and Michael Kennedy, with the assistance of Marilee Lawrence, *The Tradeoff Between Consumption and Military Expenditures for the Soviet Union during the 1980s*, R-2927–NA (Santa Monica: Rand Corporation, November 1982). Hopkins and Kennedy examined two aspects of productivity: conventional factor productivity (of all inputs) and differences between the efficiency of imported and domestic capital equipment.

70. This base case projection may be somewhat optimistic in that it assumed a positive rate of change of factor productivity equivalent to the rate attained in the first half of the 1970s, whereas between 1973 and 1983 productivity was negative. While the economy cannot tolerate declining productivity indefinitely, it may take a number of years to achieve sustained positive growth.

71. Becker, *Burden of Soviet Defense*, pp. 19–20, 69–71.

72. Daniel L. Bond, "Macroeconomic Projections of the Burden of Defense in the Soviet Economy," in *Soviet Military Economic Relations*, Proceedings of a Workshop on July 7, 8, 1982, Sponsored Jointly by the Subcommittee on International Trade, Finance, and Security Economics of the Joint Economic Committee and the Congressional Research Service, Library of Congress, Washington, D.C., 1983, pp. 184–191. Bond also reports the results of a high and low scenario. The first

assumes extensive reform and increased East–West trade, with defense expenditures cut back to a 2.5 percent increase per year. The low scenario postulates a defense growth rate raised to 7.5 percent and poor economic relations with the West.

73. Gregory G. Hildebrandt, "The Dynamic Burden of Soviet Defense Spending," in *Soviet Economy in the 1980s: Problems and Prospects*, p. 1, pp. 331–350.

74. *Narkhoz 1978*, p. 343; *Narkhoz 1982*, pp. 46, 339.

75. In technical terms, the elasticity of consumption (with respect to defense) is considerably greater than that of GNP.

76. In terms of either input quality or the defense sector environment, which is then (somehow) transferred along with the resources reallocated.

77. Hildebrandt, "The Dynamic Burden," p. 340.

78. Weakening the military priority system would, however, diminish the momentum behind defense spending plans at any level and would therefore result in lower growth rates.

79. As Hildebrandt, p. 338, explains the contrast with the case of freezing the defense budget, "The capital goods transferred to defense in the higher [defense] growth case cost the civilian sector more output at the margin than the output gain it would obtain if defense sector growth were reduced."

80. Becker, *Burden of Soviet Defense*, sec. 5.

9
Weapons Acquisition in the Soviet Union

Stan Woods

Recent Western disillusionment with détente has been partly shaped by vast increases in the quantity and diversity of Soviet weapons. Nevertheless, observers have drawn comfort from a belief that Western technological supremacy can compensate for Soviet numerical superiority. Two assumptions lurk here. The first is that the Soviet threat can be gauged merely by applying quantitative criteria. The second is that the threat is best countered by procuring technologically advanced weapons. Both theses are contentious.

The objective of this study is to highlight the weaknesses in this pair of judgments. In pursuit of that goal, the key features of the Soviet weapons acquisition system are scrutinized in an analysis that examines institutions, relationships, and conventions. This is supplemented by an appraisal of the system's performance and its outputs. Initially, however, some observations are in order about weapons acquisition systems in general, identifying features common to any weapons policy, in the Soviet Union or elsewhere.

Preliminaries and Perspectives

Weapons acquisition is a process that transforms national resources into usable military hardware. The character of any nation's weapons acquisition system is determined by diverse considerations: the size and economic capacity of the country, the strength and variety of its technological base, the priority attached to military preparedness, and the perceived utility of military power. The threats and opportunities that confront the state, and the military doctrine that emerges as a result of these threats and opportunities, also play important roles.

A procurement strategy seeks to furnish the nation's armed forces with the best possible military equipment to meet the threat posed by a potential adversary (or adversaries). The successful conception, development, and production of technically advanced weapons comes about as a result of a dynamic and flexible relationship linking military doctrine, potential threat, and national economic and technological capabilities. Accordingly, the acquisition process must be iterative to allow responses as conditions change and as elements of the environment react with one another.[1] New technological possibilities for weapons may prompt revision of doctrine; alternatively, perceived technological backwardness in crucial mission areas may cause a change in resource allocations to specific projects or produce new and innovative procedures for dealing with shortcomings.

The essence of weapons acquisition is uncertainty. At the inception of any new program, great uncertainty exists about the final quality and technical performance of the desired output, about the length of time it will take to develop, and about the ultimate cost of the undertaking. A correct relationship between design continuity (that is, inertia, conservatism, and potential technological obsolescence) and progress (or dynamism, inspiration and innovation) is crucial to the successful provision of effective armaments.

The substitution of the old by the new is the motor of weapons acquisition. The problem is how one decides when hardware has become obsolete and how one chooses among the many competing predevelopment ideas for new systems. The dilemma has been sharpened over recent years by the increasing rapidity of technological change. In turn, this has led to a concomitant reduction in the operational life of modern weapons systems. An often spurious belief has arisen that existing weapons, even when they are new, are necessarily obsolescent in comparison to paper designs yet to be produced.[2] As a result, everywhere R&D now consumes a significantly higher percentage of total acquisition funds than hitherto. This has meant increased unit costs and shorter production runs.

The procurement of a specific weapon is the result of a process that comprises three distinct stages: the R&D stage; the large-scale industrial manufacture of the weapon, or production stage; and the final delivery of equipment to the military customer for operational testing and service. In practice, however, the distinctions are not so formalized or clear-cut:

> Design is reiterative and repetitive, as models are evaluated, revised and tested once again. Once production is underway, improvements in individual components can be made which do not constitute a change in the basic system.[3]

In short, although notionally and administratively divisible, in reality procurement is necessarily a continuous, overlapping process.

The R&D stage can itself be subdivided into three interlocking phases. The first of these, often associated with feasibility study (in Western nomenclature), concentrates on matching information and experimental results derived from scientific research with the military's operational needs and demands. The final characteristics of the proposed weapon need not be specified at this juncture; as a result the feasibility study is the least expensive of the three phases. The second phase is project definition and involves determining exact performance, development time, and costs specifications. Scale models, perhaps even crude prototypes, may be constructed before the decision is taken to proceed to the third and final phase. Full development is the most costly of the phases since resources must be allocated to cover large-scale equipment development, including prototype testing, plus some preproduction costs.

There are two basic styles of military R&D. A nation can adopt either a radical or a conservative approach to the translation of paper ideas into usable military hardware. Both strategies see R&D as future oriented, aiming at the development of weapons that are superior to and different from existing hardware. Yet there are profound differences between them. The former sees the nature of R&D as a quest for radically different weapons sytems by means of a design-from-first-principles approach. In this view, new weapons are militarily more effective if they take advantage of new technologies or if they are based on the latest advances in the state of the art. The latter is a strategy that, in contrast, relies on incremental modification of already-deployed systems.

There are advantages and disadvantages with each. The radical approach is almost prohibitively expensive. Performance specifications are continually upgraded as advances in the state of the art hold out the promise of ever-greater capability. Weapons programs rarely stay within their budget. Delivery dates constantly slip past. (The last 5 percent of performance always consumes a disproportionate share of resources.)

On the other hand, attempting to press the limits of existing scientific knowledge and engineering art can produce situations where the conservative approach cannot compete effectively. The more incremental approach, if pursued to its extreme, has an immanent tendency to hinder creative innovation and may lead to design stagnation. This holds out the possibility of technological ambush (being left behind in the arms race) with all that that implies.

Three groups play a major role in the weapons acquisition process in any society: the military (with their doctrine, history and traditions), the political leadership (with all of its priorities, values and aspirations), and the R&D community combined with the defense industry as a whole. The production of new weapons is not the result of a rational progression of events but is the output of a complex web of iterative relationships among these groups.

Weapons policies will differ according to the relative importance of the three groups in the national acquisition system. Various questions relating to their position and performance are crucial to a consideration and evaluation of a national weapons policy. For example, which group has ultimate responsibility for decisions about the level of financial commitment to defense is of vital importance to the place that defense takes in the scheme of national priorities.

Intragroup relationships are significant too. Within the military hierarchy, interservice rivalry may play a critical role in equipment selection. Thus a preference for (say) land-based, as opposed to sea-based, ballistic missiles could reflect an inherent bias on the part of an influential military group rather than a choice debated and accepted by all interested parties. The level of access to higher echelons of defense policymaking enjoyed by field and lower-grade officers may also affect the style of a national acquisition system.

Moreover, specific questions relating to the position and functions of defense industry and the R&D establishment have an important bearing on national weapons policies. How freely does scientific, technical, and design information permeate the system? Can personnel move unhindered among different research areas as the interdisciplinary nature of modern R&D requires? What access do research groups have to higher policymaking bodies? How high is the caliber and performance of research personnel employed in the defense sector? Finally, what is the extent of technology and information transfer from foreign scientific communities?

At a more fundamental level, the balance struck among science, technology, and design is crucial to the success of weapons procurement. Although conceptually separate, they are inextricably intertwined. Any society must combine all three whenever it seeks to create useful artifacts. Science, or basic research, aims to advance the frontiers of knowledge and establishes empirically sound principles, which technology then embodies in physical components through manufacture. Design can be defined as the practical solution of specific problems by means of an original arrangement of these components.[4]

This brief discussion of the science-technology-design nexus would be incomplete without a proviso. It is very easy when discussing weapons production to confuse two essentially different notions: military effectiveness and the level of technology. There is no necessary correlation between them. A higher level of technology does not inevitably produce more effective weapons. The opposite is also true: a superior weapon is not always a reflection of a stronger technological base. Within certain limits, although beginning with less sophisticated components, innovative and creative designers can produce weapons not inferior to foreign counterparts. In other words, "Design is the process whereby the whole is made greater than the sum of its parts, and consequently it intervenes in the relationship between technological level and military effectiveness."[5] This distinction is a worth-while one, particularly in light of the style of Soviet weapons design.

Effective equipment need not be high performance, multirole, and technologically advanced. Any evaluation of weapons perceived to be technologically inferior should examine not what they do but how well they do it, particularly in competition with enemy systems. Technological superiority and combat effectiveness are not synonymous. A bad design, whether it is simple or sophisticated, will not be effective. There are many examples where sophistication has been a positive hindrance in the field because of difficulty of maintenance or repair (or simply in terms of ease of operation).

Soviet Weapons Acquisition System

Although ultimate authority for the Soviet Union's military dispositions rests with the political leadership, administrative responsibility for many matters has devolved to a range of institutions. Consequently a description of the various agencies (and relationships) concerned is mandatory before any assessment of their performance can be made.

Overview

Since the inception of the Soviet state, national security has been accorded a very high priority. Defense has been privileged in respect of both the volume and quality of its share of scarce resources.[6] It is in the years since 1960, however, that the levels of Soviet defense spending have been at their most spectacular and since then that Western concern has been most evident.

Between 1958 and 1960 Khrushchev embarked on a radical mission to reorient Soviet military policy away from the labor-intensive combined-arms approach, which had previously served the Soviet Union so well, toward a minimum deterrence posture founded almost exclusively on possession of a nuclear retaliatory capability. In 1960 defense accounted for 8.5 percent of GNP in the Soviet Union.[7] Military outlays have risen steadily since then and in 1982 accounted for between 11 and 13 percent of GNP.[8] This general trend has occurred in tandem with a falling rate of economic growth. In the 1950s the Soviet growth rate was about 7 percent. Through the 1960s and 1970s it fell to a low of approximately 3 percent per annum and is expected to decline further in the 1980s.[9]

These figures stand in striking contrast to the pattern of U.S. defense-to-GNP ratios over the same period. Proportionately, U.S. defense spending was at its highest during the Vietnam war, when it accounted for 9 to 9.5 percent of GNP. It has since declined steadily and in 1982 absorbed about 6 percent. (It must be emphasized that the U.S. GNP is almost twice as large as its Soviet counterpart. Furthermore, defense's share of GNP may edge up again in the 1980s because of the Reagan administration's plans to increase arms spending significantly.)

Just as there are disparities between U.S. and Soviet defense-to-GNP ratios, there are also striking differences in the distribution of expenditure within their respective defense budgets. In 1955 spending on personnel accounted for 45 percent of the Soviet Union's outlays; by the mid-1970s it consumed only 13 percent. Trends in the United States went in the opposite direction: personnel costs increased from 42 percent of the defense budget in 1964 to over 50 percent in the late 1970s.[10] On the other hand, Soviet procurement expenditures increased from 25 percent in 1955 to more than 65 percent in 1980. Before 1960 expenditure on equipment consumed more than 50 percent of the U.S. defense budget; since then this proportion has declined to around 30 percent.[11]

In the Soviet Union, these movements reflect an increasing emphasis on the procurement of high-quality and technologically sophisticated weapons in large numbers. Because of this, the unit cost of Soviet military hardware has risen considerably. The offsetting factor is that most Soviet troops are poorly paid conscripts. In the United States, by contrast, the high cost of all-volunteer forces has squeezed procurement, and this tendency has been reinforced by self-imposed budgetary restraints and uncontrollable unit-cost escalation.

Although real rates of economic growth have been declining, the Soviet Union has continued to build up its military power with little or no respite. Even conservative Western estimates put the annual increase in Soviet military outlays in the region of 4 to 5 percent. Some analysts have argued that 8 percent per annum might be nearer the mark.[12] If these figures are accurate, total Soviet military expenditures have increased two- or three-fold over the last twenty years. Moreover, unless the Soviet economy unexpectedly improves its performance or the Kremlin alters its priorities, by 1985 Moscow's defense budget will amount to 15 percent of GNP.[13]

It is a reasonable assumption that the high level of and steady increase in military spending have had a deleterious effect on the Soviet Union's rate of economic growth.[14] Yet high and growing expenditures have been accepted by a majority of the Soviet ruling elite. Clearly their motivations reflect more than a desire for mutual deterrence; it is believed that military power has political payoffs. The Soviet Union's leaders want their state to be perceived as a superpower throughout the world and to wield concomitant global influence. These aspirations are pursued against the backdrop of traditional Russian imperialist ambitions and an expansionist Marxist-Leninist ideology, combined with a long-standing preference for massive combined arms operations as an integral part of modern war.

Institutional Structure

Because of the closed nature of Soviet society, any analysis of the Soviet Union's weapons acquisition system has to be based partly on speculation. No one is certain exactly how the military share of the national budget is determined. What is known, however, is that four groups are involved in the formulation of procurement policy the political leadership, the armed forces, the defense industry, and the R&D community.[15]

Political Leadership. It is a cardinal rule of the Soviet political system that security policy, defense, and foreign affairs come directly under the civilian leadership's supervision. Many observers, however, have noted the absence of a civilian role in Soviet military affairs, and it seems probable that the day-to-day defense decision-making machinery is so managed as to prevent nonmilitary groups from challenging the dominant position enjoyed by the armed forces. Military policy is the domain of the professional soldier, and this fact alone makes it difficult for civilian voices to be adequately heard.[16] However, three civilian bodies within the political elite are quite definitely involved in the process of weapons procurement: the Politburo, the Defense Council, and the Central Committee's Secretariat.

The Politburo is the supreme decision-making body in the Soviet Union. It is therefore important to scrutinize the relationships that exist among this body, the Communist party as a whole (CPSU), governmental institutions, and the military hierarchy. Put simply, governmental institutions—the Supreme Soviet, its Presidium, and the Council of Ministers—have a largely symbolic, legitimizing role. The CPSU controls the direction of all policy and is itself subordinate to the Politburo. The Poliburo ultimately decides the direction of armaments policy and the range and reach of Soviet military power generally.

The military have not been successful in obtaining formal, institutionalized, political influence in major decision-making bodies.[17] Marshal Zhukov (between 1956 and 1957) and Marshal Grechko (between April 1973 and April 1976) have been the only professional military representatives on the Politburo; both served as minister of defense. Moreover, Grechko's promotion to full Politburo status did not guarantee an increased role for the military in national policymaking. He owed his position to Brezhnev's personal patronage rather than strong pressure from the armed forces.[18]

Although there has been a long history of direct Politburo intervention in weapons procurement, its participation in virtually every aspect of Soviet life probably results in a cursory consideration of most issues. Indeed the delegation of responsibility to lower bureaucratic levels was a key characteristic of the Brezhnev incumbency. The trend has been toward scientific policymaking in which the claims of expertise and technical competence are recognized.[19] In the defense realm, therefore, most attention focuses on major budgetary and allocative problems. The competitive relationship with the West necessitates a thorough examination of strategic, as opposed to lower-level, issues.

The Defense Council is the second-ranked military decision-making body in the Soviet Union. Military affairs at the highest level have tradition-ally been supervised by an institution that has linked the political elite and the military leadership. In the past this body was known as the Main, or Supreme, Military Soviet.[20] Currently this council fulfills the function, representing the interests of the CPSU in military affairs at the highest level. It has been described as a military-political subcommittee of the Politburo, and indeed its permanent membership comprises only those full Politburo members who also have military responsibilities.[21] Brezhnev was known to be its chairman, and since he was simultaneously head of state and general secretary of the CPSU, he stood in an ideal position to ensure consistency between military policy and state policy.

The council has three prime functions: to gather and analyze informa-tion in order to make recommendations and provide guidelines for the full Politburo, to make and review decisions about the defense of the Soviet Union, and to ensure that decisions taken by the Politburo are carried out. It is basically a time-saving body, undertaking much preliminary work that otherwise would have to be done by the Politburo. Its major responsibility is approval of the current defense program and of five-year (and longer-term) military plans.

To perform these functions, the Defense Council requires expert advice and information, particularly since all of the permanent members (exclud-ing the minister of defense) have other areas of responsibility. Two agencies provide this advice: the Institution of Advisors to the Defense Council and the Institution of Permanent Consultants to the Defense Council. The former focuses its attention on the broad sweep of Soviet military policy. Its membership includes first deputy ministers of defense, high-ranking For-eign Ministry and Council of Ministers' officials, the president of the Academy of Sciences of the USSR, and several other interested parties. The last body is concerned with the details of defense planning rather than the major issues. Hierarchically it is one step lower than the Institution of Advisors and comprises individuals drawn from the Ministry of Defense (of deputy, not first deputy, rank) and from other political and industrial agencies. Scientists and designers are also intimately involved at this level. As a result, the political leadership is able to keep abreast of the latest military and scientific developments.

The Defense Council's increasing reliance on externally provided information and analysis suggests that responsibility for day-to-day man-agement of Soviet military affairs rests with the armed forces themselves. The Main Military Council must play a key role in this respect. Its membership includes the minister of defense, his first deputy chairman and deputy chairmen (all of whom are professional officers), the heads of the Main Political Administration of the Soviet Army and Navy (MPA), plus the chairman of the Defense Council. In addition to performing an administrative role, this body is the source of alternative policies and options that are presented to the Defense Council and the Politburo for consideration. These are crucial to the ordering of national priorities. Without the considerable assistance of the military, political leaders would be unable to make reasoned and rational choices. The military have managed therefore to obtain a potentially decisive voice in the formulation of Soviet defense policy, despite being formally excluded from the major decision-making bodies.

The secretariat of the party's Central Committee plays a pivotal role in all aspects of life in the Soviet Union by virtue of its position at the apex of policymaking. It controls policy formulation and implementation, as well as information flows and analyses. Four of its twenty functional departments have direct links with the defense sector: two departments—Defense Industry and Machine Construction—jointly oversee the nine defense industrial ministries; the Department of Administrative Organs is involved not only in ensuring compliance with CPSU instructions but also with the selection and promotion of party members; and the MPA, which operates simultaneously as a department of the secretariat and as a directorate of the Ministry of Defense, has responsibility for party political education and indoctrination within the armed forces as a whole.

These departments have a more comprehensive, all-embracing view than any of the individual ministries that they supervise and a self-consciousness that extends beyond the goals of these ministries. Despite this, it is unlikely that they dominate the ministries. It is more probable that they become allied with and, to an extent, reliant on them. The secretariat therefore is unlikely to be a source of independent analysis on military-industrial questions.[22]

Armed Forces. The military's involvement in weapons procurement occurs at a number of levels: in the specification of requirements, in the acceptance of new designs, in the monitoring of production, and in the acquisition and integration of new equipment into actual use. Three major military institutions are involved: the Ministry of Defense, the General Staff, and the main staffs of the five Soviet armed services.

The Ministry of Defense is staffed almost exclusively by professional military officers. The exception to this rule was the former minister of defense, Dimitrii F. Ustinov, a civilian who had a long-term involvement with defense industry. Although notionally a governmental body, the ministry sees its first priority as representing the interests of the military establishment to the political elite. Because of its expertise and its monopoly of

information relating to defense, the Soviet military hierarchy wields disproportionate influence in comparison with the military in Western countries.
Ustinov has three first deputy ministers of defense: the commander in chief
of Warsaw Pact Forces, the chief of the general staff, and a deputy responsible
for administration. The five service commanders hold the rank of deputy
minister of defense. The senior Ministry of Defense official responsible for
weapons acquisition, particularly in respect of those projects with high
priority or costs, is the deputy minister of defense for armaments. In October
1970 Colonel General Engineer N.N. Alekseev was appointed to this post
and has remained at it for over ten years.[23]

The General Staff wields enormous power and influence. Its primary
function in the procurement process is to monitor and evaluate proposals for
new weapons rather than to initiate them. It has grown in importance in this
regard over recent years because of widespread disappointment with standards of efficiency and innovation in the armaments sector. An impression
achieved currency in the 1960s that weapons acquisition arrangements were
adequate for the production and incremental improvement of weapons
already being manufactured but deficient as far as innovation and the
development of new-in-principle weapons were concerned. In response to
this widely felt concern, a Scientific-Technical Committee was established.
Its function, by all accounts, is to exploit new scientific and technical
discoveries with a view to matching them to military requirements. Because
of this and other reforms, it has been noted that "professionalism, which had
always been the hallmark of the military leaders controlling weapons acquisition, moved from competence based on the *use* of weapons to an emphasis
on technical experts who know how to *build* them."[24] It is indisputable that
the officer corps today has higher levels of technical skill, training, and
expertise than it did during Stalin's time. As a result, the military's position
as the sole source of informed advice on defense matters has been strengthened.[25]

The General Staff is preeminent in questions concerning the formulation and evaluation of Soviet military doctrine and weapons choice. During
wartime it would transform itself into the Soviet high command and would
have responsibility for directing military operations. Very little information
exists about interservice rivalry within the Soviet armed forces, but the
General Staff's pivotal position would give it a major role in the resolution
of such conflicts.[26]

The main staffs of the five military services account for the overwhelming majority of requests for new weapons. There are four areas from which
these requests emanate:[27]

1. The Armaments Directorates maintain intimate links with industry and
    R&D institutions.

2. The Scientific-Technical Committees probably perform a similar role to that of the General Staff's committee of the same name but at a lower level. These bodies are aware of the state and level of research in particular weapon areas and of the nature of weapons required. Consequently they sit in a perfect position for making recommendations.

3. The operations staffs are made up of officers directly involved in battlefield-level military planning who are excellently placed to make detailed requests for weapons.

4. Field commanders and other lower-grade officers have the perspective of the equipment user and are able to make proposals based on thoroughly defined tactical-technical requirements. (Their requests are probably channeled through one of the other three agencies described)

The Soviet defense sector differs from its civilian counterpart in several profound ways. Differences directly relevant to this study include the secret nature of all military affairs in the Soviet Union and the consumer power of the armed forces.

The confidential nature of all defense issues is a vital determinant of the style of Soviet military decision making. The secrecy that surrounds the defense effort makes it virtually impossible for outside groups to challenge proposals made by the military or participate in budgeting for defense. It follows that the political pressure that affects resource allocation for military purposes in liberal democracies is much reduced in the Soviet Union.

In contrast to the situation that prevails in the Soviet civilian economy—where the supplier (or industry itself) determines what is to be produced and in what quantities—the consumer plays the key role within the military sector. The Defense industry has no choice but to comply with a decision to produce a weapon once it has been taken. Defense customers can reject military hardware at any stage in the production process, and quality control is strict. Moreover, the defense industry has been given privileges and incentives of its own lest it be unable to satisfy military demands.

The secret nature and consumer power of the Soviet military have not resulted, indeed could not result, in the total subordination of the civilian economy. There is a trade-off between guns and butter, and the Soviet leadership recognizes this fact. Allocation of resources to defense must fit with national priorities as embodied in the economic plans. There are three concurrent plans: a one- (or two-) year plan, a five-year plan, and a long-term (fifteen- to twenty-year) plan. Major adjustments to any one would be costly and complicated. Planners are notoriously inflexible and conservative, disposed to protect their domain at all costs. Despite this, the rapid pace of technological change in modern weapons development often necessitates major alterations to the military industrial program in being. Periodic confrontation between the Soviet military and GOSPLAN (the state planning agency) is therefore inevitable.

GOSPLAN cannot unilaterally reject demands from the military, however. To curb potential military profligacy, a special agency acts as a buffer or arbitrator between the adversaries. It serves both to moderate the unnecessary demands of the military and to promote their legitimate requests. If conflicts cannot be resolved, the party itself adjudicates, and a Central Committee military-industrial department has been constituted for just such a task.[28] The armed forces are in this respect continuously under party scrutiny.

Defense Industry. The third actor in Soviet weapons acquisition is the defense industry. There are nine defense-industrial ministries.

1. The Ministry of Defense Industry is responsible for the production of armaments and munitions (tanks, artillery, armored vehicles, small arms and ammunition, fuses, primers, propellants, explosives, and possibly some tactical guided missiles).

2. The Ministry of Aviation Industry has responsibility for aircraft and aircraft spares, as well as for a selection of aerodynamic missiles.

3. The Ministry of Shipbuilding Industry undertakes the design and manufacture of all ships for the Soviet navy and of a large percentage of the merchant and fishing fleets.

4. The Ministry of Electronics Industry produces a range of electronic components.

5. The Ministry of Radio Industry produces communications and other electronic systems for the military and civilian markets.

6. The Ministry of General Machine Building undertakes construction of strategic ballistic missiles and space vehicles.

7. The Ministry of Medium Machine Building runs the Soviet atomic energy program and manufactures warheads.

8. The Ministry of Machine Building was established in 1968; its functions are not known with certainty. It may be that responsibility for missiles and space has been divided, with this ministry handling the latter. Another possibility is that it has taken over the munitions part of the Ministry of Defense Industry's business.

9. The Ministry of the Means of Communication produces telecommunications equipment.[29]

These nine ministries also produce for the civilian market; Brezhnev once said that 42 percent of defense production is consumed by the civilian sector.[30] In return, the defense-industrial sector receives help from certain nominally civil industrial ministries: the ministries of Instrument Manufacturing, Means of Automation and Control Systems, Tractors and Agricultural Machine Building, Chemical Industry, and Automobiles Industry.[31]

The coordination and control of the defense industry is exercised through the Military-Industrial Commission, a working organ of the Council of Ministers. Its membership includes the minister of defense and representatives for the nine defense-industrial ministries, GOSPLAN, and the Central Committee Secretariat.[32] It is not a planning organization—responsibility for this lies solely with GOSPLAN—but it is able to influence the directions and goals of military-industrial planning by virtue of its pivotal position. It has responsibility for coordinating military research, development, and industrial production. It is also a source of information, analysis, and evaluation. This gives it a significant influence on the type and quantity of weapons produced. Weapons-related manufacture is accorded the highest priority in the Soviet Union; this is the agency responsible for policing that priority.

The Soviet defense-industrial sector differs from its counterparts elsewhere in the world in several major respects. Of particular importance are its autarkic nature and the remarkable length of tenure of top decision makers.

Powerful incentives within Soviet defense industry impel decision makers toward autarky. Secure and stable sources of supply—of raw materials, semifinished goods, or manufactured spare parts—are notoriously difficult to guarantee. This, combined with the stern pressure on managers to meet output goals, has led to vertical industrial integration wherever possible.

It is hard to control organizations outside the area of one's own responsibilities. Because of this defense-industrial managers have sought to colonize and control enterprises producing parts essential to the achievement of their own output goals. During the 1960s, for example, it has been reported that over 90 percent of the essential components required by the Ministry of Aviation Industry were produced in enterprises that came under that ministry's direct supervision.[33] (The civilian sector attempts to follow this strategy too but without much success. Within the defense sector, it is facilitated by the priority and preference given to defense throughout the economy as a whole.)

The leading defense industrialists are not a coherent interest group but a diverse collection of individuals responsible for producing a wide range of products for five separate military services. Their long-term incumbency and myriad interrelationships, however, have bred a powerful inclination toward continuity in procedures. The intense emphasis on production in the 1939–1945 war—and Stalin's insistence that any dislocation of plants be kept to a minimum—influenced the organization and procedures for weapons development and manufacture. Leading defense managers have learned that continuity is the best guarantee of meeting targets even in peacetime. There are no prizes for the introduction of new products and technologies if production goals are not met. New technologies require new sources of supply, and this, given the highly bureaucratic and inefficient distribution network, causes difficulties. In short, real problems exist that can act as a brake on innovation in the Soviet defense sector.[34]

Research and Development Community. The Soviet Union's R&D institutions occupy an intermediary position between the military on the one hand and defense industry on the other. The R&D function is fractured vertically and horizontally. In vertical terms, effort is divided between two kinds of organization. Research institutes are the most prestigious R&D performers. They tend to concentrate their investigations on the initial and middle stages of the R&D cycle—the realm of basic and applied research—although there is evidence that some are involved through to the full-scale production stage. Design bureaus are found mainly in the industrial ministry network. They engage in the middle and later stages of military R&D for the most part. Although these bodies are the major performers of Soviet military R&D, other, less important, agencies are involved too. These include research laboratories, technological institutes, experimental production facilities, and pilot plants.

The relationship between research institutes and design bureaus profoundly influences the Soviet R&D process. Because many separate bodies engage in military-oriented R&D, an efficient feedback of technical information is vital to any project's success. The chief instrument of information transfer is the vast array of technical handbooks produced for the design bureaus by the research institutes. These handbooks aim to ensure that designers work within accepted, proved, technical limits. They indicate approved structures and acceptable materials and list manufacturing techniques. Their existence is a reflection of the institutes' monopoly of research and test facilities. It is said that this style of R&D inhibits designers from exploiting new technologies that could lead to important weapons developments. But to argue this is to ignore the military effectiveness of many Soviet weapons and rely on assertions about their low technological content. Yet it is effectiveness that matters, not technical complexity.

R&D bodies are also separated in horizontal terms. They can be affiliated to the defense industrial ministries, the Ministry of Defense, or the Academy of Sciences of the USSR.[35]

Each of the defense industrial ministries controls a number of institutes and a network of bureaus. The design bureau is a fairly autonomous body since it is not usually financially dependent on the industry concerned. As a result there is little incentive to overdesign a weapons system. This reduced tendency to gold plate hardware is reinforced by the imperatives of Soviet military doctrine, the traditions of the armed forces, and the inclinations of the defense industry managers themselves. It stands in direct contrast to the preferences of most Western defense industrial managers.[36]

The R&D institutions of the Ministry of Defense concentrate over-whelmingly on applied research. There are two types of such institutions. First, the command and staff academies of the various armed services per-form a research function with a military operational bias in areas such as weapons application, tactical utilization, and assessment of the possible capabilities of potential future systems. Second, a number of scientific research institutes come directly under the aegis of the Ministry of Defense itself.

The Academy of Sciences' role in weapons research has been increasing over the last twenty to thirty years. This is a reflection of the fact that weapons development—particularly that which is new in principle or exotic—is com-ing to depend increasingly on basic scientific research. Before World War II, the general and applied sciences were the wellsprings of innovation; now fundamental scientific principles are the major source. In line with this change, scientists are not only involved in the development of new weapons, they are increasingly being drawn into the officer corps itself. (This is a trend evident in every advanced nation, not just in the Soviet Union.)

In combination with the State Committee for Science and Technology and Gosplan, the academy determines the overall progress of Soviet science and technology. The extent of its involvement in defense R&D is not known precisely, but there is sufficient information for some speculation.[37]

The military themselves have an overriding influence on decisions about weapons procurement and deployment, and it is unlikely that the academy has any influence in these respects. But in exploring the potential military applications of basic research, the academy probably plays an important role. Until reorganized in 1961, its primary function was to ensure that the results of research in the applied sciences promoted Soviet industrial and economic development. The focus then shifted, however. The academy came to be responsible for the natural sciences and humanities while retain-ing its major links with applied research and with industry. At present, therefore, it is involved at every level of science and technology in the Soviet Union.

It has helped to foster advances into a small number of very advanced military technologies. Work on lasers, high-energy particle beams, nuclear energy, ICBM, and space technology—all areas with direct military rele-vance—is now performed under the academy's auspices. Its role here results from a concern felt in the 1960s that the R&D cycle was not flexible enough to cope with rapidly changing scientific opportunities. This prompted a managerial reorganization—including Colonel General Engineer N.N. Alekseev's appointment as deputy minister of defense for armaments in 1970—and the academy was drawn much more into military R&D.

The academy and industry interact on two levels. At the lowest level, links probably exist in the form of an informal scientific-technical complex that involves institutes of the academy, design bureaus, and industrial plants. This arrangement serves to ease the problems of information feedback and dissemination of technical knowledge.

Because of its unique concentration of specialized personnel and expertise, the academy's involvement in military R&D will almost certainly increase in the future. In fact, prospects for Soviet military technology depend significantly on the performance of the academy.

So far as the higher direction of science policy in the Soviet Union is concerned, a key institution is the State Committee for Science and Technology (SCST). This body's terms of reference are to manage and construct Soviet state policy in the area of science and technology; to utilize and disseminate scientific advances throughout the national economy; to identify and monitor the most significant R&D research areas currently under investigation; and to forecast future trends and organize a national scientific-technical information service. Although the SCST's military-related functions are not known in the West, some interaction with the military must occur.

What of the highest levels? The top political leadership has at times had a crucial influence on the evolution of R&D in the Soviet Union. Stalin's involvement in particular has been well documented. Although he did not conceive of new weapons himself, he did provide the impetus for several extremely important crash programs, including the nuclear weapon and ballistic missile developments. It is unlikely that the present leaders' involvement matches that of their predecessors, if only because of the increased complexity of modern weapons. But they can help overcome obstacles to innovation by direct intervention in the R&D cycle. The government has often set up special-purpose agencies in high-priority weapons areas that have ignored existing institutional boundaries, the aim being to improve the efficiency of the innovation process.[38]

Procedures in Brief

To complete this survey of the Soviet weapons acquisition process, something should be said about procedures. There are difficulties here because of lack of firm knowledge of the Soviet way of procurement. Enough is known, however, to offer a summary account of what probably happens in the Soviet Union between the initial proposal for a weapon and its ultimate full-scale manufacture and acquisition.[39]

Once a proposal for a weapon has been approved, exploratory work is done by a research institute under the supervision of a scientific-technical commission. The commission, composed of both military men and industrialists, is the linchpin of the R&D cycle. It provides the detailed specifications of the projected weapon. These are presented in a document called the tactical-technical instruction, which serves to regulate the future progress of the weapon program.[40] This dossier presents detailed information on the reason for the development of the weapon in question and its projected operational and cost specifications.

The tactical-technical instruction is the basis on which the military reject or accept development work. Once it has been drawn up, it is delivered to several specially-chosen design bureaus, which produce completed paper designs on the basis of the specifications in it. These designs are subsequently returned to the scientific-technical commission, which recommends one or more of them for further development. Prototypes are then constructed, which are eventually run in competition with each other. If a production decision is taken, a document called the technical conditions is prepared.[41] This text is the basis for military control of the production phase. Quality control is also ensured by the involvement of the chief designer throughout the production process and is reinforced by the position of the scientific-technical commission. Because the latter is funded by the Ministry of Defense (and is institutionally independent of the research institutes, design bureaus, and industrial plants), it has no material interest in selecting any particular design.

Style of Soviet Weapons Acquisition

The translation of technical discoveries into usable military hardware is always difficult and demanding. Many observers, however, have asserted that the structure of weapons acquisition in the Soviet Union—cast as it is in the mold of the Soviet economic system as a whole and suffering from the same maladies—conspires to make procurement more problematical than in, say, the United States. In particular, the system is believed to frustrate innovation and encourage design conservatism. Military technology is therefore alleged to be inferior to that of the West.

Each element in this argument is open to question. For instance, it is not true that Western innovation is always radical, never conservative and it is certainly not always successful. Nor is Soviet weapons design invariably conservative. When it is, moreover, this is often because of deliberate choice, and the resultant weapons systems are not necessarily inferior.

Characteristics

To elucidate the character of the design and development process in the Soviet Union, a useful starting point is consideration of the thesis that it reflects the application of three principles: simplicity, standardization, and evolutionary change.[42] There is some truth in this, but it is not the whole truth. Soviet designs are often simple—meaning rugged, lacking detailed finishing, and tailored to a single role—and frequently they are able to perform the task required of them and no more. From the fact that many, but by no means all, systems fit this description, it cannot be inferred that they are any less effective, however. In fact, real operational benefits result from Soviet designers' preference for weapons containing a minimum of exotic materials or sophisticated subsystems and for employing the most advanced technology only if it is vital to successful performance of the combat mission.

The Soviet Union does seem to favor standardization, or use of off-the-shelf components and subsystems in a range of different equipment. For example, the same turboprop engine was used for the Tu-22 (Bear) strategic bomber developed in 1955 and the An-22 (Cock) heavy logistic transport aircraft introduced in 1965, while the Tu-22 itself incorporated systems and structures developed for the Tu-16 (Badger). It is significant, however, that tried and tested subsystems have frequently been combined into extremely effective weapons. In fact, such creative improvisation is a notable feature of Soviet military design. The ZSU-23/4 (Shilka) antiaircraft gun illustrates this very well. "There is little new about this system—*except its design as a system.*"[43] Its chassis is a close relative of the amphibious PT-76 light tank introduced in 1952, and the electronics are of a similar vintage. The engine is a six-cylinder derivative of a 1930s tank propulsion unit, and the guns are modifications of World War II models. The ZSU-23/4 is not therefore a technologically advanced weapon in terms of chassis, propulsion, radar acquisition, or firepower, but it has demonstrated its military effectiveness; and it is this criterion—rather than any dubious level of technology comparisons—that must be used to evaluate military hardware.[44]

There are managerial advantages in standardization, too. Longer production runs, easy interchangeability of equipment and components between different weapons systems, and reduction in production, training, and logistical costs are three of the more obvious ones.

As for evolutionary change (or exploitation of design inheritance), there is an apparent Soviet preference for cautious, step-by-step modification of hardware rather than radical design innovation. Techniques and components are specified for designers' use in the research institutes' technical handbooks. Moreover, an inefficient supply network often necessitates repeated employment of identical components. The Soviet space exploration program illustrates this well. The Voltok launch vehicle, designed in

1954 but repeatedly improved since then, has been involved in all three manned programs.[45] In contrast the United States has used a different launch vehicle for each of its major efforts (with the exception of the Apollo and Skylab programs, which both used Saturn V rockets). This reliance on well-tested equipment and the slow development of new and more powerful rocket carriers (for example, Proton from 1965) may have resulted in the loss of an initial Soviet advantage in rocket thrust. But the incremental method does have payoffs, particularly in vehicle standardization and production line manufacture (with its concomitant economies of scale). And it is not slavishly adhered to. Design from first principles is not alien to Soviet designers. Indeed, new demands are impelling them to seek new solutions to novel military problems. The Soviet Union's ability to meet these challenges should not be underestimated.

It remains generally true, however, that conservatism is a key factor in Soviet weapon designs. The United States has initiated the substantial majority of important military equipment developments. Nuclear armaments, strategic bombers, nuclear-powered ballistic missile submarines, and MIRVs first developed and deployed by the United States. The Soviets have rarely introduced a new type of system before the United States (an exception being the Soviet deployment of the first ICBM, the SS-6). In this respect the general level of military technology in the Soviet Union is lower than in the United States. This fact is not at issue; the inferences drawn from it are.

Reasons for Conservatism...(1)

If it is accepted that Soviet designers and force planners are driven by conservative impulses, why is this? There are two alternative explanations. The first is that the stultifying nature of the Soviet procurement system ensures that only lowest common denominator proposals for new weapons can be accepted. The second is that a strategy of conservative weapons acquisition has been deliberately chosen by Soviet policymakers to provide cost-effective weapons. On this latter argument, the conservative approach emerges as an optimal procurement philosophy (given historical, doctrinal, demographic, and economic constraints).

Taking up the first thesis, it is the case that the Soviet economy has severe deficiencies that militate against successful R&D. It is relatively efficient in the mass production of straightforward heavy-industrial objects. It is less so in the development of high-technology goods. Innovation is said to be inhibited by the brittle, centrally controlled planning process, widespread bureaucratic inertia, and the lack of managerial imagination.

Yet despite starting from a significantly inferior technological base, the Soviet Union has surprised the West on several occasions. Soviet designers have been successful more than once in putting into service weapons thought to be beyond their technological capability. (The unexpectedly swift development and deployment of nuclear weapons, ICBMs, and MIRVs may be cited as evidence.)

It is generally held that a command economy on the Soviet model and efficient R&D do not go together. However, Soviet military R&D is thought to be quite effective and certainly more so than comparable civilian production. The word *effective* is used advisedly here. What is at issue is not the efficiency of Soviet military, compared with nonmilitary, R&D or indeed compared with U.S. military R&D (although both of these comparisons are significant in respect of the East's ability to maintain a substantial defense effort in the long run). Rather, it is the capability of the Soviet Union to produce militarily effective weapons.

One reason why a command economy is often less good at innovation than a market economy is that in the latter, R&D is tied to the commercial success of the outputs produced. Responsiveness to market forces is absent from the Soviet weapons acquisition process. But, ironically, the U.S. procurement process does not have a free market either. It is the buyer (the military) who usually decides what type of system is required.[46] Government funds are provided before the initiation of the R&D phase, and officials often cancel the project before its completion. The price of the equipment is not determined by market competition but rather by an amount that covers the development costs plus a previously negotiated fee. The government has the bargaining power of a monopsonist (that is, a single buyer). Moreover, since individual weapons projects require vast expenditures, the private funding of their development is virtually impossible. By financing weapons development, the government acts in two capacities: that of buyer and investor.

The situation is not identical in the Soviet Union, but it is analogous. Because responsiveness to market forces is absent from the Soviet system, successful innovation and production are heavily dependent on the customer's ability to define his needs accurately and completely. The military in the Soviet Union possesses consumer sovereignty.[47] This demand power lubricates a cycle of R&D that otherwise might suffer from bureaucratic inertia. Exhaustive military screening of weapons proposals and comprehensive and stringent military involvement throughout the acquisition process ensure that weapons procurement is tied to military needs.

The military also benefits from the generous allocation of resources to defense. Incentives, financial and otherwise, are superior to those elsewhere in the economy, although the gulf has lessened. Yet despite this, many of the brightest engineers and scientists now attempt to avoid defense jobs in favor of positions in nonmilitary areas. This may come from a desire to escape to the more competitive, less secretive, and restricted atmosphere of the civilian sector.[48] Nevertheless, it is likely that the strong military connections with the Academy of Sciences ensure that the very best brains are always involved in work of military relevance.

Furthermore, there is nonmarket competition in military R&D in the Soviet Union in two crucial respects. First, there is a measure of competition with the West in the military sphere that is totally absent in civilian production. Successful manufacture of effective armaments is imperative. The producer of a cheap but unreliable household article in the Soviet Union does not face stiff outside competition. On the other hand the deployment of inferior antitank weapons, judged as they might be by real criteria, could be an expensive mistake. Weapons production is not only about price but also about performance, and poor performance on the battlefield results in defeat.

Second, competitive evaluation is as much a principle of Soviet weapons procurement as any of the triad of simplicity, standardization, and evolutionary change. A competition is run among several prototypes prior to a full-scale production decision. This competition acts as a spur to innovation and as extra insurance. In the aviation industry the ratio of prototypes to production models is approximately two to one, for example.[49] As a result, outlays on development account for only 26.6 percent of total Soviet R&D funds. Because the production decision is usually taken when the original preprototype design has been accepted, however, the comparable U.S. figure is much greater, as high as 64 percent.[50] (In the Soviet Union prototypes are authorized in order to discover information on equipment costs and performance; this may be critical to a decision to proceed to full-scale production.)

By adopting this method, the rapid introduction of weaponry into the field is facilitated. The Soviets attempt to deploy new systems as quickly as possible. They are prepared to cancel a series in the middle of its production run when sufficient data have been acquired. In contrast, the Western style demands that hardware should be fully refined and developed before it becomes operational. In this respect, R&D can acquire a momentum independent of military operational needs. Once the benefits of a technological breakthrough are foreseen, there may emerge a reluctance to put that equipment into a service until it has been developed to the maximum extent. Advanced weapons on paper, however, can never destroy enemy systems in the field. The Soviet practice of prototyping enables a weapon—albeit not a fully refined weapon in every case—to reach operational status very quickly.

Lead times in weapons development are always substantial, but the Western style results in longer ones than those experienced in the Soviet Union. This means more expensive weapons since performance, mission, and vulnerabilities are all upgraded. The attempt to field a system that contains no obsolete technology is doomed given the rapid pace of technological change. By contrast, a strategy that combines evolutionary changes—

based on tried and tested components and subsystems, the frequent conversion of existing platforms, and a belief in single-role weapons—aids the solution of this cost-effectiveness problem.

High levels of defense expenditure have caused concern within the Soviet political and military leaderships for the past twenty years. Since the 1960s there has been a growing emphasis on cost-effectiveness as a criterion of force planning.[51] It has been realized that the last 5 percent of weapon performance is disproportionately costly. In the Soviet view, numbers of systems in the field compensate for technological inferiority.

The financial foundations of Soviet military R&D have been little affected by this pressure for cost-effectiveness. Western firms have found that to sustain the highly sophisticated personnel involved in weapons development is very expensive, particularly when no new orders are forthcoming. But once such teams have been disbanded, they cannot easily be reformed. The experience of the U.S. aerospace industry during the last decade highlights this dilemma. The Vietnam war ensured a massive demand for military aircraft during the 1960s. With the cessation of hostilities, this virtually disappeared, and the numbers of personnel involved in aerospace R&D declined considerably. In the Soviet Union, the situation has been different. There is an inclination toward the steady-state maintenance of R&D teams in order to take advantage of technological breakthroughs when they occur. This approach helps to explain annual production of 4,000 tanks when 40,000 are already in stock.[52]

The Soviet military has been fairly successful in overcoming economic constraints on effective R&D. Moreover, it is clear that Soviet designers should be able to take advantage of foreign scientific or technological breakthroughs more easily than their Western counterparts can absorb Soviet advances, if only by virtue of having an almost hermetically sealed society. Large-scale import of foreign designs and technology therefore could help to provide the solution to many economic bottlenecks and has been assuming increasing importance over recent years.

The conclusion to be drawn is this: to ascribe to the system the conservatism that is observable in many areas of Soviet weapons development—notably the classical items (small arms, armored fighting vehicles, some ships and naval subsystems, and even selected aircraft)—is too simplistic. Technological inferiority is not endemic to the Soviet way of procurement. What, then, of the alternative explanation: that the conservative approach, where observed, is the result of deliberate choice?

Reasons for Conservatism . . . (2)

There are a number of reasons for believing that the Soviet style of weapons design has been selected advisedly. Past experience of conflict—particularly between 1939 and 1945—has played a crucial role in shaping Soviet military doctrine. It explains, for example, the strong emphasis on massive force concentrations and mobility (or shock power) for large combined arms theater operations. The Soviet high command learned two lessons from their hard-fought and painful success. The first was that an enormous, generally unskilled conscript army requires weapons that are easy to operate and maintain, simple to produce, and relatively inexpensive. This is a philosophical approach radically different from that adopted by the volunteer forces of the United States. The other lesson was that after 1945, the West, especially the United States, was far ahead in technologically advanced fields, particularly electronics, jet propulsion, and nuclear weapons.

The Soviet Union has made powerful and sustained efforts to overcome such technological backwardness. The late Marshal I.I. Iakubovskii (ex commander in chief of Warsaw Pact forces) argued that there were two basic tasks for a Soviet weapons policy: "the development and creation of fundamentally new weapons systems, and the further development of so-called classic arms for the purpose of increasing their effectiveness."[53] The pursuit of these objectives has continued to this day. In many areas, the Soviet Union has not matched Western technical prowess, and design philosophy sensibly reflects that. In other areas, however, Soviet designers have produced weapons that are neither simple, standardized, nor evolutionary.

U.S. hardware is reputed to be qualitatively superior to Soviet weapons. This qualitative lead is thought by many observers to compensate for clear Soviet numerical advantages. But because the Soviets often have different mission requirements from their U.S. rivals, purely technological comparisons are dubious criteria for judgment of a weapon's military effectiveness.

A qualitative technological difference between two adversaries may be an irrelevant difference. One side may have selected alternative performance goals and therefore different, but not necessarily inferior, technology to achieve them. Weapons designers often do not aim for similar objectives since procurement reflects asymmetrical military doctrines, R&D styles, and national political aspirations. A comparison of the structures of the Soviet and U.S. fleets illustrates this point very well.

The missions of the two navies are dissimilar. The U.S. fleet has been designed to ensure control of the sea; the Soviet fleet has been designed for sea denial.[54] A strategy of sea control aims to employ naval power to secure the use of the sea for one's own forces. By contrast, the objective of sea denial is merely to prevent the adversary from using the seas to his own advantage. The former is harder to implement than the latter.[55]

The U.S. fleet has been built around carrier task forces and nuclear-powered ballistic missile submarines (SSBNs). The Soviet navy has been designed to counter these systems. Soviet vessels therefore have a large offensive surface-to-surface missile capability and considerable antisubmarine warfare (ASW) potential. U.S. maritime forces operate within a defensive screen provided by fixed-wing tactical aircraft; they also employ this air power offensively. As a result, there is less need for a large ship-to-ship missile capability.

Sea denial lays a heavy emphasis on firepower and mobility. In general, Soviet vessels have been faster and more heavily armed than their U.S. counterparts. U.S. craft usually spend long periods at sea. Sustainability and habitability therefore are two major design goals. Consequently, U.S. ships are larger than Soviet ones because of a requirement for extra space for sanitation, messing, kitchens, and stores.[56]

The U.S. navy has emphasized the survivability of its ships as platforms from which force can be projected onto the shore. Until recently Soviet craft have been designed for fast, mobile antiship and ASW operations. These are different design priorities and mission requirements from those adopted by U.S. naval planners. While the Soviets have made few breakthroughs in extending the state of the art in naval design, they deploy a formidable and effective fighting force. Moreover, a willingness exists to update weapons, electronics, and propulsion systems wherever and whenever necessary.[57]

Given broadening foreign policy interests, it is unlikely that the Soviet Union will continue to rely exclusively on a sea denial strategy. Indeed, given current Soviet procurement patterns—particularly the introduction of the Kiev class very short takeoff and landing cruisers (of which there are now three commissioned and one on its way)—it appears that the emphasis has shifted toward sea control. Furthermore, recent reports suggest that a new Soviet nuclear-powered aircraft carrier, of approximately 50,000 tonnes and capable of operating about fifty conventional takeoff and landing aircraft (probably modified MiG-27s), will put to sea by the end of the 1980s.[58]

These indications of a shift toward sea control illustrate a common Soviet policy of attempting to master a particular mission area before widening the arc of concern. Immediately after 1945, the role of the Soviet navy was merely to defend the home base. Accordingly, naval procurement patterns emphasized small patrol craft, short-range diesel submarines, and land-based maritime attack and reconnaissance aircraft. In response to the emergence of a U.S. carrier and SSBN threat, the Soviets developed a powerful ASW force and introduced several classes of large surface combatants armed with antiship missiles.

These ships had low endurance and comparatively poor crew habitability standards. In the future, the desire for a sea control capability may presage the doctrinal justification for carrier task groups on the U.S. model. For example, only recently have Soviet replenishment-at-sea procedures been improving. Habitability standards are now much better, and this, combined with the procurement of larger, more endurable, ships, suggests that a shift in Soviet naval priorities may be afoot. If this is true, Soviet designers will be forced to satisfy similar mission requirements to the United States.

The inference is that the conservatism apparent in many areas of Soviet weapons design arises out of past experience of armed conflict and the asymmetric mission priorities and requirements of the Soviet armed forces. But there is also another, more comprehensive, explanation. Soviet designers and force planners often have a different approach to what, in military terms, constitutes quality. They have distinctive ideas about what technology can do for military effectiveness on the prospective battlefield. For Moscow, weapons are of high quality when the technology embodied in them reflects the operational or tactical state of the art. For the United States, on the other hand, hardware is of a high quality where operational requirements are satisfied by equipment that reflects the state of the art in technical terms. Particularly telling in the light of these observations is the remark of an Israeli general who used both Soviet and U.S. equipment: "American weapons are designed by engineers for other engineers, whereas Soviet weapons are developed for the combat soldier."[59] There is no lack of evidence for this characaterization of the U.S. style.

Since the 1950s the United States has sought to combat a numerically superior Soviet military threat by means of highly advanced military hardware. This has resulted in increasingly complex weapons produced with high performance, not cost-effectiveness, in mind. Over the years, the cost of a U.S. tank has increased tenfold and that of an aircraft nearly one hundred-fold (in constant dollars). Yet U.S. defense budgets have increased by a mere 15 percent (in constant dollars) since the early 1950s. The weapons procured, therefore, have been fewer in number and more expensive.[60]

Yet despite this, the U.S. military has adopted a combat doctrine based on firepower and attrition. This aims to destroy enemy power by eliminating forces and equipment at a faster rate than the adversary can either tolerate or reciprocate. To attempt to counter the Soviet Union by employing this type of doctrine seems curious, however. Soviet forces are marginally inferior only in technological terms, and their quantitative advantages provide adequate compensation for this inferiority. To expect to prevail in any war of attrition using low numbers of highly sophisticated weapons against a technically advancing opponent with numerically superior forces is illogical at the very least. At worst, it is profoundly dangerous.

The reliability, durability, and sustainability of high-technology weapons must be doubted, and sophisticated equipment requires superior manpower to operate and maintain it. The U.S. decision to procure the Abrams M-1 tank highlights these problems. While the tank has a top speed of 45 miles per hour—and outpaces every Soviet tank—its high-performance gas turbine engine becomes less effective in a dusty environment, a condition that often prevails on battlefields. On average the tank malfunctions every 40 to 50 miles. It consumes nearly 2 gallons of fuel for every mile it travels. This has necessitated the construction of an expensive fuel bowser, which now accompanies tank units in the field. It also boasts a targeting system that employs lasers, thermal detection techniques, and computers to lock onto a target. As yet, however, it has not been used effectively during trials; it has proved to be too complicated and unreliable. A fully operational M-1 will be a formidable armored fighting vehicle, but its record does not inspire confidence that it will work purposefully for long enough and in sufficient numbers to play a decisive role on the battlefield.[61] Such gold-plating is eschewed by Soviet planners who tend to opt for reliable workhorses in preference to temperamental thoroughbreds.

In general, Soviet systems are trustworthy. Although they may not match Western equipment on a one-to-one basis, they are nevertheless effective. And they are of high quality too if quality is judged by military criteria. They are produced in great numbers, which serves to counteract any technological shortcomings.

Soviet Systems in Lebanon, 1982

The performance of Soviet weapons systems in Lebanon has, however, cast doubt on judgments such as these. For many people the swift destruction of the Soviet-equipped Syrian forces by Israeli units during June and July 1982 reinforced the assumption that Western technological superiority compensates for Soviet numerical advantage. This study is not the place for a detailed analysis of the military lessons of the Lebanese campaign; however, some preliminary remarks relating to the conflict are in order.

It is clear that Israeli forces overwhelmed their Syrian counterparts in three crucial areas. In air combat about eighty Syrian planes were reportedly shot down, mainly MiG-21s (Fishbed) and MiG-23s (Flogger), though some Su-22s (Fitter) and even a couple of reconnaissance MiG-25s (Foxbat) were destroyed as well. The Israeli air force lost no aircraft to enemy jets and only one frontline plane—an F-4E Phantom—to ground fire. In the air-to-surface battle, twenty-three Syrian surface-to-air missile (SAM) sites were destroyed. In the land conflict, the Israelis, with total air supremacy, wiped out over 400 Syrian tanks and lost only about 10 tanks of their own. Over half of the Syrian tanks destroyed were T-62s. Although approximately 10 T-72s—the latest Soviet main battle tank—were lost, the majority of the remainder were older T-55s.[62]

To infer from this chastening catalog of Syrian setbacks that Soviet military hardware is junk and, by extension, that U.S. high-tech weaponry is all conquering is, however, crudely overoptimistic and ill advised.[63] There were reports of general Syrian disenchantment with the performance of their Soviet-built equipment. But the Soviet Union has suggested, albeit obliquely, that the explanation for Israel's successes lay not in the inferior quality of the Syrians' hardware but in the inadequate performance of their soldiers.[64] Although this Soviet claim could have been predicted, it should not be lightly dismissed.

For several reasons, the results of a limited war between Israel and Syria in Lebanon cannot be extrapolated to a prospective European conflict. These relate to the quality of Syrian troops compared to their Soviet counterparts, to the numerical differences between what happened in the Lebanon and what might transpire in Europe, and to the type of equipment used by the Israelis. There was a vast gulf in quality of manpower between the protagonists in the Bekaa Valley. It was the skill, professionalism, and battle experience of Israel's forces that carried the day. Had the Israelis used Soviet weapons, the result would probably not have been different. In tactical terms, on the ground and in the air, the Syrian forces were handled very poorly by all accounts. As in 1973–1974, "Their ability to read the battlefield correctly and interpret what was going on remained very low."[65] And a high-ranking Israeli air force officer remarked:

> Russian aircraft are very good from what we know of their abilities and from what we've seen they can do. The problem was that their [Syrian] pilots didn't do things at the right time or in the right place. They flew in a way difficult to understand. That's why their losses were so high. . . . They could have flown the best fighter in the world, but if they flew it the way they were flying, we would have shot them down in exactly the same way. It wasn't the equipment at fault, but their tactics.[66]

The West would be foolish to luxuriate in a false sense of security following the war in Lebanon. Soviet troops will neither be so poorly trained nor so tactically naive.

The clash in the Bekaa Valley did not duplicate the massive numerical advantage in men, tanks, artillery, SAMs, and aircraft possessed by the Soviet Union in Europe either. Thus some Western observers' contention—that a few high-tech planes are more than a match for numerous but less sophisticated systems—is clearly facile. The Israelis probably outnumbered the Syrians by three to two in numbers of tactical aircraft, while in the land battle there was a rough parity in numbers of tanks and men—force ratios quite unlike those on the Central Front.

Reports that Israel's success in the Lebanon was achieved primarily through using state of the art technology imported from the United States also tell less than the whole story. In the air, Israeli-built Kfir fighters were extremely successful, in some cases outperforming the F-15 and F-16 jets.[67]

The imaginative use of remotely piloted vehicles (RPVs), or drones—designed and constructed in Israel—had much to do with the destruction of Syrian SAM sites.[68] The Israeli electronics industry appears to be ahead even of U.S. firms in this area of warfare. On the ground, the Israelis deployed three types of tank: the U.S. M-60 Patton, modified British Centurions, and a new tank of exclusive Israeli design, the Merkava. This last performed best of all. Indeed, the M-60 was reported to be the least capable of the three. Although few T-72s were destroyed, it appears that the Merkava's 105 mm projectile did penetrate the Soviet tank's heavy frontal armor, something that other Western tanks cannot guarantee.

It is evident that the result of the clash between Israel and Syria in Lebanon is neither the outright condemnation of Soviet equipment nor the ringing endorsement of U.S. weaponry that many have suggested. The Israelis themselves believe that very few such lessons can be drawn. All that can be said with certainty is that "certain Soviet-made weapons in Syrian hands ... were shown to be not up to scratch with the sophisticated US-made (and Israeli-made) weapons in Israeli hands."[69]

High Technology

Returning to the mainstream of this survey, it is appropriate to note that the contrast between Soviet and U.S. procurement styles has been somewhat overdrawn. The Soviet Union has not invariably opted for quantity; there are quite a few high-quality weapons in its inventory.[70] On the U.S. side, the high-technology approach has come in for some telling criticism from Washington's military reformers, much of it to do with the meaning of quality: "The Pentagon defines quality in technical terms: high technology equals quality. The military reform movement defines quality tactically, in terms of the characteristics that are most important in actual combat."[71] There is common ground here because, for the Soviets too, quality is tightly related to military effectiveness. They reject technological complexity for its own sake. The weapon must be of high quality, but it is quality judged by tactical criteria, not simply by the level of embodied technological fanciness.

This is why Soviet weapons are often simple in comparison with overly sophisticated U.S. equipment. And it is why Soviet hardware is notoriously poorly finished by Western standards. In the trade-off between production costs and high weapon capability, Soviet designers tend toward the former when possible. Low production costs permit the procurement of large numbers of sturdy, reliable, and militarily effective systems. On the other hand, the quest for high weapon capability can result in extremely expensive, unreliable equipment, which may perform poorly in battle.[72]

As well as being simple, Soviet weapons frequently use standardized components. Military benefits accrue from using tried and tested subsystems.

Longer production runs allow greater economies of scale, and standardized hardware is easier to maintain because components and subsystems are easily interchangeable.

Many Soviet armaments are also products of an evolutionary approach to design. This reduces production, training, and logistical expenditures. Evolutionary design does not give rise to the spectacular successes of radical innovation, but neither is it prone to spectacular failure.

Yet despite this general penchant for a conservative style of procurement, the Soviet Union can, when necessary, be innovative. Designers have recognized that there are certain military areas where a conservative or incremental strategy will not suffice. In these areas it is clear that a radical, or design-from-first-principles, approach is inescapable. The Soviet Union is capable of pursuing such a strategy when new problems emerge that are not susceptible to conservative solutions.

Summary Case Studies

There is very little evidence of a Soviet drive for main battle tank (MBT) standardization, although simplicity has long been a key aim of Soviet tank designers. With the T-34 (many of which are kept in mothballs for emergency or export) and the new T-72, the Warsaw Pact deploys five MBTs, though for all practical purposes there are only three: the T-54/55, T-62, and T-64/72. All of these tanks have different guns—100 mm rifled, 115 mm smooth bore, and 125 mm smooth bore, respectively—each without interchangeability of ammunition.

In design terms the T-62 was only an incremental or evolutionary advance on the effective T-54/55. The T-64/72, however, is a generational jump. The development of Chobham armor in the West during the 1970s meant that the T-62 had been developed to the limit of its potential; its gun could no longer ensure penetration of enemy armor. In response, the 125 mm gun was introduced. This proved too large for a T-62 turret ring, and a totally new design was required.[73] This includes an automatic loader that allows reduction in crew size from four to three. (The T-64/72 was the first tank in the world with this characteristic.) It also possesses unconventional frontal armor and movable armored plates along the side of the hull.[74]

A comparison of Warsaw Pact and NATO tanks is outside the scope of this study. Suffice it to say that Soviet designers have been in the forefront of tank design since the production of the superb T-34 during World War II. The T-34 had a rough finish, but this did not reduce its combat capabilities. By all accounts the German Panther overwhelmed a T-34 on a one-to-one basis, but it was expensive and more complicated to transport, operate, and maintain. As a result, it was defeated by the rugged, reliable, and numerous T-34. Such information is directly relevant to an evaluation of current Soviet MBT design.[75]

Soviet ballistic missile R&D has also reached a high level of competence. Since the 1960s seven new ICBMs have been developed. During the 1970s four ICBMs were flight tested; all were significantly more penetrating than their predecessors, and all embodied completely new techniques.[76] The Soviet Union has also embarked on preflight tests with two fifth-generation ICBMs.[77] Both are solid fueled, and one is reportedly a large mobile system approximately the size of MX. Two more fifth-generation missiles are under development, and these are believed to be storable liquid fueled. Undoubtedly standardized components and subsystems have been incorporated into several missiles. And missile design has relied heavily on an evolutionary approach. Nevertheless, Soviet progress in ICBM technology suggests that neither simplicity, standardization, nor evolutionary change was exclusively or rigidly pursued by design teams. Indeed it can be argued that Soviet ICBM engineering has demonstrated a flexibility and an innovative dynamism that makes it superior to comparable U.S. work. A decision to proceed to full production of a prototype depends overwhelmingly on the quality of the proposed system. This has meant the procurement of a wide range of complex, nonstandardized systems that are the products of radical—not conservative—innovation.

At the highest levels of sophistication, Soviet competence can be separated into two. First, there are high-technology sectors—which may be military-related—where indigenous technology is inferior to Western equipment. Dependence on foreign technology here is necessarily high. (Examples are the Soviet computer and chemical industries.) Second, there are other areas where Soviet technological and innovatory performance is equal to, or even high than, that of the West. These are overwhelmingly located in military-relevant industrial sectors.

In the past there have been bursts of Soviet innovative energy that resulted in rapid technological advance. The nuclear weapons program provides an example of this and was accelerated by Stalin's direct involvement, as were the ICBM and space projects. Soviet efforts in space are an impressive testament to a considerable technological prowess, and Soviet designers have been responsible for extending the state of the art on several occasions. Such achievements have continued to this day.

The Soviets have sent three times as many craft into space as the Americans. A reusable space vehicle has long been a priority of Soviet planners. Experts now believe that the Soviet Union will develop a space transportation system by the late 1980s that is similar to the U.S. space shuttle but uses a fly-back booster.[78] This program is code named Raketoplan. The space ship (called Albatross) is much smaller tha the U.S. shuttle, and unmanned prototypes have already flown into space and successfully returned. The project is in two phases. Phase 1, which is expected to be completed by 1985, involves the transportaion of a spacecraft on an expandable, vertically launched booster; phase 2 is revolutionary and envisages a reusable booster and spacecraft.

Albatross, moreover, is thought to possess an orbital maneuver capability. If so, this gives it more flexibility than its U.S. rival constrained as it is to a single orbit. Over 80 percent of Soviet space missions have military applications, and Albatross must have a satellite transport and interceptor role, as well as conventional civilian, scientific-technical information-gathering missions. Soviet space technology is highly advanced and of very high national priority. It demonstrates that the Soviets do not slavishly pursue a conservative strategy of design. They have recognized that in many areas effective performance of the military mission relies of necessity on a high-technology design from first principles approach. The conservative style is jettisoned in these circumstances.

Soviet advances in laser and particle beam technology also show a capacity to produce new-in-principle equipment when circumstances so demand. Despite massive obstacles, these technologies hold out the possibility of accurate and effective ABM defense and an antisatellite capability. Soviet research into energy beams reflects a long-term commitment and had reached sizable proportions as early as 1967. The Soviet Union is currently thought to be six years ahead of the United States. It has been predicted, moreover, that the Soviets will test these weapons during the 1980s. If this occurs, Soviet scientists will have effectively undermined the hypothesis that they are ineffective innovators. Soviet science is highly advanced and at least the equal of U.S. science. Future weapons developments at the high-technology end of the scale are coming to depend increasingly on the exploitation of pure scientific principles. Soviet science has an excellent track record; it will continue to compete effectively.

Concluding Remarks on Style

The forces that animate Soviet weapons acquisition are different from those that drive U.S. procurement. The contention that Soviet armaments are inferior to U.S. hardware is therefore overly simplistic.

No one would deny that there are structural weaknesses in the Soviet economy as a whole that inhibit technical progress. But Soviet military R&D has overcome them and can produce high-quality weapons. Certainly many Soviet systems are simple, and many do rely on standardized components and subsystems. Also many, if not most, clearly are products of an evolutionary design process. Overall, therefore, the Soviet approach to military innovation is conservative; however, that does not connote inferiority. In fact, the approach is based on deliberate choice. The system is functional, taking full account of Soviet constraints and preferences.

The key point is that the Soviet Union's past experience of conflict and the different mission requirements of its armed forces have resulted in the adoption of a distinctive definition of military quality. Quality is gauged not in technical terms but according to tactical and operational criteria. Technical complexity for its own sake is eschewed. Tactics and technology are symbiotically joined, with the aim of producing weapons that are effective as battlefield systems. The approach is epitomized in the exhortation that Mikhail Mil, the famous helicopter designer, is reported to have addressed to his design teams: "Make it simple, make it rugged, make it reliable and make it work." Put another way, there is a conscious effort to select the right weapon for the mission. This means systems that are advanced but less inherently complex than comparable U.S. systems.

The Soviets have recognized that design conservatism is counterproductive in certain military areas, however, and they are aware of the possible shortcomings of an exclusively incremental strategy:

> The dogmatic utilization of this method [conservative design] can result in slowing down the rate of technological progress. ... Upon reaching a certain stage in the development of a given ... design, it is necessary to forgo the design inheritance method and to look for new solutions with the purpose of substantial improvements.[79]

Accordingly, a radical, nonstandardized style of design is adopted, as required, in sectors where it is important to avoid what may be called technological ambush (where there is no compensation for being technologically inferior). The examples of ICBMs, space exploration, and particle beam technology demonstrate that, when given the requisite support, Soviet planners, scientists, and designers can produce state of the art weaponry that compares favorably with U.S. equipment.

Conclusion

The conventional wisdom in the West makes some contentious judgments about the institutional structure and style of Soviet weapons acquisition. It holds that effective procurement in the Soviet Union is handicapped by excessively centralized procedures implemented by an unimaginative bureaucracy. It holds that the Soviet approach to weapons design is conservative and produces low-quality systems (by U.S. standards). These are dubious assertions, and Western policymakers are ill advised to accept them. Most Soviet systems are not inferior to U.S. equipment. Where it matters—on the battlefield—they can be expected to perform at least as well as, and probably better than, U.S. hardware.

The institutional arrangements of Soviet weapons acquisition are undoubtedly complex; however, they are functional. Certainly there is nothing in the account of procurement procedures in the first half of this study to suggest that faults in the system condemn the Soviet Union to military inferiority. Indeed, the high priority accorded to defense within the Soviet economy and the political leadership's role in military decision making combine to facilitate effective procurement. Moreover, the focal position of the armed forces in defense policy formulation and their intimate links with the defense-industrial sector and R&D institutions enable them to define exactly the types of weapons they require. This consumer sovereignty lubricates an acquisition cycle that otherwise might suffer from bureaucratic seizure.

The style of procurement in the Soviet Union is functional too. The approach reflects the historical, demographic, doctrinal, and economic constraints under which Soviet force planners and designers operate. There is a disposition to apply the three principles of simplicity, standardization, and evolutionary change and a predilection for conservative design. But this does not connote inferiority. Rather, it has resulted in a distinctive Soviet definition of what constitutes quality in military terms. A weapon of high quality is not one that simply embodies state of the art technology but one that satisfies stringent operational criteria. This is tactical, not technical, quality. (Where state of the art systems are required, however, Soviet scientists have shown that they can be as innovative as their Western counterparts.)

The conclusion is clear. Western efforts to characterize the Soviet Union's procurement apparatus as inefficient and its outputs as inferior are mistaken. The Soviet weapons acquisition system is highly successful in the production of effective hardware. In fact, given the problems that frequently beset the West's high-tech approach to military design, a pertinent question is, Would more respectful attention to the Soviet system and its style not be worthwhile?

Notes

1. Arthur J. Alexander, *Armor Development in the Soviet Union and the United States* (Santa Monica: RAND, R-1860–NA, 1976), p. 4.

2. An example of this tendency is the furor surrounding the delivery of the new U.S. M-1 Abrams tank.

3. John A. McDonnell, *The Soviet Weapons Acquisition System* (Halifax, Nova Scotia: Centre for Foreign Policy Studies, Dalhousie University, March 1979), p. 19.

4. For a lucid discussion of these distinctions and the role played by design in the Soviet Union, see Raymond Hutchings, "Soviet Design: The Neglected Partner of Soviet Science and Technology," *Slavic Review*, no. 4 (1978): 567–583.

5. David Holloway, "Soviet Military R&D: Managing the 'Research-Production Cycle,'" in John R. Thomas and Ursula M. Kruse-Vaucienne, eds, *Soviet Science and Technology: Domestic and Foreign Perspectives* (Washington, D.C.: George Washington University, 1977), p. 190.

6. It is recognized that the exact measurement of the burden of Soviet defense is fraught with difficulties. For a brief but excellent presentation of the literature and problems involved, see Abraham S. Becker, *The Burden of Soviet Defense: A Political-Economic Essay* (Santa Monica: RAND, R-2752, October 1981), pp. 3–21.

7. W.T. Lee, "Soviet Defense Expenditures," in William Schneider, Jr., and Francis P. Hoeber, eds., *Arms, Men and Military Budgets* (New York: Crane, Russak, 1976), p. 265.

8. Becker, *Burden*, p. 16.

9. Ibid., p. 1.

10. Lee, "Soviet Defense Expenditures," pp. 282–283.

11. Becker, *Burden*, p. 17.

12. *Guardian*, March 18, 1982.

13. Defense spending is only one of a range of factors that has contributed to a decline in the growth rate of the Soviet economy; the rapidly depleting accessible energy reserves, the decline in the growth rate of the labor force, and perennial agricultural problems are also relevant.

14. This section is based on published sources, particularly Arthur J. Alexander, *Decision-Making in Soviet Weapons Procurement*, Adelphi Paper Nos. 147–148 (London: International Institute for Strategic Studies [IISS], Winter 1978–1979) and Edward L. Warner, *The Military in Contemporary Soviet Politics* (New York: Praeger, 1977).

15. David Holloway, "Military Power and Political Purpose in Soviet Policy," *Daedalus* (Fall 1980): 25.

16. William E. Odom, "The Party-Military Connection: A Critique," in Dale R. Herspring and Ivan Volgyes, eds., *Civil-Military Relations in Communist Systems* (Boulder, Colo.: Westview Press, 1978), p. 40.

17. J. Hough, "The Brezhnev Era—The Man and the System," *Problems of Communism* (March–April 1976): 1–17.

18. For a succinct history of the antecedents of the Defense Council see Alexander, *Decision-Making*, pp. 14–15.

19. Warner, *Military*, p. 46.

20. Alexander, *Decision-Making*, p. 12.

21. For details of Alekseev's appointment see ibid., p. 17, and also *The Directory of the USSR Ministry of Defence and Armed Forces Officials* (Washington, D.C.: National Foreign Assessment Center, CR8011888, 1980).

22. Alexander, *Decision-Making*, p. 17.

23. Roman Kolkowicz, *The Soviet Military and the Communist Party* (Princeton: Princeton University Press, 1967), pp. 309–321.

24. See Roman Kolkowicz, "Interest Groups and Soviet Politics: The Case of the Military," in Herspring and Volgyes, *Civil-Military Relations*, pp. 17–19, for a brief elucidation of this issue.

25. Alexander, *Decision-Making*, pp. 18–19.

26. Very little research concerning this very important body has been done, but for a brief discussion, see Michael Checinski, *A Comparison of the Polish and Soviet Armaments Decisionmaking Systems* (Santa Monica: RAND, R-266Z-AF, January 1981), pp. 57–58, 67–68.

27. Andrew Sheren, "Structure and Organization of Defense-Related Industries," in U.S. Congress, Joint Economic Committee, *Economic Performance and the Military Burden in the Soviet Union* (Washington D.C.: Government Printing Office, 1970), pp. 123–132, and Alexander, *Decision-Making*, pp. 21–24.

28. David Holloway, "The Soviet Style of Military R&D," in Franklin A. Long and Judith Reppy, eds., *The Genesis of New Weapons Decision Making for Military R&D* (New York: Pergamon Press, 1980), p. 143.

29. Vernon V. Aspaturian, "The Soviet Military-Industrial Complex—Does It Exist?" *Journal of International Affairs* 26 (1972): 15.

30. Alexander, *Decision-Making*, p. 21.

31. Arthur J. Alexander, "Weapons Acquisition in the Soviet Union, the United States and France," in Frank B. Horton, Anthony C. Rogerson, and Edward L. Warner, eds., *Comparative Defense Policy* (Baltimore: Johns Hopkins University Press, 1974), p. 427.

32. Simon Kassel and Cathleen Campbell, *The Soviet Academy of Sciences and Technological Development* (Santa Monica: RAND, R-2533, December 1980), pp. 10–11.

33. John A. McDonnell, *The Soviet Weapons Acquisition System* (Halifax, Nova Scotia: Center for Foreign Policy Studies, Dalhousie University, March 1979), p. 4.

34. See Kassel and Campbell, *Soviet Academy*, and Simon Kassel, *The Relationship between Science and the Military in the Soviet Union* (Santa Monica: RAND, R-1457, July 1974).

35. Arthur J. Alexander, *The Process of Soviet Weapons Design* (Santa Monica: RAND, R-6137, March 1978), p. 20.

36. Arthur J. Alexander, *R&D in Soviet Aviation* (Santa Monica: RAND, R-589, 1970), p. 9, and Holloway, "Soviet Style," pp. 146–147.

37. Ibid.

38. Ibid.

39. McDonnell, *Soviet Weapons*, p. 29.

40. Alexander, *Armor Development*, p. 48.

41. For a brief overview of Soviet rocketry, see Milan Kocourek, "Rocketry: Level of Technology in Launch Vehicles and Manned Space Capsules," in Ronald Amann, Julian Cooper, and R.W. Davies, eds., *The Technological Level of Soviet Industry* (New Haven: Yale University Press, 1977), pp. 490–522.

42. Merton J. Peck and Frederic M. Scherer, *The Weapons Acquisition Process* (Boston: Harvard University, 1962), chap. 3.

43. Holloway, "Soviet Military R&D," p. 204.

44. Mikhail Agursky and Hannes Adomeit, "The Soviet Military-Industrial Complex," *Survey* 24 (Spring 1979): 114–117.

45. Alexander, *Weapons Acquisition*.

46. Nancy Nimitz *The Structure of Soviet Outlays on R&D in 1960 and 1968* (Santa Monica: RAND, R-1207, 1974), p. 41.

47. For an expansion of this theme see Holloway, "Soviet Military R&D," p. 209.

48. For a brief exposition of this "no feast or famine" argument, see Alexander H. Flax, "The Influence of the Civilian Sector on Military R&D," in Franklin A. Long and Judith Reppy, eds., *The Genesis of New Weapons: Decision Making for Military R&D* (New York: Pergamon Press, 1980), pp. 117–120.

49. Michael J. Deane and Mark E. Miller, "Science and Technology in Soviet Military Planning," *Strategic Review* (Summer 1977): 80.

50. Ken Booth, *Navies and Foreign Policy* (London: Croom Helm, 1977), pp. 117–119.

51. James W. Kehoe, "Warship Design: Ours and Theirs," *United States Naval Institute Proceedings* (August 1975): 56–65.

52. Jan S. Breemer, "The New Soviet Aircraft Carrier," *United States Naval Institute Proceedings* (August 1981): 30–35.

53. J.W. Kehoe and K.S. Brower, "U.S. and Soviet Weapon System Design Practices," *International Defence Review* 15 (1982): 706.

54. James Fallows, "Muscle-Bound Superpower: The State of America's Defense," *Atlantic* 244 (October 1979): 63.

55. Craig Oliphant, "The Performance of Soviet Weapons in Lebanon," *Radio Liberty Research*, RL68/83, February 7, 1983, and "The Lesson of Lebanon," *Defence Attache*, 4 (1982): 25–28.

56. The quotation is from *Washington Times*, October 15, 1982.

57. Galia Golan, "The Soviet Union and the Israeli Action in Lebanon," *International Affairs* 59 (Winter 1982–1983): 7–8.

58. Israeli Chief of Staff Eitan, quoted in *"Lesson of Lebanon,"* p. 26.

59. "Bekaa Valley Combat," *Flight International,* October 16, 1982, p. 1109.

60. Ibid., p. 1108.

61. "Surveillance Integration Pivotal in Israeli Successes," *Aviation Week and Space Technology,* July 5, 1982, pp. 16–17.

62. Oliphant, "Performance," p. 2.

63. Michael Handel, "Numbers Do Count: The Question of Quality versus Quantity," *Journal of Strategic Studies* 5 (September 1981): 237.

64. Gary Hart, "What's Wrong with the Military?" *New York Times Magazine,* February 14, 1982.

65. Steven J. Zaloga, *Modern Soviet Armour: Combat Vehicles of the USSR and Warsaw Pact Today* (London: Arms and Armour Press, 1979), p. 25.

66. Ibid., p. 7.

67. For a full discussion of the capabilities and techniques used by these missiles, see *The Military Balance 1981–82* (London: IISS, 1982), and "Soviet Nuclear Arsenal Continues to Proliferate," *Aviation Week and Space Technology,* June 16, 1980, pp. 67–76.

68. "Soviets Testing New Generation of ICBMs," *Aviation Week and Space Technology,* November 3, 1980, pp. 28–29.

69. "Soviets Developing Fly-Back Launchers," *Aviation Week and Space Technology,* November 6, 1979.

70. From a Soviet textbook on aviation technology quoted in Alexander, *Weapons Acquisition,* p. 431.

71. Gary Hart, "What's Wrong with the Military?" *The New York Times Magazine*, 14 Feb. 1982.

72. As mission requirements become more demanding in the future, Soviet simplicity must give way to increasing complexity. However, it will be complexity which continues to match technology to Soviet tactical and operational necessities.

73. Steven J. Zaloga, *Modern Soviet Armour: Combat Vehicles of the USSR and Warsaw Pact Today* (London: Arms and Armour Press, 1979), p. 25.

74. A new tank—the T-80—has been identified by NATO as a variant of the T-72 with composite armor.

75. *Ibid.*, p. 7.

76. For a full discussion of the capabilities and techniques used by these missiles, see *The Military Balance 1981–82* (London: IISS, 1982), and "Soviet Nuclear Arsenal Continues to Proliferate," *Aviation Week and Space Technology*, 16 June 1980, pp. 67–76.

77. "Soviets Testing New Generation of ICBMs," *ibid.*, 3 Nov. 1980, pp. 28–29.

78. "Soviets Developing Fly-Back Launchers," *ibid.*, 6 Nov. 1979.

79. From a Soviet textbook on aviation technology, quoted in Alexander, "Weapons Acquisitions," p. 431.

10

The Soviet Union and the East European Militaries: The Diminishing Asset

Dale R. Herspring

Despite the key importance Moscow has assigned the East European armies in Warsaw Pact strategy and the important role they have been expected to play in helping maintain political order, recent trends suggest that their value to Moscow is diminishing in the first area and limited in the second. On the external front, the increasing qualitative disparities between East European and Soviet weapons systems, as well as nagging—if not increasing—questions concerning their political reliability, are not only undermining Moscow's strategy of coalition warfare in relation to NATO but may be forcing the Kremlin to make some significant changes in its strategy for fighting a war in Europe. Internally, despite the actions taken by the Polish military on December 13, 1981, to help maintain communist rule in Poland, a careful analysis of the Polish experience over the past four or five years, as well as the East European historical record in general, suggests that the government-party's ability to utilize the armed forces in an internal crisis is much more limited than is generally assumed in the West.

Conceptually, the role and function of East European militaries can be divided into two broad categories: external, or the deployment of the armed forces against foreign enemies, and internal, or the use of the military to maintain or strengthen political stability, especially during periods of systemic crisis. For purposes of this chapter, the external role of the military refers primarily to Moscow's perception of the utility of the East European militaries in an East–West conflict in Europe, although mention will also be made of their value as a tool for maintaining discipline within the socialist commonwealth. The internal role of the military refers to the armed forces as an institution that can be relied upon to step in to help maintain systemic order and control by the party in a crisis situation. As the historical analysis will demonstrate, the role and function of the East

---

The opinions expressed in this chapter are those of the author and do not represent official U.S. government policy.

European militaries, and their consequent value to the Soviets, have changed over time in both areas.

Historical Evolution of the East European Armies

1944–1948: The Seizure of Power

While Soviet and East European military historians have argued that the origins of most of the East European armies can be traced back to the common struggle against the Germans during World War II,[1] in fact, with the exception of the Polish and Czechoslovak armies, most of the others (Slovaks, Hungarians, and Rumanians as well as Germans) fought on the Eastern Front against the Soviet Union.[2] Furthermore, even in the case of the Polish military, the memories of the Katyn Forest massacre, Stalin's partition of the country, and Moscow's relatively harsh treatment of those Poles who fell under its control contributed to an intensification of historical animosities on the part of Poles.[3] As a consequence, Moscow hesitated to introduce a strong system of political controls in the Polish army when it was first created. For example, large numbers of nonparty members were utilized within the political apparatus. One official source reports that only about 13 percent of all political-educational officers were members of the party in December 1944.[4] And only 5 percent of officers assigned to the Main Political Administration (MPA), the most central and politically sensitive component of the political apparatus, belonged to the Communist party.[5]

Even after the close of World War II, hostility toward the Soviet Union and communism was strong enough throughout the region that the Soviets hesitated to Sovietize fully the East European militaries. In the Polish case, for example, although the MPA continued to function, its importance as a politicizing agent actually decreased. The political officers' school was closed in 1946, and by 1948 only 50 percent of all political officer positions were filled in the armed forces.[6] Political indoctrination efforts were aimed at imparting a basic understanding of Marxism-Leninism but were not required, and measures traditionally employed as control devices in communist militaries such as self-criticism were largely ignored.

Despite this go-slow policy toward Sovietizing the militaries, Moscow did begin to take steps aimed at neutralizing the militaries while laying the groundwork for building a sense of loyalty toward the newly evolving socialist systems. Thus, hostile elements were removed from the officer corps and replaced by individuals with the proper class background. As a prominent Polish sociologist put it, "For understandable reasons, socio-political criteria took precedence during the period when the army was created—even at the expense of many purely professional criteria."[7]

Little thought was given during this period to the possible deployment of these forces against an external foe. Their equipment was insufficient and antiquated—often of World War II vintage—training rudimentary, cadre unqualified, and neither the Soviets nor the East European leaderships showed any concern with removing the armed forces from their emasculated condition. From Moscow's point of view, the task was to neutralize the armed forces, and if this meant making them militarily irrelevant, so be it.

1948–1952: Stalinism

With the imposition of Stalinism in Eastern Europe in 1948, all aspects of the various political systems were expected to imitate the Soviet model. This included the armed forces. As a result, national command positions were immediately filled with communist or pro-communist officers, often individuals with little or no military experience. The neutral officers appointed to senior positions only a few years earlier were quickly shunted aside. Furthermore, the process of recruiting new officers from hitherto disadvantaged classes (the worker or peasant classes) was intensified. Thus by 1950 the percentage of officers with a worker or peasant background was 82 percent in Bulgaria and 60 percent in Hungary; by 1952 it was 67.7 percent in Czechoslovakia, and by the end of 1953 it was 50.3 percent for Poland.[8]

In addition to personnel policies, other areas of military life were affected by the Sovietization of the East European militaries. Soviet doctrine, training patterns, and internal organization were also introduced. Even the traditionally distinctive East European uniforms were modified to the point where they were almost indistinguishable from those worn by the Soviets.

To ensure East European military subordination to Soviet command, a number of direct channels of control were introduced by the Soviets. Thousands of military officers were assigned to the East European militaries as advisers, although in some cases they were actually incorporated into the national armies as regular officers. The most conspicuous example of the latter was in Poland where Soviet Marshal Konstantin Rokossovsky became Warsaw's defense minister.[9]

Moscow also moved at this time to intensify politicization within the militaries. In Poland, for example, the political officers' school was reopened, and the number of political officer positions was increased. The post of deputy commander for political affairs was introduced at the company level, thereby bringing the political apparatus down to the main working level. Furthermore, throughout Eastern Europe the MPA was given responsibility for the politicization process, and its actions came under increased scrutiny by the party leadership. In addition, the party organization was revitalized, and the basic party organization was introduced at the regimental level. Party meetings and discussions began to be held on a regular basis.

Concurrent with Sovietization of the East European militaries, the Kremlin began to devote attention to building up Eastern Europe's military capabilities. By 1949, for example military conscription had been introduced throughout the region (except for the German Democratic Republic)[GDR]), and by 1953 the East European armies had expanded to 1.5 million men, organized into roughly sixty-five divisions.[10] In addition, Soviet equipment began to replace the East Europeans' largely outdated armament inventory. As a Bulgarian source noted in reference to this period; "The troops gradually received new protective weapons (the self-loading rifle 'Simonov', 'Kalaschnikov' submachine guns), better developed air defense systems, jet aircraft, modern tanks, etc."[11]

While from the Soviet standpoint there was little reason to trust in the internal or external reliability of the various East European militaries at this time, Moscow could at least take comfort in the fact that the basis for a more dependable military had been laid. Furthermore, insofar as a future East–West conflict is concerned, Stalin "may have intended their build-up as a supplement to that of the Red Army itself, which was designed to alter the military balance in Europe to the advantage of the Soviet Union."[12]

1953–1959: Post-Stalinism and the Founding of the Pact

The aftermath of Stalin's death was a period of major transition for the East European armies. Most of the more extreme forms of Sovietization were eliminated. For example, traditional East European military uniforms and songs were reintroduced. In addition, status of forces agreements were concluded with Poland (1956), Hungary (1957), Rumania (1957), and East Germany (1957), thereby regularizing the presence of Soviet troops, and in the case of Poland guaranteeing their noninterference in Polish domestic affairs.[13] The Soviets also agreed to a Rumanian request and in 1958 withdrew all Soviet forces from that country.

From a military standpoint, the most important form of renationalization concerned the recall of large numbers of Soviet advisers and military officers from the East European militaries. This was most evident in Poland where Marshal Rokossowski and almost all of his fellow officers were returned to the Soviet Union. They were replaced by native communist officers, many of whom had been purged and imprisoned during the Stalinist period.

In addition to the renationalization of the armed forces, the role of the political apparatus was deemphasized. In Poland, the post of deputy commander for political affairs at the company level was abolished and the time allocated to ideological indoctrination courses shortened. The communist youth organization was abolished, and the focus of party activity shifted from the political apparatus to the party organization. Since only half the officers and even fewer enlisted personnel were party members, the net result was to weaken party influence within the military.

Although ostensibly created as a loosely organized socialist military coalition, to counter "possible aggression," the Warsaw Pact, founded in 1955, was equally important to the Kremlin as an institutionalized substitute for Stalin's personalized system of asserting Soviet hegemony over the East European militaries.[14] From the military standpoint, for example, article 5 of the treaty provided for a joint military command, and one was established in Moscow in 1956. Nevertheless, in military terms it remained a paper organization during this period. The primary Soviet history of the pact lists only one major military exercise during this period, involving naval, air, and ground forces from the Soviet Union and Bulgaria.[15] As Thomas Wolfe put it, "The Soviet Union made no effort to weld the Warsaw Pact into an integrated military alliance" during its early years.[16]

Despite Moscow's neglect of the pact during its first five years, important changes occurred in the East European militaries. East European forces were cut back by 464,000 men.[17] Concurrently vigorous efforts were made to improve the educational qualifications of the remaining officers and noncommissioned officers. In Poland the proportion of officers with academic degrees rose from 12 percent in 1956 to 20 percent by 1962, in Czechoslovakia from 4.8 percent in 1956 to 14.4 percent in 1963, and in Bulgaria by 1960 between 15 and 20 percent had academic degrees.[18]

With regard to equipment, the motorization of infantry units was pushed, new armored units were established, and tactical forces were modified to permit operations under conditions of nuclear war. T-54s gradually replaced T-34s, MiG-17s were added, and improved communication and transportation systems were introduced.[19]

Despite the modernization of East European forces and the creation of the pact, their utility to the Kremlin in a strictly military sense was severly limited at this time. The lack of qualified personnel, training deficiencies, especially in the area of combined operations, and the disparity in equipment held by front-line Soviet forces and East European armies meant that their use in conjunction with Soviet forces in an East–West confrontation would be problematical.

If equipment and training shortcomings presented the Kremlin with problems at this time, they were nothing when compared with the questions raised concerning the overall political reliability of East European forces. The uprising in East Berlin in 1953 was put down by Soviet forces, due in large part to Soviet concerns over the reliability of East German paramilitary forces. During the Hungarian revolt in 1956, some units fought against the Soviets "with valor, courage, and heroism reminiscent of the best traditions of Hungarian military history," while the army as a whole stayed out of the fight.[20] Furthermore, in the aftermath of Moscow's suppression of the revolt, the army was decimated by a purge that left large gaps in the ranks of the officer and noncommissioned officer corps.

From the Soviet standpoint, the events in Poland in 1956 presented an even more dangerous challenge. Not only do the Poles occupy a strategic piece of real estate and possess the largest non-Soviet pact force, but most senior ranks in the polish military were at that time occupied by Soviet officers. When troops in Poznan refused to put down demonstrations in June, Polish authorities were forced to call in security forces from Warsaw. Furthermore, in October, shortly after Gomulka assumed power, Polish forces played a critical role in ensuring a Polish solution to the leadership question. Khrushchev and his compatriots arrived at Okecie airport unannounced and uninvited in an effort to oust Gomulka. At the same time, Soviet troops in Poland left their barracks and began to move on Warsaw. Meanwhile, Polish forces took up defensive positions around the city, making it clear they were prepared to fight. The threat of resistance by Polish forces at a critical juncture appears to have played an important role in Khrushchev's decision to back down and accept Gomulka. For Moscow the message was ominous: not even the presence of Soviet officers in the senior ranks of the Polish military could ensure loyalty on the part of the Polish military. If anything, these three events made it clear to the Kremlin that serious problems would have to be overcome before the East Europeans could be considered reliable.

1960–1968: The Buildup and Czechoslovakia

The significant increase in attention paid by the Soviets to the pact as a military organization after 1960 appears to have been primarily associated with Khrushchev's plan for shifting reliance in Soviet defense planning and doctrine away from traditional emphasis on ground forces toward greater importance for strategic nuclear forces. He apparently felt he could justify—at least partially—the cutbacks he planned in Soviet ground forces by getting East European military forces to assume a larger role in pact strategy.

To implement this new strategy, major steps were undertaken to upgrade East European forces shortly after Marshal Grechko took over as pact commander in chief in 1960. A new pact doctrine called coalition warfare was developed. This doctrine assigned the East Europeans a key role in any East-West conflict. In such a conflict they would be expected to participate jointly with Soviet forces in rapid offensive military operations against NATO. As a result of this new doctrine, East European forces were assigned increasingly important roles. The Poles were eventually given their own front commanded by a Polish general (the so-called Northern Front), and East German and Czechoslovak forces were assigned important roles in conjunction with Soviet forces on the Central and Southern fronts, respectively.

To make this new doctrine workable, East European military equipment was upgraded. The process of replacing the World War II vintage T-34 with the more modern T-54/55 was completed, and MiG-21 and SU-7 aircraft as well as antitank missiles and self-propelled guns were introduced into pact inventories. Some East European forces began to be supplied with nuclear-capable delivery vehicles (although the weapons themselves were kept in Soviet hands). Standardization of weapons systems was pushed, and a nascent East German aircraft industry was dismantled in 1961. Poland renounced further work on advanced jet aircraft in 1967.[21] Considerable effort was devoted to improving the qualifications of officers. By the end of this period, for example, the percentage of officers with an academic degree in Poland had risen from 18 to 30 and in East Germany from approximately 6 to 13.[22]

A major change also occurred in the area of multilateral training exercises. Where there had been only one in the pact's first five years, there were nineteen between 1960 and 1968. Furthermore, while some of the early exercises could be viewed primarily as propaganda devices, by the mid 1960s they had taken on an increasingly important military meaning.

Finally, increased attention was given to the pact's high-level military organs. They began to meet on an annual basis, and while details on the agenda of their meetings are lacking, information available from Soviet and Polish sources suggests they were primarily concerned with operational matters such as the coming year's training program.[23] Broader defense-related questions appear to have been dealt with by the pact's highest political organ, the Political Consultative Committee (PCC). For example, conditions in the Warsaw Pact forces were discussed at the 1963 PCC meeting.[24]

The increased attention given to training, equipment, and personnel, as well as the greater concern being paid to the pact's defense organs, gave the impression that the Soviet Union was assigning greater weight to the role of the East European militaries. Two developments, however, raised serious questions on Moscow's part concerning the pact's overall military utility.

In late 1964, the Rumanians unilaterally reduced their term of service from twenty-four to sixteen months, which led to a cut of 40,000 men from the Rumanian armed forces. In addition, the Rumanians argued that pact military expenditures were excessive, succeeded in obtaining a reduction in the size of the Soviet military liaison mission in Bucharest, demanded a consultative voice i matters related to nuclear weapons, refused to permit pact troop maneuvers on Rumanian soil, declined to participate in joint maneuvers with combat troops in other countries, and finally proposed that the position of the pact's military chief rotate among member states.[25] These actions not only undercut Moscow's efforts at upgrading and improving cooperation among pact members but also raised serious questions about the utility of Rumanian forces in the Southern Region in the event of a war. These developments, as well as the northern tier's more strategic location—may help to explain the greater attention paid by the Soviets to forces in the northern tier.

Following on the Rumanian deviation came an even more unsettling development insofar as the Soviets were concerned. In 1968 with the rise of reformist elements in Czechoslovakia, certain segments of the Czechoslovak military—concentrated to a large degree in the political apparatus—began to express open dissatisfaction with Moscow's domination of the pact's leadership councils and side with Dubcek in his efforts to democratize Czechoslovakia. Insofar as the domestic Czechoslovak front was concerned, it has been argued by one Western analyst that conservative officers, opposed to the liberal internal policies advocated by Dubcek may have planned to intervene in an effort to save the Novotony regime.[26] In fact, a letter sent to the crucial December 1967 Central Committee meeting apparently contained an implied threat by the army to intervene on Novotony's behalf, and certain units of the army were actually placed on alert, while a number of officers planned to "intervene if the Party's deliberations went against Novotny."[27] The plot was reportedly neutralized by younger pro-Dubcek elements in the officer corps. Despite its inaction during the Soviet invasion—it was ordered not to resist—shortly after the Husak regime was installed, the Klement Gottwald Political Millitary Academy was closed, and a large-scale purge of pro-Dubcek forces followed. According to one source, as a result of the purge and reorganiztion of the officer corps, personnel in some branches were 10 to 30 percent below normal. In the air force, it was admitted to be 20 percent below normal, making it impossible in the first years of 1970 even to hold proper training and evaluation exercises.[28]

Despite all of Moscow's efforts to upgrade the East European forces, the Rumanian and Czechoslovak events suggest that serious problems remained insofar as the reliability of these two pact members were concerned. Not only did the Romanian military support Ceausescu in his defiance of Moscow, important elements of the Czechoslovak army criticized Soviet leadership techniques in the pact and supported liberal elements in the country at a critical juncture.

It could, however, be argued that the period was not a total loss to the Kremlin. After all, the Soviets were able to convince five of their six allies (the Rumanians opted out) to participate in the invastion of Czechoslovakia in 1968. This could be used as evidence to show that the East Europeans are reliable in an intrapact policing role. In my opinion, the importance of this event has tended to be overestimated in the West. Ross Johnson put it best when he noted:

> The invasion of Czechoslovakia demonstrated that the Soviet Union could mobilize some of its East European allies to interfere in the internal affairs of one of them; it did not demonstrate, however, that East European forces could contribute effectively to military operations against one of their number.[29]

There are rumors, for example, that the East German forces aroused considerable resentment on the part of the local populace and had to be quickly withdrawn; that serious morale problems existed among Polish troops (who were embarrassed at being involved, even against a traditional enemy); and that the Hungarians had little heart for the exercise.[30] With the exception of the Soviets, who had morale problems of their own, only the Bulgarians appear to have supported the action. And this occurred against a largely passive population. Thus even an apparent victory in Moscow's efforts to utilize the pact for its own ends left unanswered important questions concerning the reliability of East European troops when asked to carry out Soviet orders.

1969–1979: Reassessment and Reorganization

Despite Soviet concern over pact reliability in the aftermath of the Czechoslovak events, Moscow still felt the East European contribution important. Consequently efforts were made to strengthen pact unity. The most important change in this regard was the introduction of modifications in pact structure. Although raised within pact councils as early as 1966, they were not formally announced until the March 1969 PCC meeting in Budapest. First, a Committee of Defense Ministers (CDM) was created as the pact's supreme military consultative organ. The CDM appears to have taken over some of the broader policy-oriented functions previously dealt with by the PCC. As one Soviet source put it, the CDM "works out joint recommendations and proposals for organizing the defense" of the Warsaw Pact and deals "with other questions requiring joint agreement."[31]

The Budapest meeting also established a Military Council, which appears to be subordinate to the pact's joint command. This council seems to be responsible for some of the planning and quality control functions formerly assigned to the defense ministers and chiefs of staff. For instance, in discussing the work of the Military Council, Marshal V.G. Kulikov, the current commander in chief of pact forces, has stated that it analyzes "the results of combat and operational activities for the preceding year and determines the tasks of the armies and fleets for the coming year."[32]

The third organ that emerged as a result of the 1969 reforms, the Technical Council, does not appear to have a precursor. Not much is known about this body except that it deals with "the development and modernization of weapons and technology, the coordination of the efforts of the unified armies in the area of scientific research and experimental design work of a defensive nature."[33] Yet the relative frequency with which it is mentioned in Soviet and East European writings on the pact suggests that it plays an important integrative role: To quote Marshal Kulikov, "Its creation speeded up the outfitting of the armies and the Warsaw Pact states with new types of weapons and equipment."[34]

As a result of these changes, responsibilities in the military sphere became more differentiated. Very broad political-military issues are discussed within the PCC, whose meetings usually include defense ministers as well as foreign ministers. Specific multilateral military issues are handled within the CDM, and the Joint Command oversees the implementation of "decisions by the Communist and Workers' Parties of the [member] States."[35] The actual planning and organizing of military activities such as "maneuvers, exercises, and war games" are carried out by the staff of the Joint Command.[36]

Since it was established, the CDM has met annually. The Military Council convenes twice a year on the average, once during the spring and once toward the end of the year. There is no information on how frequently the Technical Council meets.

While formally at least giving the East Europeans a greater role in pact decision making—a deputy minister of defense serves as pact deputy commander and relays directives from the pact chief to the national command—most observers agree that in fact key authority remains in the hands of the Soviets.[37] In a wartime situation, for example, East European forces would not be commanded through the pact but directly from a Soviet front or theater headquarters. If anything, the new structural changes improved Moscow's ability to coordinate and integrate pact efforst in the military sphere.

Another manifestation of the mounting effort at pact integration in the military sphere was the sudden increase in pact military maneuvers. During the first fourteen years of its existence, the pact held only twenty military exercises, but there were twenty-one in the period from 1969 to 1972—eleven of them in 1969 alone.[38] This striking increase in military exercises appears to have been designed primarily to give pact forces extensive training on a multilateral level, a prerequisite for efficient deployment of pact forces under the doctrine of coalition warfare. Such a conclusion is borne out by the great number of certain types of exercises largely ignored in the past. During 1969–1971, for example, five air defense–air force exercises took place, whereas there had been only one previously. Similarly, four rear services exercises were held between 1969 and 1972.

Apparently satisfied that the groundwork for multilateral cooperation had been laid, pact officials let the number of multilateral maneuvers drop off after 1972. But pact military cooperation of a new type, which has generally been overlooked in the West, began to emerge in the mid-1970s. This consists of bilateral cooperation among East European armies, in which the Soviet Union appears to be only minimally involved. Such cooperation is particularly prevalent among the northern tier countries. For example, Polish officers attend East Germany's Friedrich Engels Military Academy, and Polish, Czechoslovak, and East German forces train together—without the presence of Soviet military units—and use each other's facilities.[39] Such training significantly increases the ability of these forces to operate independently of Soviet troops either in rear areas or on a seperate front.

In spite of the progress Moscow made in improving the functioning of the pact as a military organization, major problems began to surface during the 1970s. First, although some Western commentators have suggested that modernization was proceeding apace in the East European forces, the real situation was quite different.[40] According to figures published by the Arms Control and Disarmament Agency, with the notable exception of East Germany, military expenditures in region increased only gradually throughout period, certainly not in sufficient amounts to cover even the minimal costs of expensive contemporary weapons systems.[41] This failure on the part of the East Europeans to allocate sufficient funds to cover the costs of contemporary weapons systems during the 1970s is borne out by an analysis of their actual holdings.

Air Forces: Most writers on the pact point to the acquisition by East Europeans of MiG-23s and advanced Sukhoi aircraft during the 1970s as an example of how these military forces are being updated. However, a careful review of East European holdings as of 1979 (table 10-1) suggests that

Table 10-1
Selected East European Air-Ground Holdings, 1979

Country	Air Force	Ground
Poland	MiG-17, 21, Sukhoi -7; some Sukhoi 20	T-54/55
GDR	MiG-17, 21	T-54/55
Czechoslovakia	MiG-17, 21; some 23s	T-54/55
Hungary	MiG-21	T-54/55
Bulgaria	MiG-17, 19, 21; some 23.	T-54/55
Rumania	MiG-17, 21	T-54/55

Source: International Institute for Strategic Studies, *The Military Balance, 1979–80* (London: Institute for Strategic Studies, 1980), pp. 14–16.

although the Soviets were moving ahead to introduce the latest aircrafts into their own forces in the region, with a few notable exceptions little was being done to upgrade the East European air forces with modern aircraft such as the MG-23 and Sukhoi planes.

Armies: At a time when there was talk of new tanks and other equipment being introduced in the East European inventories, the record shows that the T-54/55 remained the main battle tank in non-Soviet pact forces, (table 10–1).

Navies: With the exception of East Berlin which began a major buildup in the early 1970s, little was being done by other pact leaderships to modernize their fleets.[42] The vast majority of the Polish fleet was constructed in the late 1950s and mid-1960s, and little was being done to push new construction in the Bulgarian and Rumanian navies.

Most weapons systems require considerable lead time, and it could be argued that the delay between a push by Moscow and actual acquistion by the East Europeans of the weapons is related to this process. Although the acquisition of new weapons may be somewhat influenced by this process, this does not appear to be a major problem in Eastern Europe. After all, the equipment was Soviet designed, and since it was being introduced into frontline Soviet units at this time, if a high enough priority had been assigned to its acquistion, it could have been obtained. If was clearly available.

The second major problem area for the Soviets during this period occurred in Poland.[43] In 1970 riots occurred in Gdansk, and although the circumstances are still unclear, the best available information indicates that the military was involved in the suppression of demonstrations by workers. However, despite their involvement, the Polish military reportedly refused to go along with orders from one of Gomulka's representatives in the Gdansk area to use overwhelming force to put down the demonstrations.

This event had two important consequences for the Polish military. First, it had a devastating and demoralizing impact on the Polish officer corps and was the subject of considerable soul searching and debate within the armed forces. Second, the event showed not only that the military would not unquestionably follow the orders of the political leadership but convinced the high command that the military should at all costs avoid involvement in internal Polish politics.

The 1976 crisis in Warsaw centered around price increases that led to work stoppages by workers in and around Warsaw. According to Polish sources, the Polish military played a key role in Gierek's decision to back down quickly. Jaruzelski's now famous statement, "Polish soldiers will not fire on Polish workers," convinced Gierek of the need to avoid a confrontation.[44]

Taken together, these two events showed that far from being a reliable tool in the hands of the party leadership, the Polish military's utility is an internal crisis was limited. If it was to be utilized successfully at all, it would have to be carefully orchestrated.

By the end of the 1970s, it must have been clear to Moscow that not only were the East Europeans not doing their share in modernizing their armed forces but that serious questions existed concerning the reliability of one of the Pact's key members.

1980–1985: The Problems Increase

From the Soviet perspective, events in Eastern Europe since 1980 have expanded the problems Moscow faces in utilizing the East European militaries for its own ends. In fact, the difficulties faced by the Kremlin have reached the point where the Soviets may have to consider some major changes in pact strategy in the event of an East–West conflict in Europe.

Polish Experience. The actions of the Polish military over the past five years have been far from reassuring to the Soviets. During August 1980, the Polish military remained neutral and refused to become involved in what was viewed as an internal political struggle. Admiral Janczyszyn, commander of the Polish navy, is reported to have stated in the time that he would not permit the use of Polish troops to put down strike activity by Polish shipyard workers and instead called on the party's Central Committee to approve the Gdansk accords.[45]

Throughout the fifteen-month period preceding the declaration of martial law, the Polish military stayed in the background. Some Polish sources claim, for example, that Jaruzelski was offered the position of first secretary, at the time of Gierek's ouster but turned it down. When he did accept it in February 1981 as the internal political struggle was heating up in Poland, any possibility for him to find a compromise solution to the strike ended with the Bydgoszcz incident in March. At that time, in an effort to gain official recognition, members of Rural Solidarity had been occupying government buildings. Shortly after Polish labor leader Lech Walesa met with General Jaruzelski and hopes had risen over the possibility of a negotiated settlement to the country's problems, the police attacked those occupying the buildings, seriously injuring a number of them. The result was an intensification of passions on both sides as Solidarity called for punishment of police officials. Walesa reportedly described the affair "as an obvious provocation against the Government of General Jaruzelski; he plainly did not mean that Solidarity members had acted provocatively."[46] It is generally believed in Poland that the incident was staged by hard-line elements within the security services and Polish leadership—perhaps with

Soviet support—to prevent any accommodation between the government-party and Solidarity.

Throughout the remainder of the year, Poland fell further into internal disarray. The party steadily lost cohesiveness, and there was increasing talk of a full-scale takeover of the party by liberal elements. Frustrated by its inability to get an increasingly beleaguered government-party apparatus to live up to its promises, Solidarity became increasingly radicalized to the point where Walesa's leadership of the union was in serious question at the September 1981 trade union congress. In fact, he succeeded in maintaining control but only by the smallest of margins and after making a number of concessions to more radical elements in the union.

While we probably never know exactly who was behind the declaration of martial law on December 13 (to what degree it was a Polish decision on the result of intense Soviet pressure), contrary to the general Western perception, military involvement was minimal. Regular military units were often not even aware of the declaration of martial law. Furthermore, I am not aware of a single incident in which regular military units were involved in the use of force against civilians. The task of implementing the more onerous aspects fell on the shoulders of the security forces, in particular the dreaded ZOMOs. Military participation in the early days was limited to actions such as: manning of checkpoints on highways and main urban intersections, two- to three-man patrols in major cities, the transportation of ZOMOs around the country (by the air force), and providing communication support for the militia or an occasional drive past key points in tanks or similar equipment in an effort to intimidate the populace. If the West misjudged events in Poland, it was not because it underestimated the ability of the Warsaw leadership to utilize the military in an internal crisis; it was a failure to recognize the tremendous buildup of security forces that had occured during the six months prior to the declaration of martial law.

When it came to a crisis, Warsaw went out of its way to avoid utilizing regular military units in confrontation situation. The leadership was too unsure of how the soldiers would react if called upon to use force against other Poles. In short, it went out of its way to avoid testing the validity of Jaruzelski's 1976 statement that "Polish soliders will not fire on Polish workers."

Since December 1981, the Polish military has been used in a variety of functions. First, in addition to General Jaruzelski and those immediately around him, a number of other senior Polish officers have taken on high-level positions. Second, they have acted as trouble-shooters, For example, officers at the level of colonel were assigned to provincial governors who used them to help eliminate supply bottlenecks or deal with other logistical problems. Finally, they served on inspection teams that were assigned the task of ensuring that party and government bureaucrats throughout the country were carrying out the General's orders (they frequently were not). While many of these officers returned to their barracks after martial law ended in July 1983, large numbers are still active in the civilian bureaucracy. In fact, the outlook is for prolonged military presence in the civilian sphere. A return to complete civilian rule would put the same individuals who brought about the 1980 crisis back into power, something the general appears determined to avoid.

The Polish experience has a number of implications for the Soviet Union. First, although the situation in Poland is clearly better than it was on December 12, 1981, to date Jaruzelski has not always done things the way the Soviets would have preferred. He has resisted suggestions to return power to the party. Poland has the strongest church in any other communist country—if not in all of Europe. The general has not cracked down as hard on dissidents as the Kremlin would prefer. Argriculture remains predominately in private hands. The media are relatively open by communist standards, and the universities retain a significant degree of autonomy. The lesson is that East European generals cannot always be counted on to do Moscow's bidding.

Second, although senior military officers and the security organs were able to hold the line this time, the Kremlin must have continuing concerns over stability in Poland in a real crisis situation. After all, the 1981 takeover took place in the face of a largely passive populace. What if there is resistance next time and the internal security organs prove insufficient? What will the regular army do if called upon to use its weapons?

Finally, looking at Poland's key role in the Warsaw Pact (fifteen divisions with its own front), Moscow must be worried about the large number of officers who have been engaged in nonmilitary activities. Such activities are likely to detract from the Polish military's combat readiness. Furthermore, the bitterness on the part of the average Pole over the events of the past four years, as well as continuing support for the ideals of Solidarity, are certain to have an important impact on morale and combat readiness.

Modernizing the East European Militaries. In spite of some efforts to modernize them, East European militaries appear to be falling further behind Soviet forces in the region.

Air Forces. At a time when the Soviet forces will soon have MiG-29s and SU-27s, the East Europeans are far behind.[47] The predominant aircraft in

Table 10-2
Selected East European Air-Ground Holdings, 1984

Country	Air Force	Ground
Poland	MiG-17, 21; a few MiG-23s; SU-7; a few SU-20s being added	T-54/55, 70 T-72s; only 800 BMP-1 (1/2 of those required to meet Soviet norms), 0T64 and obsolescent 0T62
GDR	MiG-21; a few MiG-23s	T-54/55, large number of T-72s. 40% of combat infantry vehicles are modern and artillery holdings adequate
Czechoslovakia	MiG-15, 21; smattering of MiG-23s, SU-7	T-54/55s, 100 T-72s
Hungary	MiG-21; MiG-23s beginning to appear	T-54/55, with a few T-72s
Bulgaria	MiG-17, 21; a few 23s	T-54/55, with a few T-72s. Combat infantry vehicles outdated and major shortfalls in artillery
Rumania	MiG-17, 21; a few 23s IAR—93s	Similar to Bulgaria

Source: International Institute of Strategic Studies, *The Military Balance, 1984-85* (London: International Institute of Strategic Studies, 1984), pp. 24–28.

the region remain the MiG-21 and SU-7, although MiG-23s and SU-20s are beginning to appear in East European inventories (table 10-2).

Armies. After carefully analyzing the state of northern tier forces, one writer has concluded that there are major disparities between Soviet and East European forces. Looking at the Polish army, this writer concludes: "At best, the Polish Army would be hard-pressed to keep up with better organized and equipped Soviet forces and could not be expected to do well some of the very important things that Soviet units could do and Soviet doctrine requires."[48] The Czechoslovak army is in somewhat better shape than the Polish, but it too has serious shortcomings. All in all, "the Czechoslovak Peoples Army, like the Polish Peoples Army seems ill-structured and ill-equipped to perform a first echelon role."[49] Finally, even the East German army, the most modern of all East European militaries, is still inferior to Soviet forces in the region, which are "receiving the newest equipment, tanks, self-propelled artillery and air defense missiles of a much faster rate than the NVA."[50]

Navies. With the exception of the East German navy, all of the pact fleets have serious deficiencies. The largest, the Polish navy, is quickly sinking into obsolescence. The Rumanian navy is small and outdated, and the Bulgarian navy is in need of new ships and equipment.

To the Soviets, the situation among the East European militaries must appear bleak. The quality of their equipment, although improving, lags far behind that of Soviet forces. And although figures from the Arms Control and Disarmament Agency suggest that East European military budgets are increasing, this is not reflected in new weapons systems.[51] One option for the Soviets would be to increase pressure on the East Europeans to purchase more modern weapons. Given the region's serious economic problems—Poland is only the most obvious case—such an approach, if carried out, could have serious impact on these countries' economies. In view of the close tie between economic and political stability in the area, it could also have significant political ramifications. However much the Kremlin may prefer modern militaries in Eastern Europe, it is doubtful they are prepared to push the East Europeans in that direction if the result is likely to be increased political instability.

There is also some question as to whether the East Europeans (with the exception of the East Germans) will agree to a significant increase in military budgets. By and large they appear to have other priorities particularly resolving internal economic difficulties while preventing a further deterioration in East–West relations. Recent East European assertiveness on issues such as INF counterdeployments (only the East Germans and Czechoslovaks accepted the SS-12s, and there are rumors that the move was opposed by almost all East European pact members) as well as participation in the 1984 Olympics (the Rumanians went, and the Hungarians and Poles held out until the last minute) suggest that within limits, the East Europeans are becoming increasingly willing to assert their independence on some issues.[52]

If the past forty years is any indication, the Soviets still have a long way to go before problems of political reliability will be overcome. The Hungarian revolt in 1956, the Czechoslovak crisis of 1968, and the Polish events in the 1970s and 1980s raise questions concerning their reliability at home and in an East–West conflict. And although, the Soviets may attempt to deal with such problems by pushing cooperation among the various political apparatuses as one writer has suggested, it is unlikely that they will overcome the problem in the foreseeable future.[53]

The Soviet Dilemma

The increasing technical gap between Soviet and East European weapons systems, together with continuing questions concerning the latter's political reliability in a NATO–Warsaw Pact confrontation, present Soviet military planners with a number of problems.

Compensating for East European Forces

One of the major consequences of the Czechoslovak invasion in 1968 was the permanent stationing of five Soviet divisions in Czechoslovakia. The presence of these forces together with the modernization of Soviet forces in Eastern Europe has to a degree helped compensate for shortcomings on the part of East European forces. Since 1968, however, the situation within the East European armies has worsened from Moscow's point of view. One way of dealing with this situation would be to station a greater number of Soviet troops in the region. Alternatively, Moscow could allocate some of its divisions from the western regions of the Soviet Union for service in Europe in an emergency.

Both options have drawbacks. The first is likely to be resisted by the East Europeans and would be a matter of concern to the West Europeans, who would be alarmed by the presence of greater numbers of Soviet troops in the area. It would complicate Moscow's efforts to drive a wedge between the United States and its Western European allies and undercut the Kremlin's peace policy in Western Europe. The second alternative would create problems in a crisis situation. The mobilization and movement of such forces into position prior to the opening of hostilities wold provide NATO with increased warning time.

Greater Reliance on Nuclear Weapons

Moscow could compensate for the reduced utility of the East Europeans by modifying pact strategy to eliminate or shorten a conventional stage of a European conflict by moving more quickly to the use of theater nuclear weapons. Such a step would not only increase the danger of a central system exchange, it would almost certainly be picked up by the West during peace time, help legitimize NATO's reliance on nuclear weapons in the minds of many West Europeans, and create difficulties for Moscow's attempt to downplay the existence of a Soviet threat. To date, I am not aware of any movement toward greater reliance on nuclear weapons by the Soviets in a NATO–Warsaw Pact conflict.

Conflicts Must Be Short and Successful

Although there is no doubt that the Soviets can mobilize and East Europeans for an East–West conflict and ensure their participation, potential problems with reliability place a premium on a short, successful campaign. Should the Soviet Union suffer reverses or become bogged down, problems with East European troops could quickly emerge. As a consequence, assuming the Soviets decide to utilize the East Europeans, Soviet military planners will be under strong pressure to pick exactly the right time and place to ensure the quick success of any operation against NATO. This obviously limits flexibility in the planning of operations.

Ensuring the Integration of Pact Weapons Systems

The increasingly obsolescent East European weapons systems will make combined arms operations more difficult. The pact's continued reliance on a high level of exercises helps somewhat, but as one writer put it with reference to the less technical East Europeans, "the national armies are becoming rapidly less capable than their Soviet counterparts and less able to execute Soviet combined arms operations."[54]

Moscow could eliminate the discrepancy between its forces and those of its allies by supplying them with modern weapons free of charge. To date, however, the Soviets have not done so. As one East European specialist on national security questions put it in a conversation with me, "We won't be supplied with the latest equipment for three reasons: first, the Soviets want to make money off of the sale of weapons and we don't have the hard currency. Second, they don't think we will do our part in an East–West conflict and don't want to waste the weapons. Third, they don't trust us and are afraid some of our pilots, for example, will defect to the West with the latest equipment." Assuming the trends outlined in this chapter continue, the pact's difficulties in carrying out combined arms operations will grow.

Maintaining Supply Lines

Given the strong anti-Soviet sentiments throughout Eastern Europe, Moscow must also contend with potential problems in ensuring the security of its rear echelons in an East–West conflict. This is particularly true of Poland, where anti-Soviet feelings are strong and through which Soviet forces in East Germany are normally resupplied. In a European conflict, the Soviets could try to send supplies by sea, as they did during the height of the Solidarity period, but in view of West German naval air and undersea capabilities, such an approach is fraught with dangers and uncertainties.

Keeping the Peace in Eastern Europe

The recent Polish experience shows that while the military can be useful in helping to maintain order, serious questions remain not only about its readiness to carry out Moscow's will but concerning its ability to keep the situation under control if serious bloodshed errupts as well. This means that Moscow must continue to be prepared to use its own forces in a policing role in peacetime and that disturbances in rear areas could not only cause serious logistical problems but instability at a time when Soviet forces were engaged elsewhere.

Observers in the West have traditionally devoted a considerable amount of attention to NATO's deficiencies, both political and technical. While such attention is appropriate and needed, there has been a tendency on the part of most Western analysts either to ignore the pact's problems or at a minimum to downplay them. As I have tried to show, the problems for the Soviets are real and getting worse. It is doubtful, despite all of its problems, that many NATO generals would be prepared to trade their own forces for those of the other side.

It has often been observed that the Soviet soldier is not ten feet tall. This analysis indicates, however, that despite the attention and effort the Soviets have put into the pact and its East European components, it is also not ten feet tall. In fact, recent trends suggest that relative to Soviet forces, the pact's figurative height is decreasing. The problems for the Kremlin will continue and require actions on the part of the Soviets to deal with them. Although it is not clear how the Soviets will react, the situation is important enough to warrant more careful attention on the part of Western analysts than has hitherto been the case.

Notes

1. For a discussion on their origin from the Soviet point of view, see A.V. Antosyak *et. al.*, *Zarozhdenie narodnykh armiy stran-uchasnits varshavskogo dogovara* (Moskva: Izdatel'stvo nauka, 1975).

2. See, for example, Peter Gosztony, *Hitlers Fremde Heere* (Düsseldorf: Econ Verlag, 1976).

3. For an analysis of the Katyn Forest massacre, see J.K. Zawodny, *Death in the Forest* (Notre Dame: Notre Dame University Press, 1962).

4. Ignacy Blum, *Z dziejów Wojska Polskiego w latach 1944–1948* (Warszawa: Ministerstwo Obrony Narodowej, 1968), p. 180.

5. *Ibid.*

6. Tadeusz Konecki, "Zawodowe Szkolnictwo Ludowego Wojska Polskiego w Fierwszym Powojennym Dziesiecioleciu," *Wojskowy Przeglad Historyczny*, no. 2 (1974): 341.

7. Jerzy Wiatr, "Sozio-politische Besonderheiten und Funktionen von Streit-kräften in sozialistischen Ländren," in Rene Konig, ed., *Beitrage zur Militärsoziol-ogie* (Köln and Opladen: Westdeutscher Verlag, 1968), 104.

8. For Bulgaria, see Marian Jurek and Edward Skrzypowski, *Tarcza Pokoju* (Warszawa: Ministerstwo Obrony Narodowej, 1975), p. 240; for Hungary, Sandor Mucs and Erno Zagoni, *Geschichte der Ungarischen Volksarmee* (Berlin: Militär-verlag der Deutschen Demokratischen Republik, 1982), p. 170; for Czechoslovakia,

Jan Liptak and Milan Spicak, "Die Tschechoslowakische Volkasarmee in der Periode des beschleunigten Aufbaus einer Armee sozialistischen Typus," *Militärgeschichte* no. 2 (1975): 189; and for Poland, Major Marian Jurek, "Dorobek XX-Lecia ludowego korpusu oficerskiego," *Wojsko Ludowe*, no. 7 (1964): 44.

9. In addition in Poland the chief of the general staff, the commander of ground forces, and the heads of all the service commanders of all four military districts were former Soviet officers.

10. Thomas W. Wolfe, *Soviet Power and Europe, 1945-1970* (Baltimore: Johns Hopkins Press, 1970), p. 43.

11. A. Semerdshiew, F. Christow, and S. Penkow, *Geschichte der Bulgarischen Volksarmee* (Berlin: Militärverlag der Deutschen Demokratischen Republik, 1977), pp. 193-194.

12. A. Ross Johnson, "Has Eastern Europe Become a Liability to the Soviet Union? (II)—the Military Aspect," in Charles Gati, ed., *The International Politics of Eastern Europe* (New York: Praeger, 1976), p. 40.

13. A. Ross Johnson, Robert Dean, and Alexander Alexiev, *East European Military Establishments: The Warsaw Pact Northern Tier* (New York: Crane, Russak, 1982), p. 22.

14. I.I. Yakubovskiy, ed., *Boyevoyoe sodruzhestvo bratskikh narodov i armiy* (Moskva: Voyenizdat, 1975), pp. 90, 86.

15. *Ibid.*, p. 273.

16. Wolfe, *Soviet Power and Europe*, p. 148.

17. These figures were arrived at on the basis of data in Stephan Tiedtke, *Die Warschauer Vertragsorganization* (Munich: Oldenbourg, 1978), pp. 23-24.

18. For Poland see Dale R. Herspring, "Technology and the Political Officer in the Polish and East German Armed Forces," *Studies in Comparative Communism* (Winter 1977): 393; for Czechoslovakia Jan Liptak et *al.*, *Die Tschechoslowakische Volksarmee* (Berlin: Militärverlag der Deutschen Demokratischen Republik, 1979): 180; and for Bulgaria, Semerdshiew, Christow, and Penkow, *Geschichte der Bulgarischen Volksarmee*, p. 219.

19. Liptak et al. pp. 164-165, and Autorenkollektiv des Deutschen Instituts für Militärgeschichte, *Zeittafel zur Militärgeschichte der Deutschen Demokratischen Republik 1949 bis 1968* (Berlin: Deutscher Militärverlag, 1969) p. 87.

20. Ivan Volgyes, "The Military as an Agent of Political Socialization: The Case of Hungary," in Dale R. Herspring and Ivan Volgyes, *Civil-Military Relations in Communist Systems* (Boulder: Westview, 1978), p. 152.

21. A. Ross Johnson, "The Warsaw Pact: Soviet Military Policy in Eastern Europe," in Sarah Meiklejohn Terry, ed., *Soviet Policy in Eastern Europe* (New Haven: Yale University Press, 1984), p. 262. Despite the abandonment of work in these areas, some of the East European states have continued to produce Soviet-designed weapons under license (for example, the Poles are building tanks and ships, the Hungarians and Czechoslovaks infantry equipment and artillery pieces).

22. Herspring, "Technology and the Political Officer," p. 393. The lower educational level on the part of East German officers can be partially explained by the fact that the East German military was not formally established until 1956.

23. V.G. Kulikov, ed., *Varshavskiy Dogovor–soyuz vo imya mira i sotsializma* (Moskva: Voyennoye Izdatel'stvo, 1980), pp. 274–279, and Jurek and Skrzypowski *Tarcza Pokoju*, pp. 338–348.

24. N.N. Rodinov et al., Organizatsiya Varshavskogo Dogovora, 1955–1976 (Moskva: Izdatel'stvo Politicheskoy Literatury, 1975), p. 75.

25. Johnson, "Has Eastern Europe," p. 44.

26. Robert W. Dean, "The Political Consolidation of the Czechoslovak Army," Radio Free Europe Research, Czechoslovakia/14, April 29, 1972, 15.

27. Galia Golan, *Reform Rule in Czechoslovakia* (Cambridge: Cambridge University Press, 1973), p. 183.

28. Condoleezza Rice, "Warsaw Pact Reliability: The Czechoslovak People's Army (CIA)," in Daniel N. Nelson, ed., *Soviet Allies: The Warsaw Pact and the Issue of Reliability* (Boulder: Westview, 1984), 135.

29. A. Ross Johnson, "The Military in Eastern Europe—Loyalty to Whom," (paper prepared for a conference, Eastern Europe—Stability or Recurrent Crisis? Arlie House, Virginia, November 13–15, 1976).

30. Even in the primarily Hungarian areas, the Hungarian army was viewed as an occupying army by a hostile population, and the army responded by trying to return to Hungary as soon as possible.

31. K. Savinov, *Moguchiy faktor mira i stabil'nosti v mezhdunarodykh otnosheniyakh* (Moskva: Mezhdunarodnyye Otnosheniya, 1980), p. 17.

32. Kulikov, *Varshavskiy Dogovor*, p. 167.

33. Savinov, *Moguchiy faktor mira i stabil'nosti*, p. 19.

34. V. Kulikov, "Chetvert' veka no strazhe zavoevanniy sotsializma i mira," *Voyenno-istoricheskiy Zhurnal*, no. 5 (1980): 26.

35. *Ibid.*

36. *Ibid.*

37. See, for example, Johnson, "Has Eastern Europe," p. 51, and Malcolm Mackintosh, "The Warsaw Pact Today," *Survival*, (May–June 1974): 122–126.

38. Material on pact exercises is taken from Kulikov, *Varshavskiy Dogovor*, pp. 272–293.

39. See, for example, the references to GDR–Polish cooperation in a 1975 speech by General Heinz Hoffmann, the GDR minister of national defense, during the visit to East Germany by the then Polish Defense Minister Wojciech Jaruzelski in *Zolnierz Wolnosci*, March 14, 1975. See also the Polish report of the result of the visit in ibid, March 15–16, 1975. There have been numerous other references to widespread Polish–GDR military cooperation in *Zolnierz Wolnosci* and *Volksarmee*. Such cooperation, at least in the form of Polish officers attending the East German military academy, does not appear to have been affected by events in Poland during the past five years.

38. Material on pact exercises is taken from Kulikov, *Varshavskiy Dogovor*, pp. 272–293.

39. See, for example, the references to GDR–Polish cooperation in a 1975 speech by General Heinz Hoffmann, the GDR minister of national defense, during the visit to East Germany by the then Polish Defense Minister Wojciech Jaruzelski in *Zolnierz Wolnosci*, March 14, 1975. See also the Polish report of the result of the

visit in ibid, March 15-16, 1975. There have been numerous other references to widespread Polish–GDR military cooperation in *Zolnierz Wolnosci* and *Volksarmee*. Such cooperation, at least in the form of Polish officers attending the East German military academy, does not appear to have been affected by events in Poland during the past five years.

40. For example, John Erickson, "The Warsaw Pact—The Shape of Things to Come?" in Karen Dawisha and Philip Hansen, *Soviet-East European Dilemmas* (London: Holmes and Meier, 1981), 164, and Johnson, "Warsaw Pact," p. 265.

41. Arms Control and Disarmament Agency, *World Military Expenditures and Transfers, 1972-1982)* (Washington D.C.: Arms Control and Disarmament Agency, 1984).

42. For a detailed discussion of the East German naval buildup and a comparison of the Volksmarine with the Polish navy, see Dale R. Herspring, "GDR Naval Build-up," *Problems of Comunism* (January–February 1984): 54–62.

43. The following description of the 1970 and 1976 events in Poland is taken from Johnson, Dean, and Alexiev, *East European Military Establishments*, pp. 51–53.

44. Dale R. Herspring and Ivan Volgyes, "Political Reliability in East European Warsaw Pact Armies," *Armed Forces and Society* 6, no. 2 (Winter 1980): 279.

45. As recounted to me by a number of Polish sources.

46. Kevin Ruane, *The Polish Challenge* (London: British Broadcasting Corporation, 1982), pp. 137–138.

47. James H. Hansen, "Countering NATO's New Weapons. Soviet Concepts for War in Europe," *International Defense Review* 17, no. 11 (1984): 1619.

48. Richard C. Martin, "Disparities in Modernization between Warsaw Pact Armies Opposite NATO's Central Region" (paper delivered at the Conference on Security Implications of Nationalism in Eastern Europe, U.S. Army War College, Carlisle Barracks, Pennsylvania, October 23–24, 1984), p. 10.

49. *Ibid.*, p. 17.

50. *Ibid.*, p. 19.

51. Arms Control and Disarmament Agency, *World Military Expenditures*, pp. 19–42.

52. Ten years ago the idea of East European leaderships' raising questions if not opposing the Soviets on a key security question such as INF counter-deployments would have been unthinkable.

53. Christopher Jones, "The Political Administration of the Warsaw Pack and the Reliability of the East-Bloc Armed Forces," in Nelson, *Soviet Allies*, pp. 67–97.

54. Martin, "Disparities in Modernization," p. 4.

Index

About the Contributors

Desmond Ball is senior fellow and deputy head of the Strategic and Defense Studies Center of the Australian National University. He has been a research associate of the International Institute for Strategic Studies in London and a research fellow at Harvard University. His most recent books include *Politics and Force Levels: The Strategic Missile Program of the Kennedy Administration* (1980) and *A Suitable Piece of Real Estate: American Installations in Australia* (1980).

Abraham S. Becker is a senior economist of the Rand Corporation. His books include *Military Expenditure Limitation for Arms Control* (1977), *Soviet National Income, 1958–1964* (1969), and a Rand monograph, *The Burden of Soviet Defense: A Political-Economic Essay* (1980).

Rose Gottemoeller is a research associate of the Rand Corporation. She previously served in the U.S. Information Agency, and the Department of Commerce. Her research included a study of U.S.–Soviet agreements on science and technology for the National Sciences Foundation.

Dale Herspring is deputy director of the State Department's Office of East European Affairs. He has served in many State Department posts in Washington and Eastern Europe and as special assistant for Soviet and East European Affairs for the Department of Defense. His books include *The Soviet Union and Strategic Arms* (1984, with Robin Laird), *Civil-Military Relations in Communist Systems* (1978, with Ivan Volgyes), and *East German Civil-Military Relations (1949-1971): The Impact of Technology* (1973).

Benjamin Lambeth is a senior staff member of the Rand Corporation. He has served in the Office of National Estimates of the CIA and the Institute for Defense Analyses and worked at the Georgetown Center for Strategic and International Studies. He is the co-author of *The Soviet Union and*

Arms Control: *The Superpower Dilemma* (1970, with Roman Kolkowicz).

Jeffrey Richelson is assistant professor at the American University School of Government and Public Administration. He has been a senior fellow at the Center for International and Strategic Affairs and an analyst for the Analytical Assessment Corporation.

Anne T. Sloan is assistant professor of Political science at the State University of New York, Albany. Previously she was assistant professor of government and international studies at the University of South Carolina.

Stan Woods most recently was a research assistant at the Aberdeen University Center for Defense Studies. He is author of *Pipeline Politics* (1983) and *Weapons Acquisition in the Soviet Union*.

About the Editors

Roman Kolkowicz is a Professor of Political Science at the University of California, Los Angeles, where he was the Founding Director of the Center for International and Strategic Affairs. His work in the field of Soviet foreign and strategic policies has appeared in *World Politics, Comparative Politics, ORBIS, Aussenpolitik, Journal of Strategic Studies,* and other journals. His most recent publications include *Soldiers, Peasants and Bureaucrats; National Security and International Stability;* and *Arms Control and International Security.*

Ellen Propper Mickiewicz is professor of political science at Emory University and editor of the journal *Soviet Union.* Her publications include *Media and the Russian Public, Handbook of Soviet Social Science Data, Soviet Political Schools,* and a number of articles in the *Journal of Communication, Public Opinion Quarterly, Slavic Review,* and other journals.